A HISTORY OF EUROPEAN DIPLOMACY
1451–1789

A HISTORY OF EUROPEAN DIPLOMACY 1451–1789

BY

R. B. MOWAT

PROFESSOR OF HISTORY IN THE UNIVERSITY OF BRISTOL
FORMERLY FELLOW AND TUTOR OF
CORPUS CHRISTI COLLEGE, OXFORD

[redacted]

ARCHON BOOKS
1971

First published 1928
Reprinted 1971 with permission
in an unaltered and unabridged edition.

ISBN: 0-208-01021-1
Printed in the United States of America

PREFACE

This book is an historical study, from the point of view of diplomacy, of how wars have been made, concluded or prevented. The essential test-question for diplomacy, when it appears before the bar of universal judgment, will be: Has it, on the whole, helped to diminish warfare? The studies made for this book seem to point to the conclusion that diplomacy began as a means by which each sovereign aimed at preventing aggression from his neighbours; it became ultimately, on the whole, from about the middle of the seventeenth century, and without putting off its national attachments, an international agency for avoiding wars, or for localizing or concluding them after they had begun. The diplomatists were, as a whole, faithful to the idea of the Christian powers as being a system or family of states, each of which was morally bound not to encroach on the other, and none of which should preponderate over the rest. This idea substituted a conception of a society of independent units for the old idea of the Roman Empire relegated for ever to the limbo of the past.

There is a striking passage in Gulliver's *Travels to Brobdingnag*. He had several conversations with the King of Brobdingnag about England and the other states of Europe, about war and politics and other public affairs. The king was not sympathetic:

> He professed both to abominate and despise all mystery, refinement, and intrigue, either in a prince or in a minister. He could not tell what I meant by secrets of State, where an enemy or some rival nation were not in the case. He confined the knowledge of governing within very narrow bounds, to common sense and reason, to justice and lenity, to the speedy determination of civil and criminal causes; with some other obvious topics which are not worth considering. And he gave it for his opinion, that whoever could make two ears of corn or two blades of grass to grow upon a spot of ground where only one grew before, would deserve better of mankind, and do more essential service to his country, than the whole race of politicians put together.[1]

[1] *Travels to Brobdingnag*, Chap. VII.

Only a perverse mind would condemn the work of the soldier, politician, and other public servants as being merely destructive or obstructive. The age of the Goth and the Hun, who fought frankly for fighting's sake or for plunder, is long past. But if these simple causes of war have practically ceased to operate, the complexities of modern life have given rise to many others. It is the claim, in particular, of the diplomatic profession that, viewed as a whole, it is found throughout the centuries chiefly engaged either in preventing wars from beginning or in stopping those that have begun. In so far as it has succeeded in these objects, it has conformed to the standard of public service of the King of Brobdingnag, and has contributed to the growing of two blades of grass where only one grew before.

R. B. MOWAT.

BRISTOL,
October, 1928.

CONTENTS

Part I.—THE DEVELOPMENT OF THE EUROPEAN STATES SYSTEM

CHAP.		PAGE
I	The Rise of the Diplomatic Profession	1
II	Congresses and the Eastern Question	7
III	Louis XI and Charles the Bold	12
IV	The Italian Expedition	23
V	The Partition of Italy	28
VI	The League of Cambrai	32
VII	England and the New Diplomacy	37
VIII	Habsburg and Valois	44
IX	The End of the Wars of Italy	50

Part II.—THE WARS OF RELIGION

X	The Counter-Reformation	59
XI	The League	70
XII	The Armada	73
XIII	The Common Cause	77
XIV	Calvinists and Roman Catholics	84
XV	The Outbreak of the Thirty Years' War	90
XVI	The Thirty Years' War down to the Peace of Prague	93
XVII	The Peace of Westphalia	104

Part III.—THE AGE OF LOUIS XIV

XVIII	The Peace of the Pyrenees	115
XIX	Louis advances towards a Natural Frontier	123
XX	The Treaty of Nymwegen	133
XXI	The Treaty of Ryswick	141
XXII	The Partition Treaties and the Will of Charles II of Spain	154
XXIII	The Peace of Utrecht	165
XXIV	Scandinavia and the Slavonic States	183
XXV	Turkey and Europe, to the Peace of Passarowitz	200

Part IV.—THE EIGHTEENTH CENTURY

CHAP.		PAGE
XXVI	Twenty-five Years of Peace. I—The Quadruple Alliance of London	207
XXVII	Twenty-five Years of Peace. II—Walpole	216
XXVIII	A General War	225
XXIX	The Reversal of Alliances	236
XXX	The Seven Years' War	248
XXXI	The Decline of the Empire	262
XXXII	The End of Poland	267
XXXIII	The Sick Man of Europe	278
XXXIV	The Last Years of the Ancien Régime	283
	Epilogue	298
	Index	301

A HISTORY OF EUROPEAN DIPLOMACY, 1451—1789

PART I

THE DEVELOPMENT OF THE EUROPEAN STATES SYSTEM

CHAPTER I

THE RISE OF THE DIPLOMATIC PROFESSION

During the Middle Ages warfare never ceased in one part of Europe or another. About the middle of the fifteenth century, however, social and political changes are discernible, which may be taken to begin modern history. In this modern period, from about the year 1451, warfare is far less common than in the Middle Ages. Nevertheless, war does arise, war on the grand scale, as it were in great waves, with long intervals of general or comparatively general peace between the waves. Each wave of great war is ended by diplomatic action, by a peace treaty or peace congress. Every such war, as brought to an end by diplomacy, is followed by about thirty or forty years of peace. Thus the close of the Hundred Years' War between France and England in 1451 was followed by a relatively peaceful period of forty-three years. In 1494 the celebrated expedition of Charles VIII of France began the "Italian Wars," the great struggle for Italy between France and the Empire, which lasted intermittently until concluded by the Treaty of Cateau-Cambrésis in 1559. This treaty was followed by nearly sixty years, during which there was no general war in Europe, although there were terrible civil wars in France and in the Netherlands, as well as maritime war between Spain and England, and between Spain and Turkey. War on the grand scale began in 1618 with the great religious struggle in Germany, which drew every state into its vortex at one time or another and lasted until 1648.

The Congress and Treaties of Westphalia inaugurated an era when there was no warfare on the grand scale (although France and Spain were not at peace with each other all the time) for twenty-four years. This period of relative peace was broken by the great assault of Louis XIV upon the existing States-system in 1672. An age of war on the grand scale ensued until the Congress and Treaties of Utrecht in 1713 gave rest to an exhausted Europe. There followed twenty-seven years of normal international life, without grand-scale warfare, until Frederick II of Prussia invaded Silesia in 1740 and began the gigantic struggle which ended with the Peace of Paris, 1763. For just thirty years Europe again had rest, until the French Revolutionary Wars began in 1792. After this Continental Europe was wracked by struggling armies until 1814. Then the Treaties of Paris and Vienna settled (with few exceptions) the frontiers of Europe for fifty years. In 1854, with the Crimean War, an era of struggle of nationalities opened; and conflicts between the Great Powers followed each other with breathless haste until 1871. After the Franco-German War and the Treaties of 1871 Europe, except in the Balkan fringe, had peace for forty-three years, when the greatest war in history commenced. After over four years of strife which became literally world-wide, the Conference of Paris and the Treaty of Versailles began the era of peace in which we are still living.

It is clear that diplomacy has not achieved its end, which is perpetual peace. It concludes a war when one or more of the parties are exhausted; and by day-to-day adjustments it prevents or defers fresh outbreaks of the fratricidal contest within the community of civilized states. Diplomacy is the father and mother of the "normal" periods of history when there is no war on the grand scale. Its ideal object is to prevent the recurrence of the catastrophes, which until now have always ended such periods after they have endured only a generation or two.

It is true that for centuries peace was not considered to be the first and constant aim of a diplomatist. He tended to regard himself simply as a servant of his sovereign and to look upon his duty as being to gain, by personal adroitness, ingenuity and subtlety, some advantage for his master. Such was the diplomacy of the Age of Machiavelli and of many subsequent years. Gradually, however, a more wholesome view prevailed; the diplomatists continued, naturally, to be the servants of their particular states, and to represent their interests, but they came to regard all civilized states as forming a cultural, if not a political society, with a common interest in peace. The diplomatic profession or *corps* became European, like the knights of chivalry in the Middle Ages. Information, gossip, and rumours circulated among the men of "*la Carrière*," the diplomatists formed a "great village" though often divided into opposite camps. The bias in favour of peace among the *corps diplomatique* was inevitably developed by the fact that in general an outbreak of war marks a diplomatist's failure, while the solution of a crisis without loss of blood or treasure has always been justly regarded as a great success on the part of those in charge of a negotiation.

Permanent or continuous diplomacy came into existence sometime between the middle of the fifteenth and the middle of the sixteenth centuries. In the Middle Ages there were no permanent diplomatic residents at the European Courts, nor indeed had sovereigns any conceptions of foreign policy. States, when their interests conflicted, fought each other; and when one side or both were exhausted, they made peace. There were traditions, not policies. For instance, it was a tradition of the Plantagenet kings of England that they should hold and acquire French territory; it was a tradition of the French Monarchy that it should try and maintain influence in Milan and in Naples. The only conceptions of unity among the sovereigns of Europe were the unity of the Holy Roman Empire which was a fiction, and that of the Catholic Church which was a fact but was not able to prevent chronic, ruinous warfare. Yet, impotent as the Imperial and Catholic ideas were to prevent anarchy between states, they stood in the way of any other conception of the political unity of Europe.

The collapse of the Empire and the decay of the Papacy in the later Middle Ages stripped Europe of even the pretence of unity. Monarchs became in theory and in practice absolute and uncontrolled,[1] and now they wielded that terrible instrument, a standing army. Towards the end of the Middle Ages the establishing of standing armies enormously increased the danger to which every state was exposed from its neighbours. At the same time

[1] See R. Koser, *Die Epochen der absoluten Monarchie in der Neueren Geschichte*, in *Historische Zeitschrift* (1889), XXV, 250 ff.

inside Italy, feeble states had found safety in the practice of negotiation, and in a "system" of balance of power. It did not take long for the men of other countries to discern this. Soon in Central and Western Europe and Scandinavia (where there was a common intellectual culture) negotiations and the system of balance of power began to fill the void left by the failure of the Imperial and Catholic ideas, and these things—negotiation and the system or policy of balance—produced a "society of European states," which however glaringly imperfect was vastly better than the congeries of warring atoms which Europe presented in the later Middle Ages.

The monarchies and governing aristocracies (every state in Europe was either one or the other) could not conduct international negotiation or maintain a balance of power by using only occasional ambassadors. Moreover, the standing army of a neighbour was a thing which required continual watching. Every sort of government needed information about its neighbours, for it had frequently to take precautionary measures. This information could only be effectively obtained and continually supplied by someone permanently resident in the neighbour-state; at the same time if the information was bruited about it might precipitate the catastrophe which it was meant to avert, and might rupture the good relations which it was meant to preserve. Therefore two essential qualities of the diplomacy which was arising at the close of the Middle Ages were permanent representation and secrecy. Instead, as in the Middle Ages, of the dispatch of a grand, occasional envoy, exciting attention by the unusual journey, proudly defying the hostile people among whom (with some inward nervousness) he parades, and advertising by the very fact of his mission the tremendous issues that are at stake, we have the permanent diplomatic resident, a familiar figure at the court, a foreigner, yet not an enemy, speaking the common language of diplomacy, behaving like a man of the world, accepted, in spite of his obvious nationality, as a member of an international profession. If he sends home reports and writes things which the sovereign, to whom he is accredited, would be indignant to hear, no harm is done, for the reports are confidential. He never approaches court with a herald and proclaims his master's animosity to the house-tops, and the better he does his work, the less will be heard of it. Being only human he will often make mistakes, and his motives will sometimes be bad. Nevertheless, his profession makes him normally pursue two objects: one, to furnish correct information; two, to help his master to maintain the inter-state balance, on which, experience was proving, the safety of each state depended. Once in a while, a sovereign might arise who aimed not at maintaining the balance but at overturning it and establishing a dominating empire; in such a case his diplomacy would become the handmaid of war, not of peace. But these cases are the perversions, not the normal conditions, of international affairs.

There are a fair number of claimants to the honour of having originated permanent diplomacy. Louis XI of France,[1] Ferdinand of Aragon, and Francis I of France have been given the credit. On the other hand, historians have pointed to fifteenth-century Italy as the home of permanent, organized diplomacy. The Papacy may be called the first really international institution of Modern Europe; indeed, from the early Middle Ages it had friends—abbots, bishops or cardinals—at almost every court; and from time to time certain of these might be designated as legates or *nuncios* specifically to represent the interests of the Holy See. At the French Court there seems to have been a permanent resident representative of the Pope throughout most, if not all, of the Middle Ages. The object, however, of this representative was not so much to transact business between the French Crown and Papal Chancery, as to watch over the existing rights in France of the Papacy and Catholic Church.

The characteristics of the diplomacy of Modern Europe, as distinct from that of the Middle Ages, are that it is permanent, secular and secret. The first mission which was stated to be permanent by the authority which accredited it was sent by the Duke of Milan, Francesco Sforza, to the Republic of Genoa in 1455. The Duke of Savoy accredited in 1460 an envoy to the Papal Court, instructed to remain there permanently, and to deal with secular as well as spiritual affairs. Nicodemus, a man of agreeable speech, and therefore called "Sweet Nicodemus," was maintained under Cosimo de Medici and his successor at Florence as diplomatic representative of Milan (down to about 1469).

[1] Louis XI assigned a great rôle to diplomacy, but he did not maintain permanent, resident missions. He preferred to send an ambassador to deal with a particular affair, and to bring him home as soon as the piece of business was completed. See A. Degert, *Louis XI et ses ambassadeurs*, in *Revue historique* (1927), T. 104, p. 1 ff.

The republic of Venice was at its zenith in the last half of the fifteenth century; and by reason of its wealth, and of its widespread commercial as well as of its political connections, it had the best opportunities for gaining information from abroad, as well as the greatest incentive to ensure competent diplomatic representation. A permanent mission appears to have been maintained by Venice at the court of Louis XI of France, from the year 1478; in 1495 an ambassador was accredited to the court of the Emperor Maximilian. The reports of the Venetian ambassadors to their headquarters, the Signory, have been, since they were made public in the nineteenth century, famous for their wealth of information and their keen insight into political and social affairs.

At first foreign diplomatists—powerful, well-connected men, who continually sent secret reports to their home governments—were regarded by the country in which they lived, with some suspicion. They could only be received on a footing of strict reciprocity. Philip de Commines when he went to Venice in 1494 found representatives of all states there.[1] When two important states established permanent diplomatic connections, other states could not afford to dispense with a similar advantage. So the system of permanent ambassadors became almost universal in Europe, and a code of customs regulating their behaviour and their rights grew up and was maintained by the sanction of the principle of reciprocity. Only Turkey stood outside the diplomatic community. The Sultan received permanent embassies, but he maintained none himself until after 1791, the year of the Treaty of Sistova.

[1] Commines, *Mémoires*, VII, 19. For this chapter in general, see D. J. Hill, *A History of European Diplomacy* (1906), Vol. II; O. Krauske, *Die Entwickelung der ständigen Diplomatie* (in Schmoller, *Staats und Sozialwissenschaftliche Forschungen* [1885], Band V, Heft 2); De Maulde-la-Clavière, *La Diplomatie au temps de Machiavel* (1892). Cp. J. J. Jusserand, *The School for Ambassadors* (1925); J. E. Neale, *The Diplomatic Envoy*, in *History*, XIII, 204 (Oct., 1928).

CHAPTER II

CONGRESSES AND THE EASTERN QUESTION

"The Hundred Years' War" between France and England absorbed the attention and energy of Western Europe, contributed to the decline of the Papacy, and prevented any concerted effort being made to withstand the advance of the Turks. By 1451, however, the Hundred Years' War was over, and conditions became favourable for the defence of the Continent. The religious unity of Europe was still unbroken. France had emerged from the Hundred Years' War with an organized, veteran, standing army, small but capable of great expansion, and led by officers schooled in the great war, expert in utilizing the discoveries of science. Feudalism—always an unsuitable system for offensive warfare—was decaying; instead, the formerly loosely compacted states were becoming solid, national organizations, with stable frontiers and centralized authority. The striking-power of such nation-states was tremendous.

When Constantinople fell to the Turks in 1453, and the last Emperor of Byzantium met his death unknown in the mêlée, a shock was given to the public conscience of Europe, surely as great as that caused by the fall of Jerusalem in 1187. The Papacy, the acknowledged spiritual head of Central and Western Europe, was alive to the crisis, and eagerly called for concerted action against the Turks. Yet nothing was done.

The Emperor, Frederick III, shrewd, pacific, sagacious, might have been expected to take action, both as the highest secular dignitary of Europe, and also as the chief territorial sovereign (being Duke of Austria) towards the south-east. When Constantinople fell, however, he did nothing. He continued his innocent amusements, and "sat idly at home, planting his garden and catching birds." "Would Julius Cæsar," cried Matthew Döring, the Franciscan, "if he came back from the underworld and knew the name of Christ, longer have borne the presumption of the

Turks!"[1] Æneas Sylvius wrote (June 12, 1453) to the Pope, Nicholas V, that historians would say of his pontificate: "In his time Constantinople was taken and plundered by the Turks." Nicholas showed some energy. He issued a summons throughout Europe to a crusade; and he took the practical step, using as negotiator a noble-hearted Augustinian monk, Simonetto of Camerino, of making peace between the mutually suspicious and hostile Italian states. With difficulty, Milan, Venice, Florence and Naples were persuaded to agree to the Pacification of Lodi, April 9, 1454.

Urged by the Pope, Frederick III convened a Congress at Regensburg, to which he invited the kings of France, England, Scotland, Hungary, Poland, and Denmark. The Congress met in April, 1454, but the Emperor himself did not attend, nor did any of the kings, nor their representatives except some Poles. The magnificent and luxurious Philip, Duke of Burgundy, came, and was really ready to send or head an expedition against the Turks; but he found almost no support and the Congress broke up amid the lamentations of Æneas Sylvius, who had attended on the part of the Emperor.

Alfonso Borgia, Calixtus III, who became Pope in 1455, was an aged Spaniard, seventy-seven years old, with all his nation's hereditary animosity against the Moslems. In some of his negotiations he made use of one of the most ascetic and inspiring of the Friars, John of Capistrano, a member of the Observants, the strictest branch of the Franciscans. Capistrano, who was a friend of Æneas Sylvius, was a small, dried-up, bald-headed man, with a grey beard, a red face, and long arms reaching to his knees; he ate hard bread and slept on the ground in the snow, and his passionate words could raise pious foundations, as it were, out of the bare earth.[2] Calixtus urged a crusade upon apathetic Europe, and sent the Papal war-galleys to reinforce the Knights of St. John at Rhodes. John Hunyadi, Governor of Hungary for King Ladislas, helped by Capistrano as Papal legate, smote the terrible Mohammed II, "the Conqueror," at Belgrade and relieved this vital fortress (July 21, 1456).

[1] See B. Gebhardt, *Matthäus Döring der Minorit*, in *Historische Zeitschrift* (XXIII), 1888, 274; see also Creighton, *History of the Papacy* (1897), III, 140.

[2] See S. Voigt, *Johannes von Capistrano*, in *Historische Zeitschrift* (X), 1863, p. 52 ff.

On the death of Calixtus III in 1458, Æneas Sylvius became Pope, taking the name of Pius II. He convened a European Congress at Mantua, and presided there himself in 1459. Deputies, more or less important, came from all the great states, including the Empire, France and England; but they had no powers to offer actual quotas of troops and money; and all Pius' eloquence could not induce them to undertake an organized expedition. Even the attendant cardinals of the Pope gave him little help; they disliked Mantua, the food, the wine, the heat, and the perpetual croaking of the frogs in the marshes. Besides, as they told Pius, he could not conquer the Turks single-handed. The Congress of Mantua accomplished nothing for Europe (May, 1459, to January, 1460). While it was going on Pius was labouring to promote the establishment of new Military Orders to fight the Turks.[1]

So far the Papacy had shown itself to be the one truly international organ of diplomacy; and although it failed to unite Europe against the Turkish menace, the fault was not the Pope's. The next effort was to be made by the Emperor. In October–November, 1473, a great conference took place at Trèves between Frederick III and Charles the Bold of Burgundy. The real cause of the Conference was Charles' hope to be elevated to the rank of king by the Emperor; but other things were discussed too. The question of a crusade was referred to a commission which reported that nothing in this direction could be done until Charles the Bold was reconciled with Louis XI of France.[2] The method of effecting this reconciliation was referred to a second commission which, apparently, never reported. A great opportunity was missed, for the wealth, the energy, and the idealism of Charles the Bold, would have found their suitable outlet in an expedition for Europe against the Turks. Instead, the last of the mediæval heroes was to waste his strength and to lose his life struggling frantically in the toils of Louis XI.

Venice, having heroically defended its possessions on the Albanian or Greek mainland against Mohammed II, the Conqueror, made a Treaty of Peace and alliance with the Porte in 1479 and ceded Scutari. Mohammed profited by this infamous compact to attack

[1] See N. Bregion in *Sitzungsberichte der K. B. Akademie der Wissenschaften zu München* (1912), p. 55 (*Pius II Rüstungen zu Türkenkrieg*).

[2] Cp. *De Congressu Frederici III et Caroli . . . apud Treverin facto*, in *Rerum Germanicarum Scriptores* (ed. Struvio, 1717), II, 304.

and storm Otranto, which was in the Kingdom of Naples (August, 1480). This conquest was, however, only temporary. The Knights of St. John successfully defended Rhodes, and in the following year Mohammed II died. A Venetian diplomatist has left a careful description of the Conqueror's successor, Bayezid II—his olive complexion, his preoccupied expression, his austerity, sobriety, love of horse-exercise, his devotion to religious rites and almsgiving.[1]

By the end of the fifteenth century the states of Europe were hopelessly divided, and in their hostility to each other were quite ready to make political profit out of alliance with the Turks. Djem, a younger brother of Bayezid II, had rebelled against the Sultan, and, being defeated, had fled for refuge to the Knights of St. John at Rhodes (1482). The Knights saved Djem's life, but agreed with Bayezid to keep him prisoner in return for 45,000 ducats a year. The money was regularly paid by Bayezid. Djem was sent to a domain of the Knights in Auvergne. In 1489 Innocent VIII, who was desirous of promoting a crusade and who, like all the other monarchs, regarded Djem as a most valuable pawn, obtained the custody of him from the Knights of St. John, and the right to receive the annual payment of 45,000 ducats from Bayezid. Impassive and gloomy, Djem entered Rome on a white palfrey and rode in "stolid silence" amid a great procession.[2] A closely-guarded prisoner, he was sumptuously lodged in the Vatican. Innocent summoned a Congress to meet at Rome for the organizing of a crusade. Djem was to be placed on the Sultan's throne; in return he promised to Innocent to withdraw the Turks from Europe. The Congress met in Rome, in the summer of 1490; it was well attended and a working plan for a crusade was actually drafted.

On July 30 (1490) the envoys dispersed to obtain full powers from their governments. Nothing more happened; a contemporary authority wrote that the crusade was only prevented by the sudden death of the great warrior-king of Hungary, Matthias Corvinus.[3]

Innocent VIII died in 1492. His successor, Rodrigo Borgia, the notorious Alexander VI, out of dislike for the Neapolitan claims of the French king, Charles VIII, became the ally of Alfonso

[1] Baschet, *La Diplomatie Vénitienne* (1882), 219–20.

[2] Pastor, *History of the Popes* (trans. 1898), V, 299.

[3] Sigismondo de' Conti, *Le storie de' suoi tempi*, II, 4 (quoted by Pastor, *op. cit.*, V, 310).

of Naples. Charles VIII had a fantastic and vague idea of conquering Constantinople, if he was successful in conquering Naples. Alexander VI, on the other hand, was on good terms with the Sultan Bayezid, exchanged letters with him, and accepted the annual payment for Djem. Whether Charles VIII seriously intended to go on crusade is uncertain; in any case, as Alexander VI pointed out to him, the way to begin a crusade was not to attack a Christian state.

In December, 1494, Charles VIII entered Rome. He demanded to have possession of Djem, who was now kept in the strong castle of St. Angelo. Alexander handed over "The Grand Turk" to be held by Charles during the crusade on which the king declared that he was embarking. The French monarch with his army then passed on victoriously to Naples. He entered it almost without a blow. Now was the time for him to go on crusade, but he preferred to dally in the soft air of the earthly paradise. Djem died, probably of drunkenness, not of poison, on February 25, 1495. The king made this an excuse for abandoning all thought of a crusade.[1]

[1] For this chapter in general, see M. Creighton, *History of the Papacy* (1897), III–IV; L. Pastor, *History of the Popes* (trans. 1894), III–V; De la Jonquière, *Histoire de l'Empire Ottoman* (1914), I; Franz Lindner, *Die Zusammenkunft Kaiser Friedrich III mit Karl der Kühnen von Burgund im Jahre* 1473 *zu Trier* (1876).

CHAPTER III

LOUIS XI AND CHARLES THE BOLD

The struggle between one of the most "modern" of French kings and one of the most "mediæval" of dukes, attracted from the first the attention of Europe. It was the theme of the authentic and romantic memoirs of Philip de Commines, one of the most sagacious diplomatists of his age. It has been described, in the grand style, by Sir Walter Scott, in *Quentin Durward* and *Anne of Geierstein*. The interest of the struggle lies far deeper than the personal antagonism of the champions, the subtle, persistent Louis, and the heroic, misguided Charles. For Louis represented the spirit of national monarchy, powerful, exclusive, acquisitive; Charles was impelled, though he knew it not, by the spirit which transcends racial nationalism, for he aimed at building up a state from men of diverse race, history and language, to be bound together by a common loyalty and a common function in Western Europe, the function of keeping apart the French and Germans who in those days could not live at peace.

It is no more correct to say that the attempt of Charles the Bold to establish a "Middle Kingdom" was bound to fail, than it would have been correct to prophesy that the attempt to make a big Habsburg or Hohenzollern state was bound to fail. Charles the Bold's subjects had as much racial kinship and as good (or as bad) frontiers as the Prussians who were welded together by the Great Elector, Frederick the Great, and Bismarck. The Habsburg Monarchy, as it existed for five hundred years, had much less racial or geographical unity. Charles the Bold failed simply because he was a worse diplomatist than Louis XI, and because he had no sons to help him, and to carry on his work when he was gone. But it was chiefly lack of diplomacy that ruined him. Had he understood the new Italian "system" of balance of power, he could have preserved his state.

The territories which Charles the Bold inherited on the death of his father, Philip the Good, in 1467 had come into the possession of the Burgundian family by marriage and the accidents of the "feudal system," in much the same way as the Habsburgs acquired their lands. The Burgundian territories were the Duchy of Burgundy and the County of Burgundy (Franche Comté), and the Netherlandish fiefs of Flanders, Artois, Brabant, Limburg, Hainault, Holland, Zealand, Luxemburg, Antwerp and Malines.

By the Treaty of Arras, September 21, 1435, when Philip the Good abandoned the English alliance (originally made with Henry V) and gave his support to the French Crown, Charles VII ceded the towns and seigneuries on both banks of the Somme (*de l'un côté et de l'autre*), with the stipulation, however, that he could redeem them by a payment of 400,000 gold crowns.[1] The acquisition of the Somme towns (Amiens, St. Quentin, Corbie, Abbeville) brought the Burgundian power within 80 miles of Paris. For every province, district or town, the Duke of Burgundy was the "man," the vassal, either of the King of France or the Emperor; but feudalism was dying, liege homage was merely a name, and might soon have been forgotten altogether. Charles the Bold was rich beyond the dreams of avarice. His dominions were populous. He had many professional soldiers in his pay; he had a nobility and a bourgeoisie who could have made excellent diplomatists and administrators. But he lacked policy.

Charles the Bold was a man of attractive character, generous, chivalrous, chaste; he was fond of reading, especially in knightly history, and he had a wholesome love of open air—hunting in the forest of Soignies near Brussels, or fishing with daring sailors off the coast of Holland. Philip de Commines said that Charles the Bold never showed a sign of either fatigue or fear. The dresses of the Burgundian courtiers were famous for their magnificence. Charles could dress splendidly; but he seems to have felt more at home in his armour.

Very different from Charles was the man who was going to be his rival. He had a mean presence, and his dress and deportment did nothing to set off the insignificance of his person. He wore a doublet and mantle of grey fustian, and a shabby felt hat ornamented with leaden images of the Virgin. He liked to live in darksome places—in a gloomy, frowning castle

[1] Dumont, *Corps diplomatique* (1726), Tome II, partie II, 309–15, Art. XX.

like Loches, containing *oubliettes* and cages for "overmighty subjects."

In the fifteenth century sovereigns had not yet gained a monopoly of diplomatic business ; their vassals were still in the habit of entering into treaties as well as of maintaining their own armed forces. Charles, while only Count of Charolais, in the lifetime of his father, Philip the Good, had made a treaty of alliance with the Duke of Brittany, another of the great vassals of the King of France. This happened about the same time (1463) as Louis, making an unprecedented financial effort, redeemed the Somme towns which had been ceded to Philip of Burgundy at the Treaty of Arras. The friction existing between Burgundy and France was further increased by an act of Charles, who was residing at the Hague, in 1464. He caused a ship of Dieppe, which had put in at Gorcum on the coast of Holland, to be seized. Charles evidently thought that the skipper or owner of the ship was a pirate, a spy or a conspirator. He refused redress, although Louis sent a special embassy to claim it, to the court of Philip the Good at Lille. When in 1465 a number of discontented French nobles rose in arms against Louis XI, Charles joined actively in their revolt. He won a battle at Montlhéry, and maintained a desultory siege of Paris. This struggle, called the "War of the Public Weal," was fairly sanguinary, and it might have gone on for years ; it was very costly in treasure of which the king had little. So Louis offered to make peace with Charles and the other nobles. The terms were registered in the Treaty of Conflans, October 10, 1465.

By this treaty Louis regranted to Burgundy the Somme towns, in return for a payment of 200,000 crowns, and with the condition that he would not redeem them again during the lifetime of Charles. Louis also agreed that, in the execution of this treaty, he would subject himself to the decision of the Pope, and also permit himself to be sued "in all courts, as well ecclesiastical as civil." The other powerful vassals who had taken part in the revolt were suitably rewarded, so that Philip de Commines wrote : "The public weal was converted into private advantage—*le bien public estoit converti en bien particulier.*" [1]

The struggle between Louis XI and Charles the Bold was fought, as it were, in a series of "rounds." The first round, which ended with the Treaty of Conflans in 1465, had been won by Charles.

[1] Commines, I, xii.

He had gained back the Somme towns ; and Louis had been further weakened by having, at the same time, to give up Normandy, as an appanage, to his own brother Charles.

The second round in the struggle is concerned chiefly with Liège. This was an ecclesiastical principality, ruled by the bishop, who was a member of the Holy Roman Empire. The city of Liège was a prosperous place of over a hundred thousand inhabitants, highly industrialized, conspicuous to all the country around at night by the alternate gloom and glare of its furnaces. The Burgundian dukes naturally coveted it, for it lay between their northern and southern possessions. Accordingly when the citizens in 1466 rose in rebellion against their prince-bishop, who was a friend of the Duke of Burgundy, Charles the Bold invaded Liège, and imposed upon the citizens the " Piteous Peace." Not only was the authority of the bishop fully restored but also the citizens undertook that no alliance should be made without the consent of the Duke of Burgundy, who was to be recognized as hereditary protector of Liège. The Liègeois were not to maintain any fortresses on those parts of their frontier which marched with Burgundian possessions. The treaty was ratified on January 24, 1466.

Liège and its policy were by this treaty completely subordinated to the will of the Duke of Burgundy, and brought wholly within his political system. Louis XI, however, counter-balanced this increase of power on the part of Burgundy, for his brother Charles was not equal to the task of ruling Normandy, so Louis took it back into his own hands. Nevertheless, the position of Burgundy seemed unchallengeable. The duke was regarded throughout Western Europe as " the representative of Chivalry and the champion of Feudalism," and he had also prestige of a more valuable kind in the modern world of diplomacy that was just beginning. " Governments like that of Venice which regulated their conduct by the nicest rules of a scientific policy, saw the importance of cultivating the friendship of a sovereign whose power was already so considerable, and who had given such proofs of his determination to extend its limits." [1] Such was the condition of affairs when Philip the Good died in June, 1467. During the forty-eight years of his reign his numerous possessions had gained nothing but good from their union, and had enjoyed almost continuous peace and prosperity.

[1] Kirk, *History of Charles the Bold* (1863), I, 453.

The new duke, Charles the Bold, was not so pacific as his father. Louis XI realized that a war would quickly come. He took a step which brought out sharply the difference in outlook between himself and his antagonist. He summoned the French Estates-General (April, 1468) and appealed to their sense of nationality. Sacrifices, he said, would be necessary. "The matter was one which concerned the universal weal and the perpetuity of the kingdom, and not the mere interests of the king, who being mortal had temporary fee in the dominions over which he ruled."[1] Charles the Bold could make no such appeal. His states had no organic unity between themselves, no appreciation of the perpetuity of the whole, which is the sense of nationality.

Opposing forces were now in arms, and a clash seemed imminent. But Louis, always eager to use policy rather than arms, proposed negotiations, and even offered to confer with his adversary on Burgundian territory. Attended by only one or two officials and a single company of archers, having received a warrant of safe-conduct, written and signed by Charles, he went to Péronne (October 9, 1468). While he was there a revolution, which Charles believed to be caused by agents of Louis, and which in part probably was so caused, broke forth in Liège. Charles, in spite of the safe-conduct, at once closed the gates of Péronne, and held Louis virtually a prisoner.

The result was inevitable. Louis had to accept an agreement (Treaty of Péronne), October 14, 1468, which greatly strengthened Charles' position; in particular it released the courts of Flanders from the appellate jurisdiction of the Parlement of Paris. The treaty also contained the stipulation that if Louis violated any of its terms, the Duke of Burgundy and his heirs should be absolved for ever from their allegiance to the Crown of France.

Thus Charles the Bold won the second "round" of the struggle. Louis XI is one of the three kings who were made captive by their adversary, and had to assent to galling conditions. The first was John, captured at Poitiers by the Black Prince, in 1356. Louis was the second. Francis I, taken by the army of Charles V at Pavia, in 1525, was the third.

The third "round" of the contest between Charles the Bold and Louis was chiefly concerned with the last step in the Burgundian march to greatness, the gaining of complete independence and a crown. But this step was never to be completed.

[1] Chastellain, quoted by Kirk, I, 181.

In the years 1469–1474, between the second and the third (and last) round, Charles' strength was steadily increasing. In 1469 he married Margaret, sister of Edward IV, the powerful Yorkist King of England. The alliance was a decided check to the foreign policy of the French monarchy, which was bound to support the House of Lancaster, because of Margaret of Anjou, wife of King Henry VI (Henry was then a prisoner in the Tower of London). The Yorkist-Burgundian alliance received a shock in 1470 (October), when a Lancastrian revolution drove Edward IV from the throne and compelled him to flee for refuge to the court of Charles the Bold. Edward, however, returned to England with Burgundian help (March, 1471), defeated and killed the Earl of Warwick at Barnet (April), and routed Queen Margaret's forces at Tewkesbury (May). After this Edward IV was firmly seated on the throne, and the weight of Yorkist England was thrown on the side of Charles the Bold.

The Burgundian dominions went on growing. In 1473, taking advantage of civil troubles in Guelders, Charles acquired possession of that duchy. In 1469 Charles had, by the Treaty of St. Omer (May 9, 1469) concluded with Sigismund of Austria, purchased (Sigismund retaining a right of redemption) the Habsburg possessions in Southern Alsace (the Sundgau) and in the Breisgau or Black Forest region. In 1473 Charles made an arrangement with Réné, Duke of Lorraine, by which he became protector of that duchy against the French Crown, and by which the Lorraine frontier towns were to be permanently garrisoned by Burgundian troops. Thus at last Charles had lands, either directly under his rule or wholly within his political system, from the mouth of the Rhine upwards to where the Swiss Confederacy began at Bâle. In the surrounding regions he had a large measure of support from the public opinion of the feudal nobles who justly regarded him as the champion of the "feudal system" on which their own power and privileges depended. In the same year, 1473, Charles and the Emperor Frederick III had the famous conference at Trèves, which lasted amid the festivities and meetings for eight weeks.[1] The grand old city on the Moselle was the capital of the ecclesiastical principality of Trèves. The magnificent Burgundian nobles easily outdid in splendour the Imperial German court. Charles' prestige was at its height. Carpenters were erecting the

[1] See above, p. 9.

C

scaffolds, and jewellers were preparing the crown, for the great ceremony at which he was to be made a king by the Emperor, so that at last the House of Burgundy would stand forth in Europe an independent monarchy. But in the night of November 25 the old Emperor and his son with some half-dozen attendants slipped away in a barge on the dark and rapid stream of the Moselle, their tradesmen's debts unpaid and Charles still uncrowned.

The conflict between Charles the Bold and Louis XI was absorbing a great proportion of the energies of Christendom. Like the Hundred Years' War, recently concluded, it prevented any union of the Western states against the Turk. The Treaty of Péronne of 1469 was of short duration. Louis XI denounced it in 1470, and recaptured most of the Somme towns by force of arms. The papal court was at this time a highly conscious international centre. "No nationality is excluded from its offices and dignities."[1] It was alarmed at the paralysis of Western Europe caused by the endless Franco–Burgundian dispute. A legate—Cardinal Bessarion—was sent to France in 1472 to mediate in the conflict, but he had no success. Meanwhile Burgundy, Brittany and England were leagued together to support Charles the Bold.

Louis, on his side, was spinning his webs. Never was there a diplomacy more active. Although he did not maintain permanent embassies, he sent out frequent missions, open and secret. "He knew all persons of any authority or worth in England, Spain, Portugal and Italy."[2] Commines, who also writes this, says: "King Louis knew better the art of separating people than any man that I ever knew." He knew also the art of combining. The Swiss countries neighbouring to Alsace, though having mainly a peasant population, were guided by politic burghers of Bâle, Lucerne and Berne. The acquisition of a large portion of Alsace by Charles the Bold naturally alarmed them; the "Middle Kingdom," if successfully established, might absorb Switzerland. Louis had, as agents or allies, the prominent Bernese family of Diesbach. He was successful in mediating between Sigismund of Austria and the Swiss Confederation, who together in conference at Constance made, on March 30, 1474, the Eternal Compact (*Ewige Richtung*).[3] By this agreement the conflict of two hundred years between the Swiss and the Habsburgs came to

[1] See note in Pastor, IV, 194. [2] Commines, I, chap. 10.

[3] Dirauer, *Geschichte der Schweizerischen Eidgenossenschaft* (1887), II, 181.

an end. The victors of Morgarten and Sempach could afford to be generous. The money was found by which Sigismund could redeem from Burgundy his lost possessions in Alsace and the Schwarzwald. The offer of this money (which Charles refused) made war between Burgundy on the one hand, and the Swiss and Sigismund on the other, almost inevitable. A rising of the people of Alsace, who drove out the Burgundian garrisons, brought the war to the doors of the Swiss. In August (1474) an embassy from Louis XI appeared in Berne and in Lucerne. A treaty, dated on October 26, 1474, at Lucerne registered the defensive alliance of the Swiss Confederacy and Louis XI; a substantial subsidy, in case of war, was promised from France. The making of this coalition of Austria, the Swiss, and France was, says Philip de Commines, "one of the wisest things the king ever did." It was also one of the most difficult.

In 1475 the war reached its intensest point. Charles' army was never more numerous nor in better order.[1] He had only one real ally, but a substantial one—Edward IV of England. "But it was a whole year before the English army could be raised and set in order."[2] When Edward did at last invade France through the English fortress of Calais, Louis met him with diplomacy rather than with arms, and bought him off by the Treaty of Picquigny.

The negotiations were first conducted by heralds and other envoys who passed between the armies, and were concluded at a personal interview between the two kings. The place chosen for the interview, Picquigny, was a castle and small town about nine miles from Amiens. Commines writes:

> The town lies low; the river Somme runs through it, and it is not fordable or wide near it. On the one side, by which our king was to come, was a fine champaign country; and on the other side it was the same, only when the King of England came to the river, he was obliged to pass a causeway about two bow-shots in length, with marshes on both sides, which might have produced very dangerous consequences to the English, if our intentions had not been honourable. And certainly as I have said before, the English do not manage their treaties and capitulations with so much cunning and policy as the French do, let people say what they will, but proceed more ingenuously, and with greater straightforwardness in their affairs; yet a man must be cautious, and have a care not to affront them, for it is dangerous meddling with them.

[1] Commines, IV, chap. 1. [2] *Ibid.*

A wooden bridge was constructed over the river. In the middle of the bridge was a barrier of lattice-work. King Edward IV and Louis XI met, one on each side of the barrier, and conversed with each other through the lattice (August 29, 1475). The Treaty of Picquigny was concluded on the same day and was contained in four separate documents or agreements. The chief terms were that Edward IV should receive a lump sum of 75,000 gold crowns, and should take his army back to England; he was also to receive an annual pension of 75,000 gold crowns, during the lifetime of both kings, payments to be guaranteed by the bond of the bank of the Medici of Florence. All new charges imposed upon French traders in England or by English merchants in France were declared to be abolished. The allies of France or England could be comprehended in the peace if they so desired. The two kings entered into "true, sincere and perfect amity." This important treaty marks the real end of the Hundred Years' War. England ceases to chase the phantoms of the Middle Ages and prefers to secure commercial advantages. It was the policy of the "New Monarchy."

The catastrophic end of Charles the Bold was not far off. With the intention of gaining a protectorate over the ecclesiastical principality of Cologne, like that which he had acquired in Liège, he had laid siege to Neuss on the Rhine in July, 1474. The princes of the Empire rallied to the defence of the Archbishop of Cologne. After ten months Charles was forced to raise the siege of Neuss. When Edward IV made the Peace of Picquigny, Charles saw no other course open but to conclude with Louis XI a truce, with a nominal duration of nine years. In spite of his failures against the Archbishop of Cologne and the King of France, his design of forming a "Middle Kingdom" seemed at last on the eve of being accomplished.[1] He marched into Lorraine and without much difficulty conquered the whole duchy. Duke Réné took refuge at the French Court. On December 18, 1475, Charles, having summoned the Estates of Lorraine to Nancy, which he had just captured, declared that Lorraine would be the centre of his kingdom and that Nancy would be his capital. Then he passed on with his war-worn army to his native Duchy of Burgundy. But there was to be no rest for either troops or duke. In February, 1476,

[1] See the remarks of Otto Cartellieri in *Geschichte der Herzöge von Burgund* (1910), Band I, *Vorwort.*

he marched through the Jura with his army, to quell the Swiss, who seemed now to be the last obstacle in the way of his design for a Middle Kingdom stretching from the North Sea to the Alps. He met the forces of the Swiss Confederacy on the plain of Grandson by Lake Neuchatel on March 2, 1476, and was signally defeated. Charles retired with a considerable portion of his army, but without any of his valuable furniture and stores, to Lausanne (the Bishop of Lausanne was a ruling Prince of the Empire), and rested for a time by the lovely Lake of Geneva. In June he set off to Berne, the supreme object of his vengeance. Laying siege on the way to Morat, he again suffered a defeat at the hands of the levies of the Confederacy who came to relieve it (June 22, 1476). Charles escaped to the territory of Gex which belonged to his ally, the Duchess Yolande of Savoy. From Gex he went to the Duchy of Burgundy and pressed his weary subjects for money with which to raise another army. Meanwhile Réné had reopened the war for Lorraine and had recovered Nancy. Charles marched to Nancy, followed by the indomitable Swiss, who felt that the fate of their country depended on that of Lorraine. On January 5, 1477, he met the forces of Réné and the Swiss outside Nancy and was defeated and killed. He was forty-three years old.

On receiving news of the defeat of Charles, Louis XI immediately gave orders to his governor of Champagne to occupy the Duchy of Burgundy and Franche Comté, in spite of the claim or right of Charles' only child, Mary. The occupation of the duchy was carried into effect without any difficulty, but Louis failed permanently to hold Franche Comté. He sent Philip de Commines, who since 1473 had been in his service, finally to take over the Somme towns and districts. Flanders and the other adjacent Low Countries strenuously resisted the advance of French troops. To check the French the Dowager Duchess Margaret and her Council hastily agreed to a marriage which the Emperor Frederick III had long been pressing—the marriage of Mary to Maximilian of Habsburg. This was celebrated at Ghent on August 18, 1477, Maximilian being eighteen years old, and Mary twenty. The accession of the Habsburgs to the side of Mary and the danger of intervention from Edward IV of England (brother of the Dowager Duchess Margaret) induced Louis XI to cease hostilities and to enter into a truce in 1478. In March, 1482, Mary died, after being thrown from her horse while hunting, leaving a son and a daughter to Maximilian. Louis XI was still striving to obtain more of the late duchess's dominions, but death was claiming him too. Anxious to settle matters while he still had the power, he entered into negotiations with Maximilian and concluded peace by the Treaty of Arras, December 23, 1482. He died in his sixty-first year, on August 30, 1483.[1]

[1] For this chapter see J. F. Kirk, *History of Charles the Bold* (1869); Philip de Commines, *Mémoires*; P. F. Willert, *The Reign of Louis XI* (1876); H. Pirenne, *Histoire de Belgique* (1908), Tomes II, III; C. I. Scofield, *The Life and Reign of Edward IV* (1923); Rausch, *Die Burgundische Heirat Maximilians I* (1880). For the Trier (Trèves) Conference: Moltzer en Winkel, *Frederik III en Karel de Stoute te Trier*, in *Bibliotheek van Middelnederlandsche Letterkunde* (1891).

CHAPTER IV

THE ITALIAN EXPEDITION

The design of Charles the Bold to erect a Middle Kingdom between France and Europe had signally failed, and his dominions (except for the Duchy of Burgundy and the Somme towns, united to France) had passed almost intact, with the marriage of Mary, to the House of Austria. The titanic efforts of Charles the Bold, far from keeping France and " the Germanies " apart, had brought them closer together, with the balance preponderantly tipped in favour of the Germans. When, about 250 years later, Louis XV of France visited the tomb of Mary of Burgundy at Bruges, he remarked: " Here is the origin of all our wars."

When Charles VIII became King of France in 1483 at the age of thirteen, his sister Anne de Beaujeu, commonly called *Madame*, was made regent. France was now a fairly consolidated state. With the death of Réné of Lorraine, Anjou and Provence, Louis XI had acquired Anjou and Provence, although Réné's grandson was permitted to become Duke of Lorraine. This duchy, however, remained ever afterwards closely related to the French Crown until annexed to France in 1738.[1] Burgundy was gained for France on the death of Charles the Bold; but Flanders, Brabant, and other neighbouring Low Countries, including Luxemburg, definitely escaped from French hands and were included in the Habsburg dominions. Only the Duchy of Brittany remained as a type of the great mediæval fiefs, nominally under the suzerainty of the French Crown, but in fact independent—paying no taxes to the French treasury, sending no representatives to the Estates-General, repudiating any jurisdiction of the Parlement of Paris, and exercising the extreme feudal right of entering into treaties and military alliances with foreign sovereigns. The last Duke of Brittany, Francis II (died 1488), had a daughter, Anne, to succeed

[1] Technically Lorraine had its own sovereign duke until the death of Stanislaus Leczynski in 1766; see below, pp. 222–3.

him. Maximilian of Habsburg, the widower of Mary of Burgundy, was ready to marry her; and the council of Brittany, to save the independence of the duchy, consented. Such a signal triumph of the Habsburg marriage policy (which was always pursued by diplomatic means and never by threats or deeds of war) failed on this occasion. Maximilian was married by proxy to the Duchess Anne, in 1490, but the marriage was never completed. A French army sent by the energetic Regent Anne proved a more decisive influence, and on December 6, 1491, the Duchess Anne and Charles were married in prison. A military expedition of the English, led by King Henry VII in person in support of Breton independence, did not arrive in France until October, 1492. This campaign was almost an exact replica of the campaign of Edward IV in 1475, which was concluded by the Treaty of Picquigny. Henry VII laid siege to Boulogne, but forbore to assault the town, which was not in a very good condition for resistance. Throughout the siege commissioners on the part of the French and English crowns were negotiating.

> Meanwhile, a peace was concluded by the commissioners, to continue for both the kings' lives. Where there was no article of importance; being in effect rather a bargain than a treaty. For, all things remained as they were; save that there should be paid to the King seven hundred and forty-five thousand ducats [£186,250 sterling], in present, for his charges in that journey: and five and twenty thousand crowns yearly, for his charges in the aids of the Bretons. . . . And the truth is, it was paid both to the king, and to his son, king Henry VIII longer than it could continue upon any computation of charges.[1]

This treaty was concluded at Étaples on November 3, 1492. Henry VII thus showed that he had adopted the new system of conducting international affairs, and that he sought to attain his ends by policy in preference to using war. He gained external peace, and also what he equally needed, a useful store of money, for, wrote Bacon, "he foresaw at that time a storm of inward troubles coming upon him; which presently after broke forth."

For Charles VIII, writes the same wise authority, the Treaty of Étaples was equally decisive, "for that it assured unto him the possession of Brittany, and freed the enterprise of Naples."

[1] Bacon, *Life and Reign of Henry VII* (edition 1870), p. 327. The crown equalled six shillings and twopence. See Bridge, *History of France* (1921), I, Appendix, especially p. 258.

The Regency of Anne of Beaujeu came to an end in 1493. She had checked the resurgent feudalism of the French nobility, and she had acquired Brittany for the Crown. Yet because she had not made any use of Philip de Commines, that observant writer and eminent diplomatist makes scarcely any mention of her in his famous memoirs, except to say that she tried to dissuade Charles VIII from making the expedition to Italy.[1] The short-sighted, stuttering, and misshapen King of France, with the spindly legs and the protuberant paunch, had fed his mind on the romances of chivalry, and had decided to undertake a dazzling expedition of conquest into Italy, and, as he hoped, into the Near East. As soon as Anne of Beaujeu ceased to direct the councils of the king, he had made up his mind to go on the fateful journey, and had negotiated, in addition to the expensive Treaty of Étaples with England, still more expensive treaties with Spain and Austria. By the Treaty of Barcelona, January 3, 1493, he formed a defensive alliance with Ferdinand and Isabella of Spain, and ceded to them Cerdagne and Roussillon, provinces which were partly on the side of the Pyrenees towards France. By the Treaty of Senlis, May 23, 1493, he surrendered all rights over Franche Comté and Artois to Maximilian of Austria. Having thus abandoned territories on his eastern and southern frontiers which were indispensable to the security of France, Charles took up the ruinous policy (it must be remembered that he did not originate it)[2] of seeking for empire in Italy. For sixty years French arms and diplomacy ploughed the sands until Henry II at last turned his back on Italy, and reverted to the wholesome policy of gaining the "natural" frontiers on the east and south.

The states which between them divided Italy had for some years successfully maintained their independence by the policy of nicely adjusting the balance of power in the peninsula. This system was now to be subjected to a terrific strain or test, when the powerful state of France thrust its armies and its diplomatists into Italy, and strove for dominion there—a catastrophe which was in part due to invitations from various Italians, of whom the last and most seductive was the usurper, Ludovico, Duke of Milan.

[1] Commines, VII, chap. 5.

[2] For previous history of the French in Italy, see *L'Expedition de Charles VIII en Italie,* by J. Vaesen, in *Revue des Questions Historiques,* XLV (1889), 574; a very suggestive article.

Charles VIII had some claim to the crown of Naples, as heir of Réné of Anjou and Lorraine, titular king of Naples of the Angevin line; actually the kingdom was in 1494 in possession of Alfonso II, of the Aragonese dynasty, which had succeeded to Naples by conquest in 1442.

On August 23, 1494, Charles VIII set forth from Vienne with about 30,000 troops and large numbers of non-combatants. He marched through Savoy (a weak duchy under French influence) and passed into Piedmont by the Mont Genèvre Pass. The invasion presented no great difficulty. The Italian states through which the route lay either offered a way-leave or were compelled to provide one. On December 31, 1494, Charles VIII entered Rome and forced the Pope to sign a treaty, allowing to the French army passage through the papal dominions, and giving to Charles the custody of Prince Djem.[1] By February 22, 1495, the French, without much fighting, took possession of the city of Naples. In Bacon's words, Charles conquered Naples—or was it all Italy?—"in the felicity of a dream." Among the pleasaunces and gardens of Naples, gorgeous with flowers, and rich with citrons and oranges, the French army gave itself up to the enjoyment of ease and luxury. All authorities—even Commines who defends the French cause—agree that the French behaved loosely;[2] they lost the reputation of *saintliness*, which the Italians of the later Middle Ages had ascribed to them. And while the king and army were wasting their time and strength in Naples, the wise Venetians were forming plans to disencumber the peninsula from the foreigner.

Commines had been sent by Charles VIII on a diplomatic mission to keep Venice quiet, in the summer of 1494. He had a splendid reception from the Signory, and resided at Venice eight months at their expense; and every other ambassador—for all the diplomatic threads of Europe seem to have been concentrated in Venice in those months—was treated in the same way. Commines consistently explained to the Signory that Charles VIII had only two objects in coming to Italy—to make good his just claim to the Kingdom of Naples, and then to pass onwards to fight the Turk; but the Signory was not convinced. The news

[1] See above, p. 11.

[2] Delaborde, *L'Expedition de Charles VIII en Italie* (1888), pp. 575–6, makes a sort of defence of the army.

of the fall of Naples hastened the course of their diplomacy. On March 31, 1495, the League of Venice was concluded between the Signory and the ambassadors of the Pope, Maximilian of Austria, Ferdinand of Spain, and Ludovico, Duke of Milan. Next day Commines was invited to attend at the Signory and was gravely informed of the League. Its objects were: "the defence of Christendom against the Turk; the defence of Italy; the preservation of their own states." Commines, "sick at heart," put the best face he could on the matter, telling the Signory that he had known of the negotiations and had fully warned his master. He immediately sent off urgent warnings to Charles at Naples, and to the authorities at Paris, imploring them to dispatch reinforcements. He then departed from Venice and hastened to join the king. They met at Siena after Charles had started on his homeward march. At Fornovo, about sixteen miles south-west of Parma, on July 6, 1495, the French army by hard fighting escaped defeat at the hands of the army of the League of Venice. On October 23, Charles VIII recrossed the Mont Genèvre into France.[1]

While the French king had been preparing his Italian expedition, Spain and Portugal had been dividing the great world overseas. Disagreeing about their shares there, John II of Portugal and Ferdinand of Spain applied to Pope Alexander VI for a decision. The Pope drew a line from north to south one hundred leagues west of the Azores, and assigned to Spain all the lands to the west (Bulls of May 4, 1493). This arrangement was modified in a conference held at Tordesillas on the river Douro. The Treaty of Tordesillas, between Portugal and Spain, June 7, 1494, allotted to Portugal all lands east of a straight line drawn from Pole to Pole, at a distance of 370 leagues west of Cape Verde. Spain was to have all lands discovered west of this line.

[1] H. F. Delaborde, *L'Expedition de Charles VIII en Italie* (1888); J. H. Bridge, *A History of France from the Death of Louis XI* (1924); C. M. Ady, *A History of Milan under the Sforza* (1907); Sanudo, *La Spedizione di Carlo VIII in Italia*, in *Archivio Veneto*, III (1873). Pastor and Creighton are invaluable.

CHAPTER V

THE PARTITION OF ITALY

The "system" of the Balance of Power had often been put into practice among Italian states, in order that the predominance of any one Italian power—whether Venice, Florence, Milan or Naples—might be prevented in the Peninsula. In 1454, by the celebrated "Peace of Lodi," the chief Italian states had even combined in an alliance to prevent the French royal house from interfering in the peninsula and extending its influence there. The Venetians, in forming the League of 1495, had successfully put the system into operation again. But the system of Balance of Power has shifting foundations; it has never achieved permanence. The adjustment of 1495 had an existence of four years.

The Treaty or League of Venice of 1495, which was meant to endure for twenty-five years, revealed not only to the baffled Commines, but to the whole of Europe, the new system of international adjustment. The system itself only failed because, in 1498, Venice herself put an end to it by recklessly changing over to the side of France, lured by the prospect of gaining more territory on the Italian mainland.

During the fifteenth century the Venetians, partly in order that they might establish a strategic frontier against Milan, partly to compensate themselves for the advance of the Turks from the east, had extended their power over small towns or principalities on the Italian mainland westward to the River Adige, and beyond that river almost to Adda. In 1498 (April 7), Charles VIII, against whom they had created the League of Venice, died, falling down suddenly, at the age of twenty-eight, in his palace at Amboise, while he was watching a tennis-match. He had no children and so was succeeded by the head of the cadet (Orleans) branch of the House of Valois; this was Louis, Duke of Orleans, who, as king, is known as Louis XII. He was an athletic man, although thin and inclined to stoop, a chivalrous knight, and a careful administrator. His honour, his lands and his rights were his chief concerns; and therefore as combining in himself Orleanist claims on Milan and Angevin claims on Naples, he descended once more into the Italian arena. But he was cautious enough first to prepare the way by diplomacy, helped by the councils of one of the most active and daringly political of prelates, Georges d'Amboise, Archbishop of Rouen. He found the Venetians surprisingly ready to ally themselves with him; indeed, the initiative seems to have come from them. A debate was held in the Council of the Pregadi. Some of the senior councillors questioned the policy of French alliance, but the "forward" party carried the day, and offered to assist Louis XII on condition that he would guarantee to them Cremona and the territory known as Ghiara d'Adda, on both sides of the river of that name ("Treaty of Perpetual Confederation," Blois, February 9, 1498).[1] As the object of Louis XII was stated to be that he should gain Milan, and all its territory except the part which was to be the share of Venice, this is one of the first of the long series of Partition Treaties, which have been a feature of modern international relations; the war which ensued is the first War of Succession or Partition.

At the same time Pope Alexander VI was won to the French side by Louis XII's consenting to the marriage of Alexander's son, Cesare Borgia, with the beautiful and charming Charlotte d'Albret, cousin of the king. The Pope on his side gave a bull of dispensation to Louis so that he could marry Anne of Brittany, widow of Charles VIII, and thus keep this duchy for the French Crown. Georges d'Amboise was also made a cardinal. The interests of Crown and Papacy were thus cemented together. The Swiss, at war with the Empire, had made an alliance with France, March 16, 1499, allowing Louis to recruit troops in Switzerland, and promising in return for a subsidy that no Swiss recruits would serve Louis' enemies. In July (1499) the French king was able to announce that his allies were England, Scotland, Spain, Portugal, Sweden, Denmark, Norway, the Swiss, the Papacy, Venice and certain princes of the Empire. The French army immediately marched to North Italy and without difficulty conquered Milan. Duke Ludovico Sforza fled for refuge to the court of Emperor Maximilian at Innsbruck. Venice, according

[1] Sanudo, *Diarii*, II, 522–56.

to her bargain, took possession of the Cremonese and Adda territory.

The international crisis of 1499-1500 brought great gains to the Swiss, through their energy and decision. For shortly before they took Bellinzona [1] they had ended their old troubles with the Habsburgs. The Emperor Maximilian, striving to regain lost rights, had suffered a defeat (he himself was not present) at Dornach in 1499. Ludovico Sforza, involved in hostilities with Louis XII, had seized the occasion to offer mediation between the Empire and the Swiss, for their war was preventing all chance of his ever receiving support against France. A peace-conference, under Milanese mediation, met at Bâle (August-September, 1499), and on September 22 the Treaty of Bâle recognized the Swiss Confederation as a " companion " (*Glied*) of the Empire. Although this did not amount to a formal recognition of independence (which was not gained until the Peace of Westphalia), it was a practical separation of the Swiss from the sovereignty of the Emperor.[2]

The Peace of Bâle was a brilliant diplomatic success on the part of Ludovico, for next year, February-March (1500), he was able to return to Lombardy with German and Swiss troops (paid for by him, of course), and to recapture Milan. In April the French and Milanese forces faced each other at Novara, which was held by Ludovico. But there were Swiss companies on both sides and they refused to fight. They made a military convention with the French commander, La Tremoille, that the Swiss in Ludovico's army should march away safely, and that if the French could find Ludovico, they could take him. As the Swiss soldiers marched out of Novara, Ludovico dressed as one of them, was discovered and made prisoner. He was taken to France, where he died at Loches, eight years later. The Swiss companies, in returning home, took possession of the Milanese territory of Bellinzona (the inhabitants had already asked the Swiss Confederation to admit them to their union), claiming it under an old promise of Louis XII as Duke of Milan. This occupation is the foundation of the Swiss canton of Ticino.

Milan was now firmly (as it seemed) in French hands. Maximilian recognized this fact and made a truce. For a year, Europe, except for the Turks, was in complete peace. Christendom was

[1] See below, p. 30.

[2] Dirauer, *Geschichte der Schweiz. Eidgenossenschaft*, II, 363.

still undivided; a crusade was the subject of general talk. Louis XII sent envoys and made a treaty of alliance with King Ladislas of Bohemia and Hungary, and with King John Albert of Poland (July, 1500). He dispatched a fleet to the Archipelago to help the Knights of St. John against the Turks. The fleet was, however, unsuccessful; and Louis almost at once was plunged into the complication of war in Italy. The fair promise of the year 1500 vanished like a dream. It was ruined by the fatal tendency which pushed every dynasty to extend its possessions.

On November 11, 1500, French and Spanish plenipotentiaries signed the secret Treaty of Granada, for the partition of the Kingdom of Naples: the claim of Aragon and Anjou was to be divided. Spanish and French armies descended upon Naples, captured it, and then quarrelled. This began the Franco-Spanish wars for Italy, which lasted with intermissions for nearly sixty years.[1]

[1] Guicciardini, *Istoria d'Italia*, Libro Quarto (there is an English translation in one rare volume by Geffray Fenton, published in folio in 1599); Kohler, *La Conquête du Tessin par les Suisses*, in *Rev. historique*, XLV (1891), pp. 308–23. For a very complete account of the Swiss undertakings, see E. Gagliardi, *Der Anteil der Schweitzer an der italienischen Kriegen*, 1494–1516 (1919).

CHAPTER VI

THE LEAGUE OF CAMBRAI

In the first years of the fifteenth century, it seemed as if diplomacy was going to give to Western Europe a "universal peace." It is true that the French and Spanish monarchs were bickering over the partition of Naples. Yet on August 10, 1501, a treaty was signed at Lyons on behalf of Louis XII and the Archduke Philip of Austria. Philip's son Charles (later the Emperor Charles V) was to marry Claude, the only daughter of Louis XII; "with this event began the splendid dream of a united Europe."[1] As, however, Charles was only eighteen months old at the time, and his *fiancée* two years, the marriage project was perhaps not to be taken very seriously. Yet three years later a remarkable treaty, signed on September 22, 1504, at Blois, on behalf of Louis XII and the Emperor Maximilian and the Archduke Philip, united the Habsburg and Valois monarchs as "one soul in three bodies" (*una anima in tribus corporibus*).[2] Their immediate object was to maintain the *status quo* in Italy. Thus would be settled the quarrel over Naples, which the French had absolutely lost to Spain. The Archduke Philip's son, Charles, who was to marry Claude, was to have Naples.

The fair design of a Habsburg-Bourbon union, which would have brought peace to Europe if honourably intended, was really corrupt; for a secret supplement of the Treaty of Blois contained a project for a partition of Venice in concert with the Pope Julius II.

This energetic and even fiery ecclesiastic was just short of sixty years old when he was elected Pope, in October, 1503. He was a prelate of enormous wealth (drawn from numerous rich benefices which he had held) and of liberal tastes. A man of the Renaissance, interested in painting, architecture and literature, a great builder of villas and palaces, a father of a family (although a

[1] Hill, *A History of European Diplomacy*, II, 232.
[2] Dumont, IV, Partie I, 55.

priest), he was also a soldier and statesman. He had seen Cesare Borgia, the son of Alexander VI, annexing one dominion after another from the petty lords of the Romagna ; and he now planned to take in all those lordships into the Papal State and to establish a solid Temporal Power in Italy. Raphael's famous picture of Julius as he sits in his chair, his grand head reflectively inclined, his lips closed and firm, expresses the deep designs and the strong will of the terrible old man.

As soon as he was elected Pope, Julius had Cesare Borgia arrested and compelled him to surrender Romagna to the Papacy. Having secured this, Julius let him go. The brilliant adventurer, so admired by Machiavelli, went to Naples, where the Spanish government arrested him. Imprisoned in Spain, he escaped to France in 1506, and met a soldier's death in the service of the King of Navarre against a rebellious vassal.

The Venetians, even more alarmed by the Pope's annexations in Romagna than they had been by Cesare Borgia's, made the great mistake of occupying Faenza and Rimini, in order that they might have a "strategic frontier." This brought down upon them the wrath of Julius, and he entered into the Secret Treaty of Blois on the side of France and the Empire. Although the marriage contract of the Treaty of Blois was never completed, and the Habsburg-Valois union was really doomed, it lasted just long enough for the Emperor Maximilian and Louis XII, with the Pope Julius II and King Ferdinand of Spain, to make the League of Cambrai, December 10, 1508. On November 22 the Archbishop Georges d'Amboise, now a cardinal, entered the quaint old Picardy city with a grand retinue of over four hundred cavaliers. Soon after came Margaret of Austria, daughter of Maximilian and Governor of the Netherlands, a capable woman, devoted to family and to politics. The League of Cambrai began with a treaty concluded by Margaret and Amboise. The ostensible object was to fight the Turks. A supplementary secret treaty of the same date (December 10, 1508), between the Emperor, Pope and King of France, designated the Venetians as the enemy—each state was "to recover its possessions occupied by them." [1]

All princes who had any claims upon Venice, or rather upon its lands and possessions, were to be invited to join in the operations. The frontiers of Milan and Naples were to be readjusted in favour

[1] Guicciardini (ed. 1819), chap. VIII, p. 7 ; Dumont, IV, Partie I, 109–16.

of Louis and Ferdinand, those of the Empire and Austria in favour of Maximilian, and those of the States of the Church in favour of the Pope.[1]

The war which now ensued recalls to the historian a later war, that of 1672, fought by Louis XIV for the destruction of another free, commercial republic, Holland. The view of the French Court in 1508 in regard to the Venetians was that "those fishermen must be driven back into their lagoons to catch fish." The Venetians, on their part, girded themselves for the struggle, believing that once for all they would drive the French from Italy. They were supported by the flower of the Italian knighthood. With cries of "Italy! Liberty!" they met the French (who had crossed the Adda from Milan) at Agnadello, May 14, 1509, and were utterly overthrown. This was the end of the secular greatness of Venice and of the hopes of Italian patriots for centuries. The Venetian Government resigned itself to giving up all its territories on the mainland, content, if by extraordinary efforts of war and diplomacy, it could save the city of Venice and its islands.

Fortunately, diplomacy could be a strong aid to the weak though still valiant right arm of Venice. The Signory, whose relations with England had not been good, sent a skilful negotiator, Badoer, as permanent ambassador to the court of Henry VII—the first permanent embassy in England. Badoer suggested to Henry VII that the French were becoming too powerful in Italy. This consideration might not move the cautious old king, the ruler with the "few hairs, few teeth, and a face that no painter would envy, studying his advantage more than his reputation." He was now dying. Badoer delivered his message. The king answered (through his councillors) that "he was pleased with the peace between the King of the Romans and France but much displeased to hear that France was coming against the Signory of Venice; which was not going against Infidels."[2] The son who succeeded to the throne, the brilliant, ambitious Henry VIII, was soon ready for action. His father-in-law, the crafty Ferdinand, with the whole Kingdom of Naples in his hands, was thinking that the conquest by France of Venice, in addition to Milan, would make France a

[1] Ranke, *Latin and Teutonic Nations*, Bk. II, chap. III, § 4. The Kingdom of Naples was concerned because it had pledged some Apulian harbours to Venice.

[2] *Letters and Papers, Foreign and Domestic, of the Reign of Henry VIII* (1920), I, 3.

danger to himself in the Italian peninsula. But most of all was Pope Julius II moved. His invitation to the French, his League of Cambrai, had succeeded only too well. Venice had been chastised, but at the cost of all Italy, doomed now, as it seemed, to become part of a French Empire. Quickly he threw all his weight —his wealth, his prestige, his unique opportunities for exercising diplomatic influence—on the side of Venice. While, inspired by their doge Leonardo Loredano (whose strong and noble countenance still looks out from Giovanni Bellini's painting), the Venetians were fighting for their lives, Pope Julius was sending letters to King Ferdinand and the Swiss.

In February, 1509, Louis XII himself, always careful about money, had terminated his alliance with the Swiss. Rather than pay subsidies to the Confederation, he would hire Swiss for his army individually. This he did, but it left the Confederation free to conclude an alliance, March 14, 1510, with Pope Julius II. This was arranged by the Pope's agent, the famous Matthäus Schinner, Bishop of Sion.[1] In return for a subsidy the Confederation was to send 6,000 men against the Pope's enemies. When next year a courier, with the armorial bearings of Schwyz sewn on his tunic, went forth to receive the subsidy, he was seized by the inhabitants of Lugano (Francophile subjects of the Duchy of Milan) and drowned in the lake. This violation of the courier's diplomatic immunity (for he had the sacred character of a herald) aroused the indignation of the Swiss, and brought them, not simply as auxiliaries of the Pope, but as principals, into the war against France. Ferdinand of Aragon in the same year, October 5, 1511, joined with the Pope in an alliance, now to be called the Holy League.

France was left with only the alliance of James IV of Scotland, and the Emperor Maximilian. Scotland had no troops to send, Maximilian's were not dependable. Mediation was tried. Scotland had an envoy in Italy called Murray; Maximilian sent his most active diplomatist, Matthäus Lang, Bishop of Gurk (a lay official of the Imperial Chancery),[2] who was equal to the most arduous journeys. But the mediation of those men between the Emperor and the Pope was unavailing. Louis XII was furious

[1] See Gagliardi, *Der Anteil der Schweitzer*, I, 831.

[2] Lang was not ordained priest until 1519, after he had become Archbishop of Salzburg.

and swore that he would overthrow the Papacy itself. His armies and those of the Holy League met on the plain of Ravenna on Good Friday, April 9, 1512. The French and Spanish commanders-in-chief, Gaston de Foix and Ramon de Cardona, spoke across one of the irrigation canals that intersect the plain. "Shall we fight to-day?" asked the Spaniard. "If you will, we are ready," answered Gaston. They broke the white staves which they held as a sign that they met in peace.[1] When evening fell the French were victors on the field, but Gaston de Foix, aged twenty-three, the flower of French chivalry, the genius of their high command, was no more.[2]

[1] Ranke, *Latin and Teutonic Nations*, p. 333.

[2] See also Le Glay, *Négociations diplomatiques entre la France et l'Autriche durant les trente premières années du XVIe siècle* (1845); also Guicciardini, Pastor, Creighton. There is some interesting material in L. M. Ragg, *Crises in Venetian History* (1928).

CHAPTER VII

ENGLAND AND THE NEW DIPLOMACY

The new Diplomacy, the policy of balance, which had its centre in Italy, did not leave even the distant state of England out of the system. The affair of Brittany, which Anne of Beaujeu was doing her best to annex to France, inclined Henry VII to anti-French courses. Ferdinand and Isabella of Spain, anxious to recover Cerdagne and Roussillon from France,[1] desired English support. It was on such calculations that the Treaty of Medina del Campo, March 12, 1489, was based, negotiated by Dr. Thomas Savage (one of Henry VII's chaplains, afterwards Archbishop of York), and Richard Nanfan, Deputy-Lieutenant of Calais, in the Spanish camp, south of Valladolid. It provided for the future marriage of the Princess Katharine of Aragon (then aged three) and Arthur, Prince of Wales (aged two and a half years). Spain and England became allies in war against France. This war, however, did not prevent the union with France and Brittany in 1491. Nevertheless, although Henry VII made peace with France at Étaples in 1492, alliance with Spain, based on the Treaty of Medina del Campo, remained the corner-stone of English foreign policy until the divorce of Katharine of Aragon and the breach with Rome.

After the invasion of Italy by Charles VIII in 1494, and his astonishing conquest of the Kingdom of Naples, the alliance of England was cultivated more intensely than ever by the states seeking to check the preponderance of France. Pope Alexander VI and Ferdinand of Spain urged Henry VII to join the Holy League. This created a favourable atmosphere for negotiations with Ferdinand's son-in-law, the Archduke Philip, the ruler of the Netherlands. Thus was concluded the "Treaty of Peace and Intercourse," [2] which Bacon in his *Life of Henry VII* calls the Magnus

[1] In 1493 Charles VIII ceded the provinces to Spain. See above, p. 25.

[2] Rymer, *Fœdera* (1711), XII, 578–90.

Intercursus, signed at London on February 24, 1496. The chief English commissioner for negotiating this treaty was Richard Fox, Bishop of Durham. The chief Burgundian commissioner was Philip, Lord of Benves, Captain-General and Admiral. The treaty restored the commercial intercourse which had been interrupted for ten years through the support given by Flanders to Yorkist pretenders to the English throne. The treaty enacted that trade should take place freely between England and Flanders, subject only to such dues as had been levied in the previous fifty years. On July 18, 1496, Robert Sherburne, who had been sent on mission to Rome, gave the English adhesion to the Holy Alliance. Thus Henry VII ensured that the Anglo-Spanish Marriage-Treaty of 1589 (Medina del Campo) would be implemented. His accession to the Holy League did not involve him in actual hostilities with France, for Charles VIII had already lost the French conquests in Italy and died two years later, before he could make a fresh expedition to retake them.

In 1501 the Infanta Katharine came to England and was married to Prince Arthur. Next year another momentous marriage treaty was concluded. The negotiations for this originated in a frontier incident on the Scottish border. In 1498, during a truce, some fighting had taken place at Norham, the great castle on the Tweed, of which the Bishop of Durham was the lord and defender. Fox, who was the best English diplomatist of the time and who also, as Bishop of Durham, was partly responsible for the peace of the Border, went to Melrose to regulate the troubles with the Scots. There he took occasion to open a proposal for a marriage alliance of England and Scotland. The plan was too revolutionary to be at once accepted; but in 1501 Scottish commissioners arrived in London and met Fox, who held a commission from Henry VII, to negotiate a marriage. The sweet-tempered and thoroughly practical bishop (no longer of Durham, but now of Winchester) carried his task, through many months of arduous conference, to a successful conclusion. The marriage treaty of June 24, 1502, put an end to the secular conflict of Scots and English, and united the Thistle and the Rose for the first time in 300 years. On August 7, 1502, James IV and Margaret Tudor were married in Holyrood Abbey. Although the marriage was not happy, and did not ensure lasting peace, it was effective for the rest of the reign of Henry VII.

This king never let an opportunity slip. In 1504 Queen Isabella of Castile died. Her daughter Juana and her son-in-law the Archduke Philip, became Queen and King of Castile. In 1506 they sailed from the Netherlands for Spain, but stress of weather compelled them to land on the coast of Dorset. Henry VII invited them to Windsor, entertained them royally, and persuaded Philip to agree to a treaty of alliance and to leave behind him an authority for a treaty of commerce. The commercial treaty (signed at London on April 30, a week after Philip's departure) admitted English woollens to the Netherlands. The merchants of the Netherlands naturally disliked losing their monopoly of the home market; but the name, Malus Intercursus, commonly applied to this treaty, is not found anywhere before Bacon's *Life of Henry VII*.

King Henry VII died on April 21, 1509, and was succeeded by his surviving son, Henry VIII; Arthur, the elder son, had died in 1502. On June 3, 1509, Henry VIII married the widow of Arthur, with a dispensation granted by Pope Julius II. Thus the political connection with Spain, or at least with Aragon, became stronger than ever; and in 1513 Henry VIII joined the League of Cambrai. By this time the French, in spite of their victory at Ravenna, had lost all their possessions in Italy—the Duchy of Milan, and even Genoa. Henry's part in the war was personally to lead the invasion of Northern France, and to send an expeditionary force to Guienne. The League of Cambrai, however, was not interested in the mediæval design of the English to hold French provinces; and so Henry's ardour in the cause of the League soon cooled. Influenced by Fox, who was still, according to reports of the Venetian ambassador, powerful in the king's councils, and by Wolsey, a new and rising star, Henry made peace with France at London on July 10, 1514. Louis XII undertook to renew and to increase the Étaples pensions which had not been paid during the war; and he also engaged himself, being now a widower, to marry Henry VIII's sister Mary. The marriage took place and ensured an Anglo-French alliance. It was the greatest revolution which had ever occurred in English foreign policy.

Thomas Wolsey was one of the three great diplomatists of the early sixteenth century, of whom two were clergymen. The other was the councillor of Louis XII, Georges d'Amboise, who died in 1510. The third was a layman, Mercurino Gattinara, an official first of Maximilian, and subsequently of Charles V. Wolsey's rise was sublime. He was the son of an Ipswich wool merchant, became a Fellow of Magdalen College, Oxford, took a country living, became chaplain to Richard Nanfan, the Deputy of Calais, and so became attached to the king's service. His power of work was enormous, his ambition insatiable, his capacity for handling diplomatic affairs almost unrivalled. By the year 1515 Richard Fox, Bishop of Winchester, hitherto the chief adviser, was beginning to divest himself of secular affairs so that he might devote himself exclusively to good works. Wolsey became Henry VIII's right-hand man. He was a true European, not unmindful of the interests of his own country (nor indeed of himself), but with a belief that he had a responsibility for Europe as a whole and for the general peace.

The French alliance which Wolsey had made in 1514 suffered a blow from the sudden death of Louis XII in January, 1515, three months after his English marriage. Henry VIII at once ordered Wolsey to procure the return of the dowry of Mary, the young widow. Wolsey sent as ambassador an active and magnificent nobleman, Charles Brandon, later Duke of Suffolk. The Duke succeeded in obtaining partial return of the dowry ; and for himself he gained a wife, marrying (apparently in February, 1515) Mary, with whom he had for long been in love, before he returned to England. Francis I of France, sure that Mary could not now be given as a bride to any of his enemies, went off to Italy, renewing the policy of Charles VIII and Louis XII (August, 1515).

The League of Cambrai had been dissolved long before this, when the French, after the battle of Ravenna, lost Milan. Venice had saved herself by her own exertions and through the assistance of the Holy League. When her safety was assured she returned to her old policy of peace and of alliance with France. The Venetians were no longer in fear of partition ; and their diminished strength prevented them from aspiring to control Italy. So they let the French have their own way.

Julius II died in 1513. The terrible old man, who had aimed to be "lord and master of the game of the world,"[1] had not scrupled to engage in sanguinary war, actually at the age of sixty-eight commanding troops in person, amid the snow before

[1] Domenigo Trivixan, MS., quoted in Ranke, *History of the Popes,* I, chap. 2.

the walls of Mirandola in 1511. When he died he left the papal Temporal Power, of which he was practically the creator, supreme throughout Central Italy from Piacenza to Terracina.

The new Pope was Giovanni de' Medici, Leo X. He was a statesmanlike man, who studied to be agreeable to all persons, and was anxious to live at peace and to enjoy his tenure of the Papacy. He had no desire to plunge into political adventures; the only thing he feared was that the French, if they regained Milan from the Sforzas, would take away Parma and Piacenza from the Papal States; the only political object which he earnestly desired was to extend the influence and wealth of the Medici family in Florence and elsewhere. Accordingly in 1515, when Francis I of France was openly preparing to invade Italy for the purpose of gaining Milan, Leo X entered into union with the Emperor Maximilian, Ferdinand of Spain, Milan, Florence, and the Swiss, to resist the French (February, 1515). In order to secure the neutrality, if he could not have the support of England, he granted Wolsey's ardent wish by making him a cardinal (September, 1515). The weight of the French attack fell upon the Swiss, who, under the redoubtable Cardinal Schinner, held a position at Marignano, guarding Milan. At the battle of September 14, 1515, the French gained an overwhelming victory. This was the end of the commanding rôle which the Swiss had played on the European stage in the period of the Renaissance. The Canton of Ticino is the surviving witness of this brief period of Swiss military ascendancy. "The battle of Marignano was a check to the spread of republican ideas, because it dispelled the charm of success which had hitherto accompanied the republican organization in war. By this battle the way was cleared for the assertion in European affairs of the monarchical principle." [1]

The victory of Marignano has been considered the opening or reopening of the secular struggle of France and the Empire. In the long run it may be considered in this light, but actually it was at the moment the prelude to a sustained and successful effort made by the Western monarchs to secure a universal peace. Francis I was content with gaining the Duchy of Milan. He re-annexed Parma and Piacenza to the Duchy of Milan and then made peace with the Pope. On January 23, 1516, Ferdinand of Spain died, and was succeeded by his grandson, called Charles V (Charles I of Spain), who

[1] Creighton, *History of the Papacy*, V, 243.

was also heir to the Burgundian and Austrian dominions. Charles was a cool-headed young man, naturally inclined to peace, fond of administration, and of hunting, blessed with a healthy appetite. He was no knight-errant like Francis I. Advised by his Walloon councillor, the Seigneur de Chièvres, he decided to seek peace, not war, with France. On August 13, 1516, the Treaty of Noyon was made. Charles was to marry Louise, the daughter of Francis I (she was only one year old), and to her the French claims to Charles' Kingdom of Naples would be made over. The Emperor Maximilian, grandfather of Charles V, acceded to the treaty in December, 1516. Wolsey seized the occasion to intensify negotiations with all states—with Leo X, the Venetians, Maximilian, Charles V, Francis I. Western Europe was in a condition of equilibrium, and, if England were determined to favour no one party, peace might be maintained indefinitely, for the continental monarchs were in desperate need of money, and England had both money and men; she was then, as Montesquieu said of her later, *la puissance médiatrice de l'Europe*. After an elaborate exchange of special embassies a treaty of alliance was signed, under the mediation of the Pope, between France and England at London on October 2, 1518. The treaty, which took the form of a league against the Turks, enunciated the principle not simply of Anglo-French peace, but of "universal peace." The signatory powers mutually guaranteed each other's possessions; other powers were to be invited to adhere to the peace, which would then be under the guarantee of the principal contracting parties (*principaliter contrahentes confoederati*). All the numerous allies of the contracting parties were stated to be comprehended within the league.[1]

The adhesion of Charles V was given in Saragossa on January 14, 1519, two days after the death of his grandfather, the Emperor Maximilian. The ratification of Leo X was given through the legate at London on December 2 (1519). Europe—at least Western Europe—was thus left in control of three young monarchs, Charles V, Francis I, Henry VIII, who were in alliance with each other and pledged to maintain the peace. The Universal Church and

[1] Full text in Rymer, XIII, 624–31. See also Busch, *England under the Tudors* (trans. 1895); Brewer, *The Reign of Henry VIII* (1884); Busch, *Drei Jahre Englands Vermittlungspolitik* (1884); Pollard, *Henry VIII* (1905). The monumental, invaluable series of Public Record Office volumes, published by H.M. Stationery Office under the title of *Letters and Papers, Foreign and Domestic*, begins with the death of Henry VII.

the Papal State, represented by Leo X, who had also worked for the concord of all the sovereigns, was a member of this "holy alliance." Apart from the Turks, there was a real, a universal peace, which already in effect had been unbroken since the end of the Marignano campaign. How long would this peace endure ?

CHAPTER VIII

HABSBURG AND VALOIS

Since the battle of Marignano, when the King of France had gained (or regained) Milan, there had been peace in Europe; and the brilliant success of Wolsey in 1518 had turned this into the guaranteed Universal Peace, which endured for three years more.

The power of the French monarchy was very high. France was the most solidly united people on the Continent. The authority of the French king was the most absolute. The monarchy had triumphed over all other civil authorities during the agonies of the Hundred Years' War; it now triumphed over the Church. By the Concordat negotiated between Francis I and Leo X in August, 1516, the French chapters lost their right to elect to the vacant bishoprics and abbeys. Instead, the king was to nominate, and the Pope was to institute a prelate to the vacant place; nor had the Pope any right to refuse institution to the person nominated by the king.

Between Francis I and Charles V there were plenty of latent subjects of dispute, besides their eternal claims to Naples and Milan. The existing peace was obviously temporary and provisional; nevertheless, a provisional state of affairs often has a curious habit of enduring; and Wolsey was honestly anxious to make it endure.

On January 12, 1519, the Emperor Maximilian died. The obvious candidate for the vacancy was his grandson Charles V, lord of the Austrian territories (through his grandfather Maximilian), of the Netherlands (through his father), of Spain and the Indies (through his mother). Francis I of France also was a candidate; and finally Henry VIII, rather late, entered the lists. His representative was Richard Pace, a brilliant young ecclesiastic, friend of Erasmus, and personal secretary of King Henry. He now held the position of Secretary of State. He had already performed important diplomatic duties abroad, before he was sent to Frankfort.

"Here," wrote Pace, "is the dearest merchandise that was ever sold." All the three candidates spent a great deal of money. On June 28, 1519, Charles V was elected "King of the Romans." That the empire was now a purely national German affair was shown by the fact that the electors, before registering their decision, made Charles sign a capitulation, in which he undertook to confer no office on anyone but a German.[1]

Although the Imperial Election further ruffled the international surface of Europe, already by no means smooth, Wolsey still hoped to maintain the Universal Peace, and his own position as its organizer. He busied himself in exchanging visits between Henry and the two monarchs. Charles V visited England in May, 1520—the first foreign monarch to come since the Emperor Sigismund in 1416. In June, 1520, the famous meetings with the magnificent pageantry on the "Field of the Cloth of Gold" took place. Henry and Francis conferred together, but, although Charles V was near at hand, at Gravelines, Wolsey never sent him a summons—the international atmosphere, even on the Field of the Cloth of Gold, was not sufficiently serene. Wolsey would have liked to confirm the Universal Peace by forming a general confederacy; instead, he had to content himself with making separate treaties between England and each of the two monarchs. The new Anglo-French treaty was made during the Conference of the Field of the Cloth of Gold, at Calais on June 6, 1520. The treaty between England and Charles V was made on July 14, 1520, also at Calais. By these acts existing treaties were renewed and the friendship of England with both parties confirmed. The peace endured, with the help of more conferences and embassies organized by the indefatigable Wolsey, until after another year he made, rather unaccountably, a secret treaty of alliance between England and Charles V against France on August 25, 1521. Here ended his glorious fabric, the Universal Peace.

Wolsey met his match in Gattinara. This active Piedmontese, devoted to the interests of his great employer Charles V, belonged to the school of diplomatists described in the early part of More's *Utopia*, men who study how to promote their master's interests, and who judge the chances of war or peace solely from the point of view of their master's particular advantage. It was nothing

[1] See Hartung, *Die Wahlcapitulationen der Deutschen Kaiser*, in *Historische Zeitschrift*, Band 107 (1911), pp. 321–30.

to Gattinara that Wolsey looked upon Europe as a Christian community of states which should live in universal peace; he was determined to gain the support of English men and money for war against France which he regarded as the natural and hereditary enemy of his master.

Mercurino Gattinara was born in 1465 at Vercelli. At the age of twenty-five he became Doctor of Law of the University of Turin and took up the profession of an advocate. The Duke of Savoy, Charles I, attached Gattinara to his person as a legal official. In 1508 he went with Margaret of Austria, widow of the Duke of Savoy, to the Netherlands, where she was to be Governor for the Emperor Maximilian. Here he met the young Charles V, then only six years old. Gattinara for the rest of his life was one of the few familiars of Charles. He knew all the famous diplomatists of the period—the Seigneur de Chièvres, Georges d'Amboise, Wolsey and the rest. Able lawyer, expert official of the Chancery, man of the world, discreet, prudent, industrious, devoted, Gattinara was the ideal servant for the morbid, moody Charles V. He was an austere man of inflexible will, ate only once a day, wrote everything with his own hand, read all the dispatches, and spent himself in the service of his master. He died at Innsbruck in 1530.[1]

It cannot be asserted that Charles V personally desired to dominate Europe. Obstinate, irresolute, honest, conscious that he was lord of more territories than one man could manage, Charles had no designs of world-empire. His long wars with Francis I were the result of his views and the views of Francis and of their respective advisers, who all held that independent states were enemies to each other, always on the look-out to snatch an advantage—a world of armed enemies. To encircle a neighbour with hostile alliances was considered to be legitimate self-defence. Gattinara was determined to use diplomacy to construct such a scheme of defence. The French, naturally, felt their existence to be endangered, and took counter-measures. A war for the defence of rights arose and only terminated after thirty-eight years with the exhaustion of both sides.

[1] See Gaudenzo Claretta, *Notice pour servir à la vie de Mercurin de Gattinara*, in *Mémoires et Documents publiés par la Société Savoisienne d'histoire et d'archéologie*, T. XXXVII (1898), 247–59. See also the detailed description of Gattinara in Alberi, *Relazioni degli Ambasciatori Veneti al Senato* (1840), Serie I, Vol. II, p. 55.

Charles' system of alliances was begun with a treaty negotiated with Pope Leo X during the Imperial Election, in the summer of 1519. Leo, who had at first favoured the candidature of Francis I, soon saw that this was hopeless, and on June 17 agreed with Charles V, for this one time (*ipse solus*) that the Empire might be held along with the Kingdom of Naples, which was always held in fee from the Pope.[1] Such union of the Empire and Naples the papacy had consistently and at the cost of terrific sacrifices resisted since the days of Frederick II. This treaty was secret and remained so for nearly 300 years.[2] On May 8, 1521, inclined further to the Emperor by the Protestant outbreak of Martin Luther, Leo took a further step by concluding, through the Cardinal Raffaello de' Medici, and Jeronimo Adovno, a Genoese, who had much influence at the courts of both Leo and Charles, a treaty of alliance with Charles V "for the establishing of a universal peace, for the undertaking of a general war against the Turks, and for bringing all things to a better condition and form." France, on account of her "desire of taking Milan and Genoa, and of dominating Italy," was to be coerced.[3]

The Pope "cannot have been unaware that the exaltation of Cæsar (i.e., the Emperor) would be the depression of himself. But the bad fortune of Italy induced him to do that which no prudent man would have done."[4]

The Imperial negotiator of this instrument was a Castilian, Juan Manuel, who had performed many diplomatic missions for Charles V. Hostilities between Francis I and Charles V had already begun (March, 1521). Wolsey by patient, tireless diplomacy arranged a tripartite conference at Calais, the chief representatives being himself for England, Gattinara for Charles V, and Duprat for Francis I. Wolsey was recognized as mediator, but Gattinara seems to have been determined to make the conference a failure. It lasted, with interruptions, from August 7 to November 28, 1521. As a peace-conference it was a dead failure. Actually while the conference was in progress Wolsey had gone to Bruges, lodged in Charles' palace, interviewed the Emperor in many conversations,

[1] Pastor, *Popes*, VII, 285.

[2] Text published by Nitti, *Documenti circa la politica di Leone X*, in *Archivio della R. Società Romana*, XVI (1893), pp. 218–22.

[3] Text in Dumont, IV, Partie III, Supplement, pp. 96–9.

[4] Francesco Vettori, *Sommario della Storia d'Italia dal* 1511 *al* 1527, in *Archivio storico Italiano*, prima serie, Appendice, Tome VI (1848).

and concluded with Charles a secret treaty of alliance against France (August 25, 1521).

The English fleet was to guard the Channel when Charles should go to Spain to obtain supplies for the war; and the contracting parties were to declare themselves open enemies to the King of France in March, 1523.[1]

The pacific Cardinal, the author of the Universal Peace, being convinced apparently that war to the death between Charles and Francis was inevitable, had decided that England must be on the stronger side, and so he bound her to Charles. Besides, the influence of Charles could make Wolsey Pope, and Leo X could not live much longer. It was a disgraceful treaty. "The impotence of Wolsey dated from the day when, abandoning his position as a possible ally to either contestant, he placed his king in bonds to one to despoil the other. Thus, through abandoning the principles of truth and justice, he fell from the greatest height to which any European statesman had ever attained."[2] Nor did he gain the papacy. Leo X died on December 1, 1521, and Charles used his influence to have Adrian of Utrecht elected. In 1523, when one of the most powerful French magnates, the Constable of Bourbon, turned traitor and joined Charles V, the Anglo-Imperial allies made agreements which, if carried out, would have effected a dismemberment of France, if not its destruction as an independent state.[3]

Wolsey, although he was now involved in a policy of offensive war, engaged in it, probably on purpose, without much energy. The glittering prize of the papacy still escaped him. Pope Adrian VI died in 1523, and the Cardinal de' Medici, Clement VII, was elected. Francis I by this time had lost Milan, which was now once more under a duke of the Sforza family; however, French troops occupied Milan again in 1524. In spite of the enormous strength of the coalition which was against him, Francis I was not faring badly. On December 12, 1524, Clement VII believing (with good reason) that the Papal States and the Medici in Florence had less to fear from the French than from the Imperialists, made

[1] Busch, *Drei Jahre,* 132–4. See also dispatches in Brewer, *Letters and Papers of the Reign of Henry VIII* (1867), Vol. II, Part 2, pp. 620–1.

[2] Hill, *op. cit.,* II, 366.

[3] League between Charles V, Henry VIII and Duke of Bourbon, Aug. 4, 1523, in Brewer, *Letters and Papers of Henry VIII,* Vol. III, Part 2, p. 1317.

a secret alliance with Francis and with Venice; [1] but on February 24, 1525, the defeat and capture of Francis I at Pavia put Europe at the feet of Charles V. England, the natural mediator on the Continent, the guarantor of the *status quo*, had actually used all its weight to ensure universal domination to him. Charles, who was at Madrid when he received the news of Pavia, retired quietly to his bedroom and prayed.

[1] Jacqueton, *La Politique extérieure de Louise de Savoie*, in *Bibliothèque de l'École des Hautes Études*, T. 88 (1892), p. 67 n. The text of this treaty has not been published. For further details on the period see Armstrong, *The Emperor Charles V* (1910); Creighton, *Cardinal Wolsey* (1888); Alberi, *Relazioni degli ambasciatori Veneti al senato* (1846), Serie II, Vol. III.

CHAPTER IX

THE END OF THE WARS OF ITALY

France was now plainly faced with the same fate as had threatened Venice after the creation of the League of Cambrai and the battle of Agnadello. On this, however, as on other occasions, the state marked out for extinction has been saved, partly by its own efforts, partly by the self-interest of its neighbours, who see, at last, that its ruin will bring their own ruin with it.

The French king was a prisoner, but the government of France was taken over with dauntless courage by Louise of Savoy, mother of Francis I. She saw at once that the policy of balance, so grievously departed from by England, might still save the situation. She sent a mission to London, with instructious to point out to Wolsey the consequences of France's ruin. The mission succeeded, and on August 30, 1525, England made peace and a defensive alliance with France at Moore (one of Wolsey's mansions), asking for no territorial cession, and stipulating only for an indemnity of 2,000,000 crowns, at thirty-five sous to the crown. The diplomatists, who negotiated this important treaty for France, were Jean Brinon, an advocate, President of the Parliament of Rouen, and Jean Joachim de Passano, a Genoese man of affairs who was a sort of financial agent for the French Crown in its dealings with Genoese bankers.[1] A valuable concession which these able diplomatists gained from Wolsey was that the Treaty of Moore should be immediately made public, and this took place on September 6. It was probably this announcement of alliance between England and France, quite as much as any generosity on the part of Charles V, which accounted for the comparatively light terms accorded to Francis I as a condition of his release. Edward Lee, afterwards Archbishop of York, was sent by Henry VIII and Wolsey on embassy to Charles V, with instructions to advise Charles to exact nothing more than a ransom from Francis. Actually, the Treaty of Madrid,

[1] Jacqueton, *op. cit.*, pp. 16, 53–4.

January 14, 1526, released Francis on condition that he should cede the Duchy of Burgundy (as taken by Louis XI from "Madame Marie, grandmother of the Emperor") to Spain, marry the sister of Charles V, and indemnify him for certain charges. The Pope was to be asked to summon a Congress of States to deal with the question of universal peace and of war against the Turks.[1] "Henceforth Charles was only to have subjects or allies on the continent"; [2] nevertheless, the terms of the Treaty of Madrid were surprisingly moderate. Francis signed the treaty with the deliberate intention of breaking it. It is difficult to see why Charles V did not stipulate that Burgundy should be actually given into his hands before he let Francis go—probably the cautious Emperor wished to avoid war with England.

On returning to France, the king was able to conclude with Pope Clement VII and the Venetians an alliance called the League of Cognac, May 22, 1527. The object of this "Holy Alliance," as the treaty called the confederacy, was stated to be the expulsion of the Imperialists from Italy. Also, in order to take advantage of the hostility between Charles V and the Turks, Francis entered into relations with the Porte. It was Louise of Savoy, while Francis was a prisoner, who had taken the first step, by sending an envoy to Constantinople immediately after Pavia. This envoy, whose name is not known, was murdered on his way through Bosnia. In 1528, however, Antoine de Rinçon was more successful, and carried through an exchange of friendly letters with the Sultan, Suleiman I, at Constantinople.[3]

After Francis had repudiated the Treaty of Madrid the indignant Charles challenged him to single combat; but Francis, although he liked to appear as a knight of chivalry, preferred to behave as a prince of Machiavelli. On May 6, 1527, the army of Charles V captured and sacked Rome. Clement VII, a prisoner, had to abandon the League of Cognac. Nevertheless, everything was not going well for Charles V. In 1526 at Mohacs the armies of the terrible Suleiman had brought about the defeat and death of Louis, the last Angevin king of Hungary. The advance of the Turk continued and threatened Vienna itself. The question of the divorce of Katharine of Aragon and Henry VIII seemed likely to make Henry VIII a permanent enemy. The Reformation and the

[1] Dumont, IV, Partie I, pp. 400–10. [2] Jacqueton, *op. cit.*, p. 252.
[3] De la Jonquière, *Histoire de l'Empire Ottoman*, I, 163.

ambitions of the territorial princes in Germany were breaking up the Emperor's power there. Charles, however, would obstinately have continued the war, and so would Francis, but the French Queen Mother, Louise of Savoy, and the Governor of the Netherlands, Margaret, aunt of Charles V, exchanged letters and at last actually met at Cambrai, which was an episcopal principality claimed by both the King of France and by Charles V.[1] A subterranean passage joined the lodgings of the two princesses. After prolonged conferences they made the Peace of Cambrai, August 3, 1529. This treaty was practically the same as that of Madrid, except that Charles V resigned himself to do without Burgundy or any territorial cessions. Francis agreed to give up all his claims in Italy, and to pay an indemnity of 2,000,000 crowns. He recognized Charles' complete sovereignty in Flanders and Artois. This peace, in breaking for ever the bonds which had attached to France for a hundred years the regions on the left bank of the Scheldt, was the triumph of the policy of the former Dukes of Burgundy.[2] And at last Francis I and Charles V were at peace.

The great revolution in French foreign policy took place when the French Crown abandoned the policy of beating the air in Italy, and adopted instead a practical scheme for strengthening the eastern frontier. The first hint of this momentous change comes in 1532, when, taking advantage of the divisions caused by Protestantism in Germany, Francis I sent Guillaume du Bellay to negotiate with the Schmalkalde princes. The League of Schmalkalde (a small town in electoral Saxony) was an association of German Lutheran princes and towns, formed on December 31, 1530, for the defence of their religion. Guillaume du Bellay undertook three successive missions into Germany, and in 1532, May 26, concluded the Treaty of Scheyern ; Francis I thus became the ally or protector of the Duke of Bavaria, the Elector of Saxony, the Landgrave of Hesse and other princes.[3]

Francis I, however, could not abandon his dream of Italian dominion. The Peace of Cambrai endured from 1529-1535. On the death of Francesco II (without an heir), the last Sforza Duke of Milan (who was a protégé of Charles), Francis I began the weari-

[1] Dubrulle, *Cambrai à la fin du Moyen Age* (1903), pp. 336-8. Cambrai was not definitely united to France until the Treaty of Nymwegen, 1678.

[2] Pirenne, *Histoire de la Belgique*, III, 101.

[3] *Mémoires de Martin du Bellay*, II, 142, in *Société de l'histoire de France* (1910), T. 350.

some war again for the duchy (October, 1535). Pope Clement VII, whom Charles V had taken prisoner in 1527 (although he afterwards made peace with him), had died in 1534. His successor, Paul III (Alexander Farnese), was anxious to end the war which, along with the Protestant schism, was dividing Christendom. In 1538 he arranged a conference between Charles V and Francis I at Nice. The aged pontiff (seventy years old) went himself to Nice, which was in a Savoyard territory. Paul III and Francis I remained on land. Charles V came in a galley and did not leave it. The result of this curious conference was a truce, concluded for ten years (June, 1538). On July 14 of the same year the two antagonists actually met on French soil at Aigues Mortes, conversed together and slept in the same chamber. The news of this reconciliation and the prospect of an alliance of these two Catholic monarchs against the now schismatic England, frightened Henry VIII into acceding to the proposal of his minister Cromwell for a Protestant marriage. The King of England, hoping for Lutheran support, married Anne of Cleves. But the *entente* between Francis and Charles was soon shown to be illusory, and Henry VIII felt safe in putting away the plain-featured Anne of Cleves, Lutheran alliance and all.

The friendly understanding made between Francis I and the Sultan Suleiman in 1528 was confirmed in 1535 by a treaty of peace, friendship and commerce negotiated at Constantinople by Jean de la Forest. This agreement established the régime of Capitulations, and accorded extra territoriality to French subjects in Turkey. Thus Francis was the ally of the Austrians' greatest enemy, who by the year 1540 had won nearly all Hungary. In 1541 Antoine de Rinçon, who followed upon La Forest as ambassador at Constantinople, after a vacation in France, was murdered on the way back to his post, at Casale in Montferrat. There appears to be no doubt that the Imperial Governor of Milan was anxious to gain possession of Rinçon's dispatches, which would have shown that Francis I was conspiring to unite Venice and the Turks in a war against the Empire. The dispatches, however, were not found in Rinçon's baggage. This atrocious murder of an ambassador showed up the hollowness of the truce between Francis and Charles. War broke out again in 1542 (July), but peace was patched up by the Treaty of Crépy near Laon, in September, 1544. Francis I by this time was really sick of the policy of Italian conquest.

In the treaty he conditionally abandoned his claim to the Milanese. He was busy arranging to subsidize the Lutheran German princes against the Emperor,[1] when death carried him off in 1547, a soured and disillusioned old *roué*, at the age of fifty-three.

Francis was succeeded by his son, Henry II, a peacefully intentioned, business-like man who had become taciturn and melancholy in a period of captivity in Spain as hostage for his father after the Treaty of Madrid. He was determined to make peace, but he realized that he could not negotiate favourably unless he did some hard fighting first. He fought the English in 1550 and captured Boulogne, which the late King of England, Henry VIII, had taken. At the same time he made a decision which was the most momentous in French history since Charles VIII invaded Italy in 1494: he decided definitely to abandon Italy and to turn to his eastern frontier. This policy is said to have been debated by Henry II and his advisers in a council held at Fontainebleau in 1551, when the Maréchal de Vieilleville advised the king to seize the Free Imperial Cities of Metz, Toul and Verdun.[2] But Henry II seems independently to have made up his mind and had an ambassador in Germany, Jean de Fresse, Bishop of Bayonne, disguised as a trader, making a treaty of alliance with Maurice of Saxony and the Lutheran princes (October 15, 1551). There was also one of these princes, the Margrave Albert of Brandenburg-Culmbach, in France, *incognito* as Paul von Biberach, and giving himself out to be merely an official of the Margrave. On January 15, 1552, he met King Henry II at the royal hunting lodge of Chambord, where Henry ratified the alliance already concluded in the previous October with the German princes. Henry was to have the cities of Metz, Toul and Verdun, which he was to hold only as a member of the Empire. On his side he was to supply money and troops in the war of the confederates against Charles V. The allies bound themselves to conclude peace only in common.[3] Next month a supplementary treaty

[1] The Lutheran princes already regarded themselves as practically independent sovereigns, with the right of making war on the Emperor if he interfered with their religious position. See Karl Müller, *Luthers Äusserungen uber des Recht des bewaffneten Widerstands gegen den Kaiser*, in *Sitzungsberichte der K.B. Akademie der Wissenschaften* (1915), 8 Abhandlung, p. 1 ff.

[2] *Mémoires du Maréchal Vieilleville*, Livre IV, chap. VII, in *Coll. universelle des mémoires particuliers* (1787), pp. 297–8.

[3] Ranke, *Deutsche Geschichte in Zeitalter der Reformation* (ed. 1873), Band 5, p. 164. The Treaty of Chambord is in Dumont, IV, Partie III, p. 31.

with Maurice of Saxony was concluded at Friedwald in Hesse (February 19, 1552).

The Treaty of Chambord was a spirited document, and is of considerable interest in other respects besides its importance in religious history. It declared that Charles V was endeavouring to reduce the Estates of the Empire from their ancient liberty, and to bring them into "a bestial, insupportable and perpetual servitude." It stated that the purpose of the confederates was "to restore to her ancient liberty our very dear country and German nation"; and it agreed in business-like terms that their method would be to "march straight against the person of the Emperor."

Maurice was as good as his word. The great campaign was opened in March, 1552, and while Henry II succeeded in capturing Metz, Toul and Verdun, Charles V only escaped becoming a prisoner of Maurice by a romantic and secret ride from Innsbruck to Villach in Carinthia. While he was there Maurice and his confederates negotiated with Charles V's brother, Ferdinand of Austria (who was favourable to the claims of the Protestants),[1] a separate peace by the Treaty of Passau (August 2, 1552), securing religious liberty to the Lutheran princes, but Charles refused to accept the treaty. The war with France went on. Charles V failed in a great effort to retake Metz at the end of the year 1552. Modest, speaking little, not elevated in prosperity, not depressed in adversity,[2] Charles, by the year 1556, made up his mind to abdicate the throne. His brother, Ferdinand, Archduke of Austria and King of Hungary, became Emperor; Philip II, son of Charles, became King of Spain, and lord of the Italian possessions, the Netherlands and the Indies. Before this, Charles had consented to the Religious Peace of Augsburg, made by the Imperial Diet, meeting at that city (1555); religious toleration was granted to Lutheran princes and cities only.[3] The "Ecclesiastical Reservation" contained in the Augsburg Treaty declared that Church property converted to

[1] See W. Maurenbrecker, *Zur Beurtheilung des Kurfürsten Moritz von Sachsen*, in *Historische Zeitschrift* (1868), XX, 332–3.

[2] Alberi, *Relazioni*, Serie I, Vol. II, p. 62.

[3] See K. Brandi, *Passauer Vertrag und Augsburger Religionsfriede*, in *Historische Zeitschrift* (1905), Vol. 59, p. 259. The Text of the Peace of Augsburg is in Dumont, IV, Partie III. The important sections of it are given in English translation in B. J. Kidd, *Documents illustrative of the Continental Reformation* (1911), pp. 363–4. The term used for Lutherans is those who "espouse the Augsburg Confession."

Lutheran uses down to the time of the Treaty of Passau should remain in Lutheran hands, but that no such conversions or "secularizations" would be lawful after 1552.

Philip II continued the war with France. As the husband of Queen Mary Tudor he had the alliance of England. In 1557 his army defeated the French at the battle of St. Quentin, but next year the French captured Calais from the English. Everybody was sighing for peace, but the war had become a settled tradition and nobody knew how to break it off. "Yet it was only necessary to find a mediator who would put the word *peace* forward; for the two Princes would rather have their skulls cracked than mention it."[1] M. de Vieilleville, who was in the King's Council, found the way out. He sent a monk, "eloquent and bold," to the King of Spain. The devout Philip listened to the monk and began official negotiations. As a matter of fact he had already been putting forward very definite proposals for a peace through a certain highly placed French prisoner of war.[2]

Plenipotentiaries were appointed: for Henry II, the Constable Montmorency, the Cardinal of Lorraine and the Duchess of Lorraine; for Philip II, the Duke of Alva, Bishop (later Cardinal) Granvelle, the Prince of Orange (William the Silent), and the Duchess of Eboli (mistress of Philip II). England was represented by Thomas Thirlby, Bishop of Ely, Henry, Lord Howard of Effingham, and Nicholas Wootton, Dean of York. The peace conference was held at Cercamp and began on October 12, 1558. A truce of arms was declared, and Cercamp was neutralized for the period of negotiations. In January, 1559, the peace-conference transferred itself from Cercamp, where their quarters in an old abbey were very bad, to Le Cateau in the Cambrai district, where the bishop put his *château* at their disposal. England, although Mary, the Catholic Queen of Philip II, was dead and the Protestant Elizabeth was on the throne, acted still as the ally of Spain. Calais, the restoration of which was obstinately demanded by the English, was the great obstacle to peace. At last the complete treaty was drafted and signed on April 2, 1559. France was to keep Calais for eight years and then to give it back to England or else pay 500,000 crowns. On the other hand, France recognized Philip II as sovereign of Milan and Naples. Metz, Toul and Verdun, not belonging to Philip

[1] *Mémoires du Maréchal de Vieilleville* (1787), Livre VII, chap. 18.

[2] L. Romier, *Les Origines Politiques des Guerres de Religion* (1913), II, 289.

II, were not mentioned in the treaty, although sharp discussions took place in the conference concerning them. France remained in possession of the three cities, without any acknowledgment by the Emperor, who was not represented at the conference.

The Treaty of Cateau-Cambrésis, on account of the large cessions which it made to Spain, was highly unpopular in France. Yet it was the most statesmanlike act which the French Crown had undertaken in sixty years. It put an end to the exhausting wars for Italy; it also terminated the wars fought by England for French territory since the year 1066. It registered the definite swerve of French policy from the aim of Italian empire to the aim of making a "natural" eastern frontier in Lorraine and Alsace. Cateau-Cambrésis was the first of the series of great European treaties. Its chief provisions, except as regards Italy, still stand in the public law of Europe.[1]

[1] For this chapter see Merriman, *Life and Letters of Thomas Cromwell* (1902); Ranke, *Deutsche Geschichte in Zeitalter der Reformation* (1873); A. de Ruble, *Le Traité de Cateau-Cambrésis* (1889); Lindsay, *A History of the Reformation* (1906); Imbart de la Tour, *Les Origines de la Reforme* (1914), Tome III; *Mémoires de Martin et Guillaume du Bellay*, ed. Bourilly et Vindry, in *Société de l'Histoire de France*, T. 338, 350, 356, 387; *Calendar of State Papers, Foreign*, 1558–9 (ed. Stevenson).

PART II
THE WARS OF RELIGION

CHAPTER X

THE COUNTER-REFORMATION

Old Europe, the Europe of the Middle Ages, had broken up before the Reformation. Nation-states, absolutely independent national sovereignties, were coming into existence throughout the later Middle Ages and had reached something like complete development in the course of the Italian Wars which ended in 1559. Thus Europe was already in fragments when the Reformation came and the last theoretical union of Christendom was shattered. At the same time, while religion divided the Protestant states from the Catholic, it tended to unite the Protestant states among themselves. Thus religion was both a cause of union and a cause of division until the era of toleration, or of comparative toleration, came with the Peace of Westphalia in 1648. So long as the period of religious wars lasted, so long as states which differed in religion recognized no relations between themselves except relations of force, diplomacy could do almost nothing. Diplomacy had been active from about 1453 to 1559, in the period of the nation-states. It lapsed into something like futility and ineffectiveness between 1559 and 1648; after 1648 it entered into its grand period; and the rule of international law, often denied in practice, but almost always recognized in theory, began. In the period of Wars of Religion, however, diplomacy, as a whole, was concerned with little more than conspiracies and intrigues.

The Reformation was chiefly Lutheran in Germany, Calvinist and Zwinglian in Switzerland, Calvinist in Scotland, the Netherlands, and France so far as it took place there; in England it was neither Lutheran nor Calvinist, but something essentially national and characteristically English. The religious differences which prevailed between the Protestant countries made the Reformation only a very incomplete form of union. The Roman Catholic countries, on the other hand, had the same faith, and, like the Protestants, they had also the ardour of reform. For there was a reform movement, known as the Counter-Reformation, within the boundaries of the Catholic Church, between the years 1520 and 1570, that is, contemporaneous with the Protestant Reformation at its widest. The Reformation of the Catholic Church was carried out by the General Council of Trent, which began its sessions in 1545 and ended them in 1563. The Spiritual right arm of the Counter-Reformation was the Jesuit Order established in 1540; and the Roman Catholic monarchs provided the military resources.

The Peace of Cateau-Cambrésis marked a profound change in French policy. It was not merely that Henry II had transferred his aim from the pursuit of phantoms in Italy to the pursuit of realities on his eastern frontier—this was a right and proper step, although taken perhaps a little too soon. As he was winning the war in 1558 he might have refused to consider peace unless France's claims to Metz, Toul and Verdun were explicitly, instead of tacitly, admitted; for as things stood after the peace which was eventually made, Metz, Toul and Verdun had still to be fought for. But the Treaty of Cateau-Cambrésis marks something much more than an "orientation" of French policy from Italy towards the left bank of the Rhine. It marks a subordination of the French Crown to that of Spain. For Henry II made peace at that particular time, 1559, largely because he was alarmed at the growth of the Protestant heresy in France. For some years previously, France had been fighting against Spain with the support of the Protestants—the German Protestant princes. In 1559 Henry II abandoned this policy and began a work of extermination of his own Protestant subjects—an effort which brought French policy for years into a position of subordination to Spain, for Spain was, throughout the whole sixteenth century, the one consistent, immovable antagonist of the Reformed faith. This subordination of French policy to Spanish, this blind, unreasoning determination to crush the Huguenots, was ruinous to France for the fifty dreadful last years of the sixteenth century. From the hopeless slough of this "orthodox" and "Spanish" system France was at last saved by Henry IV, and by Richelieu who turned their diplomacy to gaining once more the alliance of Protestantism abroad, after establishing toleration at home.[1]

That French policy and diplomacy was for years after 1559 directed to the support of a great anti-Protestant Coalition seems impossible to be doubted. The Treaty of Cateau-Cambrésis contained a clause binding Philip II of Spain and Henry II of France to employ their power for bringing about the convocation of a General Council for the reformation and reduction of the whole Christian Church to a true union and concord. Privately Henry II had made up his mind to go much further than this: "I swear," he said to one of his councillors, "that if I can settle my foreign affairs, I will make the streets run with the blood and heads of this infamous Lutheran canaille."[2] This evidence supports the famous story related by William the Silent, Prince of Orange, in his *Apology*. As a great nobleman and as one of the chief diplomatists of Philip II, he was sent to Paris as a hostage for the execution of the Treaty of Cateau-Cambrésis. King Henry riding with the Prince in the Forest of Vincennes casually spoke to him about the plans which he was concerting with Philip of Spain for the extermination of the heretics. "In order not to fall into contempt with the King as if secrets were kept from me, I answered so that the King was not undeceived. This led to a complete exposition on his part of the establishment of the Inquisitors. . . . Thus nets were to be spun in which the nobles and the people of the land were destined to be entangled, so that the Spanish and their adherents should gain control over them, which they never could have acquired in any other way."[3]

Henry II was setting about actively to extirpate heresy within his kingdom, and to organize an anti-Protestant league abroad, when death met him on the point of Montgomery's spear in a tournament (July, 1559). During the period covered by the reigns of the next two kings (Francis II, died December 5, 1560; Charles IX, died May 30, 1574) diplomacy played only a petty part in France, England, Germany, Spain and Italy. It was an era of blood and anarchy. The "drive" of the Roman Catholic monarchs against the Protestants was in full force—a period of violence in

[1] Cp. Romier, *op. cit.*, II, 285–92.

[2] *Ibid.*, II, 287, quoting State Archives of Modena, Alvarotti, May 22, 1558.

[3] Dumont, V, Partie I, pp. 384–406, especially p. 392, column 2 (December 30, 1580).

which diplomacy was inevitably subordinated to war. The outstanding event was the last session of the Council of Trent, which, after having been suspended for years, met in 1563, reformed the discipline of the clergy, and issued a definite creed—the "Creed of Pius IV." [1] This provided, as it were, a definite constitution through which the Counter-Reformation or, as it is often called, the Catholic Reaction, could work. The Catholic Reaction had immediate effects: it produced civil war in the Netherlands and in France; in Spain it brought about the literal extirpation of the Protestants. In Germany, however, the Religious Peace which was negotiated at Augsburg in 1555 was, on the whole, maintained for over sixty years.

The centre of European diplomacy had once been in Venice, next in France; during the early period of wars of religion from 1559 to 1583 the diplomatic centre was England. For the England of Queen Elizabeth truly held the balance of power. It was the only powerful Protestant state of Europe; to it the struggling Reformed peoples of the little states of Germany and the agonized Huguenots of France looked for help or at least for a refuge. Against England Pope and Spaniard employed first their blandishments, next their conspiracies, finally their military strength; and to each new device Elizabeth offered a secret diplomacy that was artful, persistent, widespread and daring.

A correspondent of Sir William Cecil (Burghley) in an address to the Lords of the Council described the condition of England from the domestic and also from the international point of view at the accession of Queen Elizabeth in 1559: "The Queen poor; the realm exhausted; the nobility poor and decayed; good captains and soldiers wanting; the people out of order; justice not executed; all things dear; excesses in meat, diet and apparel; division among ourselves; war with France; the French king bestriding the realm, having one foot in Calais and the other in Scotland; steadfast enemies but no steadfast friends." [2] In addition, Philip of Spain was plainly threatening Elizabeth with the choice of alliance or of war with the most powerful military and naval state in the world; or rather, he maintained that the Spanish alliance made through his marriage with the late Mary Tudor was

[1] See A. L. Richter, *Canones et Acta Concilii Tridentini* (1853).

[2] Domestic MSS., quoted by Froude, *History of England* (1893), VI, 111. This was written before the Peace of Cateau-Cambrésis.

still in force.[1] Moreover, through her grandmother, the princess Margaret of England, Mary, Queen of Scotland and wife of Francis II of France, had a strong claim to the English throne. At this time England had no army, some half-dozen ships in the royal navy, and a woman for ruler whose title to the crown was disputed.

The Regent for Mary Queen of Scots was her mother, Mary, of the powerful French house of Guise. Under the Regency the government of Scotland was largely French and wholly Catholic. But the majority of the Scottish people had been converted to the Reformed religion by John Knox. A civil war began, and the Regent's division of French troops was besieged in Leith by the Protestant Scots Lords. Cecil (afterwards Lord Burghley), Queen Elizabeth's chief adviser, induced the Queen to send an English squadron to the Firth of Forth to co-operate with the Scots Lords in the siege of Leith. The difficult negotiations in regard to this momentous expedition were carried out secretly between Cecil and Richard Maitland of Lethington, a man of extreme caution, foresight and skilfulness. "The mark I do always shoot at," wrote Maitland to Cecil (April 9–10, 1560), "is the union of these two kingdoms in perpetual friendship." The siege of Leith was being prosecuted with prospect of success, but the negotiations by which the affair would have to be closed were so delicate that Cecil went in person to Leith in May, 1560. While the siege was still in progress an intercepted letter informed Cecil that the French were unable to hold out much longer, and that they would accept any peace-terms short of explicitly abandoning the claim of Mary Queen of Scots to the English Crown. On the seventeenth of June, a conference and a meal took place between Cecil and the French and Scottish commissioners on the sands of Leith. The English, whose camp was well supplied with stores, provided ham, capons, chickens, wine and beer. The French officers contributed what they could—one chicken and a piece of baked horse, and six delicately roasted rats.[2] Nevertheless, the French were not at the last extremity, for the salmon were coming in from the sea and were being netted by the garrison in Leith. The conference failed to come to terms. At last, however, after further negotiations,

[1] *Calendar of State Papers, Spanish*, 1558–1567, p. 14 (Philip to Ct. de Feria).

[2] Froude, *op. cit.*, VI, 390. The quotation from the Maitland-Burghley correspondence given above is from Froude, VI, 347 : Scotch MSS. Rolls House are cited in each case.

the Treaty of Edinburgh was signed on July 6, 1560. The French troops were to be removed from Scotland, only natives were to be officers of state in Scotland; Elizabeth's right to the English Crown was acknowledged, although no renunciation was made of the claim of Mary Queen of Scots.[1]

Thus Scotland was saved from the French, and the success of the Reformed religion there was assured. In December, 1560, Mary's husband, Francis II, who appears in official documents as "King of France and Scotland," died childless. He was succeeded by his brother Charles IX; and Mary, no longer Queen of France, returned to Scotland. Her stormy career there concluded with her flight to England in 1568 and her imprisonment by Elizabeth. From this time the relations of England and Scotland were untroubled; Mary's son, James, and Elizabeth entered into a defensive and offensive alliance (1586)[2] which endured until James succeeded to the English throne in 1603, and thus the aim which the diplomatist Maitland had avowed to Cecil was realized.

The Spanish danger, which overhung England, did not become acutely menacing so long as Philip II thought that he could stop the Reformation there by diplomacy rather than by war. Philip had an ambassador, Count de Feria, in England, who reported on Elizabeth's accession: "The more I reflect on this business, the more clearly I see that all will turn on the husband which this woman will choose." Of the various possible suitors, Philip II seemed the best. "If she marry out of her own realm," wrote de Feria, "may she place her eyes on your Majesty."[3] Although Elizabeth declined Philip's proposal for marriage, which was actually made through de Feria, the Spanish king still hoped to control England through arranging some other Catholic union for Elizabeth, for instance with Ferdinand or Charles, Archdukes of Austria, so he deferred year after year using force against the independently-minded heretic. Besides, if Philip overcame England by force he could scarcely help allowing the Catholic Mary Queen of Scots, great-granddaughter of Henry VII, to succeed to the throne—and thus French influence, not Spanish, would triumph.

In 1562, after the soldiers of Francis, Duke of Guise, had

[1] Treaty in Rymer, *Fœdera*, XV, 593–7.

[2] See Rait and Cameron, *King James's Secret* (1927), pp. 10, 11.

[3] Froude, VI, 134–5, quoting Simancas MS. For negotiations concerning Austrian suitors, see V. von Klarwill, *Queen Elizabeth and some Foreigners* (1928), pp. 10, 58 ff.

massacred some Protestants at Vassy, religious civil war broke out in France. It was waged on both sides at this time with almost inconceivable atrocity. "The year 1562 was one of the most lamentable in French history. Never had the country presented such a terrible spectacle, not even during the Hundred Years' War, when the misery was not nearly so widespread."[1] Passion ran so high that the Huguenot chiefs offered Havre to Queen Elizabeth as security for Calais which, according to the Treaty of Cateau-Cambrésis, was to be returned by England in 1567, unless France paid a ransom of 500,000 crowns. Elizabeth, though loth as ever to involve herself in diplomatic engagements which would necessitate war, was overcome by apprehension of a general coalition against her. Her banker, Sir Thomas Gresham, reported from Antwerp (which, like all banking centres, was a great mart for news): "There be none other communication, but that if M. de Guise had an upper hand of the Protestants, the French king, the king of Spain, the Pope, and all those of that religion would set upon the Queen's majesty for religion's sake."[2] On September 20 (1562) an agreement was concluded with the Prince of Condé, the Huguenot leader who held Normandy. Condé handed over Havre to the English garrison, on condition that Elizabeth should give up the town, if she received Calais according to the stipulations of the Treaty of Cateau-Cambrésis.[3]

The Anglo-Huguenot alliance of 1562 was perhaps the only serious blunder of Elizabeth's diplomacy. When it became known it shocked the whole of France, and caused all the moderates to join the Royalist Catholic side. At Dreux (November 19, 1562) the Huguenots in their white tunics met the Catholics, who bore crucifixes on their hats. The crucifix triumphed. Most of Normandy was recovered by the Royalist forces. After enduring a desperate siege the English surrendered Havre (July 29, 1563). Elizabeth had only involved herself in war with France, thus virtually cancelling the obligation of the French king to restore Calais in 1567.

Elizabeth had all through this war professed that her quarrel was only with the House of Guise, who were all-powerful at the French court, and not with the Crown of France. Accordingly her ambassador, Sir Thomas Smith, was at Paris in the years after

[1] L. Battifol, *The Century of the Renaissance* (1916), p. 206.
[2] Gresham to Cecil, August 8, 1562, in Froude, VI, 580.
[3] Treaty of Hampton Court between Elizabeth and Condé, September 20, 1562, in Dumont, V, Partie I, pp. 94, 95.

the fall of Havre, in spite of the nominal condition of war, and Paul de Foix, the French ambassador, was in London. This war resembles the struggle between Great Britain and Napoleon in the year after Trafalgar: the English could not fight the French on land, and the French could not fight the English at sea. So the antagonists did not meet in battle. Common sense pointed to an abandonment of *amour-propre* on both sides, and on April 11, 1564, Smith was able at last to conclude with Charles IX the Treaty of Troyes. The French Crown redeemed, by a payment of 120,000 crowns, the four hostages who had been left in England as security for the execution of the Treaty of Cateau-Cambrésis. Thus England and France re-entered into peaceful relations. The return of the hostages amounted to a tacit renunciation of Calais by the English for all time. Here ends the last trace of the Mediæval Anglo-French struggle for territory on the Continent.[1]

The Treaty of Troyes had been concluded by Charles IX in the course of a great progress which he made with his mother, Catherine de Medici, throughout his dominions. In May, the month following the Peace of Troyes, the court was at Lyons; gradually the tour was extended through the south and south-west of France. In the spring of 1565 the progress was resumed through Languedoc; by June Bayonne was reached. Here the King and Queen-Mother were met by the Queen of Spain, who was sister to Charles IX and by the grim Duke of Alva. It was commonly believed in all Reformed countries that in these interviews at Bayonne in the summer of 1565 a policy was concerted between France and Spain for a European league against the Protestants and for the extirpation of heresy.

In France the Crown certainly continued to bear hard upon the Huguenots, although not consistently; and intermittent, ruinous civil war continued. In the Netherlands the Spanish authorities were carrying out a policy of religious persecution which was steadily goading the Dutch into rebellion. The English seamen who were now sailing on every sea were, almost to a man, Protestant. They deliberately challenged Spanish authority wherever they went. Nevertheless, Philip II maintained correct diplo-

[1] There were really two Treaties of Troyes, both dated April 11, 1564, one dealing with peace, the other with the hostages: Rymer, XV, 640–8. The Treaty of Cateau-Cambrésis had stipulated for 500,000 crowns (see above, p. 56).

matic relations with England, and had an ambassador permanently at London. So long as Mary Stuart was alive, it was unlikely that Philip would attempt to conquer England. In 1568, at one of her interviews with the Spanish ambassador de Silva, Elizabeth, who always conversed with him easily in Latin and Italian, plainly explained her danger: she said (according to de Silva's dispatch) "that reports had reached her of some league or confederation, supposed to exist between the Pope, the Emperor, your Majesty, the King of France, and the Christian princes, the object of which was the settlement of religion, and, in consequence, with a special direction against herself." The Spanish ambassador replied that he "was surprised at her listening to such extravagant nonsense." [1] However, although Philip was not meditating conquest at the moment, England's danger was serious enough. In September, 1569, de Guerau, the Spanish ambassador who followed de Silva, advised Philip to arrange a Continental blockade against this country. He believed that if Europe refused to trade with England till she was reconciled to the Pope, Cecil would be overthrown (for all the traders would blame him), and that without Cecil the Queen would do as the Catholics wished. Nothing came of this proposal.

In 1570 the doom of Protestant England appeared at hand. Pope Pius V excommunicated Queen Elizabeth. It was believed in England that this could not have happened without the approval of Spain and France. In 1571 a plot was arranged between the Duke of Norfolk, the Spanish ambassador de Guerau, and Ridolfi (an Italian banker in England) for a rising against Elizabeth which, if accompanied (as was obviously understood by the conspirators) by the assassination of the Queen, would be followed by a Spanish invasion. Philip II was quite conversant with the plot, for Ridolfi went to Madrid and explained it. Enough was discovered by Cecil's agents to justify Elizabeth in expelling the Spanish ambassador; but a state of war did not ensue. In France, rebels continued to be secretly supported by Elizabeth—at least the Venetian ambassador was convinced that this was so.[2]

In April, 1572, the smouldering insurrection in the Netherlands became open war, when some Dutch sailors who had found refuge

[1] De Silva to Philip II, June 17, 1568 (Froude, VIII, 285–6, from Simancas MS.).

[2] Report of Correr for 1569 in Alberi, *Relazioni* (1860), Serie I, Vol. IV, p. 213.

in English ports made a descent upon the town of Brill on the island of Walcheren and held it against the Duke of Alva. Many Englishmen crossed to Holland and volunteered for service with the Dutch. In the early morning of August 24, St. Bartholomew's Day, a general massacre of Huguenots was carried out in Paris and other parts of France. This put an end to all ideas of friendship between Charles IX and Elizabeth, although she had hitherto been in apparently serious negotiations concerning a possible marriage between herself and a brother of the French king. Nevertheless, war did not come. The French ambassador remained at the English court. On November 8, 1576, the seventeen provinces of the Netherlands, which had been resisting the Spanish authorities without a concerted union, made the Treaty of Ghent among themselves, for common defence ; but although the Dutch sent a mission to London, Elizabeth refused to give them aid. In 1578, after an interval of six years since the expulsion of de Guerau, the Spanish embassy in London was again filled, this time by Don Bernardino de Mendoza. While maintaining correct relations with Spain, the Queen even entered again into the marriage negotiations with France—her "last matrimonial adventure," as Froude calls it. The Duke of Alençon, brother of Henry III, was the suitor. For three years the Alençon marriage negotiations prevented the French Government from taking any active part in Europe against the English or the Dutch. In 1580 a volunteer force of eight hundred Spaniards and Italians sailed from Corunna for Ireland, where a rebellion was in progress. The force landed in the south of Ireland and entrenched itself at Smerwick. When the English captured the force, the garrison was treated as a pirate band ; all were executed, except the officers, who were reserved for ransom. In 1583 a plot was arranged between certain English Catholics and the Duke of Guise for a French landing in England. The Spanish ambassador, Mendoza, and Philip II were privy to the plot.[1] Walsingham, the Secretary of State, had spies and agents who detected one of the Catholic agents, Francis Throckmorton ; this man was arrested and tortured on the rack (November, 1583) ;

[1] Conyers Read, *Mr. Secretary Walsingham* (1925), II, 381–5. For further information on this chapter in general, see Froude, *History of England* (1893) ; Romier, *Les Origines Politiques des Guerres de Religion* (1913) ; *The Fugger News-Letters* (1924 and 1926) ; *Calendar of State Papers, Foreign,* 1558 *sqq.* (ed. Stevenson), and *Spanish,* 1558 *sqq.* (ed. Hume) ; Alberi, *Relazioni* (1860), Serie I, Vol. IV.

he made a full confession. Throckmorton's trial and execution naturally followed. Equally natural was Queen Elizabeth's action in expelling the Spanish ambassador (January, 1584). At the same time Elizabeth sent a special envoy, Sir William Wade, to Madrid to explain and soften the effect of her action. Philip, however, refused to admit Wade; diplomatic relations between England and Spain hereupon ceased.

CHAPTER XI

THE LEAGUE

In 1583 France was in a condition of uneasy religious peace. King Henry III was, as a rule, indifferent to the affairs of state, but was subject, spasmodically, to fits of extraordinary religious devotion. The Huguenots became restive, suspecting that the movement which is known as the Counter-Reformation, and which was in progress in the Netherlands and Germany, might be resumed in France. The Roman Catholic party in France, headed by the Duc de Guise, the Papal nuncio, and the Spanish ambassador, in 1582 made preparations for an invasion of England for the dethronement of Queen Elizabeth in favour of Mary Stuart. In 1583 the plan was assuming definite shape and was communicated in a *mémoire* to Pope Gregory XIII.[1] On June 10, 1584, the Duc d'Anjou, last surviving brother of the childless Henry III, died. This made the Huguenot, Henry of Navarre, heir to the throne. The Roman Catholic party had already decided to procure the recognition, in place of Henry of Navarre, of the Cardinal of Bourbon as heir.

On July 10, 1584, William the Silent was assassinated by a Roman Catholic fanatic. By the end of the year a Catholic League had been formed in France, promoted by the Guise faction. This League was the subject of intense propaganda among the lower classes, particularly in Paris, and thus it gained many adherents. Philip II of Spain lent his support, and sent as his representative with the League at Paris (November, 1584) Don Bernardino de Mendoza, the same diplomatic plotter whom Elizabeth had expelled from England. On December 31, 1584, at the Château of Joinville in Lorraine, a treaty was signed between the chief Leaguers—the Cardinals of Bourbon and Lorraine, Henry Duke of Guise and his brother, the Duke of Mayenne, on the one hand, and Philip II of Spain, represented by Jean-Baptiste de Taxis and Juan Moreo—"a

[1] Roquain, *La France et Rome pendant les guerres de religion* (1924), 260.

perpetual offensive and defensive union for the defence and conservation of the Catholic religion and the entire extirpation of all heresies of France and of the Low Countries." Philip II engaged to support the League with 50,000 crowns a month (repayable). Cambrai, which had been in the occupation of the French since 1559, and which was actually in possession of Catherine de Medici,[1] was to be restored to Spain. The Leaguers and the King of Spain bound themselves with each other to recognize the Cardinal of Bourbon as king after the death of Henry III; and meanwhile not to treat separately with the King of France or any other prince.[2]

Pope Gregory XIII sent a verbal message of approval of the Treaty of Joinville, but issued no bull or decree to this effect. In March, and the following months of 1585 the Leaguers seized Metz, Toul and other towns, and raised the people of Normandy; they issued a public declaration in which they protested against the idea of the succession of a Protestant prince (Henry of Navarre) and against the present misgovernment of the realm. Henry III, after calculating the chances of a struggle, threw up his hands and concluded with the Leaguers, through the mediation of the Queen Mother Catherine de Medici (who signed), the Treaty of Nemours, July 7, 1585. In this act the king agreed to forbid the exercise of the Protestant religion in France. He recognized the League's cession of Cambrai to Spain. The League troops were to be paid off by the king.[3] With the Counter-Reformation thus progressing in France, and, as it seemed, also in the Netherlands and Germany, the outlook was black for heretic England.

The immediate result of the formation of the League and of the capitulation of Henry III to it, was a new outbreak of religious war in France. The moderate Catholics—called "Politiques"—began to give their support to Henry of Navarre, as being the sole hope, in the long run, for domestic peace. "The Duke of Montmorency," he wrote to his friend and agent in Germany, Ségur, "has bound himself indissolvably with me. We have decided to oppose the League and to reduce them by arms. Haste to treat

[1] *Correspondance du Cardinal Granvelle*, 1584 (*Collections de Chroniques Belges inédites* (1894), pp. xli, xlii).

[2] Dumont, V, Partie I, 441–3.

[3] *Ibid.*, p. 453.

with the Prince Casimir, and raise as many soldiers as you can."[1] Next month Pope Sixtus V (who had succeeded Gregory XIII) declared by a bull (September 9, 1585) that Henry of Navarre was incapable, as a heretic, of becoming King of France. Henry's reply was a treaty signed on January 11, 1587, with John Casimir, brother of the Elector Palatine. John Casimir contracted to bring an army of *Reiters* into France, to be paid by an English subsidy.

Thus the policy which Henry II had inaugurated in 1552, when he allied himself with the Protestant princes of Germany, was adopted by Henry of Navarre. This policy was to be continued by Henry as king, and still later by the Cardinal Richelieu, who took part in the religious war in Germany (Thirty Years' War), just as John Casimir was now going to take part in France's religious civil war. The invasion, however, of John Casimir and his *Reiters* in 1587 was beaten off by the Duc de Guise. But Henry III feared the consequences of the success of the Duc de Guise and the League. In the friction which existed between the king and the duke, Paris sided with the duke. There was a day or days of barricades, and popular partisanship gave Paris over to the League (May, 1588). At the same time Philip of Spain was preparing his great descent upon England.

[1] Cp. F. von Bezold, *Briefe des Pfalzgrafen Johann Casimirs* (1882), II, 329 (an Ségur, January 5, 1586), cp. II, 423 (Pallavicini an *J.C.*, October 10, 1586). For further information on Chapter XI see Roquain, *La France et Rome pendant les guerres de religion* (1924); *Correspondance du Cardinal de Granvelle*, in *Coll. de Chroniques Belges inédites* (1894, 1896), Vols. XI–XII; Paul van Dyke, *Catherine de Medici* (1923), Vol. II; Alberi, *Le Relazioni degli Ambasciatori Venete* (1857), Serie II, Vol. IV, pp. 340 ff. (Roma).

CHAPTER XII

THE ARMADA

Ever since the rise of Nation States—each a compact, powerful, military unit—there has been no safety in Europe. A moderate and unstable degree of security has been assured for each state partly by its defensive system, and partly by intelligent association, that is to say, by alliances negotiated through diplomatic means, on the basis of the balance of power. In the second last decade of the sixteenth century, however, England, compared with her enemies, had only a weak defensive system, and she was supported by alliance with no strong state. England's danger was obvious —even terrifying. It cannot be doubted that powerful Roman Catholic princes and their supporters were deliberately working for the conquest of the country in favour of the Counter-Reformation. In February, 1586, Olivarez, the representative at Rome of Philip of Spain, discussed with Pope Sixtus V the fate of England. "I told the Pope," he wrote, "that although Your Majesty had been often invited to undertake this enterprise by his Holiness's predecessors, you had never before felt assured that you would receive the practical assistance which would be necessary. His Holiness's willingness to meet Your Majesty's views in this matter had now induced Your Majesty to take a more favourable view of his request, notwithstanding the continual troubles of Holland, and the other obstacles which have stood so long in the way."[1]

The recent events which had cleared obstacles out of Philip's way were the murder of William the Silent in 1584, the Treaty of Joinville made between Spain and the League in 1584; and the execution of Mary Queen of Scots in February, 1587. Philip now had the near prospect of controlling France, of regaining the rebel Netherlands, and of succeeding to the throne of England. With the active support of the Pope, and the victorious armies and navies

[1] Froude, XII, 45, from Simancas MSS. Cp. Report of Giovanni Gritti to Venetian Senate, 1589, in Alberi, *Le Relazioni*, Serie II, Tome IV, p. 343.

of Spain, and the wealth of the Indies, how could Philip possibly fail to win ? Philip had annexed Portugal in 1580. That England should become a Spanish province seemed almost certain. Except for making an alliance and leaving the rest to the fortune of war, the resources of diplomacy, so far as England could use them, were at an end.

The obvious allies were the rebels of Holland, whose case was even more desperate. They had lost their leader, and were just managing to struggle on under the sovereignty of their States-General, an assembly of delegates from the governing body of each province. Yet weak as they were, their alliance appealed to Elizabeth's advisers. To accept it would involve war with Spain, but this was going to come anyhow. "Her Majesty cannot provoke Spain more than she hath done," wrote one of her secret agents to Burghley in July, 1585.[1] King Philip was "a colossus outward, but inwardly stuffed with clouts."[2] About this time deputies from the States-General were at London actually offering the sovereignty of the Netherlands to Queen Elizabeth ("to beseech Her Majesty to take the United Provinces under her protection.")[3]

She refused the offer; she could not bring herself to pledge all the resources of England to guarantee the existence of the Netherlands; but she undertook to assist them actively if Spain refused her mediation[4] (Treaty of Monesuch, August 10, 1585). Elizabeth undertook to provide 5,000 men under a "Governor-General," who should be "a person of respect and quality, affectionate to the true religion," and also to supply money; in return she was to receive the towns of Flushing, Brill, and Rammekins, as pledges for repayment.[5] The military expedition, which the Earl of Leicester led in the Netherlands for the next two years, heartened the Dutch for a time, but was withdrawn in August, 1587, after many disputes and disappointments. The English garrisons, however, remained in Flushing and Brill, and certain other English forces were still maintained in the Dutch armies.

[1] Froude, XII, 16.

[2] Wm. Herle to Burghley, July 17, 1585, in *Calendar of State Papers, Domestic*, 1581–1590, p. 253.

[3] *C.S.P., Foreign*, 1584–1585, p. 488 (States of Zeeland to Valcke, May 21, 1585).

[4] *Ibid.*, p. 671 (Instructions to Smith, envoy to Prince of Parma), where the Queen also says that she refused the *sovereignty* of the Netherlands.

[5] Text of Treaty of August 10, 1585, in Dumont, V, Partie I, pp. 454–5.

While Leicester was fighting in the Netherlands Mary Stuart had been tried on the charge of conspiring against the life of Elizabeth, and had been found guilty and executed (1587). This removed the last obstacle in the way of Philip's resolution to conquer England. If he were successful, it would not be a Franco-Scottish queen, but himself, who would reign in England.

Elizabeth still tried to ward off the invasion by diplomacy. In the spring of 1588, she had Robert Cecil (the second son of Burghley) with an English commission engaged in negotiations with the Duke of Parma, Philip's commander-in-chief in the Netherlands. Ostend was held, precariously, by the English forces, whose members were now in rags and, it was said, had not been in bed for nearly two years. When one of the peace commissioners, Dr. Rogers, a canon lawyer, met Parma at Ghent, he said that Parma held in his hands, "like Jupiter, the issues of life and death." Rogers' report was sent home; he received a sharp reprimand. "Her Majesty," wrote Burghley, "can in no sort like that any speeches should be uttered as though she did beg a peace." Parma was in favour of accepting Elizabeth's overtures. He wrote to Philip that, by doing so, "you will not conquer England, but, on the other hand, your fleet will be secure." There was always the danger that Parma's troops would mutiny for want of money; 400,000 crowns which he had borrowed in Antwerp for his military chest had, "between interest and exchange," become only 300,000 when the money reached him.

Negotiations between the English and Spanish commissioners took place at Ostend, Bruges and Ghent. There is ground for believing that Philip did not mean the negotiations to effect anything more than a gain of time. During the Ostend negotiations Parma, "disguised as a rabbit-catcher," wandered among the sand-dunes, surveying the fortifications.[1] Elizabeth offered to make peace if Philip would agree to allow to the United Provinces such toleration in matters of religion "as he might with conscience and honour," and not to reintroduce the Inquisition (May, 1588). Nothing came of this offer; Burghley, Walsingham and all the strongly Protestant advisers of Elizabeth were apparently against

[1] Froude, XII, 338. For further information on Chapter XII see *Calendar of State Papers, Spanish*, 1586–1588; Blok, *History of the People of the Netherlands* (trans. Putnam, 1900), Vol. III; F. von Bezold, *Briefe des Pfalzgrafen Johann Casimirs mit verwandten Schriftstücken* (1882), II.

it, and in any case while it was being made, the Armada was actually sailing down the Tagus. The English commissioners packed up their valises and left for London; and the stately Spanish navy, overcrowded with soldiers and priests, bore away to its doom.

CHAPTER XIII

THE COMMON CAUSE

The powerful, persistent and largely successful effort of the forces of the Counter-Reformation to recover for the Roman Catholic Church and sovereigns control of all Western Europe was bound to be met by concerted resistance on the part of the Protestant States. The expression "common cause" was frequently used during this time by statesmen in England, the Netherlands and France.[1] Already in 1585 an Anglo-Dutch alliance had been made. In 1589 Henry IV of France joined this union in concert, if not in strict alliance.

Henry III, the last of the reigning House of Valois, was assassinated by a friar, and died on August 2, 1589. The nearest male heir to the throne was the "heretic" King of Navarre, Henry IV. The League, however, still refused to acknowledge him as king, and maintained their adhesion to the Cardinal of Bourbon, Henry's uncle. As the League was in control of Paris, Henry withdrew with his loyal followers to Normandy, and established himself in Dieppe, whence communication could be easily maintained with England. He retained the existing French ambassador, Paul de Chouart, in England, and sent Pierre de Mornay as additional representative to the court of Queen Elizabeth. Henry asked for an alliance, which other Protestant princes might be invited to join. Elizabeth, however, would not enter into a treaty, but she lent him £20,000 which "was handed over to the ambassadors and receipted by them at the Lord Treasurer's house in the Strand on the 7th of September."[2] On receiving this sum, Henry said that he had never seen so much money at one time. Other subsidies were given later by Elizabeth on a generous scale. She sent (autumn, 1589) an expeditionary force of 6,000 men for

[1] E. P. Cheyney, *A History of England from the Defeat of the Armada to the Death of Queen Elizabeth* (1926), I, 190.

[2] Cheyney, I, 217.

three months under Lord Willoughby. Some of the gentry in this force served as volunteers at their own charges. Henry IV continued to press Elizabeth to join a confederation of all Protestant princes which he hoped to create, but she still refused. However, she continued to support the French king with money, and she sent one of her agents, Horatio Pallavicini, to Germany to hire troops for King Henry. The Queen's ambassador in Turkey, Burton, tried, along with the French ambassador, to stir up the Turks against Spain.

The Triple concert, which almost amounted to a triple alliance, was faithfully maintained by Queen Elizabeth. At the battle of Arques in September 21, 1590, there were only a few English volunteers on Henry's side, but an English expeditionary force under Sir John Norris fought in Normandy in 1591. In the Netherlands the troops of the hero, Sir Francis Vere, maintained at a fighting strength of about 2,000 men, rendered invaluable service in co-operation with Maurice of Nassau. The English ambassador at the Hague was, in accordance with the Anglo-Dutch treaty of 1585, a member of the Netherlands Council of State. Nevertheless, the Protestant cause was not greatly triumphing. Philip of Spain, called "Protector of the Crown of France," supported the League lavishly. The Duke of Parma, who had saved the ten southern provinces of the Netherlands for Spain, invaded France at the orders of Philip II, and effected powerful military diversions in favour of the League. Henry was almost in despair; he told the English ambassador at his headquarters, Sir Henry Unton, that if Elizabeth abandoned him, he could only hope for a soldier's death. His Frenchmen were without spirit; when he died, he was to be buried between an Englishman and a Swiss.[1] On the other hand, the protection afforded by Parma did not please the self-esteem of the French. Unton reported to Queen Elizabeth that they were now "wearie of the Spanishe yoake."[2]

The Protestant coalition was not strong enough to hold its own in France against the Counter-Reformation. Here, however, the conversion of Henry IV turned the scale. On July 23, 1593, he received instruction, and promised obedience to the Catholic Church. This act secured to him national support. The *Satyre Ménippée*, a composite work written by a group of "Politique"

[1] Cheyney, *op. cit.*, I, 269.

[2] Unton to her Majestie, February 26, 1592 (*Unton Correspondence*, p. 352).

scholars and men of letters, and published in 1594, upheld the national ideal. It is a brilliant, ironical description of the objects and methods of the Leaguers, who are made out to be unpatriotic, selfish pensioners of Spain. In the same year (1594), on March 21, after a long siege, Paris was entered by Henry IV, and the resistance of the League was broken at the centre. The civil war between Henry's partisans and the League was converted into a war of the King of France against Spain.

When Henry IV accepted Roman Catholicism the English statesmen became a little alarmed lest this change should also bring about peace between him and Spain—a peace which would leave England exposed to her still more dangerous enemy. In August, however, of the same year (1593) Henry and Elizabeth entered into an agreement, to make peace only by mutual consent. In September, 1595, the Spaniards successfully invaded Picardy and captured Cambrai. Henry, who had vainly besought Elizabeth to send an expeditionary force, informed her by message that he could not sustain the burdens of war alone.[1] The United Netherlands, although not bound by formal treaty with him, sent 2,000 troops and some money.

Elizabeth disliked the idea of a binding alliance which would entail vast liabilities in men and money. And if she did consent to such an alliance she wished to receive Calais as the reward: to this Henry IV would not agree. At last, in fear that Henry would make peace with Spain, Elizabeth sent Sir Henry Unton on special mission. This loyal and manly gentleman in previous negotiations had gained the liking and confidence of the soldier king of France. Unton arrived in January at Coucy, the headquarters of the king, who was engaged in the siege of La Fère. He had many talks with the king, sometimes in the Council-Chamber, sometimes in the garden of the château along with Gabrielle d'Estrées, the king's mistress. Henry was very angry at the small support which Elizabeth had given him. Unton fell ill at Coucy of camp fever in March. Henry visited his bedside, and the dying diplomatist testified his belief in Elizabeth's good intentions. Unton died on March 23 (1596). A week later a Spanish army suddenly appeared before the walls of Calais. Henry, in alarm, at once decided to send an ambassador to negotiate a more binding alliance with Elizabeth.

[1] Cheyney, II, 115 (from Gaillard, *MSS. de Brienne, Notices et Extraits*, II, 113).

An expeditionary force under the command of the Earl of Essex was assembled at Dover. The Queen, however, still hesitated and bargained for the possession of Calais. The men at Dover, idle in their ships, could hear the booming of the Spanish guns in the siege of Calais. At last, on April 15, the Queen gave the order to sail; but on that very day Calais was captured by the Spaniards. This disaster brought over to England a fresh deputation from Henry IV, headed by the Duc de Bouillon, one of the greatest nobles of the realm. Arduous negotiations conducted with the aged Burghley and his son, Sir Robert Cecil, in a house in Greenwich Park led to the signature of a famous Treaty of Alliance, May 16, 1596. Elizabeth agreed to send 4,000 (reduced by a secret article to 2,000) English soldiers to France for six months, the cost to be repaid by the French king. Similar succour was to be sent every year, if convenient to Elizabeth. Henry IV was to be allowed also to raise troops in England. Neither party was to make peace without the consent of the other. States, enemies of Spain, were to be invited to accede to the treaty. The States-General of the Netherlands gave their adhesion by treaty signed at the Hague on October 31, after Elizabeth and Henry IV had duly ratified the Greenwich treaty. Besides guaranteeing to each other military help in the war, the three contracting parties granted freedom of trade to each other's merchants. The Protestant princes of Germany, preferring neutrality, declined to adhere to the alliance.

Although the treaties of 1596 did not, as Henry IV intended, form the basis of a grand alliance or Protestant confederation against Spain, they at least enabled the war in France to be satisfactorily concluded. In spring, 1598, Henry was ready for peace. He invited the English and Dutch to take part in the negotiations. Elizabeth was averse from treating for peace at this time because it was practically certain that Spain would refuse to include the Netherlands in the treaty, and would not make the religious and commercial concessions to England which she required. The King of France therefore made a separate peace with Spain, at Vervins, in Picardy (twenty-five miles north-east of Laon), on May 2, 1598, recovering Calais, but restoring Cambrai to Spain. The Spaniards, thus relieved from the French war, hoped now to carry out the old design of conquering England. In July, 1600, Philip III thought seriously of "nominating" the Infanta as the successor to Elizabeth. A beginning was to be made with the conquest of

Ireland.[1] The English, however, had no great difficulty now in preserving the land in safety.

The extant state papers reveal an extreme amount of espionage, treason and conspiracy at this time. There were numerous Roman Catholic English and Irish ready to sell their country to Spain. The Spaniards had their own way of conducting business with these gentry. In September, 1600, Charles Paget, brother of Lord Paget, offered to sell to Philip III for 30,000 ducats information which, he said, was "worth millions." The Council of State reported to Philip III that the offer be accepted because "if the information be really true and as important as is asserted, the money will be well spent, whilst if it is not true it will not be paid."[2]

Fortunately Governments officially cast off prejudices and prepossessions more easily than private individuals. In March, 1603, Philip III and his Council were deliberating how they should act in order to secure England for the King of Spain or one of his nominees when the expected death of Queen Elizabeth should occur. The great queen died on the twenty-fourth of the same month. Within a year the Spanish Crown was ready to conclude peace.

The Anglo-Dutch alliance endured as long as Queen Elizabeth was alive, but James I, in the first year of his reign, made peace with Spain by the Treaty of London, August 28, 1604. He endeavoured to comprehend the United Netherlands in this treaty, but neither the Spaniards nor the Dutch were yet ready.

The war went on, but at last in 1608 both parties accepted the good offices of France, England, Brandenburg, Ansbach, the Palatinate and Hesse. The chief English deputy in the negotiations was Sir Ralph Winwood ; the most active of the French was Pierre Jeannin, a lawyer, President of the Parliament of Burgundy. The mediators passed between the Hague where the Dutch authorities were, and Antwerp, where the Spaniards were. The relations between the English and French diplomatists were latterly of the frankest and most cordial kind, though it was not always so during the early part of the negotiations.[3] The treaty was signed at Antwerp on April 9, 1609.[4] It provided not for a

[1] *Calendar of State Papers, Spanish,* 1587–1603, pp. 660, 665.

[2] *Ibid.*, p. 671.

[3] Jeannin to Villeroy, January 28, 1609 (*Négociations*, p. 555).

[4] Dumont, V, Partie II, p. 99. The Anglo-Spanish Treaty of 1604 is in Rymer, XVI, 617–29.

permanent peace but for a truce of twelve years, leaving over to the future the question of the definite recognition of Dutch independence.

In the negotiation of this "Twelve Years' Truce" the influence of Henry IV's ambassador, President Jeannin, was almost decisive. He had a character of extraordinary persuasiveness and charm. "It was difficult to withstand the force of his reasoning; but it was absolutely impossible not to surrender to the insinuating manner which accompanied it. He impressed upon one's spirit a sweet and agreeable violence which one was unable and did not wish to resist." [1]

With the coming in of the Twelve Years' Truce, Europe had rest, not indeed for the whole twelve years, but for nine or ten.

Although this general peace was not secured until 1609, the governing factor in the settlement was the Treaty of Vervins which in 1598 had ended the great war between France and Spain. Henry IV, by the Edict of Toleration of Nantes, of 1598, had brought religious peace into the domestic affairs of his country. Since 1598 there had been no European war on the grand scale, although it had required twelve years more to liquidate, even provisionally, the warlike disputes between Spain and England, and between Spain and the Dutch.

It is one of the remarkable facts of history that mankind has always longed for peace, and yet has, with brief intervals of respite, always suffered from the calamity of war. Yet there is no doubt that the same people who fought desired peace. The preamble of the Treaty of Vervins cannot be taken as hypocritical verbiage:

> The kingdom of France and the Provinces of the Low Countries having suffered very great losses, ruins and desolations, by reason of the civil and foreign wars which for several years have continued; of which also the Kingdoms of Spain and England and the Country of Savoy have also felt the effects; during which time the common enemy of the Christian name, taking our ills for his opportunity, and prevailing through our divisions, has made very great and very dangerous progress and usurpations in the Christian provinces: considering which our most Holy Father Pope Clement VIII by name, desiring to apply to this a convenient remedy, and to cut the evil at the root, has delegated, etc. The Kings, moved by zeal of piety, of compassion,

[1] Wicquefort, *L'Ambassadeur et ses Fonctions*, Livre II, § VIII.

and of the extreme regret that they have and feel in their hearts at the long and heavy oppressions which, by reason of the said wars, their realms and subjects have suffered and still suffer to the present time . . . have committed and deputed M. Pompone de Bellièvre, etc. . . .[1]

[1] Dumont, V, Partie I, 561. For this chapter in general, see *Calendar of State Papers, Spanish,* and *Venetian.* P. Jeannin, *Négociations* (Michaud, *Nouvelle Collections des Mémoires relatifs à l'histoire de France,* 1854, Vol. XVIII). *Correspondence of Sir Henry Unton,* 1591, 1592, edited Stevenson for the Roxburghe Club, 1847. For valuable documentary material on the activities of Frederick of Würtemberg, see V. von Klarwill, *Queen Elizabeth and some Foreigners* (1928), 347 ff. See also below, Chapter XIV. For Papal designs in Britain, see L. van der Essen, *Correspondance d'Ottavio M. Frangipani* (1596–1606), t. I (1924).

CHAPTER XIV

CALVINISTS AND ROMAN CATHOLICS

The great war which devastated much of Germany for thirty years was seen impending, like the War of 1914–18, for a generation before it broke out; and throughout these years diplomacy laboured to prevent it. As in the War of 1914, hostilities first occurred over a local affair which, in the prevailing condition of international tension, brought one state after another into the war until nearly all Europe was involved.

The prevailing tension, which nothing but the highest and most steadfast statesmanship could have prevented from bursting forth into a great war, was not, like the later tension of Europe, "national" or "economic"; it was purely religious. The Peace of Augsburg of 1555 was not a satisfactory settlement. It did not include Calvinists. It left in some obscurity the legal position of lands or territories in the case of ecclesiastical possessors who, after 1552, should change from Catholicism to Lutheranism. The Lutherans, where they were able, had continued to "secularize" such lands, contrary to the provision contained in the "ecclesiastical reservation" of the Peace of Augsburg. The Lutheran states had protested from the first against this reservation, and it had only been promulgated, under this protest, by imperial authority.[1] The amount of secularization of ecclesiastical property carried out between 1555 and 1618 was undoubtedly very large.

The religious tension which existed in Germany was extended to Germany's neighbours. The Dutch knew that Spain still hoped to recover the Netherlands. The Gunpowder Plot (1604) kept alive in the minds of the English the apprehension of an onslaught from the forces of the Counter-Reformation. In Sweden the claim of the Roman Catholic king, Sigismund III of Poland, to the crown of Sweden (from which he had been deposed in

[1] See above, p. 55; also see for the protest, W. Maurenbrecher, *Beiträge zur deutschen Geschichte*, in *Historische Zeitschrift* (1883), XIV, 2–6.

1599) was a standing menace to the Lutheran establishment there. The kinship between the Spanish and Imperial Austrian branch of the House of Habsburg, both equally intolerant, made Henry IV of France, who, in spite of his conversion, was not favourably regarded by Catholics, anxious for his country's safety.

There are many reports upon the condition of Germany in this period written by diplomatists, and also by travellers who visited Germany in the thirty years before the outbreak of the great war. Fynes Moryson, a Fellow of Peterhouse, Cambridge, who travelled in Germany in 1592, and Thomas Coryate, the author of *Crudities*, who was there in 1608, have left full accounts. They describe a people living in considerable material comfort. The state of intellectual culture was as high as anywhere else; universities were numerous; there were reasonably good systems of internal communication by road and water, and trade was carried on with fair success, in spite of the large number of tolls and tariffs imposed by the 350 sovereign states. Men of different religions lived on the whole peacefully side by side, although the German Protestants began to fear that there would be a revival of the Counter-Reformation after Spain and France came to terms by the Peace of Vervins (1598). Two things in particular gave the Protestants ground for apprehension. One was, the prospect of the death of Duke William of Cleves, a Protestant, and childless. It was feared that a Habsburg or some strong Roman Catholic prince would obtain the Duchy, which would thus strengthen the chain of Roman Catholic territories—Franche Comté (Spanish), Mainz, Trèves, Cologne (prince-archbishoprics), Cleves, the Spanish Netherlands; thus the Rhine would become a "Priests' Lane." The second thing which caused grave apprehension to the Protestants was the occupation of the Free City of Donauwörth on the Danube in 1607 by Maximilian, Duke of Bavaria, acting on behalf of the Empire on the ground that Protestant Donauwörthers had violated the Religious Peace.

Germany had for hundreds of years been the home of Leagues. The famous League of Protestant Princes of Schmalkalde of 1537, which had proved a match for Charles V, is only one particularly famous instance of such unions. Between the years 1580 and 1608 many attempts were made to form similar unions of Protestant princes, in alliance, if possible, with France and England. But the dislike of Lutherans and Calvinists for each other, and the precarious legal position of Calvinism which had no status under the Religious Peace of Augsburg, made all unions either abortive or temporary.

In 1607, however, the apprehension caused by the Bavarian occupation of Donauwörth, combined with the active diplomacy of Christian of Anhalt, brought about the establishing of a strong union. Christian was the second son of Prince Joachim Ernst, Duke of Anhalt, and was born in 1568. He was carefully educated, and is said to have been able to speak and write Latin, French and Italian like his mother-tongue. He was also skilled in military exercises and was an accomplished knight. His career, like that of many of the more active spirits of that time, was one of both war and diplomacy. While still not fifteen years old Christian was sent by the Emperor Rudolf II in an embassy to the Sultan Murad III at Constantinople, journeying there by way of Budapest, Belgrade and Adrianople. After this experience in the Imperial service Christian accepted a post at the Saxon court. In 1588 he made a journey to Italy. Shortly after this he was designated by Queen Elizabeth of England and the Elector of Saxony to lead the army which, with the help of English subsidies, was being raised in Germany for assisting Henry of Navarre and the Huguenots in France. He was then only twenty-three years old. Christian returned from the French war with a high reputation for courage, and with a warm admiration for Henry of Navarre. It was now that he gave up Lutheranism and became an ardent Calvinist. In 1595 the Calvinist Elector Palatine Frederick IV made him Statthalter of the Upper Palatinate; and in the same year Christian married Anna, daughter of Count Arnold of Bertheim, a lady who brought him further under the influence of the Huguenot-Orange interest and policy. From this time he was, under the nominal headship of the Elector Palatine, the real head and political driving-force of the Reformed party in Germany. Tireless, skilful, ambitious, he made connections in every Protestant court in Germany; "he was the most accomplished diplomatist of the time." At Amberg, the capital of the Upper Palatinate, he transformed his bureau of Statthalter into a diplomatic Chancery in which for a time were gathered the threads of the policy of Protestant Europe. His secret agents were not merely at all the Protestant courts. They are found at Vienna, Prague, Venice, Turin. From all sides information flowed into him in an endless correspondence. Christian was the maker of the Evangelical Union of Protestant Princes. The court which he and his wife maintained at Amberg was a social centre for German Protestants.[1]

The master of Christian, the Elector Frederick IV of the Palatinate, was one of the highest of the Calvinist princes in Germany. In his capital, the noble city of Heidelberg, he maintained the state of a powerful sovereign, far beyond his real means. The Protestant League, which at last crowned the efforts of these ambitious men, was made at Anhausen in Ansbach on March 16, 1608, and included, besides the Elector Palatine, the Duke of Würtemberg, the Margraves of Ansbach and Baden, and some minor princes and cities. Naturally, it provoked a reply. On April 9, 1609, at Munich, a pact for a Catholic League was signed by Maximilian, Duke of Bavaria, with the Prince-Bishops of Passau and Würzburg, to be joined a little later by the great Rhenish Archbishoprics, Mainz, Trèves, Cologne, and some secular princes. The League took authority to raise troops and to appoint a commander-in-chief (*Oberst*); Maximilian, Duke of Bavaria, was named in the treaty as Oberst.[2] Everything was ripe now for an outburst, for the rival German leagues had taken authority to raise military forces and to conclude foreign alliances. The diplomacy of the Evangelical Union of Anhausen was the more active; besides Christian of Anhalt, who worked chiefly by correspondence, it had Christopher von Dohna (a member of one of the most numerous and remarkable families of the seventeenth century), the peripatetic envoy of the Elector of the Palatinate. Dohna's energy and powers of persuasion were brought to bear with effect at the courts of France and England. Duke Frederick of Würtemberg, another active Protestant, visited the English court in 1610. It was then that he saw *Othello* performed at the Globe Theatre.

In 1610 the outburst seemed to have come. Duke William of Cleves-Jülich had died without issue on March 25, 1609. The Habsburg Archduke Leopold, Bishop of Passau and Strasburg, immediately occupied the two duchies with troops pending the decision which the Imperial Aulic Council was to give respecting the

[1] Cp. O. von Heinemann, *Christian I von Anhalt*, in *Allgemeine Deutsche Biographie*, IV, 148.

[2] *Liga Catholica* or *Articul der Bündniss so von denen Katholischen Ständen zu Würsburg aufgerichtet*, 1610, in Dumont, V, Partie II, p. 118.

succession. The Evangelical Union held a conference at Schwäbish-Hall in Würtemberg (February, 1610). Boissise, an ambassador from Henry IV, was present. War was decided upon. Henry IV of France felt that the moment had arrived when the empire of the Habsburgs should be curtailed for ever before it overshadowed all Europe. A coalition of the Evangelical Union and France, which was also joined by England and the Netherlands, was established. Every party bound itself to contribute troops. King Henry IV assembled an army of 34,000. He was in his carriage, driving through Paris to visit the Arsenal, when he was murdered by François Ravaillac on May 14, 1610.

The general war, which seemed absolutely inevitable, was suddenly averted. The French regency of Marie de Medici cancelled the orders of the dead king and relapsed into neutrality. The Evangelical Union in alarm treated with the Catholic League and agreed to leave the succession to Cleves-Jülich to be settled by arrangement between the rival claimants. The English and Dutch forces did actually engage in brief hostilities in Cleves against the Habsburgs, who withdrew from the duchy. Hostilities ended, however, without any settlement of the religious situation in Germany.

The compromise concerning Cleves-Jülich was made and embodied in the Treaty of Xanten, November 12, 1614, by George William, Margrave of Brandenburg, who was a Protestant, and Wolfgang William, Duke of Neuburg, who was a Catholic (and a son-in-law of Maximilian of Bavaria). The treaty enacted that the disputed duchies should be divided into two parts, one including Cleves, Mark, Ravenstein and Ravensberg, the other including Jülich and Berg. The two claimants were then to draw lots, and each was to hold and rule over the part which fell to him without prejudice to the ultimate rights of the other over that part.

In the drawing of lots Cleves, Mark, Ravenstein and Ravensberg fell to Brandenburg, Jülich and Berg to Neuburg. The compromise, which was only provisional, was made through French and English mediation, and was signed by du Maurier for France and by Henry Wotton for England.[1] It endured until the Peace of Westphalia in 1648, when the provisional division was made absolute.

[1] Text of Treaty of Xanten in Dumont, V, Partie II, p. 259.

No war is inevitable. To say that the Thirty Years' War was bound to come and would best have been fought out in 1610 is an unjustified and reckless statement. The human mind is infinitely capable and ingenious; and a general war averted for a few years may by patient and energetic statesmanship be averted for ever. When the hostilities of 1610 ceased suddenly without a general war, the suffering people of Europe were given nearly ten years during which their governors, if endowed with statesmanship, might have solved their religious troubles. But statesmanship and the spirit of reasonableness were wanting. The dagger of Ravaillac was itself a proof of the intolerance which in the end brought on the general catastrophe.

CHAPTER XV

THE OUTBREAK OF THE THIRTY YEARS' WAR

Between 1610 and 1618 not a single thing was done to avert the impending struggle. In Germany the spirit of religious intolerance, far from growing less, grew worse and worse. If Germany had been a single state, this religious intolerance would at worst only have produced civil war among its inhabitants. But as the Empire consisted of some hundreds of sovereign states, which, ever since the League of Schmalkalde, had exercised from time to time the power of making foreign alliances, war from within was almost certain to become also war from without.

If it is agreed that the war which broke out in 1618 was really due to religious intolerance, there is sufficient evidence to admit of the assertion that responsibility lies chiefly with the Roman Catholics. For after 1610 the Protestants of Germany were passive; they had long since lost all missionary enthusiasm. But among the other great religious party, the Catholics, missionary zeal expressing itself in organized persecution, was stronger than ever; the Counter-Reformation was actively in progress.

The chief prince of the Evangelical Union, Frederick IV, Elector Palatine, died in 1610. His son, the ambitious Frederick V, highly educated at the splendid court of his father, was the hope of those who felt themselves threatened by the Counter-Reformation and by the Habsburg Emperor. The policy of James I of England was still kept on "Elizabethan" lines by his Secretary of State, Robert Cecil, Earl of Salisbury; accordingly Sir Ralph Winwood, Ambassador to the Dutch, was authorized to conclude a defensive alliance between England and the Evangelical Union. This he accomplished by treaty signed with representatives of the Union princes at Wesel on March 28, 1612, to endure for six years.[1] The Union maintained at the Court of James I a permanent representative, Louis Frederick, brother of the Duke of Würtemberg.

[1] Dumont, V, Partie II, 637.

This man strongly pressed for a marriage between the Elector Palatine and Elizabeth, daughter of James I, an amiable and beautiful princess, of firmly Protestant convictions. The marriage-contract, which, it was hoped, would confirm the position of the English king as head of the Protestant world, was signed on May 16, 1612. It was the last work of the Elizabethan statesman Robert Cecil, who died a few days later (May 24). The marriage took place early in 1613. On his return journey from England with his princess the Elector concluded at the Hague, on May 16, 1613, a treaty of defensive alliance, on behalf of the Evangelical Union, with the Dutch. James I maintained diplomatic relations with the Protestant Swiss cantons. Thus a general Protestant *entente* was being created for resistance to the Counter-Reformation. In consonance with this policy James I co-operated with the French regency in the successful mediation over the Cleves-Jülich dispute, which was settled by the Treaty of Xanten in 1614.

While the Protestant states were thus drawing closer together, the Roman Catholic powers were not idle. In 1617 the Bohemian Diet, as the result of much political pressure from Vienna, recognized Ferdinand of Styria, the cousin of the Emperor-King Matthias, as king-designate (or successor) in Bohemia. On June 6 of the same year Philip III of Spain and Ferdinand entered into a secret compact by which Philip resigned his hereditary claims to Bohemia and Hungary, on condition of receiving on Matthias' death some Austrian territories in "one of the Austrian provinces" (meaning probably the Austrian rights in Alsace).[1]

In 1618 (May 23) prominent Bohemian nobles and burghers, of the Reformed faith, apprehensive of the intolerant character of the king-designate Ferdinand, came to the castle of Prague to make representations to the Regents. A dispute arose in the course of which two Regents, Jaroslav von Martinitz and William Slawata with the secretary Fabricius, were thrown out of the window on to the mud of the moat, fifty feet below, without serious injury. This *coup*, the "Defenestration of Prague" of May 23, 1618, was probably deliberately planned. Naturally it started a war between the Reformed Bohemians and the Austrians. Some

[1] See two treaties of June 6, 1617, one between Philip III and Ferdinand, the other between Philip III and Matthias in Dumont, V, Partie I, 298–301, especially p. 301, where it is stated that the compensation to Spain will be in *aliqua provinciarum Austriacarum*.

big event was portended. The famous Palatinate diplomatist, Christopher von Dohna, went on mission to London and obtained the renewal of the alliance of England and the Evangelical Union, and spoke of a possible accession of his master, the Elector Palatine, to the Bohemian throne (January, 1619). On March 20 the Emperor Matthias died; and on August 26 Ferdinand of Styria was elected Emperor. Two days earlier, however, the Bohemian Estates in a General Diet, disregarding their previous recognition of Ferdinand as king-designate, elected Frederick, the Elector Palatine, to be king. This was an absolute defiance of the whole Habsburg system of government, as well as of the forces of the Counter-Reformation. The Austrian Habsburgs were already in the field and the Spanish Habsburgs immediately joined them. The Thirty Years' War was now in full course.

Only two men in Europe seem to have had a policy for averting the general war by conciliatory measures. One was Cardinal Klesl, the chief adviser of the Emperor Matthias, who maintained a tolerant religious policy in the Habsburg dominions. But Ferdinand had him dismissed from office and imprisoned in 1618, not to be released for five years. The other peaceful statesman was James I, who as early as 1611 had entered into negotiations with the court of Spain for a marriage alliance between the Spanish Habsburgs and his family. It is doubtful whether Philip III was serious on his side in these negotiations, yet they were not without prospects of success when the religious war broke out and spoiled everything. After this the persistence with which James continued to pursue the Spanish marriage project merely prevented any solidarity among the Protestant states. When Prince Charles and his friend Buckingham went on their mad journey to Madrid in 1623 they simply made their Government a laughing-stock before Europe while the last Protestant garrisons were being driven by Spain out of the Palatinate.

CHAPTER XVI

THE THIRTY YEARS' WAR DOWN TO THE PEACE OF PRAGUE

The Thirty Years' War is the first of the series of four general conflagrations which have devastated Europe; the second is the long struggle aroused by the ambition of Louis XIV, which ended in 1713; the third is comprehended in the French Revolutionary and Napoleonic Wars; the fourth is the Great War of 1914–18.

During a general war, or for the greater part of it, diplomatists turn from their beneficent function of working for peace and become instruments for extending the war and for securing victory. They labour in order to obtain active allies for their masters; and thus diplomacy becomes for a time the servant of war. Sooner or later, however, there comes a prospect of the end of the struggle, either through the success of one side or through the exhaustion of all parties; then, while the din of arms is still sounding, diplomacy ceases to serve war and reverts to its primary function, preparing the way for the conclusion that must come.

Historians have been used to dividing the Thirty Years' War into the Palatinate period (1618–24), the Danish period (1625–29), the Swedish period (1630–35), and the Franco-Swedish period (1636–48). These divisions correspond with the diplomatic stages in the struggle. The states engaged in the conflict were Austria and most of the states of the Empire, Spain, the Dutch, Denmark, Sweden, England and France. England was in the struggle very ineffectively and only for a relatively brief space of time. The meagre participation of this country in the European War undoubtedly increased the length and waste of the struggle. Towards the end English diplomacy re-entered the field, and helped in the conclusion of hostilities.

The adventure of the Elector Frederick and his wife, the Queen Elizabeth, in Bohemia was brief and disastrous. He was only a "winter-king," and lost his throne in the battle fought against Tilly, the general of the Catholic League, on the White Mountain near Prague on November 8, 1620. Christian of Anhalt, commander-in-chief of the Union forces at Prague, had been persuaded against his better judgment by the hasty Frederick and other advisers into giving battle. This was the end of Christian's grand plans and restless activity. He found a refuge for a time in Denmark, later made his peace with the Empire, and devoted himself to the administration of the Duchy of Anhalt which he had inherited through the death of his elder brother in 1618. He died in 1630 and was buried in the Schlosskirch at Bernburg.

The battle of the White Mountain was not merely the end of Christian of Anhalt's far-reaching plans. It was the end of Bohemian independence. The Elector Frederick lost his kingdom and had to fight for his hereditary lands. In May, 1621, some of the princes of the Evangelical Union meeting at Heidelberg formally declared the Union's dissolution. By the year 1626 Frederick had lost the Palatinate to Spanish armies; he and his Queen were fortunate to find a refuge in Holland. The English Crown, which had maintained a few regiments in the Palatinate, now tried to restore the Protestant and Palatinate cause by using diplomacy to arrange a powerful alliance. For "Charles I had undertaken to do what his father had avoided to the end of his life—to offer open opposition to the Spanish monarchy and its aims." [1] He carried out this resolve partly by sending a very unsuccessful expedition against Cadiz (1625), partly by subsidizing—or promising to subsidize—his uncle, the strongly Protestant Christian of Denmark.

Before the war, "the Powers of the North were in a sense strangers to Europe; the Reformation caused their inclusion in the general political system." [2] About a year before he died King James I had sent Sir Robert Anstruther, one of the best English diplomatists, to induce Christian IV to intervene in North Germany. Christian, however, required more definite assurances than James was prepared to give him. At the same time, in the latter part of the year 1624, Sir James Spens had been sent to Sweden. He found the young king Gustavus Adolphus proposing that a general league of Protestant states should be formed to

[1] Ranke, *History of England* (Eng. trans. 1875), I, 535.

[2] Koch und Schoell, *Histoire abrégeé des Traités de Paix* (Paris, 1817), I, 42.

meet by war the advance of militant Catholicism. James was not ready for such a decisive step, but he suggested that a congress of Protestant states might be brought together at the Hague. When Charles I came to the throne the congress had not yet assembled; but he himself took the important step of agreeing to furnish to Christian of Denmark a subsidy of £30,000 a month for that monarch's campaign in North Germany. On September 17, 1625, by the Treaty of Southampton, England and the States-General formed an "offensive and defensive alliance" against Spain;[1] but so far as England was concerned the hostilities, according to the treaty, were only to be pursued by sea. The truth is that the only kind of war for which the House of Commons would vote any money was a maritime war. The Congress which did actually meet at the Hague was almost a fiasco. Instead of the representatives of all the Protestant Powers, only those of England, Denmark and the States-General were present; the Swedish ambassador who came died as soon as the Congress was opened. Charles' friend and high official, the Duke of Buckingham, renewed the promise of the monthly subsidy (which had fallen hopelessly into arrears); and a triple alliance was signed at the Hague between England, Denmark and the States-General (December 9, 1625).[2] But Christian IV, who had been fighting all summer and autumn against the Imperialist and Catholic League forces in North Germany, profited nothing. The English money never arrived, for the Parliament would not vote the necessary sums. On August 31, 1626, Christian was hopelessly defeated by Tilly, the general of the Catholic League, in the Harz country at Lutter. His country was invaded, and although he successfully defended himself in his islands, the end was inevitable. The Emperor, perhaps in view of the coming war with Sweden, consented through Generals Wallenstein and Tilly to give the King of Denmark liberal terms. Christian IV made the Peace of Lübeck with the Emperor (May 22, 1629)[3] and retired from the war, without losing territory and without paying any indemnity. Nobody could now stand against the Emperor in North Germany; and the Habsburg Maritime Design, to establish

[1] The Twelve Years' Truce between Spain and the Dutch had expired in 1621. Text of Treaty of Southampton in Dumont, V, Partie II, p. 478.

[2] Dumont, V, Partie II, p. 482.

[3] *Ibid.*, p. 584.

Spanish and Austrian power in the Baltic, seemed now certain of success.[1]

England, which had been recognized from the time of Queen Elizabeth as the chief Protestant state, was now helpless through internal dissension. Sweden was the last hope. It was not merely Protestants who turned their eyes to this country; Cardinal Richelieu, First Minister of France, had the same idea—to employ Sweden to check the Habsburg ascendancy.

The strongest English advocate of a Swedish alliance was Sir Thomas Roe, a seasoned diplomatist who in 1628 was on his way home from Constantinople to London. He was a staunch friend of Queen Elizabeth of Bohemia, the wife of the unfortunate Elector Frederick of the Palatinate. At Constantinople, where he had been ambassador since 1621, Roe had vainly tried to arouse the Sultan and also Bethlen Gabor, Prince of Transylvania, to enter the war against Austria. On his journey home in November, 1628, he passed through the Netherlands and visited Queen Elizabeth in exile at Rhenen, and also Frederick Henry of Orange, the Stadtholder, at the Hague. In England Roe drew up a memorial on foreign affairs for the consideration of Charles I, pointing out, among other things, the danger to England from the establishing of Habsburg power in the Baltic. Charles was convinced; and Roe received his Instructions in June, 1629. He was to endeavour to arrange a peace between Sweden and Poland, and to use his influence to open the trade of the Baltic, which was threatened with being closed to all but Spain, Austria and their confederates.[2]

Sweden, the state which was to decide in these critical years the fate of Northern Europe, dated its existence as a modern power only from the year 1523, when Gustavus Vasa threw off the dominion of Denmark and so ended the famous Union of Calmar, made in 1397. Gustavus Vasa and his son were Protestants, but his grandson, Sigismund, who succeeded to the throne in 1592, was a Roman Catholic, and was therefore dethroned by a revolution in the royal family in 1599. Sigismund, however, had also been elected King of Poland. So when deprived of his power in Sweden, Sigismund was able to maintain with Polish forces the feud with the Swedish Crown. His successor on the

[1] See "B.E." in *Historische Zeitschrift* (XVIII), 1857, p. 424.

[2] Instructions to Sir Thomas Roe in the *Camden Miscellany*, VII, p. 10 ff.

throne of Sweden was his uncle Charles IX. In 1611 Gustavus Adolphus, the son of Charles IX, became king.

On the eastern shores of the Baltic a war for empire soon began between Sweden and the Tsar of Russia. By 1617 Gustavus Adolphus had cut off the Russians from the sea. The war between Sweden and Russia had lasted for ten years. For the last three years English and Dutch diplomatists had been trying to mediate between the two enemies. At last the Treaty of Stolbova, February 27, 1617, registered the exclusion of the Russians from the Baltic. "And I hope to God," said Gustavus in announcing the Peace to his legislature, "that it will henceforth be hard for the Russians to leap over that brook." [1]

The hereditary quarrel of Gustavus with Sigismund of Poland, who still claimed to be King of Sweden, led him into Livonia. This province too the martial Swedish king proceeded to conquer; but he could not force the Poles to admit complete defeat in the course of a seven years' war. It was to end this war that Roe went to Elbing in Polish Prussia, near where the Swedish and Polish armies were encamped. He arrived there in August, 1629, and found that Dutch, Brandenburg and French diplomatists were engaged on the same mission, mediating between the contending powers. The French ambassador, Charnacé, was extremely active; with him begins the ascendancy which French diplomacy was to exercise for nearly a hundred years.

The negotiations were being drawn out, for Gustavus would not give up Livonia, nor would the Poles recognize his possession, nor yet would they give way on their king's claim to the Swedish crown. Gustavus was very stiff on the question of titles and returned Roe's notes because they did not contain the word *Potentissimus* among the epithets assigned to him, although, as Roe wrote to Charles, there were titles "enough for any Christian king."

The negotiations were transacted mainly by word of mouth. The two mediators, Roe and Charnacé, spent their time in riding between the two camps, and in explaining the point of view of the antagonists to each other. Charnacé acted as spokesman for the Poles, and Roe for the Swedes. The sanitary condition of the neighbourhood of the camps was frightful; the quarters of the mediators were poor; there was no display, and none of the

[1] Geijer, *History of the Swedes*, p. 241.

amenities usually associated with diplomatic conferences. Terms were at last arranged and signed at Altmark, on September 25, 1629. This was not a final peace-treaty, for neither party would absolutely renounce its rights in the questions of Livonia and the Swedish crown. The terms of Altmark were a truce made between Sweden and Poland for six years. In Livonia the *status quo*, the principle of *uti possidetis*, was recognized, which meant that Sweden continued to hold most of the territory. Trade was to be free to Swedes and Poles alike on the Vistula and generally on all rivers and roads of Poland and Lithuania.[1]

Thus before Charles I of England was completely immersed in domestic troubles he was able, through Roe, to contribute materially to the cessation of war in the East (as well as to the opening of commercial routes). Gustavus of Sweden, with the harassing Polish war ended, was able to prepare for the great expedition into Germany which was to change the whole trend of history.

This was the moment when the Catholic reaction in Germany reached its highest point. The Habsburg Maritime Design was now to be enforced. This design appears to have been mooted in Spanish and Jesuit circles from about the year 1585, when the Spaniards, having retaken Antwerp from the Dutch, hoped to follow up their victory by shutting off the Dutch from either trade or other support from the side of Scandinavia. The Habsburg powers were to close the passages from the North Sea and to occupy or control the chief ports in the Baltic, placing an Imperial navy on the "East-sea."[2] After the defeat of the Danish king at Lutter, Wallenstein received from the Emperor the title of General of the Oceanic and Baltic Sea. He was going to have an Imperial fleet constructed; and as a further step towards the accomplishment of the Habsburg Maritime Design he laid siege to the city of Stralsund, a Protestant stronghold and port in the Duchy of Pomerania. The heroic resistance of the burghers (February–August, 1628) was the first definite check given to the Catholic reaction. Their resistance could not have succeeded had not Stralsund been open to the sea, over which reinforcements and supplies came from Sweden and Denmark. But for how long would

[1] Dumont, V, Partie II, pp. 594–6.

[2] For the Habsburg Maritime Design see Droysen, *Gustav Adolf* (1869), I, pp. 37, 42, 286; see also *Die Maritimen Politik der Habsburger im siebenzehnten Jahrhundert* in *Historische Zeitschrift* (1867), XVIII, 422.

the sea remain open to Protestants? This was what Gustavus Adolphus was pondering in his camp in Polish Prussia. The fiery Swede knew that if he did not come to Germany, a Habsburg fleet would soon be off the coast of Sweden. On July 22 he concluded at Dirschau a treaty of alliance for twenty years with the Hanseatic city of Stralsund "for the defence of the city and consequently for the safety of the East Sea."[1]

The Edict of Restitution, issued by the Emperor on March 6, 1629, set the legal seal on the Catholic reaction. This Act gave a final interpretation of the Treaty of Passau and subsequent Imperial laws on the subject of religion, to the effect that "immediate" ecclesiastical princes of the Empire who had become Protestant since 1552 had no right to the privileges of prelates; that all "mediate" ecclesiastical fiefs diverted to Protestant uses should be restored to the Roman Catholics; and that the Religious Peace of 1552 and the following years was applicable only to adherents of the Confession of Augsburg, that is to say, to Lutherans.[2] This edict, if it could have been put completely into practice, would have amounted to a regular revolution in the system of land-ownership in North Germany; for, as in England in the time of Henry VIII and Edward VI, in Germany many Roman Catholic properties had been "secularized," partly for the benefit of private owners, partly for the endowment of educational bodies. As a consequence of the Edict much property was actually restored to Roman Catholic corporations, but "the great events of 1631 prevented the final transfer of the great archbishops of Bremen and Magdeburg into Catholic hands."[3] Yet in 1629 there seemed no prospect or possibility of these great events.

Nevertheless, in 1630 the vast Austro-Spanish scheme of Counter-Reformation (which many of its contemporaries believed and publicly stated to be a scheme of universal empire),[4] broke down. On July 3 Ferdinand opened a Diet of Electors, a *Kurfürstentag*, at Ratisbon (Regensburg). The Diet had been summoned to deal with troubles in Italy and to recognize the Emperor's son as his future successor. At once a discussion arose which showed the

[1] Dumont, V, Partie II, p. 550.

[2] Text of Edict of Restitution in Dumont, V, Partie II, p. 565.

[3] A. W. Ward, in *The Cambridge Modern History*, IV, 112.

[4] For the alleged Habsburg scheme of Universal Monarchy, see Droysen, *Gustav Adolf*, I, 17, 37 ff.

divisions among even the Roman Catholic princes of Germany. Maximilian of Bavaria and other princes of the League protested that they could not tolerate the licentiousness of the Imperial soldiery, and that Wallenstein must be dismissed. Their opposition to the Emperor was ably, if covertly, seconded by Charles Brulart de Léon, sent by Richelieu as ambassador to the Diet, and François Leclerc du Tremblay, better known as Father Joseph, a Capuchin friar who was deep in Richelieu's confidence. Ferdinand, faced with a choice which really was between war with the Catholic princes or abdication, yielded. He agreed to dismiss Wallenstein and to reduce the Wallensteiner army. The inscrutable Bohemian received his dismissal quietly. The Emperor lost the services of his only man of genius. The forces of the League, that is, of princely independence, had won. Moreover, the forces of the Habsburg Maritime Design and the Counter-Reformation were being rolled back when they had barely reached the Baltic, for on July 4, 1630, Gustavus Adolphus and the Swedish army had landed in Pomerania.

All the stars seemed now to conspire to put a stop to the militant Counter-Reformation. For while the Swede brought forward his battering-ram against the Habsburg powers, the Frenchman wove his diplomatic mesh. At the Kurfürstentag of Ratisbon, Brulart and Père Joseph concluded a treaty of disinterestedness, France agreeing not to assist the enemies of the Empire (October 13, 1630). This treaty was not ratified by Louis XIII, because it did not give the French king the title of "Majesty" and because it conflicted with his engagements to his German allies.[1] The treaty, however, was useful in securing time for French policy to develop. A war was being fought out in North Italy owing to a disputed succession to the childless Vincent II, Duke of Mantua, who died on December 26, 1627. Spain, the Emperor and Savoy took one side, with the object of extinguishing and partitioning the duchy. France supported the claim of the Duke of Nevers. French arms triumphed. By the Treaty of Cherasco (April 6, 1631), made between France and the Emperor (the Duke of Savoy acceding to the treaty three weeks later), Nevers was recognized as Duke of Mantua; and Pinerolo, on the Piedmontese side of the Mont Genèvre Pass, and Susa, on the same side of the Mont

[1] Text of Treaty and declaration of nullity in Dumont, V, Partie II, pp. 615–18.

Cervin Pass, were to remain in the hands of French garrisons.[1] A cool-headed captain in the Papal troops, called Giulio Mazarini, who was attached as secretary to the Nuncio at Turin, took a prominent part in the mediation of this treaty, and once intervened, at the risk of his life, to prevent two opposing forces from fighting in ignorance of a truce which he had just succeeded in bringing about. His good work was noted by Richelieu, whose service he entered eight years later.

With the head of the German Catholic League, Maximilian of Bavaria, Richelieu concluded at Fontainebleau, on May 30, 1631, a treaty of defensive alliance for eight years. With Sweden Richelieu was already in close relations through Charnacé, who followed Gustavus Adolphus into Germany. France and the Republic of Venice had already by a treaty negotiated with Contarini in the French camp at St. Jean de Maurienne during the Mantuan Succession War agreed with each other to support Gustavus in Germany with a subsidy (July, 1630). Finally Charnacé brought to a successful conclusion his negotiations with Gustavus by the Treaty of Barwalde (or Bernwald), signed in the Swedish camp on January 13, 1631. The object of the treaty was declared to be an alliance, to endure for five years, for the defence of the common friends of Louis XIII and Gustavus; the security of the Ocean and the Baltic; the liberty of commerce on the coasts of these seas; and the restoration of the oppressed states of the Empire. Gustavus agreed to maintain an army of 36,000 men in Germany; to observe neutrality towards Maximilian of Bavaria and the Catholic League, and not to disturb the Roman Catholic religion in places where it was recognized by Imperial law. On his side Louis XIII undertook to give to Gustavus a subsidy of 40,000 Imperial thalers yearly.[2] Pope Urban VIII himself approved of this alliance, as being necessary to check the advance of the Habsburgs to political predominance in Europe.

Gustavus first cleared the Imperialist troops out of the valley of the Lower Oder, and later the Leaguers out of the Elbe valley. The battle of Breitenfeld (September, 1631) made it certain that Northern Germany would not fall to the Counter-Reformation. Gustavus, in accordance with his treaty with France, respected

[1] Dumont, V, Partie II, p. 9. The navigation of the Po as far upwards as Trino was to be free to the subjects of both Savoy and Mantua.

[2] Dumont, VI, Partie I, 1.

the liberties of Roman Catholics and only reinstated the Augsburg Confession in places in which it had been forcibly suppressed. This, however, was a great gain to the Protestant cause. "Thus it followed that an enterprise originated or sanctioned by the Catholic opposition for political purposes resulted in the advantage of Protestantism."[1] Yet although Gustavus behaved humanely and waged war according to the principles contained in the famous book of Grotius *On the Laws of War and Peace* (a copy of which he is said to have carried on campaign), the German people suffered terribly, as may be shown from contemporary works like Vincent's *Lamentations* and the *Theatrum Europæum*. After the hero-king's death at Lutzen in 1632, fighting against Wallenstein who had been recalled to the Imperial army, all moral purpose seemed to go out of the war.

The North German princes, never very enthusiastic over the Swedish operations in Germany, were willing to dispense with Swedish help as soon as their religious liberty was secure. The Elector John George of Saxony refused to make any binding coalition with the Swedes after Gustavus' death; and in 1634 he entered into negotiations with the Emperor through the intermediary of the Landgrave George of Hesse-Darmstadt, the Elector's son-in-law. The negotiations took place at the fortress of Pirna on the Elbe; Count Trautmannsdorf negotiated on behalf of the Emperor. An armistice was arranged between the Saxon and Imperial troops (at Laun, February 28, 1635). In April the negotiations were resumed at Prague which is about half-way between Dresden and Vienna and which was not then in the area of hostilities. On May 30, 1635, the Peace of Prague was signed.

The terms of the peace, according to the wording of every clause, applied only to members of the Augsburg Confession, that is, to Lutherans. These terms settled provisionally the vexed question of secularized property; "mediate" ecclesiastical fiefs and property, taken over by Lutheran princes *before* the Treaty of Passau, were to be held according to the terms of the Treaty of Passau; "immediate" ecclesiastical properties in the hands of members of the Confession of Augsburg without distinction; and "mediate" properties, taken over by such members *after* the Treaty of Passau, were to remain in their hands as they were on November 12, 1627, and so to remain for forty years from the date of the Treaty of Prague. The Emperor reserved the right of deciding the religion of

[1] Ranke, *Popes*, Bk. VII, Chap. IV, § 5.

his subjects in his hereditary dominions (except Silesia). This condition (although it was expressly mentioned in relation only to the Emperor and members of the Augsburg Confession) necessarily implied that elsewhere within the Empire each prince or sovereign body could settle their own religion. All Leagues and Unions within the Empire were to be dissolved.[1] Practically all Germany, Calvinist as well as Lutheran, accepted the Peace except the sovereigns of Hesse-Cassel and Weimar (who were closely bound to Sweden and France), and the unfortunate Palatine family which still claimed its lost inheritance. Maximilian of Bavaria accepted the Peace; thus the Catholic League came to an end and its army was merged in the Imperialist forces. Even the Elector George William of Brandenburg, whose dominions were painfully exposed between the Imperialists on one side and the Swedes (who refused to come into the Peace of Prague) on the other, decided to throw in his lot with Saxony and the Emperor.[2]

The negotiations of 1635 between the Emperor and John George were a serious effort to end the crushing miseries of Germany. The Preamble to the Treaty of Prague states in eloquent terms its object as being to put an end to "wretchedness, want and destruction," caused by the dissensions of warlike parties and by the armies of foreign peoples on "the soil of the beloved fatherland of the noble German nation" (*das geliebte Vaterland der hochedlen Teutschen Nation*). The sentiment of nationality, if not very vocal, was well established in the seventeenth century.

The Treaty of Prague marked the condition of stalemate in which the Protestant and Catholic forces were. Moreover, Richelieu's anti-Habsburg system was only partially succeeding. The French could gain battles in the Rhineland, but they were losing north-eastern Italy. By the Franco-Spanish Treaty of Monzon in Valencia (March 5, 1626) Richelieu had shared "protection" of the Valtelline with Spain. But he soon lost even this share; and by the "Everlasting Peace" of Milan, concluded between the Confederation of the Grisons and Spain on September 3, 1639, the Spanish gained control of the Valtelline—a vital part of the route between the Milanese and southern Austria.

[1] Treaty of Prague, May 30, 1635, in Dumont, VI, Partie I, 89–99. Saxony acquired Upper and Lower Lausitz by a separate agreement with the Emperor. *Ibid.*, p. 101.

[2] See O. Meinardus, *Protokolle aus der Zeit des Kurfürsten Frederick Wilhelm*, in *Publicationen aus den K. preuss. Staatsarchiven* (1889), XLI, pp. ix–xiii.

CHAPTER XVII

THE PEACE OF WESTPHALIA

After the Peace of Prague of 1635 the Religious War is really at an end. The remaining dismal years during which armies marched up and down Germany involved three major issues, none of which was primarily religious. One was the determination of Sweden, and particularly of the autocratic, inflexible Chancellor Oxenstjerna, to fight on until confirmed in the dominion on the German coast which Gustavus Adolphus had deemed necessary for Sweden's religious, commercial and military security. The second great issue at stake was the position of Spain in the Rhineland, for Spanish armies had conquered the Palatinate, and now controlled most of the territories along the "Priests' Lane" as far as the Dutch frontier; and the Dutch themselves, at war with Spain since 1631, were not safe; from this point of view—that of the revival of Spanish power—the European war from 1635 to 1648 may be considered as still having a religious element in it. The third issue, like the first, was purely territorial. Richelieu was vigorously carrying out his design of "restoring" to Gaul its natural frontiers; in his Political Testament he declares that this was the great aim of his twenty years of ministry. A fourth, but minor issue, was the question of the Palatinate.

It may be asked, why did diplomacy not stop the "Thirty Years' War" after 1635 if the religious question was practically settled? The answer is quite simple, and all who remember the war which began in 1914 will easily understand it. The Thirty Years' War started in 1618 owing to certain causes; but it went on so long that by the time the original causes were ready to be settled other vital interests had become involved, so that every year seemed to add to the difficulty of stopping it. So widespread and so conflicting were these interests that people almost gave up hope of a solution; and, as always happens during prolonged hostilities, society began to adapt itself to war-conditions, as if war, not peace, was to be the normal condition of mankind henceforward. At the same time the contending military forces were in a state of balance or "stalemate"; there was no prospect of a complete military decision on either side. Thus the conditions—mental, moral, social, military and even economic—were not favourable to the efforts of diplomacy. Exhaustion would not end the struggle, for Europe was meeting the drain by a steady lowering of the standards of life, the standards of material and moral civilization, so that the attrition of war might go on practically for ever.

The man who really held in his hands the decision of war or peace was Richelieu. He had constructed a grand coalition of which France was the centre and which would collapse if the cement of French soldiers, French money and French diplomatists was withdrawn. In 1634 and 1635, when the preliminary negotiations of the Peace of Prague were being conducted, the prospect seemed black for him; and in 1636 a brilliant raid of the Imperialist cavalry leader, Johann von Werth of Jülich, nearly reached Paris. Yet it was in this black period that the indomitable French statesmen "entered upon that final series of negotiations with which he was to crown his career and lay the foundations of the predominance of France in Europe." [1]

First Richelieu offered to make peace with the Emperor in return for receiving Alsace. Ferdinand refused. Having thus definitely stated his war-aim, Richelieu entered into an offensive and defensive alliance with the United Netherlands (Treaty of Paris, February 8, 1635). With the Dutchman Grotius, who was an exile from his native land and was now Swedish ambassador at Paris, Richelieu and Father Joseph kept up incessant negotiations, which resulted in the renewal of the Franco-Swedish alliance, each side binding itself not to make peace without the consent of the other (Treaty of Compiègne, April 28, 1635). Accordingly the conclusion of the Peace of Prague in May, 1635, found him already prepared for the new, and purely territorial, aspect which the war was to assume. The Treaty of Compiègne was followed in 1636 by the declaration of war on the part of France against Spain.

The diplomatists of three Powers tried to find a way out of war. The first power was the Papacy. Urban VIII sent a com-

[1] Hill, *A History of European Diplomacy*, Vol. II, p. 589.

missioner in 1636 to Cologne, where some discussions took place; but the Pope instructed his plenipotentiary not to assent to any peace which should recognize the secularization of Church property, the restoration of the Palatinate family, or the independence of the Dutch. The Papal mediation was accordingly not taken seriously by any of the combatants. The second mediator was Sir Thomas Roe. He attended a conference of Sweden, Brandenburg, and France, with an Imperialist representative occasionally present, at Hamburg at the end of the year 1639 and in the early part of 1640; and again in the winter of 1641 he attended a conference which met at Vienna. Although the war was still going on, diplomatic representatives of the belligerents were able to meet and discuss possible terms. Roe reported home that the Emperor (Ferdinand III since 1637) was sincerely desirous of peace, but that "the Spanish fox" would not consent to the restoration of the Palatinate to Charles Louis, son of the late Frederick V.[1]

Little by little these meetings, conferences, discussions contributed to the peace-movement which was acquiring momentum in spite of apparently helpless populations and even governments. The progress of the movement was undoubtedly delayed by the fact that England, the only powerful state which was neutral, was considered by the belligerents to be impotent at the time through the disputes of Crown and Parliament.[2] Where England failed France succeeded and had the honour of having a proposal accepted which actually in the long run led to peace. The Count d'Avaux, in conference with a Swedish and Imperialist representative at Hamburg at the end of the year 1641, suggested that a double conference should meet in separation, at two neighbouring Westphalian towns, Münster and Osnabrück.[3] Long-drawn-out conferences at Ratisbon, Vienna and Hamburg, apparently fruitless, had enabled two diplomatists like modern *rapporteurs*, to draft, out of the apparently hopeless medley of

[1] Roe's letters from Vienna are in the Public Record Office, *State Papers, Germany*, October–November, 1641.

[2] *Heads of the discourse of Count Lesly to Sir Tho. Roe, drawn out of the paper markt B* (P.R.O, *State Papers, Germany*, November, 1641). Leslie wrote that "rumours were spread abroad to the Emperor, Princes and Electors of the state of England," of the weakening of His Majesty's power "by the proceedings of his Parliament."

[3] Hill, *op. cit.*, Vol. II, p. 592.

contending opinions, some sort of common or agreed form. Such were *The Preliminary Articles for the Universal Peace Conference at Münster and Osnabrück*,[1] agreed upon by Count Conrad von Lutzow, one of the Imperial Councillors and Plenipotentiaries at the Conference of Hamburg, and Count d'Avaux, the French plenipotentiary. On December 25, 1641, the Preliminary Articles were signed at Hamburg by Lutzow and d'Avaux, and were stated in the preamble to comprehend not only the Empire and France but Spain also. The agreed Articles, which, as acknowledged in the preamble, were made under the mediation of the King of Denmark, were to the effect that a congress for the general peace was to assemble in Münster and Osnabrück ; and that for this purpose these two places were to be regarded as neutral, and likewise the roads between them.

Although this accord was reached by Lutzow and d'Avaux at the end of the year 1641, nearly two more years were to pass before the Peace Congress actually began its work, and nearly seven years were to pass before the final Peace Treaty was signed. After several postponements, the opening of the Congress of Westphalia was fixed for July 11, 1643.

There were considered to be two wars going on : one between the Emperor (with his allies—Spain, Bavaria and others) and France ; the other between the Emperor and Sweden. It is true that France and Sweden were strictly bound as allies against the Empire, but as they were separated by their religious aims, it was considered convenient to treat them separately. The Imperialists thought they would do best for themselves by meeting the French in some Catholic city like Cologne and the Swedes in some Protestant city like Lübeck. Naturally enough this proposal did not suit the Swedes and French, who knew that they could only gain their territorial aims by standing together. The compromise, suitable to every one, was suggested at the end of the year 1641 by the Count d'Avaux, who had for some years been Richelieu's plenipotentiary in Germany. D'Avaux' suggestion was that the simultaneous meetings, at Münster and Osnabrück, were to be counted as one Congress. These pleasant old towns are only about thirty miles apart, so that post-boys and dispatch-riders could pass from one to the other in a day. They were well situated, too, for communication with the outside world. Münster was the

[1] Text in Dumont, Tome VI, Partie I, p. 231.

meeting-place of roads that came from Nymwegen, Cleves, Cologne and Cassel, and which were continued through Osnabrück to Hanover. Osnabrück and Münster are situated on the fertile Westphalian plain; this was almost the only part of Germany which had suffered little from the ravages of war. Supplies of food were therefore easily obtained; this was an important matter, for the members of the staffs and the servants who attended the Peace Congress were very numerous. The deputies of the interested states assembled very slowly, the last to arrive being the French in April, 1644. Thus the Congress timed to open in July, 1643, really opened just one year later.

The two towns were neutralized and placed under the protection of their own magistrates and burgher militia. The intermediate routes were also regarded as neutral. Houses in the two towns were rented by the chief delegates, and the inns and lodgings were full of their retainers. Every state in Europe, except England, Poland, Russia and Turkey, is said to have been represented. A great deal of attention was paid to formalities: the story is well known how the Count d'Avaux (French plenipotentiary at Münster), when saying good-bye after receiving a visit from the Venetian mediator, Aloisi Contarini, only accompanied his guest to the foot of the stairs; but Contarini demanded that he be escorted by his host to the carriage. D'Avaux could not settle this point without corresponding with Mazarin in Paris; eventually the Venetian delegate was accorded full diplomatic honours. The chief Spanish delegate, the Conte di Penaranda, was equally punctilious. Even in his own house, he would not shake hands with the delegates of the German Electoral Princes, or give them the title of Excellency.[1] The amount of display was, as might be expected, considerable; banquets, after all, are cheaper than battles, and expensive clothes cost less than an army's equipment. France was a rich country and could support great state; Sweden was never rich, and was now fearfully exhausted by nearly forty years of war against Poland and the Empire. Yet John Oxenstjerna (eldest son of the great Chancellor), when he went out in his great carriage at Osnabrück, was escorted by a troop of Swedish horse. In his house he kept a regular court of Swedish gentlemen, with their pages and their men-servants. On the other hand, the Imperial Exchequer was, towards the end of the Congress,

[1] *Mercurio di Siri* (Paris, 1672), T. XIV, p. 8.

so depleted, that the daily needs of the court of Vienna could scarcely be met;[1] people knew this at the time, so that the Imperial prestige was not high.

The Peace Congress of Westphalia (as it was called, because Münster and Osnabrück were in the Circle of Westphalia) went on for three years, without an armistice being concluded in the meantime; and as the fortune of war swayed back and forth, so did the attitude of the plenipotentiaries become more obstinate or more conciliatory. At the moment when peace was concluded on October 24, 1648, the Swedes were besieging the city of Prague itself. The Congress-towns, however, were not exposed to the chances of war, for the Preliminary Articles, which had made them for the time being neutral territory, were observed.

The chief difficulties in the way of peace were not made by the Emperor, but by the Spanish plenipotentiaries. They were helped in this by disputes between the three French plenipotentiaries—the Comte d'Avaux, Abel Servien, Comte de la Roche des Aubiers, and Henri d'Orléans, Duc de Longueville; but in the last month Mazarin committed all the negotiations to Servien alone, in order that things might be done more expeditiously.

Negotiations at Münster were carried on always through mediators—the Cardinal Chigi appointed by the Pope, and Aloisi Contarini by Venice. These two mediators received the written proposals of either side and handed them on to the other side. At Osnabrück, negotiations were carried on directly by exchange of notes. All communications were translated into Latin. It was at Osnabrück that the most difficult questions, those of religion, were thrashed out; for this purpose the Catholic and Protestant delegates formed themselves into two separate conferences, and communicated with each other by writing.[2] Although most of the negotiating was done by exchange of notes, there were occasional oral conferences among the plenipotentiaries, at least at Osnabrück. Sometimes months elapsed between the delivery of a note and the reply, for the plenipotentiaries might have to send to Paris or Vienna for instructions. Although the negotiations were long drawn out, it must be admitted that on the whole they reached satisfactory conclusions; and Count Trautsmandorff, the

[1] *Mercurio di Siri*, T. XII, p. 565.

[2] The form of procedure is described in Koch, *Histoire abrégée des Traités de Paix* (Paris, 1817), Vol. I, pp. 130-1.

chief Imperial delegate, and Servien, who was left alone to represent France at the end, must have worked very hard. Servien indeed had great talents and much energy; but d'Avaux, whom he displaced from Münster, had an easier temper.[1]

The Peace of Westphalia was signed at Münster, on October 24, 1648. It comprised two treaties—that between France and the Empire, called the Münster treaty, and that between Sweden and the Empire, called the Osnabrück treaty; this last was dated from Osnabrück although signed at Münster.[2]

The main treaty is the Treaty of Osnabrück, which settled the religious question, and the territorial affairs of Germany except those which specially regarded France. The Münster treaty has no reference to religious toleration, but it repeats the territorial provisions of the Osnabrück text, other than those relating to Sweden. Both texts are in Latin.

The Peace of Westphalia, coming at the end of a war which neither side had won, was conceived along lines of liberal compromise. A complete amnesty and oblivion were ordained for all acts of hostility done since the opening of the war in 1618; and, with certain exceptions, all territories lost in the course of the war were restored to their owners of the year 1618. With regard to churches and church lands, both "mediate and immediate," which Protestants or Catholics had held, the year 1624 was to be taken as the test-year of possession. Those who held ecclesiastical lands in that year were to keep them. As regards religion, it was decided that where the public worship of either the Confession of Augsburg or of Catholicism existed in Germany in 1624 it should remain lawful; and where people changed their religion after 1624 they were to enjoy "liberty of conscience," which meant the right of private worship at home, but not in an assembly of several families. A subsequent paragraph in the religious chapter of the Osnabrück treaty gave the territorial ruler the right to order his nonconforming subjects, where the public worship of Protestantism had not been allowed in 1624, to leave his dominions, without, however, their losing their property; and it was under this clause that the Archbishop of Salzburg cruelly expelled his

[1] Flasson, *Hist. Gén. de la Dip. Française* (Paris, 1811), T. III, p. 222. Servien became Superintendent of Finances at Paris in 1653, and held the office with success till 1659, when he died, aged sixty-six.

[2] Vast, *Les Grands Traités du Règne de Louis XIV*, Paris, 1893, p. 5, n. 2, quoting from the Archives of the Ministère des Affaires Etrangères.

Protestant subjects in 1731. Finally all religious concessions granted by the treaty to Catholics or members of the Augsburg Confession (Lutherans) were by the same instrument secured also to members of the Reformed Religion, that is, the Calvinists.

The territorial provisions were of two kinds—one kind dealing with annexations, the other with restitutions. France was acknowledged to have complete sovereignty over the bishoprics, cities and districts of Metz, Toul and Verdun, which she had, in point of fact, occupied since 1552; the Emperor also ceded all the Imperial rights over Pinerolo (the key to the Mont Genèvre pass on the Italian side) and Breisach, "the landgraviate of Upper and Lower Alsace, the Sundgau, and the provincial prefectship over ten Imperial towns in Alsace"—Hagenau, Colmar, Schlettstadt, Wissembourg, Landau, Oberenheim, Rosheim, Münster, Kaisersberg, Türckheim. Thus began the history of Alsace in the modern French state. The King of France was also to have the right of garrisoning Philipsburg, and to send troops there by the Rhine through Imperial territory.

To Sweden was ceded Western Pomerania with Stettin and both sides of the mouth of the Oder, and the island of Wollin. Pomerania was fortunately at the disposal of the belligerents through the death of the last dukes in 1638. Sweden also acquired Rügen and the port of Wismar, the Dukes of Mecklenburg being compensated elsewhere for these losses. Finally the Swedes also obtained the Archbishopric of Bremen and the Bishopric of Verden, as principalities: thus they controlled the mouths of the Oder, Elbe and Weser, and went far on the way (which they never completed) to becoming a great commercial state.

Among the German rulers to profit by the Peace were the exiled Elector Palatine (Charles Louis, the son of the hapless King of Bohemia), who was restored to the Lower Palatinate and his capital of Heidelberg, and who was established as an eighth Elector of the Holy Roman Empire; but old Maximilian of Bavaria (he was now seventy-five) who had been at the start of the Thirty Years' War, kept the Upper Palatinate, and the senior Electoral dignity which Charles Louis' forefathers had possessed. The "Great Elector" of Brandenburg obtained Magdeburg (in reversion), and several other bishoprics. But apart from Brandenburg, the general principle of the peace was not change but restoration. The Treaty of Münster declared all the Estates of the Empire and their vassals to be restored to the same position and dignities as they had enjoyed previously to the war. All prisoners of war were to be forthwith liberated, and all the belligerent armies disbanded, except those needed for ordinary security.

With regard to the Princes and Free Cities of the Empire there were certain constitutional clauses, but the most important for diplomatic history was an article (number 65) of the Münster treaty: "It shall be free perpetually to each of the States of the Empire to make alliances with strangers for their preservation and safety; provided, nevertheless, such Alliances be not against the Emperor, and the Empire, nor against the Publick Peace, and this Treaty, and without prejudice to the Oath by which every one is bound to the Emperor and the Empire." The condition attached to this right of making alliances proved to be worthless in the future.

All tolls and tariffs, contrary to the public good, and imposed without the consent of the Emperor and Electors, were to be abolished, and freedom of commerce throughout the Empire by land and water was decreed, subject only to the lawful and accustomed charges.

The Treaties of Westphalia gave to Germany the rest which she so long sighed for, and permitted her to undertake the fruitful labours of peace. Materially the country soon recovered from the long war, but its moral and intellectual progress was not so quickly resumed, and long dull years followed in German science and literature. Sweden obtained great gains, but made nothing of them. France received by the Peace important territorial advantages, and had the credit of being a powerful and beneficent negotiator. For it was owing to Servien's labours both in Münster and Osnabrück that the often-retarded peace was at last concluded.[1] The Pope Innocent X through Cardinal Chigi had been, with Venice, the mediator at the Münster Congress; yet he so strongly objected to the secularizations that by the Bull *Zelo Domus Dei* (November 26, 1648) he condemned the Peace outright. No notice, however, was taken of this denunciation; the Pope was no longer the keeper of the public faith of Europe.[2] The States

[1] *Mercurio di Siri*, T. 13, p. 267.

[2] The Treaties of Münster (in Latin) and of Osnabrück (in the French translation) are given in Dumont, *Corps Diplomatique*, T. VI, Partie I, where the Dutch treaty of January 30, 1648, will also be found. The Treaty of Münster is reprinted in Vast, *Les Grands Traités*, I, where also a bibliography of the

themselves were to be the keepers of this public faith; for in the final articles of the Treaty of Münster all the parties to it, without distinction of religion, were bound to watch over the execution of the treaty, to endeavour by advice to bring any violator of it to an amicable composition, and finally, if peaceful means did not prevail, to defend the treaty by force of arms.

The Peace of Westphalia required all the guarantees that could be afforded it, for the authority of the Emperor was becoming little more than a name. The dilapidated condition of the Empire had been made clear in a piece of stinging anti-Austrian propaganda, published in 1640 over the name of Hippolithus a Lapide. It was written by Bogislav Philip Chemnitz, a member of a family distinguished for diplomatic service with the Pomeranian and Holstein-Gottorp dukes. Out of five brothers, Martin Chemnitz became a diplomatist under Gustavus Adolphus. Bogislav Philip served as an officer in the Swedish army. Afterwards he was employed by the Swedish Government in writing the history of the Swedish campaigns in Germany. His pamphlet or book of 1640 on the constitution of the Empire was considered to be such a telling blow that Chancellor Oxenstjerna himself was by some people supposed to have written it.[1]

The Dutch were not comprehended in the Treaties of Münster and Osnabrück because they had already made a separate peace with Spain nine months previously. This peace was contained in a treaty signed by Gaspar de Braccamonte, Count of Penaranda, and Antoine Brun for the King of Spain, and by Bartold de Gent, Jean de Mathenesse, Adrian Paaw and others for the States-General, at Münster on January 30, 1648. Having been made at the General Peace Congress, this treaty is properly regarded as forming part of the Peace of Westphalia.

The Spanish-Dutch treaty recognized the States-General and Provinces as "Free and Sovereign States," and thus ended what the Spaniards regarded as a rebellion of eighty years. The frontier between the Spanish and United Netherlands was fixed at the line of military occupation of the two parties at the moment of the con-

texts is given. The English translation of the Münster treaty, which has been quoted above, is in *A General Collection of Treaties*, London, 1710, p. 1. Dumont (Tome VI, Partie I, p. 463) also gives a French translation of the Bull of Protest of Pope Innocent X.

[1] See F. Weber, *Hippolithus a Lapide*, in *Historische Zeitschrift* (XXIX), 1873, p. 266 ff.

clusion of peace. Liberty of commerce was to exist between Spain and the United Provinces, subject to payment in each country of dues at the same rate as were imposed on the citizens of that country. Neither party was to have the right of trading with the colonial possessions of the other. The Scheldt and its mouths were to be closed to commerce from the side of the States-General, that is from the sea, for the States-General possessed both sides of the estuary.[1]

[1] Treaty of Münster, January 30, 1648, in Dumont, VI, Partie I, 429–35.

PART III

THE AGE OF LOUIS XIV

CHAPTER XVIII

THE PEACE OF THE PYRENEES

The Peace of Westphalia did not bring an end to all hostilities which were going on in 1648. The Empire and Sweden, France and the Empire, Spain and the Netherlands, ceased to fight; but France and Spain, which had been at war since 1636, continued in this condition till 1659. War was not a continuous and intense effort in those days, and during great portions of every year of the Franco-Spanish War the hostile armies were not in the field. Spain, in spite of her great defeats at the hands of the Grand Condé at Rocroi in 1643, and at Lens in 1648, and in spite of the revolt of Catalonia, engineered by Richelieu and still continuing, maintained fairly vigorous hostilities against France. After the civil troubles known as the *Fronde* broke out in France (1648–52), Spain even made considerable headway. For about a year the genius of Marshal Turenne was actually employed on the Spanish side, so high did partisan feeling rise among the French nobility; but when Turenne came back to his allegiance, the superiority of French arms was soon asserted. Besides, Oliver Cromwell thought it worth while to make a military alliance with France (Paris, May 9, 1657),[1] an alliance which was quickly followed by the victory of the Dunes (June 14, 1658), where 6,000 Cromwellian soldiers gained great distinction, fighting under Turenne against a Spanish army commanded by the Grand Condé. Dunkirk was captured from the Spaniards; and the King of Spain gave up the long struggle.

[1] The Treaty is in Latin and in French, and was drawn up and signed in Paris by Lionne and Lockhart; see Chéruel, *Hist. de France sous le ministère de Mazarin* (Paris, 1882), II, 53. Text in Guizot, *Hist. de la Repub. d'Angleterre*, II, 597; Dumont, VI, Partie II, 178, and in Italian in *Mercurio di Siri*.

On every side the Cardinal Mazarin had shown himself superior to his opponents, both domestic and foreign. Even while the civil war of the Fronde was going on he did not despair of the foreign war; and his diplomacy reached everywhere and countered all the efforts of Spain. The alliance with the English Commonwealth was a great achievement, negotiated in spite of the ties of blood existing between the French and English royal families (Charles I's queen, Henrietta Maria, was a daughter of Henri Quatre). Further, in 1658 (August 15) a defensive alliance was signed at Mayence between France and a number of the princes of the Rhine and Northern Germany, and thus a block of minor states was interposed between the Austrian Habsburgs in South Germany and the Spanish Habsburgs in the Low Countries. This alliance, known as the League of the Rhine, may be considered one of the greatest achievements of Mazarin. He had just failed to prevent the election of Leopold, Archduke of Austria, to the Empire (July 15, 1658), but his able ambassador to the Imperial Diet, the Abbé Gravel, and Hugues de Lionne took the opportunity of the presence at Frankfort of many German princes for the election and coronation of the Emperor to negotiate the League of the Rhine with the Archbishops of Cologne, Trèves and Mainz, the Duke of Neuburg, the King of Sweden (Charles X, who was also Duke of Zweibrücken or Deux Ponts),[1] the Dukes of Brunswick and Luneburg, and the Landgrave of Hesse. This treaty (dated Mayence, August 15, 1658) contained a guarantee of the Treaties of Münster and Osnabrück; on the King of France's part it secured the princes from invasion, and from military contributions, requisitions, winter-quarters and such things; on the side of the princes, it, in effect, bound them to prevent the passage of Imperial troops to the Netherlands. The result was a complete isolation of Spain, and a speedy conclusion of peace. From this time forward it was always the policy of France to protect the territories and the independence of the minor states of Germany; and the League of the Rhine was actually revived by Napoleon I in his famous Confederation of the Rhine, in 1806.[2] Mazarin's

[1] The personal union between Sweden and Zweibrücken came to an end at the death of Charles XII of Sweden without issue in 1718. Zweibrücken then passed to his second cousin Gustavus Samuel Leopold.

[2] The text of the League of the Rhine (in Latin) is in Vast, *Les Grands Traités*, I, p. 77. Dumont gives a French version, in T. VI, Partie II, p. 239.

League was twice renewed for periods of three years and endured until August 15, 1667,[1]—long enough for Louis XIV to begin, without any fear of opposition on the Rhine, his war of Devolution in May of that year.

France and Spain were not two nations fighting for their existence. They were contending over questions of boundaries, important matters indeed, but not incapable of settlement by compromise. Peace might have been made in 1648 at Münster, but the Spaniards thought (especially after the elimination of the Dutch from the war by the treaty of January 30, 1648) that they would emerge as victors owing to the internal dissensions of France. The end of the Fronde, however, and later the accession of the English navy and army by the treaty of 1657, prevented any chance of Spain's winning the war. Negotiations for peace had been begun (or resumed) in 1649 by Penaranda (who had concluded the peace with Holland in 1648) and by Lionne; they met for the purpose in Cambrai.

Hugues de Lionne belonged to an old family of Dauphiné. He was born in 1611, and was early trained to affairs in the office of his uncle, Abel Servien, in the Ministries of Finance and War. He was sent on various diplomatic missions, including one to Rome where he spent four years. Rome in the seventeenth century (the Rome of *John Inglesant*) was a religious, social and diplomatic centre for Europe, the place where were concentrated "the greatest number of men trained in political skill." [2] In this home of leisure, of the arts, of philosophy, of high politics, of ambition and internationalism, Lionne moved easily—indolent, pleasure-loving, observant, subtle, and when occasion required, energetic. When Mazarin became First Minister of France, Lionne, who had known him at Rome, became the Cardinal's chief counsellor. He was for a short time at the Congress of Westphalia, and when he returned to his office in Paris he was responsible for drafting the Instructions which were sent to Servien at the Congress. For many years after this Lionne was the directing force of French diplomacy. Dissipated and pleasure-loving, he could nevertheless, when it was necessary, work with tremendous energy. He could sit up all night to pen dispatches, and he personally wrote,

[1] Mignet, *Succession d'Espagne* (*Collection de Documents inédits sur l'histoire de France*, 1835), Tome II, 20.

[2] E. Lavisse in *Histoire de France* (1905), VII, Partie I, 141.

in his bad, careless handwriting, most of the important documents, or dictated them to an amanuensis, and thus he was personally responsible for the drafting of thousands of critical diplomatic papers.

The Cambrai negotiations between Lionne and Penaranda in 1649 came to nothing. After the Fronde was over, negotiations were taken up again with greater chances of success. In 1656 Lionne went to Madrid, although French and Spanish armies were still fighting each other, for in those days diplomatists met (not necessarily in neutral territory) and discussed peace while their Governments were still at war.

In 1656 the negotiations which were conducted by Lionne at Madrid seemed likely to be crowned with success. Mazarin had supplied him with full copies of instructions, among which was an order to introduce if opportunity offered, the question of a marriage between the young Louis XIV and Maria Theresa the heiress of the whole Spanish monarchy. Lionne in the heat of his arguments at Madrid with the minister Don Luis de Haro let fall *comme à l'aventure* the suggestion of this marriage ; for by this all problems about territory could be arranged to the convenience and without hurting the pride of either nation.[1] But the negotiations broke down because the Spaniards insisted that Condé (who had deserted to the Spanish service in 1651) should be restored to all his rights in France.

After the victory of the Dunes (June 14, 1658), Turenne could have conquered the Spanish Netherlands. Mazarin was quite aware of their importance for France. Years before he had written : " The acquisition of the Low Countries would form for the city of Paris an impregnable bulwark." [2] If France conquered the Spanish Netherlands, there would be no chance of a Spanish princess marrying young Louis XIV ; and this was now Mazarin's chief aim. In 1646 he had written to the French plenipotentiaries at Münster : " If the Infanta was married to His Majesty, we could attain to the succession of Spain, whatever renunciations we had to make of it. . . ." [3] And now he was more than ever bent on this marriage, as the sole means of turning the attention

[1] *Recueil des Instructions*, XI, p. 140—Narrative of M. de Lionne.

[2] Vast, *Les Grands Traités*, I, p. 84, from a dispatch of January 20, 1646.

[3] Vast, I, 83, quoting *Correspondance Politique, Allemagne*, in *Ministère des Affaires Etrangères*.

of the youthful and ardent King Louis from the Cardinal's niece Marie Mancini.

On May 7, 1659, as French arms were now being uniformly successful, there was no difficulty in arranging an armistice between the warring armies. Thus the negotiations leading directly to the Peace of the Pyrenees were, unlike the negotiations of the Westphalia Peace, conducted during a suspension of hostilities. The discussions were now being carried on at Paris directly between Mazarin and Don Antonio Pimental de Prado, a Sicilian nobleman, envoy extraordinary from the Court of Spain. By June 4 the two negotiators had agreed upon a preliminary treaty of 89 articles, which was then signed and formed the basis of the final peace. The conferences were resumed on August 13 between the First Ministers of France and Spain, Mazarin and Don Luis de Haro. Mazarin stayed at St. Jean de Luz,[1] and every day went to the meetings which were held on the Île des Faisans, in the mouth of the Bidassoa river, on the frontier of the two countries. There ensued a carefully fought duel of wits between these two expert diplomatists: gradually all points were agreed upon, and set forth in due order, except the affair of the Prince of Condé; Mazarin refused to treat Condé as other than a rebel, who would be pardoned indeed, but only by grace of the king. The Spaniards stood firmly on the ground that their honour was engaged, and that Condé must be restored to all his offices and property in France. It was in the midst of this *impasse* that, on September 29, a letter arrived from Condé at Brussels, bidding the Spanish Government not to defer the conclusion of peace on account of his interests—a creditable, if tardy act of generosity on the part of one who until then had shown only bravery and military genius to compensate for his complete selfishness. As events turned out, Condé did not lose greatly by his treason: after writing a letter of submission to the king, he was made Governor of Burgundy. Charles II of England, who was still an exile, was at Fuenterrabia during the negotiations, anxiously pressing his interests upon the attention of the two Powers. He effected nothing, however, and went back empty-handed to the Spanish Netherlands, to await a turn in the wheel of fortune.

After twenty-four conferences had been held, the final treaty (known as the Peace of the Pyrenees) was signed on November 7,

[1] *Mémoires du Marquis des Chouppes* (Paris, 1861), p. 195.

1659, in the *pavillon de conférence* on the Isle of the Pheasants. It is in French, contains 124 articles, and is unsurpassed in its technical perfection: "By its long and detailed preparation, its finished composition, its beautiful and majestic style, it deserves to be considered as the most harmonious monument of the diplomacy of the great century." [1] The composition of this treaty, which almost alone among the great treaties of history, contains no obscurities or inconsistencies, was due to Lionne, who acted as Mazarin's secretary, and Don Pedro Coloma, who acted second for Don Luis de Haro. The conclusion of this treaty was considered a great event in the history of France; and Mazarin, with the consent of Philip IV of Spain, gave Don Luis de Haro a present of 100,000 crowns.[2]

By article 35 Spain ceded to France a great part of Artois, namely Arras, Hesdin, Bapaume, St. Pol, Therouanne, and certain other places; in Flanders, France obtained Gravelines and Bourbourg; in Hainault, Landrecies and Quesnoy; in Luxemburg, Thionville, Montmédy, Damvillers; and Avesnes, Philippville and Marienbourg between the Sambre and Meuse (articles 36–40). Thus France made a beginning (but only a beginning) in strengthening her dangerous north-eastern frontier. The most important territorial condition, however, is contained in article 42, which declares that "the Pyrenees Mountains, which have anciently divided the Gauls from the Spanish, shall be also henceforth the division of the two same kingdoms." After the sea, there is no more satisfactory frontier than a range of high mountains, for (among other things) they so isolate from each other the peoples on either side, that there can be no disputes concerning the nationality of the respective frontiersmen. Since 1559 the frontier of France and Spain has been perfectly stable, and the only real problems which the two Governments have here had to face have been problems of land-surveying.

According to the principle of article 42, France received Rousillon and such parts of Conflans and Cerdagne as are "in the Pyrenees

[1] *Par sa longue et minutieuse preparation, par sa facture achevée, par sa belle et majestueuse ordonnance, il mérite d'etre considéré comme le monument le plus harmonieux de la diplomatie du grand siècle.* Vast, I, 89–90. The treaty is printed in Dumont, T. VI, Partie II, p. 264, and Vast, I, 93, English trans., in *General Collection,* p. 1.

[2] Referred to in Instructions of Louis XIV to Colbert de Croissy, suggesting how a bribe may be offered to Arlington; Mignet, *Succession d'Espagne,* III, 36.

on the side of France." Spain received back the whole province of Catalonia, which France had largely occupied during the Catalonian rebellion.

By article 60 France disinterested herself further in the war of Spain and Portugal (except to offer services as mediator), and promised not to aid the Portuguese any more—a promise which did not prevent Mazarin and the king from secretly sending a regiment next year. A considerable number of articles deal with the Duke Charles IV of Lorraine, who had taken sides against France and was now restored to his Duchy, but under conditions regarding fortifications, passage of French troops and such things, which placed Lorraine thereafter at the mercy of the King of France. From this time Lorraine (in which the French already possessed Metz, Toul and Verdun) was really a client state of France until its annexation in 1736. Of the rest of the articles of the Treaty of the Pyrenees, eight deal with the affairs of the Prince of Condé.

The contract of marriage between Louis XIV and the Infanta Maria Theresa is dated, like the Treaty of the Pyrenees itself, at the Isle of the Pheasants, November 7, 1659. It provided for a dowry of 500,000 crowns (5,571,800 francs) to be paid by the King of Spain; and in consideration of this payment (*moyennant le payement effectif fait à sa Majestie Très Chrestienne desdits cinq cens mille Écus d'or sol*), the Infanta was to renounce all the "greater goods and rights" to which she might have a claim "on account of the heritages and greater successions of her parents" (article 4 of the Marriage Contract). This clause embodies the customary arrangement that the lady who is to be wedded shall renounce her legal portion of the property of her parents in return for an immediate payment of a *dot* or dowry. Actually the King of Spain did not pay over the dowry of his daughter, and therefore the renunciation of her legal portion by Maria Theresa was void. But this did not give her any right to claim succession to the Crown of Spain; this question was regulated by a separate clause (article 5) of the marriage-contract.

Article 5 stipulated absolutely for the sake of peace and because the two Crowns of France and Spain were so great that they could not be reduced to one, that neither Maria Theresa nor any of her children could succeed to the kingdoms, states, lordships, or dominions which belonged to the King of Spain. This article made no mention of any condition (for instance, the payment of the dowry) attached to the stipulation. Therefore, although the Infanta's dowry was never paid, Louis XIV's wife had no claim, on this account, to advance any pretension to any right to the throne of Spain; but she certainly could claim her legal portion of the private wealth of her father.[1] Her renunciation of the Succession to the Spanish Crown remained binding.

Mazarin had not much longer to live, for already, when not yet sixty years old, he was a martyr to gout. He died on March 9, 1661. Few ministers of foreign affairs can point to such a record. From the moment when, as a neutral diplomatist in the War of the Mantuan Succession (1630), having just negotiated an armistice he had dashed in between the firing lines of contending armies crying *Pace! Pace!*, Mazarin had been working for peace, without shrinking, when inevitable, from the realities of war.

The Peace of Westphalia put an end to the miseries which had tortured Germany for thirty years; the Treaty of the Pyrenees ended over twenty years of warfare between France and Spain in a peace which, however short its duration (under ten years), was of inestimable benefit to the Low Countries as well as to France. Europe gained by his diplomatic efforts to terminate war, while France came to her legitimate heritage of Alsace, at the Peace of Westphalia, and Artois and Rousillon, at the Peace of the Pyrenees. The alliance with England made France safe from the powerful Commonwealth; the League of the Rhine ensured the eastern frontier. In the worst hours of the Fronde Mazarin "had not despaired of the State," and when he died the country of his adoption was ready to enter (under the guidance of Colbert whom he had trained) on its most fruitful period of material development. The work inaugurated by Henry IV and elaborated by Richelieu, to give to France all round a "natural frontier," had not been carried to its conclusion by Mazarin, but it had been brilliantly advanced. The marriage between Louis XIV and the Infanta set the seal to this labour of peace, and reconciled the French crown with the Spanish Habsburgs. Alas! the ambition of a prince was to turn this healing union into a fountain of wars.

[1] See A. Legrelle, *La Succession d'Espagne* (1888), p. 19. Extracts from the Marriage Contract are given by Dumont, along with the renunciation to the Spanish Crown, in Tome VI, Partie II. See also Vast, I, 176 ff. Mignet, *Succession d'Espagne*, I, 52 ff.

CHAPTER XIX

LOUIS ADVANCES TOWARDS A NATURAL FRONTIER

The Peace of the Pyrenees concluded the duel between France and Spain, and ended the wars which, beginning with the revolt of the Dutch against Spain in the late sixteenth century, rose to their intensest in the Thirty Years' War, and devastated much of Europe over a period of nearly one hundred years. We now enter upon an era of wars and negotiations, of which France is the centre, fought at first for a scientific frontier, and later for the control of Western Europe. The striving for Universal Monarchy which early seventeenth-century publicists ascribed to Spain, publicists of the late seventeenth century did not hesitate to impute to France. France is again the centre of activity; her garrisons and her armies control the Rhine valley; and her envoys turn the hearts of princes at Stockholm, Warsaw, and Constantinople.

When Mazarin died on March 9, 1661, Louis XIV took upon himself the conduct of French foreign affairs. At once it became apparent that the dignity and the interests of France had fallen into the charge of one who was in no way inferior to the Cardinal in capacity. For the first ambassador (the Archbishop of Embrun) sent to Madrid after Mazarin's death Louis drew up instructions laying great stress on the dignity due to the envoy:[1] hitherto all ambassadors had made their entry into Madrid *incognito*; but Louis demanded a public reception. The Spanish Government compromised this matter by sending a royal carriage to meet the French ambassador, but only in the name of Don Luis de Haro not of the King of Spain (June, 1661). In 1662 an affair of dignity brought about for a short time a state of war between France and the Pope. Louis' ambassador at the Court of Rome was the Duc de Créqui, who had in him more of the proud soldier than the complaisant diplomatist. On August 20 a dispute occurred

[1] *Recueil des Instructions,* XI, i, p. 175.

between some of the Duc's suite and soldiers of the Corsican regiment of the Pope's Guard. Some Frenchmen were killed; afterwards the Corsicans fired some shots at the carriage of the ambassador's wife and killed a page. The Duc de Créqui accused the Papal court of connivance in this quarrel and left Rome. Louis XIV took the Duc's side, occupied the *enclaves* of the Papacy in France—Avignon and the Venaissan (they were soon restored)—and sent the Maréchal du Plessis-Praslin with 8,000 men to the frontier of the Papal States. In vain Pope Alexander VII disbanded his Corsican regiment and dismissed his Cardinal-Governor of Rome. He only bought peace through a treaty signed by Rasponi and Bourlemont at Pisa on February 12, 1664, by which he declared the Corsican nation incapable of entering the Papal service and bound himself to send his nephew, Cardinal Chigi, to Paris to deliver in the king's presence an apology agreed upon in the treaty; and to erect opposite the barracks of the late Corsican regiment a pyramid, with an inscription of the decree against the whole Corsican nation. The language of the treaty is in the highest degree dictatorial in respect of Louis XIV, and humble in respect of the Pope.[1] Disputes about dignity and etiquette bulk fairly conspicuously in the state papers of the Age of King Louis XIV; but they are only incidents among greater events which steadily unfolded his grand territorial design.

For something over forty years the main concern of Europe was the spectacle of France pushing forward to her "natural frontiers" on the east, the Rhine and the Alps. The way to these was barred on the north-east by the Spanish Netherlands, which included Luxemburg, on the east by Spain again, which held the French-speaking province of Franche Comté (including the towns of Besançon and Dôle), on the south-east by the Duchy of Savoy, including Nice. Towards the middle Rhine the Archbishops of Trèves and Cologne interposed their ecclesiastical states on both sides of the river; and even in Alsace, most of which had been gained for France in 1648, the Free Imperial City of Strasburg held the most important passage of the Rhine.

Louis' diplomacy, which was to be supported by war if necessary, aimed at simplifying, by extending, France's frontier as

[1] The Treaty of Pisa, February 12, 1664, is printed in Dumont, VII, Partie III, 1.

it stood in 1661. On the north-east it was impossible probably to advance to a natural limit; for here the Rhine, from the neighbourhood of Nymwegen to the sea, was in the Confederation of the United Netherlands, a small Power which had a strong navy, a respectable army, and an efficient diplomacy with many allies. The most that Louis could probably hope for in this direction would be to advance the north-eastern frontier further from Paris and to straighten it, so that (1) the line of defence would be shortened, (2) this line would pass through the fortresses or towns which lay on the routes from the Netherlands into France. This advancing and straightening of the north-eastern frontier would have to be carried out at the expense of Spain, or rather of the Spanish Netherlands. In this aim, Louis XIV, though he failed of complete success, achieved notable results. Had he gained all that he required, the north-eastern frontier of France would have extended in a straight line for about 160 miles from Dunkirk (or thereabouts) to the neighbourhood of Longwy; the country, it is true, for about three-quarters of the distance, is perfectly flat, and one river after another would cross the frontier at right angles, and would provide natural routes for aggressors. On the other hand, the frontier would be comparatively short; and, as Vauban designed, it would have been a chain of fortresses—flourishing commercial cities, each on its own river, in time of peace, and impregnable strongholds in time of war.

Though Louis' achievement fell short of this, he accomplished much. Each time he made an effort to advance the north-eastern frontier and to secure a river-stronghold, the powers of Western Europe combined against him; and then his diplomatists came into the field, bargained and compromised, so that some of the gains of his soldiers were held and some were given back. Every adjustment of the frontier was the result of some such compromise, so that instead of extending directly along the shortest way between Dunkirk and Longwy for 160 miles, the frontier still twists and turns, forms long salients and admits re-entrant angles, and covers many hundreds of miles. Nevertheless, that France has a reasonably practical north-eastern frontier at all is due to the persistent efforts of Louis XIV, carried out during his long reign. In his last great effort, however—the War of the Spanish Succession—he went beyond the practical, and while he managed, with terrible expense of blood and treasure, to keep what he had gained, he failed to receive the reasonable rectifications which were still due to him, and which he undoubtedly could have obtained had he preferred to negotiate over the Spanish Succession instead of fighting.

The great efforts which Louis XIV made, before he plunged into the bottomless gulf of the Spanish Succession War, are known in their sequence as the War of Devolution, 1667, the War of 1672, and the War of the League of Augsburg, 1678–97. War, however, was only an incident in his diplomacy; and the steps in the development of his territorial policy may be better called by the peaceful terms—Treaty of Aix-la-Chapelle (1668), of Nymwegen (1678), of Ryswick (1697). Louis cannot be exculpated from the charge of using war as an instrument of policy. Undoubtedly he would have preferred to gain his objects simply by diplomacy. He had no territory to barter, but he could have afforded to purchase territory by money. Public opinion, however, was not ripe in the seventeenth century for this method of transfer. In default of the honest method of purchase could Spain, at whose expense all Louis' demands were made, yield her possessions when Louis had no equivalent to offer, without a blow to defend them? The two countries were in an *impasse*. Could France permanently refrain from claiming Lille and Armentières, not to mention Franche Comté? Could Spain refuse to fight? It was not diplomacy that created those wars; no one planned to start them deliberately. They arose from the pressure of circumstances which nothing but an international police of overwhelming strength could have controlled. It was diplomacy, however, that adjusted the final settlements; and it was diplomacy that saved for France some solid gains at least from the sacrifices of her soldiers.

The first act in the unfolding of this drama is the War of Devolution. This was the period of competition for maritime supremacy between England and Holland; and a dispute about certain forts or "factories" on the Guinea coast of Africa had provoked a war in 1665. Louis XIV, in terms of a defensive alliance which he had made with the Dutch three years before,[1] declared war upon England (January 26, 1666). The French fleet, however, took no part in this maritime struggle; the Dutch alone carried off the honours of war, by sailing up the Thames and burning Sheerness. Peace was made at Breda in the United Netherlands, between

[1] April 27, 1662, see Flassan, III, 272.

England, France, the Dutch and Denmark, the ally of the Dutch, July 31, 1667. England's solitary ally, the Prince Bishop of Münster, had made his peace over fifteen months earlier.[1] England acquired New York from the Dutch; in other respects the war was ended without territorial changes.

It is necessary to understand this brief war, and the alliances and peaces connected with it, in order to appreciate the extraordinary revolutions in fortune's wheel now to be experienced by the Dutch. On September 17, 1665, Philip IV, King of Spain and father-in-law of Louis XIV, died; and Louis XIV, without much delay, sent to the Court of Spain a claim to the whole of the Spanish Netherlands, which claim, if satisfied, would have brought his north-eastern frontier, not quite indeed to the Rhine, but to the Maas. The law of Devolution (*droit de Dévolution*), under which Louis claimed, was to the effect that children of a first marriage were preferred in respect of inheritance to children of a second; and that when one or the other parent died, the property of the deceased *devolved* at once upon the children, although the surviving parent was allowed a life-use of it. Under this law, accordingly it was claimed, that the rights as Queen of Spain, over the Low Countries, of Philip IV's wife (who died in 1664) had already devolved upon his daughter Maria Theresa before she made her renunciation on marrying Louis; secondly, that she was the proper heir, in any case, to such fiefs of Philip IV as were subject to the *jus devolutionis*, for the condition attached to her renunciation (namely the payment of a dowry) had never been fulfilled.

In May, 1667 (while the Anglo-Dutch war was still going on), the troops of Marshal Turenne crossed the frontier of the Spanish Netherlands without declaration of war. The resistance made by Spain now or in the following years to the French aggressions was quite without adequate resources, and accomplished nothing. As a military barrier in the hands of Spain, the Spanish Netherlands were wholly valueless to Holland. The Governor of the Spanish Netherlands, the Marquis of Castel-Rodrigo, did everything that could be done in the months before the war. He toured the fortresses, and strengthened them where he could. He incessantly urged the Spanish Government to send reinforcements. "Your Majesty is not unaware that for long I have been crying and pro-

[1] Treaty of Cleves, April 18, 1666, Dumont, VI, Partie III, 106. The Peace of Breda is in Dumont, VII, Partie I, 40–57.

testing," he wrote on March 16, 1667, to the Queen of Spain. "I am assured that the manifesto of the Most Christian King in his rights over Brabant is printed, and that war is decided."[1] The Dutch themselves had always to fight, with the help of such allies as they could obtain, for the barrier which was supposed to shield them. But on this occasion the ground was carefully prepared by Louis XIV through Lionne, who was at the head of the Foreign Ministry; and allies were difficult for the Dutch to secure. In 1667 (April) Louis had made one of his secret pacts with Charles II, binding the English king to neutrality; the League of the Rhine ensured that France remained the controlling influence in that quarter; and the Emperor had been placated by a secret partition treaty, a brilliant and unexpected success of the French diplomatist, Gremonville (January 19, 1668), for the division of the Spanish Empire if the young Charles II should die.[2] So the Dutch were left alone to protest. Louis, who was personally in command, with Turenne, had begun the war in May, 1667, and took Charleroi, Douai, Courtrai and Lille. Lille resisted for three weeks, but fell ultimately before the skill of Vauban.

It looked as if Louis would have the whole of the Spanish Netherlands at his feet; even the Marquis of Castel-Rodrigo, the courageous Governor, seemed almost to think further resistance useless. Then it was, however, when the fortunes of Louis stood so high, that check came from an unexpected quarter. The English Ambassador at Brussels was Sir William Temple, then thirty-nine years old, an accomplished man with a delightful nature and complete integrity of character. Knowing the menace which must ever exist for England if a great power held Belgium, Temple visited the various centres of Dutch authority to try and arrange some means of making Louis XIV desist. At the Hague he met and formed a friendship with John de Witt, the Grand Pensionary of Holland, who, though only an official of one of the seven states of the United Netherlands, determined the policy of the whole country by the vigour of his character and the wisdom of his views. England and Holland had been at war only a few months before, but now the sympathy of the British Parliament had been awakened; and Franz von Lisola, the best Imperial diplomatist, who had induced the Emperor to send him on special mission to London, was gaining friends for

[1] Text of letter in Mignet, *Succession d'Espagne*, II, 52.

[2] Vast, II, 6. Text in Mignet, *Succession d'Espagne*, II, 441.

a policy of intervention. Charles (careless as he was to the eventual fate of the Netherlands) could not take his own way. In November (1667) Temple received authority from Lord Arlington, the English Secretary of State (who had strong Spanish and Dutch sympathies), to propose a league with the United Netherlands. John de Witt agreed. The next thing was to obtain the support of Sweden. The military reputation of Sweden stood high, and Louis XIV thought that he could safely count on her help at all times. But just now the Swedish envoy at the Hague was a man of an unusual stamp, Christopher Delphique, Count Dohna, a native of Holland, who had entered the Swedish service, distinguished himself as a soldier, and had subsequently become a diplomatist. He was a strong opponent of the ascendancy of France, and was a man who would not shrink from momentous decisions. On the evening of the day on which de Witt had given his assent to the English alliance, Temple burst in unannounced upon Dohna at the Swedish embassy, saying in his frank, friendly way that ceremonies were made to facilitate business, not to hinder it; and that, considering the urgency of their master's interests, they should establish contact directly. Dohna, with equal cordiality, embraced the proposal, and listened encouragingly to Temple's views. Soon de Witt, Temple and Dohna were all agreed. But in the United Netherlands only the States-General could conclude treaties; and its members, who were merely delegates from the several constituent states, could make no new decision without their authority—which, as d'Estrades, the ambassador of Louis XIV, knew, would take six weeks to obtain. But the "new diplomacy" of Temple had a better way. He obtained an audience of the States-General, spoke to them, and persuaded them to take the risk of being approved by their constituents. The slow-moving legislators were fired to sudden energy. Appointing seven members with full powers, they retired from the scene. De Witt was one of the seven. A day's hard work (ending at one in the morning) was all that was needed now to complete the draft of a treaty, and on January 23 (1668) the Defensive Alliance was sealed by Temple and the Dutch delegates. Three days later Count Dohna attached his signature.[1] The Triple Alliance was made; the time occupied in making it, from the inception of the proposal by Temple in his

[1] The ratifications of the seven states of the United Netherlands came a month later. Lefèvre-Pontalis, *John de Witt* (Eng. trans., 1885), I, 434.

K

first interview with de Witt to the signature of the treaty, was five days.[1]

The object of the Triple Alliance, as stated in the preamble, was due to "the fear that the conflagration recently kindled by the rupture between the two crowns (France and Spain) might be communicated to their neighbours." They therefore (1) bound themselves to defend each other, (2) to compel Spain (which, though helpless, was still intransigeant) to accept the terms offered by Louis (that is, Spain was to cede Cambrai, Douai, St. Omer, Furnes); and (3)—a secret clause—to make war together on Louis XIV, in the event of his not keeping the conditions which he had proposed.[2] John de Witt celebrated the conclusion of the alliance by giving a grand ball; the young William, Prince of Orange, did the same. The Triple Alliance was well advertised, and the gazettes of Europe were full of it.

D'Estrades at the Hague had failed to keep Louis XIV apprised of the negotiations between the Maritime Powers, but the Marquis of Ruvigny, the French ambassador in London, seems to have obtained a hint of the secret clause of the Triple Alliance (perhaps Charles II told him), and so Louis learned about it on February 15, 1668. He must have realized that now he would have to be content with limited gains. Anglo-Dutch diplomacy had been too much for him. He could not fight England, Holland, and Sweden; instead, he must accept their offered mediation in his war with Spain. But he was in an excellent position to negotiate, for on February 5 he had sent Condé, who was still Governor of Burgundy, with 15,000 troops into the Spanish province of Franche Comté. In one fortnight the whole of the "Free County" was overrun, and its strong places taken. Louis himself, who had been travelling post-haste from St. Germain, arrived just in time to receive the capitulation of Dôle, the capital. With Franche Comté in his pocket he was now ready to go to the Conference table.

The Peace-Conference was held in the Free Imperial City of Aix-la-Chapelle; Temple and van Beunigen were the English and Dutch envoys. Their chief difficulty as mediators was to induce Spain to accept Louis' terms: he demanded now to keep

[1] Flassan, III, 353 n. Dohna signed conditionally on his Government approving. The approval came three months later. Dumont, VII, 68.

[2] Dumont, VII, 66–7.

either such places as he now held *or* Franche Comté. The Marquis of Castel-Rodrigo, the governor and gallant defender of the Spanish Netherlands and plenipotentiary for the Court of Madrid, would at first cede nothing. Then the mediators showed that their military force, which could be used to protect Spain from France, might instead be used to prevent Spain from prolonging a hopeless war. De Witt threatened to occupy Spanish Flanders. His hand thus forced, Castel-Rodrigo gave way; but he chose the alternative terms which should injure the United Netherlands most. He decided to keep Franche Comté and to give up the barrier fortresses of the Spanish Netherlands. On those terms the Treaty of Aix-la-Chapelle was concluded, May 2, 1668. By article 2 Louis received Charleroi, Binch, Athe, Douai, Fort de Scarpe, Tournai, Oudenarde, Lille, Armentières, Courtrai, Bergue and Furnes. By article 5, he evacuated Franche Comté.[1] It was an excellent bargain for France; Colbert de Croissy (brother of the great Colbert), French plenipotentiary, did his work well.

With the barriers in his hands, Louis could (if he had only a free hand) later at his leisure take in the rest of the Spanish Netherlands. The Triple Alliance had stopped him this time, and had shown the opposition which he must expect in the future, if he tried to take the mouth of the Scheldt. The Triple Alliance, in fact, was the beginning of the Anglo-Dutch association to which the existence of Belgium is due.

The outbreak of the War of Devolution caused a profound and disquieting sensation all over Western and Central Europe. The shadow of a universal military domination, which men had believed to impend over Europe in the time of Charles V and Philip II of Spain, now seemed to threaten the Continent from the side of Louis XIV. Against this prospect of military domination Lisola, the most active, and the most talented of the Austrian diplomatists, warned the peoples in a pamphlet which at once became famous. Lisola had gone to the Hague at the time of the negotiations for the Triple Alliance and had played a considerable part in these transactions. Like another great Austrian publicist, 130 years later, Friedrich von Gentz, the life-long opponent of Napoleon, Lisola discerned early the great conceptions of the French conqueror. The War of Devolution fired him to write a pamphlet on *The Buckler of State and of Justice against the design manifestly*

[1] The Treaty is in Vast, II, 14; Dumont, VII, 89.

discovered of the Universal Monarchy. Lisola protested against any peace now being made with France until Louis XIV should be compelled to admit the validity of the renunciation made by his wife to any rights of succession to the throne of Spain. "If this Renunciation doth not subsist, there is no way left for an Accommodation, nor means of finding any security necessary to it. The peace which shall be made cannot be but the seed of a new war."[1]

Louis XIV also had his publicists. At the diet of Regensburg his plenipotentiary Robert de Gravel laboured incessantly, and with success, by writing and speaking, to influence the opinion of the German princes against their taking any decisive step.[2] The Emperor Leopold himself was unconvinced by Lisola, and allowed the French menace to his power to advance in the Spanish Netherlands (which was part of the "Burgundian Circle") apparently without a qualm. In January, 1668, while Louis XIV was still in the full tide of military success, the Emperor, through the influence of his chief minister, Lobkowitz, who was distinctly "Gallophil," entered into the extraordinary Gremonville partition-treaty with France.[3] The Emperor, however, was soon to have a rude awakening, as indeed were many other people in Europe, who had hitherto thought that from the Habsburgs alone was a design of universal monarchy to be feared.[4]

[1] *The Buckler of State*, Eng. trans., 1667, p. 16.

[2] See F. Meinecke, *Der Regensburger Reichstag und der Devolutionskrieg*, in *Historische Zeitschrift* (1888), XXIV, 193.

[3] See above, p. 128. Cf. A. Wolf, *Fürst Wenzel Lobkowitz* (1869), p. 177.

[4] Among other opponents of the Habsburgs who later came to believe that Louis XIV was the danger was the international jurist, Pufendorf (1632–94). See K. Varrentrap, *Briefe von Pufendorf*, in *Historische Zeitschrift* (1893), XXXIV, 5. For further information on this chapter see E. S. Lyttel, *Sir William Temple* (1908); A. Lefèvre-Pontalis, *John de Witt* (Eng. trans., 1885); T. P. Courtney, *Memoirs of Sir W. Temple* (1836).

CHAPTER XX

THE TREATY OF NYMWEGEN

As a result of the War of Devolution and the Treaty of Aix-la-Chapelle France was now on a fair way to securing her two *desiderata* on the north-east—a straight and comparatively short line, and the chief towns on the routes across the frontier. Further south, Franche Comté in Spanish hands still held her back from her " natural " line of the Jura. To obtain Franche Comté on the one hand and to complete the north-eastern frontier on the other, were the aims of Louis' next effort.

The interval between 1668 and 1672 (when the next war broke out) was a great time for France. The Contrôleur-Général Colbert was at the height of his powers, and his great financial and commercial reforms were bringing France to unheard-of prosperity. In the Indies, and in Canada, a magnificent overseas empire was being built up. Peace, prosperity, the cultivation of the arts and graces of life, were making of France a smiling country. At last it seemed as if the wish of Henri Quatre was coming to pass, and that every peasant could count on having a fowl in his pot.

The War of 1672, however, stopped this steady diffusion of material prosperity ; for it began a military effort on the part of France which lasted, with only short breathing-spaces, down to 1714.

There is not the slightest doubt that Louis XIV, from the moment that the Treaty of Aix-la-Chapelle was made and he saw himself checked, planned the next war. His correspondence with Ruvigny and Colbert de Croissy (successively ambassadors in England) prove this. To Colbert de Croissy, who was going as envoy extraordinary to England, the king wrote on August 2, 1668,[1] that Charles II should be induced to break the Triple Alliance, to use all his influence to detach the Swedes also from their association with the Dutch, and to join instead a triple alliance of England, Sweden and France.[2] Arlington, it was pointed out, would be the greatest difficulty,

[1] Printed for the first time in Mignet, *Négociations relatives à la Succession d'Espagne sous Louis XIV* (Paris, 1842), III, p. 24 ff.

[2] *Ibid.*, p. 33.

being "*bon Espagnol,*" owing to a long sojourn at Madrid, and also "*bon Hollandais,*" through having married a Dutch lady. "The King (Louis XIV) has to-day so considerable an interest in breaking the Triple Alliance at present existing, and in detaching England from Holland, to unite the first against the second, that if Lord Arlington could be induced to act sincerely in this point in favour of His Majesty, His Majesty would hold any recompense very well employed in this service, even if it were necessary to sacrifice one hundred thousand crowns down, and ten thousand crowns pension annually."[1]

Arlington took some time to be won over, but after the French alliance was made he allowed his wife to accept 10,000 crowns from Louis XIV.[2] As Colbert wrote to Louis, the Dutch fleet might cause some anxiety to English merchants, but the French fleet (which the Contrôleur-Général Colbert was building up with great success) was causing almost more. Louis therefore ceased to trouble the Cabal ministers for a time, and tried to work directly on the king. In the winter of 1668 he sent Madame, the Duchess of Orleans, Charles' sister, to England, to persuade her brother; and early in 1669 he despatched a Theatine friar, the abbé Prignani, who was skilled in alchemy and therefore might ingratiate himself with the half-scientific, half-superstitious Charles. The king received Prignani cordially and took him to Newmarket; but the abbé's attempts to tell the winning horses by the stars were uniformly unsuccessful, and Charles, who was no fool at bottom, was only amused.[3] Louis XIV had the sense to recall the abbé. More success was gained by means of Charles' mistress, Lady Castlemaine. This high-born and more than usually rapacious mistress gladly received the presents which Madame Colbert de Croissy conveyed to her; and Colbert was able to report that Madame Castlemaine would do her utmost to promote a union between the two kingdoms.

On the evening of November 12, 1669, Charles privately informed the French ambassador that he had decided to re-establish the Roman Catholic religion in England.[4] His dastardly scheme

[1] Printed for the first time in Mignet, *Négociations relatives à la Succession d'Espagne sous Louis XIV* (Paris, 1842), III, p. 34. Cp. K. Feiling, *Two unprinted letters of Henrietta Stuart, Duchess of Orleans,* in the *English Historical Review* (July, 1928), XLIII, 394.

[2] Dalrymple, *Memoirs of Great Britain and Ireland* (1773), II, 82.

[3] Charles II to Madame d'Orléans, *ibid.*, p. 80.

[4] Colbert to Louis XIV, *ibid.*, p. 100.

was no other than to keep the Triple Alliance publicly in force, and at the same time to make a secret treaty with Louis; and so "he will easily come to the bottom of all the seditions which that declaration (re-establishment of Catholicism) might excite in this kingdom."[1] This is the most finished exhibition of deceit in the diplomatic history of England, otherwise on the whole clean and honourable.

The treaty of alliance between England and France was actually signed at Dover, on June 1, 1670, six days after Madame d'Orléans had come there to meet Charles. The negotiations had been most skilfully conducted by Colbert de Croissy, but no less so by Charles himself, who obtained extremely good terms from Louis. Article 1 contained the usual peace and friendship clause *à perpétuité*; in article 2 Charles declared his resolution to reconcile himself with the Church of Rome "as soon as the state of affairs of his kingdom permit him to do so"; and Louis agreed to pay to Charles 2,000,000 *livres tournois* (about £150,000 at that time) either in specie at Calais, Dieppe or Havre, or in bills of exchange on London, and to send him 6,000 troops (to coerce the English with!).[2] By article 3 the two monarchs agreed to keep the peace with Spain; Charles was "to be permitted to maintain the said treaty *conformably to the conditions of the Triple Alliance*"—so ran the shameless words. By article 4, Great Britain was bound to support Louis in his claims to the succession of Spain. By article 6, in accordance with their "resolution to mortify the pride of the States-General," the two monarchs agreed to declare and make war conjointly on them, and only to make peace concurrently with each other. France undertook the conduct of the war by land, Great Britain having only to send 6,000 foot-soldiers at her own expense; and the supreme command was to lie with the French. Great Britain, on the other hand, was to conduct the war by sea, the French having only to supply thirty vessels, at their own expense, the supreme command to lie with the Duke of York as Admiral. While the war lasted, Louis was to pay Charles an annual subsidy of 3,000,000 livres tournois. In the conquests made at the expense of the Dutch, Great Britain was to be content with Walcheren, Ecluse, and

[1] Conversation of Arlington with Colbert, *ibid.*, p. 117.

[2] Text of Treaty in Mignet, *Succ. d'Espagne*, III, 187–99. Dalrymple, *Memoirs*, II, 54, is the authority for the statement that 2,000,000 livres equalled £150,000.

Cadsand; and "the dissolution of the Government of the States-General" was to bring no prejudice to the Prince of Orange, who was to "find his advantages in the continuation and end of this war." The treaty was to be kept secret until ratified (actually it was kept secret for a hundred years). It was signed by Arlington, Clifford, Arundel, Bellings and Colbert de Croissy. Presents were given on the conclusion of the treaty to the English commissioners, or to their wives and mistresses. Charles knew and did not disapprove of these presents.[1]

This conspiracy to destroy the republic of a small and heroic nation being thus successfully hatched, the declarations of war followed in due course. The treaty was, however, the last work of the amiable and brilliant Henrietta of Orleans. She left England in the middle of June, and died suddenly, from the breaking of an internal ulcer, a week later. To complete her work a final treaty was necessary. It was made at Whitehall on December 31, 1670; the clause concerning the conversion of Charles was omitted. Great Britain was to gain more annexations from the eventual partition of Holland—viz. the islands of Goree and Woorne. The declaration of war was fixed for April or May, 1672.[2] This treaty was signed by the whole Cabal of ministers, and was the only one made known to the Government as a whole and to parliament.

Sweden likewise was with some difficulty (April 14, 1672)[3] won back to her old association with France; and the Dutch were left to face the greatest armies and navies of Europe alone.

It was not difficult for Louis to find causes for war. High duties were imposed upon Dutch goods entering France; equivalent duties were imposed by the Dutch. Remonstrances were then made by Louis XIV, and these were followed by a declaration of war on April 6, 1672. Charleroi, which had been acquired by France in 1668, was used as a starting-point, and from there Louis XIV marched for the Rhine, violating without scruple the neutral territory of Belgium (Spanish Netherlands). His army consisted of no less than 110,000 men. Among Louis' generals were Turenne, Luxembourg and Vauban, incomparably the three most eminent captains of the age. The campaign went well for the French, and all the southern districts of the United Provinces fell. Charles II

[1] Dalrymple, *Memoirs,* II, 81–2.
[2] Text in Mignet, III, 256.
[3] Text *ibid.*, 365–74.

engaged in the war with his whole naval forces, and also sent his quota of 6,000 men, commanded by the Duke of Monmouth. In this expedition, John Churchill, later Duke of Marlborough, served with distinction as a captain of foot. The whole of the United Netherlands would undoubtedly have been overrun had not William of Orange cut the dykes and flooded the country from the Scheldt to the Zuyder Zee.

This heroic prince, then twenty-one years old, had been brought forward as soon as war became certain. As his star rose, that of John de Witt declined. On August 20, 1672, John and his brother Cornelius (the latter had been falsely accused of a plot against the Prince of Orange, and had endured one and a half hours of fearful torture without weakening) were torn to pieces by the mob of the Hague.

The Prince of Orange, in the positions of Captain-General and Admiral-General, was now practically sole ruler of the United Netherlands; and consequently Charles II, who was uncle to the Prince, was less inclined to push the war to extremities. Behind their water-line the Dutch were now holding their own. Spain, feeble though she was, did not tamely watch Louis using her territory for his communications; the dashing Count of Monterey, youthful Governor of the Spanish Netherlands, actually invaded France in 1673. The Emperor likewise sent military support (Austro-Dutch Treaty of Alliance, August 30, 1673). Prince Wenzel Lobkowitz, who based his policy on friendship with France, lost his influence over the counsels of Leopold I, although he was not relieved of his office as Minister of Foreign Affairs until 1674.[1] At last the warnings and urgings of Lisola were taken to heart by the Emperor, and a policy of steady and vigorous opposition to the French was adopted. This was Lisola's last work. He died early in 1675.[2]

As with Venice when threatened with extinction by France and the League of Cambrai in 1508, so now in the peril of Holland the opinion of Europe was steadily setting in favour of the small free state as one of the barriers against a dominating universal Empire. Although the venal ecclesiastical princes of Cologne and Münster

[1] A. Wolf, *Fürst Wenzel Lobkowitz* (1869), 408.

[2] See A. F. Pribram, *Die Berichte des Kaiserlichen Gesandten F. von Lisola*, in *Archiv für Osterreich Geschichte* (1887), LXX, 3–4. For the treaty of alliance and assistance between the Emperor and the United Netherlands, August 30, 1673, see Mignet, *Succession d'Espagne*, IV, 207.

joined the French, the Elector Frederick William of Brandenburg stood firmly with the Dutch. In England Charles' policy was scarcely popular. He had prefaced the war by stopping the repayment of loans contracted by the Exchequer, and by issuing a Declaration of Indulgence to Roman Catholics and Nonconformists. Public opinion soon came round to favour the Dutch against Charles and his horde of mistresses and crypto-Jesuits. The Prince of Orange gained a brilliant diplomatic success by detaching England from the French alliance. On February 19, 1674, the Treaty of Westminster was made under the mediation of the Spanish ambassador, the Marquis del Fresno. The Dutch agreed to strike their flag to British men-of-war, and they paid an indemnity of 2,000,000 florins.

Louis saw that his design had failed; he could not break the Dutch. Their great fortress Maastricht had, indeed, capitulated to him (1673), but this was the limit of his successes. The power of the Dutch depended in reality not upon the land but upon the sea; and now that England was no longer against them, their navy could not be beaten. Louis therefore practically withdrew from the Dutch war, and concentrated upon fighting Spain. Condé had conquered Franche Comté. Turenne drove the Imperialists out of Alsace, and crossed the Rhine but was killed at Sasbach on July 27, 1675. Charles XI of Sweden, in accordance with his alliance with Louis, invaded Brandenburg from Swedish Pomerania in the same year, but was met and defeated at Fehrbellin by the Elector Frederick William (June 18). On the north-eastern frontier all the Spanish barrier towns fell before French arms.

Yet the Dutch had triumphed, after many sacrifices. The amazing web of hostile alliances which Louis XIV had spun around them—with Bavaria, Würtemberg, the Bishops of Strasburg and Liège, Neuburg, Hanover and others—broke down; and Louis (to whom de Witt in the early months of the war had offered Maastricht and all the Dutch Generality lands south of the Scheldt) had now to be content with a "satisfaction" at the expense of Spain.

Great Britain, now neutral in the struggle, offered her services as mediator. It was agreed to hold a peace-conference at Nymwegen, a Dutch town on the left bank of the Rhine, below Cleves. Temple and Berkeley were the English mediators; Colbert de Croissy, d'Estrades, now an old man, and d'Avaux represented France; van Beunigen, a former ambassador to France, and

Beverning (of whom Temple said he had never met a cleverer man), with others, represented the States-General; Spain had the Marquis de los Balbasez and the Sieur Christini à don Antonio Ronquillo. All the other states, allies of one belligerent or the other, had envoys. The Congress was opened in November, 1676, and continued for just short of two years, without the suspension of hostilities. The Dutch, aided by the vigorous diplomacy of the English (who signed a military alliance with them on December 31, 1677), gained their main point, namely the evacuation by Louis of all that he had taken from them, which included the great fortress of Maastricht. With Spain the negotiations dragged on for another month, and with the Emperor longer still. The Dutch peace was signed on August 10, 1678, to the satisfaction of all except the Prince of Orange, who in hopes of breaking off the negotiations attacked the army of Marshal Luxembourg outside Mons on August 14—four days after peace had been signed but before it had been published. The treaty with Spain was signed on September 17, and with the Emperor Leopold on February 5 (1679). These three treaties form the Peace of Nymwegen.

By the Dutch treaty, Louis evacuated Maastricht, and left the territorial settlement as it had been before the war. By the Spanish treaty, Louis gave back Charleroi, Oudenarde, Binch, Ath and Courtrai (which he had gained in 1668), but annexed instead Valenciennes, Cambrai, Maubeuge, St. Omer, Ypres, Poperinghe and Bailleul; further south he annexed the Spanish province of Franche Comté. By the treaty with the Emperor, Louis abandoned his right to garrison Philipsburg (a right acquired in 1648), but the Emperor renounced all rights upon Breisach so that France still retained a *tête de pont* on the Rhine. Charles IV, Duke of Lorraine, who was a hard-working and able general in the Imperial service, was restored to his Duchy, excepting Longwy and Nancy. Finally the Peace of Nymwegen was completed by the Treaty of June 29, 1679, between France, Brandenburg and Sweden, signed by Meinders, Minister of State, for Brandenburg, and Pomponne, Minister for Foreign Affairs, for France. Sweden was content with the terms which Louis secured for her. The Elector, after his victory of Fehrbellin, had pushed his advantage to the full, and now claimed the whole of Swedish Pomerania. But it was not Louis' interest to let Sweden (whose support he could always buy) be thrust entirely out of Germany; he therefore sent the Maréchal de Créqui with an army into Cleves, and thus provided that electric impulse which a swift blow gives to diplomacy. Frederick William gave in, and was perforce content to restore Western Pomerania to Sweden, all except the strip on the right bank of the Oder.

The Peace of Nymwegen ended Louis XIV's second great leap forward; and though it was only half-successful, it gave the finest results. By taking with his armies more territory than he need keep, he was able to bargain favourably for himself at the conference-table. By giving back the fortress of Maastricht (indispensable for the existence of the United Netherlands) he reconciled the States to seeing Spain lose Valenciennes and Cambrai. He had, it is true, to retrocede Charleroi to the Spanish Netherlands, but that place was too far forward to be really useful to him; his line now ran through Lille, Valenciennes, Maubeuge; and Vauban was making the line a band of iron. In the "middle east" of his frontier, by the acquisition of Franche Comté, the line was advanced to the Jura; France now had for a neighbour the Swiss Confederation.

The Peace of Nymwegen was the last diplomatic work on which the Maréchal d'Estrades was engaged. Born in 1607, he had become ambassador to the States-General as early as the year 1646; since then he had helped to negotiate the Peace of Westphalia; he had arranged the sale of Dunkirk by Charles II of England in 1662; had helped to conclude the Peace of Breda in 1667 between England and the Dutch, and finally was *doyen* of the French delegation at Nymwegen. As he helped to make the peaces, so he took part in the wars that preceded them, and rose to be Marshal of France in 1675. Brilliance, not depth, was his characteristic, yet it may be said that he never met his match, except once—when Temple and John de Witt concluded the Triple Alliance of 1668 in five days, under the very nose of the unconscious ambassador.

CHAPTER XXI

THE TREATY OF RYSWICK

A survey of Louis XIV's actions shows that he had a vaulting ambition to become predominant in Western Europe; besides this, he had a subordinate aim, that of giving to France a good frontier line on the south-west, the north-east, and the east. This lesser though highly important object was gained by the use of force and by the successive treaties of the Pyrenees, Aix-la-Chapelle, and Nymwegen, coupled with the Truces of Ratisbon (1684) which added Luxemburg and Strasburg. This latter year marks both the height of Louis' power and also the most nearly perfect frontier attained by France before the Napoleonic era. She held a firm line of fortresses on the north-east, the possession of Luxemburg secured the best road which led into France between the Meuse and the Moselle; Strasburg and Kehl made Alsace perfectly safe. The frontier thus aimed at and achieved might be considered perfectly reasonable, and if Louis had meant honestly to stop there, the Powers of Europe would not have intervened. Spain and the Empire were the only states to suffer and their protests never excited much sympathy.

Louis, however, had a grander design than to secure a good frontier for France; and it was because this grander design was really intolerable that the Powers of Europe joined to resist it, and in doing so thrust France back from some of the frontier-towns which she had gained, for example, Luxemburg. On the whole, however, Louis was able to retain his frontier-gains, and this was a permanent benefit to France. That he did not achieve the larger aim of becoming predominant in Western Europe is due to William III, who perceived the design and devoted his life to thwarting it.

Louis, ever since his marriage, had kept before his eyes the prospect of becoming monarch of the Spanish Empire. The secret partition treaty, known as the Gremonville treaty, of

January, 1668, concluded with the Emperor, guaranteed to France the reversion of the Spanish Netherlands, Naples and Sicily.[1] The Gremonville Convention, however, was torn up in the war of 1672. In 1679, October 25, another secret pact was made, this time with the Elector Frederick William of Brandenburg, who, though he had done well in the war against France, was now ready to be friends for 100,000 *livres* a year. By this treaty, the " Great Elector," the least scrupulous member of his opportunist House, promised to vote for Louis at the next election to the Empire,[2] as well as to endeavour, at the next vacancy of the Polish throne, to procure the election of a French candidate. Louis could generally count on the support of the ecclesiastical electors, whom he subsidized, and he was soon also to bring the Elector of Bavaria within his diplomatic system. Thus the Peace of Nymwegen was no sooner concluded than Louis XIV was setting in train schemes to make himself Holy Roman Emperor, as well as King of Spain. His immediate object, however, was to cull the fruits of his last two wars, and this he did successfully down to the Truce of Ratisbon. Spain was too feeble to stop France ; Holland without England was almost powerless, and England was laid aside, benevolently neutral towards Louis XIV, because Charles II had for the second time sold himself (for £100,000 a year) by a Second Secret Treaty of Dover (written out with the King's own hand) on February 16, 1676. The Kings of England and France bound themselves not to make any treaty with " Messieurs the States-General of the United Netherlands nor with any other crown without mutual consent." [3]

The means by which Louis exploited the gains already made were known as reunions. " In the parliament of Metz, in that of Besançon, also in the sovereign council of Alsace which sat then at Breisach, *chambers* called *of Reunion* were instituted, to examine the nature and extent of the cessions which had been made by the treaties of Westphalia and of the Pyrenees, as well as by that of Nymwegen." [4] These *Chambres de Réunion* were held in other places, like Douai, besides those already mentioned. After studying the obscurities and disputed points of the above treaties,

[1] See above, pp. 128, 132.

[2] Published for the first time from the French foreign office Archives by Vast, II, 126.

[3] Flasson, III, 422–3. Mignet, *Succession d'Espagne*, IV, 382.

[4] Koch and Schoell, I, 154.

the magistrates made their awards, as a result of which practically all the towns in the Duchy of Luxemburg (including Givet), and important parts of Flanders, including Ghent, were adjudged to belong to France. In Alsace, practically everything that had not been explicitly ceded by the Peace of Westphalia was now taken over by decrees of the *Chambres de Réunion* of Metz and Breisach; it was only in consequence of a decision of the Parliament of Breisach, March 22, 1680 (declaring in general terms all Lower Alsace under the absolute sovereignty of the King of France), that an independent Republic, the Free Imperial City of Strasburg, was adjudged to Louis.[1] About the same time Sarrebourg, Sarrelouis, Pont-à-Mousson, the Swedish Duchy of Deux Ponts and the Würtemberg enclave of Montbéliard were taken in.

The occupation of Strasburg caused an immense agitation in Europe. It had not been ceded to France in the Treaty of Münster of 1648, which explicitly enumerated the ten Imperial towns of which the King of France was to have the prefectship. On the other hand, Strasburg was mentioned ambiguously in the Treaty of Münster as a city whose liberties the king must recognize alongside of the liberties of the ten Imperial cities in the prefecture ceded to France. The Emperor had offered at the Congress of Nymwegen to subject the question of Strasburg to arbitration; but Louis XIV had refused.[2]

All treaties, like Acts of Parliament, require interpretation, but this can only be justly performed by some independent tribunal. Louis XIV, however, claimed to decide disputed points in his treaties with other countries, in his own courts. This monstrous pretension could only be met by force, and in 1683 Spain declared war (December 11). Louis was prepared for this, and the *code de guerre* of Louvois was ruthlessly put in force. The towns which Spain refused to surrender were terribly bombarded, and everything was done to show the peaceful inhabitants that it were best to give in to France.

Meanwhile the Emperor was involved in the almost overwhelming task of defending his hereditary dominions against a great invasion of the Turks. In July, 1683, the army of Kara Mustafa was in

[1] A. Legrelle, *Louis XIV et Strasbourg* (1884), 456. The city was occupied by a French garrison on September 30, 1681. Cp. J. E. Hamilton, *Alsace and Louis XIV*, in *History* (July, 1928), XIII, 107 ff.

[2] Legrelle, *op. cit.*, 422, 711. Cp. Lavisse, *Histoire de France*, VII, Partie II, p. 354.

front of Vienna. Fortunately King John Sobieski of Poland came to the help of the Emperor ; and also as it happened, Bavaria, which was usually on the side of Louis XIV against Austria, was for about twelve years (1681–92) in good relations with the Emperor. This Austro-Bavarian alliance was largely brought about by the efforts of the Papacy, alarmed at a proposal for marriage between the young Elector of Bavaria, Max Emmanuel, and a Lutheran princess, Eleonora Louisa of Eisenach. The diplomacy of the Courts of Vienna and Rome arranged to prevent this union and to substitute for it a betrothal between Max Emmanuel and the Austrian Archduchess Maria Antonia. The Elector and Bavarian troops fought with distinction against the Turks ; and Louis XIV was for these critical years (and indeed down to 1700) without his customary support in South Germany.[1]

Nevertheless, the course of injustice for long continued to triumph, culminating in June, 1684, with the capture of Luxemburg by the Marshals Créqui and Vauban. In vain the Emperor Leopold I demanded that Louis should submit the questions at issue to arbitration ; the French king would not hear of it. Attempts made to rouse the Diet of the Empire at Ratisbon proved fruitless, because Louis had bought over a number of the lesser princes, as well as the Elector of Brandenburg ; and the most the Diet could do was to conclude, on August 15, 1684, a truce for twenty years, France meanwhile keeping the places (including Strasburg) which had been adjudged to her in her *Chambres de Réunion*. The King of Spain made a truce on the same day, and on the same terms.[2] These truces mark the greatest extension of Louis XIV's power.

They were not to endure long, however. There was one antagonist whose vigilance never failed. William III, Prince of Orange, Stadtholder of the United Netherlands, was working hard to form a solid coalition against the all-embracing enterprises of France ; he was the driving force behind the Powers opposing Louis, just as Spain, which had been so flagrantly wronged, may be called the spiritual centre of the resistance. For, weak though it was, the Spanish Government never ceased to protest, and to show fight, whenever an opportunity offered. Louis, too,

[1] See K. T. Heigel, *Der Umschwung der bayerischen Politik in den Jahren 1679–1683*, in *Abhandlungen der K.B. Akademie*, München (1891), XIX, 1 ff.

[2] The Truces of Ratisbon are in Vast, II, pp. 135 ff. Dumont, T. VII, Partie I.

made some bad mistakes. In 1681 he embroiled himself with Pope Innocent XI by claiming the right of himself appointing the bishops in France. In 1685 he shamefully revoked the Edict of Nantes, and drove his Huguenot subjects into exile. By these acts he did much to estrange both Catholic and Protestant public opinion in Europe. William of Orange took advantage of every cause of irritation to build up again the European coalition.

Shortly after the conclusion of the Truces of Ratisbon the main line of the Palatinate family came to an end with the death, in 1685, of the childless Elector Charles (son of Charles Louis, and grandson of Frederick V, the Winter King). He was succeeded by Philip William of Neuburg, but the insatiable Louis XIV set up a claim, on behalf of his sister-in-law, Elizabeth Charlotte, to the landed property, and movable property, including artillery in the fortresses, of the late Elector. Elizabeth Charlotte was the sister of the late Elector Palatine and had married the Duke of Orleans. It is only fair to Louis to state that he offered to submit the claim for Palatinate property to arbitration, but this offer was declined.[1]

On June 29, 1686, Spain, the Emperor, Sweden, Bavaria and most of the German princes entered into agreements with each other, for the safeguarding of the Empire, for the defence of the treaties of Westphalia and Nymwegen, and for the maintenance of the Truces of Ratisbon. This coalition is known as the League of Augsburg.[2] Its object was purely defensive; and although it actually accomplished little in itself, it prepared the way for the union of German princes in the Grand Alliance of 1689; for this reason credit must be given to the two men through whose exertions it came into being. These were Count Ludwig Gustaf von Hohenlohe, and the Margrave Ludwig Wilhelm of Baden,[3] one of the greatest generals of the age who spent a long life in the Imperialist service.

In June, 1688, Louis XIV forced his candidate Cardinal William of Fürstenberg on the Chapter of Cologne, against the Emperor's candidate Clement of Bavaria. This attempt to control the ecclesiastical principality of Cologne further estranged Pope Innocent XI, and tended to throw him and also the Emperor

[1] Legrelle, *La Diplomatie Française et la Succession d'Espagne*, p. 296.

[2] Dumont, VII, Partie II, 131–8.

[3] See A. Pribram on *Die Augsburger Allianz*, in *Historische Zeitschrift* (1894), XXXVII, 95.

Leopold I (a sincere Catholic) decidedly on the side of William of Orange. It was owing largely to the benevolent neutrality of the Pope and Emperor with regard to his English designs, that William was able to take the risk of leaving the Netherlands and going on his fateful expedition to England, on November, 1, 1688. " By this it appeared," wrote Burnet, " what influence the Papacy, low as it is, may still have in matters of the greatest consequence." As a matter of fact the Papacy, whatever the personality of Pope or cardinals, has, since the time of the Mediæval Emperors, had a fairly consistent policy of opposition to any overmighty secular power. " There is nothing less personal than the Vatican." [1]

The result was that William III of Orange became William III of England. The immense resources of this country, which Louis had so often controlled under the venal Charles II, were now thrown on the side of the League of Augsburg, although much delicate negotiation was required before William III could induce the English to join solidly with the Dutch in the Continental War. Hostilities had actually broken out before the English Revolution occurred, Louis XIV having issued his declaration of war against the Emperor on September 24 (1688); and when William was on the point of sailing to England, Louis' armies were fighting to reduce the Palatinate. Doubtless Louis thought that an attempt at revolution in England would fail. It was the greatest mistake he ever made, and for once it is clear that his diplomacy was at fault. Barillon, his ambassador at London in 1688, should have sent him better intelligence.

William was aided in his departure for England by Prussian support. Frederick William, the Great Elector of Brandenburg, had died on May 9, 1688. Frederick III (afterwards King Frederick I) was an ardent champion of the policy of opposition to France. Throughout 1688 Brandenburg was still neutral, but was diplomatically in close relations with the United Netherlands, Frederick III himself visiting the Hague at the end of the year.[2]

The accession of William of Orange to the throne of England was followed by the formation of the Grand Alliance. This was

[1] The quotation from Burnet is from the *History of His Own Times* (ed. 1823), III, 260. For the impersonality of Papal foreign policy in general see U. Stutz, *Die Papstliche Diplomatie unter Leo XIII*, in *Abhandlungen der Preuss. Akademie*, 1925, Nr. 34, p. 3.

[2] See F. Meinecke, *Brandenburg und Frankreich*, 1688, in *Historische Zeitschrift* (1889), XXVI, 194–241.

made by two treaties concluded in May and December, 1689. The first treaty was made between the Emperor and the Dutch, May 12, 1689, at Vienna. William III of England acceded to this alliance, December 20, 1689, at Hampton Court. Spain and Savoy also joined the alliance. Sweden was not a member. The allies bound themselves in a defensive and offensive alliance, only to make peace on the terms of the Treaties of Westphalia and the Pyrenees, to maintain their association as a defensive alliance even after the conclusion of peace, and, in the event of the death of Charles II of Spain without children, to secure the Spanish succession to the House of Austria.[1] Brandenburg and most other German states, by special treaties with the Emperor, associated themselves with the Grand Alliance.

Louis had now to fight for his great possessions. His conduct of the war, directed from Paris by the detestable though thoroughly efficient Louvois, was atrocious. In 1689 the Palatinate (which the French had invaded in the previous year), before being evacuated, was given over to flames. Next year, in the Low Countries, Marshal Luxembourg took Mons, Namur and Charleroi, after defeating the Dutch at Fleurus. William III was busy with his Irish War. Even on the sea the French for a time were superior, defeating the English and Dutch at Beachy Head in 1690, and holding this superiority for two years. When William III brought over the English forces to the Continent in 1692, the allies were still in numerical inferiority, and his obstinately fought battles at Steinkirke (1692) and Neerwinden (1693) were not successful. In Northern Italy Catinat signally defeated Victor Amadeus of Savoy; and from Catalonia the Maréchal de Noailles and the Duc de Vendôme expelled practically all the Spanish forces. Nevertheless, the allies fought on. The English and Dutch regained the command of the sea. The French might win victories and take cities, but the English, Dutch and German armies were never destroyed; and the resources of the Grand Alliance seemed inexhaustible.

After four years of complete stoppage of diplomacy (1689–93), during which nothing but the noise of arms was heard, Louis XIV again reopened negotiations, using the good offices of King Charles XI of Sweden, who was neutral. But the allies would not make

[1] Treaties in Dumont, VII, Partie II, 229–69. For the negotiations between England and the Dutch in 1689, for military and naval co-operation, see G. N. Clark, *The Dutch Alliance and the War against French Trade* (1923), p. 16 ff.

peace; and as long as they held together, Louis knew that though he could win victories, in the long run he was doomed. So failing to induce the Grand Alliance as a whole to negotiate, he set himself to detach single members. Here his diplomacy won its greatest success.

The first member of the Grand Alliance to secede was Savoy-Piedmont. This country was somewhat isolated from other members of the Grand Alliance, for the Spanish garrisons in the Milanese could give little help. Piedmont retained its freedom, but the whole of Savoy was overrun by the French. Late in the year 1693, the Comte de Tessé, one of Louis' soldier diplomats (subsequently a Marshal of France), went to Turin disguised as a postilion and opened negotiations. Victor Amadeus wanted the French to give up Pinerolo and to support him in his designs on the Milanese and Mantua. Without doing anything more definite than retroceding Pinerolo to the Duke, Louis XIV was able to obtain a promise of neutrality (1695). Next year Savoy made peace at Turin, June 29, 1696; the treaty, which was kept secret, bound Victor Amadeus not merely to cease to fight for the Grand Alliance, but even to co-operate with France in an attack upon the Milanese. He also obtained Pinerolo, and the promise of marriage for his daughter with Louis' grandson, the Duke of Burgundy. Thus Louis detached Savoy. Not merely did he diminish the size of the Grand Alliance, but he obtained a sure means, if he chose, of conquering the Milanese (art. 1).[1] It was characteristic of this great king that he bound Victor Amadeus more strongly to his side by according to all Savoyard ambassadors henceforth the honours which the ambassadors of crowned heads received (art. 5). Although the Treaty of Turin was kept secret, the Imperial Government suspected it, and forestalled an attack on the Milanese by withdrawing all their troops from North Italy, and making a convention of neutrality with the Duke of Savoy.[2]

The next to break away from the Grand Alliance were no less than the United Netherlands and Great Britain, the two great champions. William III was not sovereign in Holland; he was only chief among a number of other magistrates, and he could not prevent the old burgher party from opening negotiations for peace. Louis entrusted the handling of this delicate affair to

[1] Treaty in Vast, II, 171. Dumont, VII, Pt. II. There was also a secret convention of the same date regulating military affairs. Vast, II, 158, n. 1.

[2] Treaty of Vigevano, October 7, 1696, Koch and Schoell, I, 163.

the Comte de Caillières, who had performed numerous missions in Poland, Germany and Italy. The negotiations began in March, 1696, and were carried on for months in various places—at Lillo, Leyden, the Hague, and finally in May, 1697, under the mediation of Sweden, at the château of Ryswick near the Hague. Here there took place a general Congress of all the belligerents.

Half-way between Delft and the Hague is a village named Ryswick, and near it then stood, in a rectangular garden, which was bounded by straight canals and divided into formal woods, flower beds, and melon beds, a seat of the Princes of Orange. The house seemed to have been built expressly for the accommodation of such a set of diplomatists as were to meet there. In the centre was a large hall painted by Honthorst. On the right hand and on the left were wings exactly corresponding to each other. Each wing was accessible by its own bridge, its own gate, and its own avenue. One wing was assigned to the Allies, the other to the French, the hall in the centre to the mediator. The Swedish Minister alighted at the grand entrance. The procession from the Hague came up the side alley on the right. The procession from Delft came up the side alley on the left. At the first meeting the full powers of the representatives of the belligerent Governments were delivered to the mediator.[1]

After the plenipotentiaries had arranged the number of carriages, lackeys and such other manifestations of the might of their masters as they should be allowed to support at the Congress, they fell to more serious work. The Dutch demanded that Louis should give up all the places which he had seized under judgments of the *Chambres de Réunion*, including, of course, Strasburg. William III was particularly anxious that Louis should also bind himself to give no support to the exiled James II. Louis showed himself ready to make peace on the basis of the treaties of Westphalia and Nymwegen, and to restore the *villes réunies*, including Strasburg. The envoys of the Emperor, however, made counter-claims, including the retrocession of the ten Imperial towns of Alsace (ceded at the Peace of Westphalia), a claim which the other allies were not ready to enforce.

The appearance of differences within the Grand Alliance induced the French to play a bold game by which, after all, they might save Strasburg. Still, nominally, keeping their offer of Strasburg open, they dragged out the proceedings at Ryswick, month after month, so that nothing was done. In this they were greatly helped by the attitude of the Imperialists, who did not wish to

[1] Macaulay, *History of England* (ed. Firth, 1915), VI, 2708.

make peace ; for they believed that Charles II of Spain might die at any moment, and they wished this event to find them with the Grand Alliance and the war against France still in full swing. Thus they would have a chance of asserting their claims to the Spanish Succession against France, which was very weary of war.

Meanwhile there was another man who had now made up his mind for peace, and perhaps the most unexpected of all. How William, a deep and silent man, the life-long opponent of the ascendancy of France, could at the last moment allow himself to be so easily overreached, is difficult to see. Yet so it happened. He had defeated Louis' great designs ; he had obtained a firm offer from France of the restoration of the *villes réunies*, including Strasburg, and he could with an easy mind agree to these, the "Nymwegen" terms. Such terms, however, could only be obtained by standing fast with the Empire. William made the capital mistake of showing that he wanted peace, and that he was willing to make it even alone. In July, 1697, he sent his friend William Bentinck, Earl of Portland, on a separate mission to deal directly with Marshal Boufflers, who commanded the French army in the Low Countries. Bentinck and Boufflers met secretly at the camp of Saint Renelle, near Brussels. The English Secretary of State (the Duke of Shrewsbury) knew nothing of these negotiations till they were concluded, nor did Villiers and Williamson who were labouring to bring the French to terms in Ryswick Castle.

In the course of three interviews (July 9–20) Bentinck obtained from Boufflers an engagement that Louis XIV would recognize William III as King of Great Britain and would give no support to the Jacobites. With the draft of a preliminary treaty in his valise, Bentinck returned to William, having, it must be admitted, accomplished his mission with great skill and dispatch. Louis XIV now knew that England was going to make peace. So he instructed his envoys at Ryswick to set a time-limit by which their offers must be accepted. The date fixed was September 1 ; until then the offer of Strasburg was to remain open for the Emperor to accept. With incredible obstinacy Leopold refused to accede, and the remaining allies, refusing to continue a European war for the House of Austria, signed peace on September 20, 1697, in the Salle de Conférence at Ryswick. The French kept Strasburg. On October 30 the Emperor perforce acceded to the Ryswick terms.[1]

[1] Texts in Vast, II, pp. 199 ff. Dumont, VII, Pt. II.

The Peace of Ryswick comprehended four distinct treaties between France on the one hand, and Spain, Great Britain, the United Netherlands and the Empire, respectively, on the other. By the Spanish treaty Louis restored all the places which he had occupied during the war, including, of course, Luxemburg, Charleroi and Mons; also the *villes réunies* which were on Spanish territory, with the exception of eighty-two small places [1] which rounded off his old gains. By the English treaty, Louis recognized the kingship of William III and forswore the Stuarts. Article 7 provides for the nomination of commissioners to settle disputed boundaries in the Hudson's Bay territory. The principality of Orange in the south of France was restored to William III (art. 13). The main treaty with Holland affirms the substance of the Treaty of Nymwegen. Like the English treaty, it touches on colonial matters, in article 8, by which the Dutch restored, among other places, Pondicherry to the French. The Franco-Dutch commercial treaty of the same date affirmed the principle so dear to the Dutch, that in time of war free ships make free goods, provided that they are not contraband (art. 27)—the still hotly disputed question of maritime law. The treaty with the Emperor is notable for article 16, which cedes Strasburg to France. The King of Sweden recovered Deux Ponts (Zweibrücken) and the Duke of Würtemburg recovered Montbéliard. But France had obtained what was really necessary. With the incorporation of Strasburg, Alsace became a purely French province.

With the conclusion of the Treaties of Ryswick, Europe had the opportunity of a period of stable peace, if only the Spanish Succession Question could be settled.

All Western and Central Europe was sighing for rest. Statesmen were working for it. Professors were engaged on perfecting systems of international law. Among other men of thought, none was more active than a great German. The philosopher Leibniz, who was as deeply immersed in practical affairs as in philosophy, was engaged on projects for the unification and consolidation of the German states-system; he had also endeavoured to turn the ambition of Louis XIV from Europe by inviting him to undertake a great enterprise in the East.

Gottfried Wilhelm von Leibniz was born on July 3, 1640, at Leipsic. His father was Professor of Moral Philosophy at Leipsic

[1] List in Dumont, VII, Pt. II, p. 418.

University, which the young Leibniz entered at the age of fifteen. His studies were chiefly in philosophy and mathematics, and later in law, but he also distinguished himself in the Greek and Latin classics. Leibniz meant to be a professor like his father, but in 1667 he made the acquaintance of Baron von Boineburg, chief minister of Philip von Schönborn, Elector of Mainz. Boineburg was so struck by the brilliant young doctor's ability that he invited him to Mainz and procured him a post in the administrative service of the Elector.

From this year Leibniz became one of the great publicists of Germany and of Europe. In 1668 he drafted a project of unification of the laws of Germany—a code for the 343 states which composed the Empire. In 1669 he supported with his pen the candidature of a German prince, Philip William of Neuburg, who was a Roman Catholic, to the throne of Poland. This design failed.

On the death of the Elector Philip von Schönborn, Leibniz was taken into the service of Charles Louis, Elector Palatine (son of Frederick V, Winter King of Bohemia). The Palatinate family, in spite of its misfortunes in the Thirty Years' War, was powerful and enlightened, and its influence was widespread. One of Charles Louis' brothers was Prince Rupert, the hero of the Civil War, who lived in England; another was Prince Maurice, who also fought in the Civil War and now lived in America; another, Edward, was married to a sister of the Queen of Poland; one sister was Protestant Abbess of Herford and highly influential in philosophical circles; another was Roman Catholic Abbess of Montbuisson in France, and had much to do with the religious-political circle of Bossuet; a third (Sophia) married Ernest Augustus of Brunswick-Luneburg and became the mother of George I of England. The Elector Charles Louis himself was an enlightened prince whose court at Heidelberg was a centre of German politics and culture. Through the Palatinate family Leibniz was able to enter into relations with many of the most influential courts and personages in Europe. In 1676 he entered the service of the Brunswick family at Hanover, under the patronage of the Princess Sophia. He first visited Paris as an Electoral Mainz diplomatist in 1672, and London (in the embassy of Electoral Mainz) in 1673. He travelled frequently to Paris, London, the Hague and other places, and was regarded as a citizen of the world.

Most of Leibniz's projects are of the nature of slow-growing seeds which had no result until long after his death. Between 1661 and 1670, when Louis XIV was beginning his advance towards political control of Western and Central Europe, Leibniz was doing his best to bring about the foundation of an Indo-German-Spanish Company for Eastern trade with a view to erecting a counterpoise to the overwhelming power of France.

The Thirty Years War had practically destroyed Germany as a Confederation. Leibniz had a plan for a new constitution of Germany as a close alliance of states, Catholic as well as Protestant. To make this possible, France must be diverted from meddling in Germany. Accordingly in 1672 Leibniz induced his influential friends to enable him to submit to Louis XIV, through the French Ministry of Foreign Affairs, a memorial in favour of an Egyptian expedition. "It is easier to take Egypt than Belgium," he wrote, "and the whole Orient rather than Germany." It was precisely at this very moment, as the pictures on the ceiling at Versailles show, that Louis XIV was deliberating whether he would choose peace or war with the Dutch; he chose war and sacrificed France's brilliant future overseas.

Among Leibniz's other designs was one for reconciliation of Catholics and Protestants (he was a Lutheran himself), another for the invention of a universal language. Of more immediate and practical effect was his foundation of the Royal Academy of Berlin, which, in his view, was to help on the union of Germans by intellectual culture. The accession of the House of Hanover to the throne of England was prepared for by Leibniz's writings and by his relations with men in England during the reign of Queen Anne. He died at Hanover on November 14, 1716. It is seldom possible to point to the precise and practical results of a publicist's life. He works in the realm of ideas; it is the men of action, the statesmen, who are the instruments through whom things are done in this world, but, without knowing it, they are moved by the ideas of the men of thought. Grotius, Leibniz, Burke, Gentz, Treitschke were all their time making diplomatic history, although never themselves high ministers of state.[1]

[1] C. B. Favre, *La Diplomatie de Leibniz*, in *Revue d'histoire diplomatique* (XIX), 1905, pp. 217, 545; (XX), 1906, p. 201, and XXI (1907). M. Cantor, *War Leibniz ein Plagiator?*, in *Historische Zeitschrift* (X), 1863, 97 ff., especially p. 107.

CHAPTER XXII

THE PARTITION TREATIES AND THE WILL OF CHARLES II OF SPAIN

There was a time when the wars of Marlborough roused the imagination of every Englishman, and they still live in the romantic pages of *Henry Esmond* and in the military history of Fortescue. But few people will take an interest in the genealogical controversies of the Spanish Succession, for the spirit of the age does not look kindly on family disputations concerning testaments, successions and hereditaments, when these deal with the destinies of nations. Yet many dusty folios bear witness to the reality of these disputations, and show how, not merely diplomatists and soldiers, but long-robed lawyers with their inkpots and quill pens had a prominent part in determining Europe's map.

Perhaps Mazarin had his eye upon the Spanish Succession when he made the Treaty of the Pyrenees, and married Louis XIV to Maria Theresa, eldest daughter of Philip IV, and sister of Charles II of Spain. She had absolutely renounced her rights to succession in Spain. She had also renounced her rights to her legal portion of her father's fortune ; this renunciation, according to article 4 of the Pyrenees treaty, had been made *moyennant* the payment of a dowry, and this condition had never been fulfilled. The non-payment of the dowry gave to Louis XIV no claim to the succession of the whole Spanish Empire for himself or for one of his family. Besides, the sum of 500,000 crowns, which was to have been the marriage-portion of the princess, was a trivial matter on which to try to establish a claim to the Spanish Empire. Lisola, in his famous pamphlet of 1667, unmasking the design of Louis XIV for universal monarchy, had written : "The delay in the payment of the Portion is a prejudice in a pecuniary matter, which may easily be repaired by paying the interest which the Civil Law doth appoint after the term of the payment is past ; to show that deficiency in the payment doth not annul the contract."

He went straight to the core of the matter by adding: "In truth it is a thing which occasions pity to see this Question moved between Kings, and that the ground of a War is layed upon a Subtiltie which private persons doth not dispute in justice."[1] Louis XIV had pressed for payment from the Spanish Crown down to about the end of the year 1661; but after this date he had ceased to negotiate about the dowry, and had concentrated chiefly on efforts to induce Philip IV to recognize the renunciation as null. In this effort, however, he had no success.[2]

In 1661 the negotiations in progress between the Courts of France and Spain concerning the dowry and concerning the effect of the renunciation had been interrupted in consequence of a violent quarrel in London. This quarrel occurred between the Comte d'Estrades, ambassador of Louis XIV and the Baron de Vatevile, ambassador of Philip IV, at the entry of the Swedish ambassador into London. D'Estrades had sent his carriage to the procession with an escort of 500 armed men commanded by his son. De Vatevile sent his carriage with an escort of 2,000 armed men. The French and Spanish contingents came into collision, and a regular combat took place, in which several men were killed, others being wounded. Louis XIV ordered the Spanish ambassador in France to leave the country. The incident was only terminated by Philip IV recalling Vatevile from London and making a public apology.[3]

Besides Louis XIV, there were at the time of the Peace of Ryswick only two other claimants to be seriously considered. One was the Emperor Leopold I, or some member of his family. Leopold was the son of the Emperor Ferdinand III and Maria, daughter of Philip III of Spain; and Maria had made no renunciation. Moreover, Leopold had married a daughter of Philip IV, Margaret (younger sister of Charles II). By Margaret, however, the Emperor had only one child, Maria Antonia, who had married the Elector of Bavaria, so that her rights, if any, passed to her son the Electoral Prince, except that at her marriage she had renounced those rights and made them over to the House of Austria.[4] Thus the three claimants were—Louis XIV, by reason of his marriage

[1] Lisola, *The Buckler of State*, Eng. trans., 1667, pp. 145, 151.

[2] Mignet, *Succession d'Espagne*, II, 71–85.

[3] Mignet, *ibid.*, I, 86.

[4] Heigel, *Kurprinz Joseph von Bayern*, in *Sitzungen der K.B. Akademie zu München* (1879), I, 230.

THE SPANISH SUCCESSION

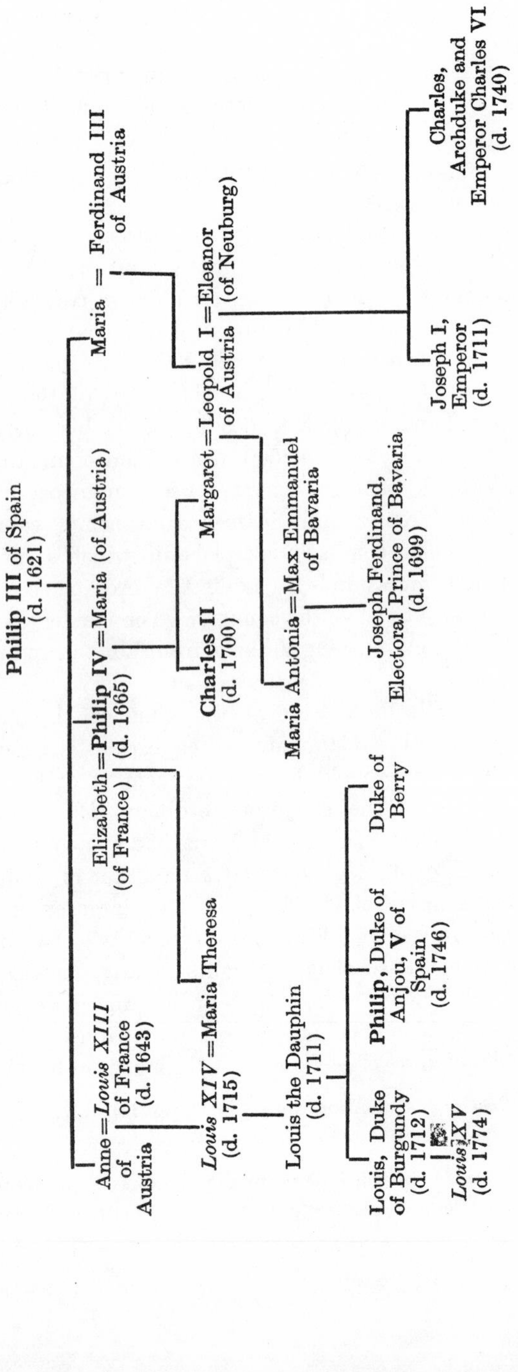

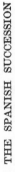

Note.—Kings of France in *italics*; Kings of Spain in **heavy type.**

with Charles II's eldest sister; the Emperor Leopold, by reason of his mother, the aunt of Charles II; and the Electoral Prince of Bavaria, by reason of his mother, niece of Charles II.

William III of England was determined that Spain and its Empire should not pass to France, for that would have meant death in two ways for the United Netherlands (of which he was chief magistrate) as well as grave danger and loss to England. For one thing, if the French obtained the Spanish Netherlands, including Antwerp and the mouths of the Scheldt, England's command of the Channel and North Sea would be gravely menaced, and the independence of the Dutch would not be worth a moment's purchase in a war with France. In the second place, the union of the Spanish overseas Empire with France would almost certainly entail the exclusion of England and Holland from trade with the Indies and South America. Spain was a slovenly and inefficient trader, and not at all a manufacturing country, so that the riches of her Empire largely went in buying English and Dutch goods, and in employing English and Dutch shipping. But the French were a different kind of people, and if they secured the Spanish overseas Empire they would develop it themselves; "Colbertism" had no place for foreign traders and shipping. Besides, as Louis XIV had a definite policy for making himself Holy Roman Emperor, and as he held Poland, Sweden and Turkey firmly in his diplomatic system, it is clear that, with Spain and the Spanish Empire in his hands, there would be nothing to stop him from becoming lord of all Europe. No one can seriously deny that the English, Dutch and Austrians had a perfect moral right to stop this. The only people involved in the Succession Question, whose interests have not so far been mentioned, were the Spanish themselves; as far as they were vocal about the year 1700 it can be said that they were decided about one thing—they did not wish their Empire to be partitioned. They had a legitimate pride in its history, its variety, its spaciousness. Yet, unfortunately, the only way in which the question could be solved was by some sort of partition. After all, however, if the Empire of Spain, the Indies and the Americas, which really owed their existence to the Spanish people, were left together, the Spaniards could not greatly object to Sicily, Naples, Milan and Belgium being detached, for these, after all, were quite external to them.

The Maritime Powers (Great Britain and Holland) worked hard

to have the question settled without a war; and it would have been so settled had not Louis XIV fallen before temptation in the end and taken the fatal leap. In the first place, by one of the articles common to the treaties of 1689 which composed the Grand Alliance, the Allies agreed to assure to the Emperor and his heirs the succession to the crown of Spain, if Charles II died childless. But the Grand Alliance came to an end in 1697, and for a time there was no more friendship between England and the House of Austria. The Spanish Succession question with its prospect of a general war was the real danger. William knew that if France and Austria could only be satisfied Europe would be at peace—indeed, if Louis XIV were in agreement with England and Austria, the other states must agree too.

Never had Europe come nearer to settling a great international war-crisis by peaceful negotiation and compromise. Louis XIV and William III, the two greatest statesmen of the age, men with the most highly developed European outlook in addition to their national sense, deliberately set themselves by diplomatic arrangements to regulate a territorial succession which, if it were left to the decision of war, offered to the winning side incomparably greater prospects of gain. "It is certain," wrote Louis XIV, "that the disposition of the peoples of Spain, the condition of my forces, and the measures which I have taken would give me just hopes of a successful war."[1] It was neither fear nor self-interest which made him accept the method of partition; it was the decision of statesmanship, which knows that war between civilized peoples is never inevitable, but can be avoided by the exercise of reason through a business-like transaction.

As soon as the Peace of Ryswick was concluded, William III sent his faithful Dutch friend, William Bentinck, Earl of Portland, as ambassador to France. Bentinck, although probably the most unpopular man in England, was a highly successful diplomatist, loyal and honest. On the French side, the Comte de Tallard was sent to represent Louis in England. This man is better known later as the loser of the battle of Blenheim; on this occasion he did better.

Through their respective envoys the two monarchs—who were incomparably the most powerful rulers as well as being the two ablest statesmen in Europe at this time—came to an excellent

[1] Quoted by Bourgeois, *Manuel historique,* I, 106.

arrangement :[1] they agreed by an instrument known as the First Partition Treaty signed at the Hague on October 11, 1698, that in the event of Charles II's death the Maritime Powers and France would support a settlement as follows : the Dauphin of France should receive a satisfaction in the possession of Naples, Sicily, the Tuscan ports, Final (about thirty miles south-west of Genoa) and Guipuzcoa (a maritime province of Northern Spain) ; the Archduke Charles of Austria would receive the Duchy of Milan ; Joseph Ferdinand, the Electoral Prince of Bavaria (son of the Elector Max Emmanuel), was to have all the rest—that is Spain, the Spanish Netherlands (where his father's governorship was extremely popular), and the Indies (including the American colonies). A secret article stated that if the Electoral Prince should die without children, his father, the Elector of Bavaria, should have his son's share of the Spanish Succession.

Thus the United Netherlands could still rely on the Spanish Netherlands as a barrier between themselves and France. Austria and France would share the Italian parts of the Spanish Empire, which parts, if they were to be under alien Powers at all, would certainly be as well off under French and Austrians as under the Spaniards. The Two Sicilies often had insurrections against Spain, while Manzoni in *I Promessi Sposi* gives a true picture of the Spanish rule in Milan. "On Joseph Ferdinand all Europe puts its hope," wrote an Austrian ambassador.[2] Unfortunately for the statesmanlike project (which in its main point—the succession of the Electoral Prince—coincided with Charles II's will), Joseph Ferdinand died suddenly on February 8, 1699, at Brussels, where he was with his father, the Governor of the Spanish Netherlands. He was only six years of age.

Count Merode-Westerloo (later an Austrian Field-Marshal), who had a post at the Elector Max Emmanuel's court at Brussels at this time, described the last scene in his Memoirs :

> On the day of his death I visited the Prince, to inform myself of his health, when the Elector himself was in the sickroom. At a sign from him I went to the bedside. He had brought a plaything, and the boy visibly made an effort to awaken the belief that he was not so ill, so as to comfort the father. The tears started from the Elector's

[1] Text in Dumont, VII, Partie II, 442–4.

[2] Quoted by Heigel, *Sitzungen der K.B. Akademie zu München* (1879), I, 304.

eyes; he was compelled to leave the room, but ordered me to stay and to play with the Prince. I did as he commanded. But as I saw how fearfully the boy suffered, I gave up and went away. Only the Jewish physician, Don Louis, remained in the chamber, with his back turned to the fireside. Since I have been told that it was he who through poison put an end to the life of the boy, I see him always stand before me.[1]

The Elector suspected an Austrian plot.

The scene then changed to Madrid, where the Marquis d'Harcourt, the French envoy, played a skilful game among the grandees and the Jesuits who ruled the Court.[2] The English minister Stanhope was a capable man and saw through the game, but could not stop it.[3] He knew how to deal with Spanish noblemen, but Jesuit confessors were outside his scope. The Imperial ambassador, however, Count Harrach, had considerable influence, and it was impossible to foretell which party, the French or the German, would end by gaining the moribund monarch's ear. Louis XIV had an active policy at Madrid throughout the years 1699 and 1700, and his ambassador Harcourt was fortunate in having the support of the Cardinal Primate, Porto-Carrero. No blame can attach to Louis for taking care that his interests were not overshadowed by the Austrian party at Madrid.

Meanwhile he was negotiating for a new Partition Treaty. The death of the Electoral Prince was considered as abolishing entirely the First Partition Treaty, in spite of the reservation made in it in favour of the prince's father, Maximilian Emmanuel, the Elector, who survived his son. It is unfortunate that an attempt was not made to substitute the father as the Spanish inheritor, now that the son was dead. Even this, however, might have required a war, for the Spanish nation itself would perhaps not have accepted the First Partition Treaty with its dismemberment of the Empire, without a blow. But it would have been a war in which Bavaria would have been on the side of the Allies. When Max Emmanuel was passed over in the renewed negotiations for

[1] Merode-Westerloo, *Mêmoires,* I, 163, quoted by Heigel, *op. cit.*, p. 306.

[2] He was appointed on December 23, 1699, and was specially instructed "to penetrate the veritable dispositions of the principal seigneurs of Spain and in general of the whole nation in the succession of the Catholic King, if that prince (Charles II) should come to die." *Instructions, Espagne*, I, p. 453.

[3] See *Spain under Charles II* (Extracts from Stanhope's Correspondence), London, 1840 *passim*. See secret article annexed to the First Partition Treaty.

the Spanish Succession, the estrangement between him and the Emperor, which had been obvious in 1692 (when his Austrian wife died), was completed. In the War of the League of Augsburg he had been on the Imperialist side. Henceforth he was to be wholly in the French interest.[1]

Louis XIV and William III set themselves to work at making a new arrangement. The Electoral Prince being eliminated and no satisfactory third party at hand, the problem now was, leaving the other two claimants (France and Austria) still in the field, to divide the late Electoral Prince's portion between them. In the arrangement which was come to, it must be admitted that Louis XIV did not show himself grasping; William was in no position to back his demands with force, the English parliament in December, 1698, having compelled him to reduce the army to the number of 7,000 men. The Second Partition Treaty "to avert a new war in Europe," as the preamble stated, was signed by Portland and Tallard for England and France at London on March 13, 1700, and by Heinsius and others for the United Netherlands at the Hague on March 25.[2] The terms were like those of the First Partition Treaty, with the Electoral Prince's portion distributed mostly in favour of the House of Austria; for while the Dauphin was to have (as before) Naples, Sicily, Final and Guipuzcoa, Milan was to be given to the Duke of Lorraine, who in return was to hand over his Duchy of Lorraine to the Dauphin.[3] The Archduke Charles (younger son of the Emperor Leopold I) was to have all the rest—Spain, the Indies, the Spanish Netherlands. But with incredible obstinacy, the Emperor refused to accede to the treaty. Rather than have the assurance of all the Spanish Empire, except in Italy, for his second son with the consent of the Powers of Europe, he preferred to wait and try to gain the Italian possessions too. By refusing to make the Peace of Ryswick along with his allies he had lost Strasburg; now by refusing to consent to the Second Partition Treaty he lost Spain; and in addition he helped to plunge Western Europe into twelve years of

[1] See Heigel, *Kurprinz Joseph Ferdinand von Bayern und die Spanishe Erbfolge*, in *Sitzungsberichte der K.B. Akademie zu München* (1879), I, 238–80.

[2] Dumont, T. VII, Pt. II, p. 477.

[3] This would have been rather a satisfactory result. The House of Lorraine was exposed to exile or confinement in every war which France waged. When in the middle of the eighteenth century it was transferred to Italy (Tuscany) it proved to be an adaptable and efficient sovereign there.

war. Any fair view of the facts will show that Leopold I, quite as much as Louis XIV, was responsible for the Spanish Succession War.

The Second Partition Treaty was announced to the Court of Spain, and caused only indignation there; the Spaniards neither wanted to see their Empire split in two, nor did they like other people to settle their affairs. Macaulay has brilliantly described the intrigues around the death-bed of Charles II. The result was in favour of France, but not wholly unfavourable to Spain. A will was actually drafted, perhaps even signed, leaving the entire Spanish possessions to the Archduke Charles; then a reversal of the tide of sympathy caused it to be burned. By the next will, dated October 2, 1700, Charles II, "recognizing that the renunciations of Maria Theresa, wife of Louis XIV, were made with a view to preventing the union of the two Crowns of Spain and France," left his dominions, "without exception of any part of them," to the Duke of Anjou, Louis XIV's second grandson. He added the condition that the two realms of France and Spain should never be joined together. If the Duke of Anjou died or became heir of France, the Spanish crown was to pass to his brother the Duke of Berry; if this prince were to die or become heir of France, then to the Archduke Charles of Austria; failing him, the Duke of Savoy.[1] Thus the Duke of Anjou, the Duke of Berry and the Archduke Charles were placed consecutively in the order of succession to the undivided Spanish Empire; and if one refused the succession, the next would have it. Charles II died on November 1, 1700. His will, as far as can be judged by any test, satisfied the bulk of the Spanish people.

When the will was communicated to Louis XIV, he was faced with a tremendous problem. The matter was most carefully considered in Council by him, and it must not be supposed that he merely fell before a brilliant temptation of the prospect of Empire. The same brilliant prospect had been present to him after the Peace of Ryswick, and he had decided, instead, for moderation, and for the Partition Treaties. He had agreed that the Spanish throne and the bulk of the Spanish Empire should devolve upon the Archduke Charles of Austria. But the Austrian family themselves refused to accept the Second Partition Treaty, and the Spaniards had unanimously spurned it with indignation. Would Louis have

[1] Text of will of Charles II in Dumont, VII, Partie II, 486.

been justified in making war to force the Spaniards to abandon a French prince and to take an Austrian prince, when the Austrians had resolved *not* to carry out the treaty for which Louis would be fighting the Spaniards ? Again, if Louis refused to allow one of his grandsons to accept the Spanish throne, then by the terms of Charles II's will that throne would pass entire to the Austrian Archduke, and so the Partition Treaty would be nullified. The same courier as had brought the will to Paris would pass on to Vienna.[1] It seemed as if, whatever Louis did, the Partition Treaty would have to be abolished ; if he took the whole Spanish Empire, the treaty was broken ; if he let it go to the Archduke, the treaty was equally broken. And, again, it seemed as if, in any case, there would be a war ; if he accepted the Spanish inheritance, Austria and the Maritime Powers would fight him ; if he stood by the Partition Treaty and tried to induce the Spaniards to accept it, he would equally have to fight them (and to fight them in favour of the perfectly ungrateful Austrians, who had selfishly refused the Partition Treaty). It was a terrible dilemma, and Louis might well say, as Torcy, his Foreign Minister, remarked, that if he had to fight, he had better fight for his own children than against them.

Still, by accepting the Spanish inheritance entire for his grandson, Louis broke the Second Partition Treaty, when the ink of his plenipotentiaries' signature was scarcely dry upon it. The treaty was probably impossible of enforcement as it was, now that Charles II had left a last will and that the Spanish people had definitely signified their assent to this will. What Louis should have done was to look for another solution, to ask his co-signatories to suppress the Second Partition Treaty, and with Austria and Spain to find some settlement which would be less offensive to Europe than the succession of France to the whole. In not approaching his co-signatories he did wrong. But to approach his co-signatories with a proposal for a modified partition would have been to reject the will of Charles II ; and then the whole heritage would at once have devolved on Austria. And Austria, by standing outside the Second Partition Settlement, had left

[1] "*Le même courier depêché en France, passoit en Vienne.*" Torcy's *Mémoires* (La Haye, 1756), I, 152. Castel de Rios, the Spanish Ambassador, had orders from the Junta to send the courier straight on to Vienna, in case of Louis refusing the offer. *Ibid.*, p. 149.

herself free to accept the whole Spanish Empire, and to rob France of the legitimate rewards of the concessions which she had made. The House of Austria, unscrupulous, cynical, selfish, is one of those responsible for the general war. Louis was responsible too; for if he had stood by the Second Partition Treaty, and had let the Austrians grasp at the whole Spanish Empire according to Charles' will, he would have kept his word; and England and Holland would likewise have stood by the treaty and insisted on France acquiring Spanish Italy. But he would not take the risk involved in this proceeding, more especially as he was doubtful whether England and Holland would really fight for him against Austria in support of the terms of the Second Partition Treaty.[1] He preferred to take the risk involved in himself grasping at the whole.

When the Spanish courier arrived with the text of the will at Paris the Marquis of Castel de Rios, Ambassador for the Court of Spain, communicated the terms of it and asked for an audience. Louis was at Fontainebleau; he had to decide quickly, so he at once held a Council at which were present the Dauphin, the Chancellor (Comte de Pontchartrain), the Minister of Finance (Duc de Beauvilliers) and the Minister of Foreign Affairs. The arguments recapitulated above were put forward. Only the Duc de Beauvilliers gave a vote to hold by the Partition Treaty, "persuaded that the war, inevitable consequence of the acceptance of the will, would cause the ruin of France." [2] The fatal decision was, however, taken and the acceptance personally notified by the King in an audience which he granted at Fontainebleau to Castel de Rios. On December 3, 1700, the seventeen-year-old Duke of Anjou left for his new kingdom; on departing he had been given by his grandfather a paper of wise counsel and advice. The old king embraced him affectionately and said: "*Adieu, mon fils: il n'y a plus de Pyrénées.*" [3]

[1] Torcy, who was present at the Council of Fontainebleau, mentions as an argument in favour of Louis' decision that the English and Dutch would not have fought to support the Partition Treaty in favour of France against Austria. Perhaps the French were right in believing this. Torcy, *op. cit.*, I, 154.

[2] Torcy, *loc. cit.*, I, 156.

[3] *Œuvres de Louis XIV* (Paris, 1806), II, 466. The "Mémoire remis par Louis XIV à son petit fils" is found in pp. 440–66.

CHAPTER XXIII

THE PEACE OF UTRECHT

"It is seldom that the English nation thinks unanimously," remarks Torcy. The English people had only recently finished a long, arduous and costly war, and "the ancient phantom of Universal Monarchy touches the English less than the horror of the taxes which they would be obliged to pay for a new war." [1] William III was sufficiently determined, but England was a constitutional country, and his hands were bound. Louis XIV, however, having been compelled, as he felt, to break one treaty, thought that he might as well break another; and impelled by a generous sentiment, he resolved when the exiled James II of England was dying in the château at St. Germain-en-Laye to recognize, contrary to the Treaty of Ryswick, the claim of the Prince of Wales (James III, the Old Pretender) to the throne of Great Britain (September 16, 1701). England, the sagacious Torcy remarks, was unanimous in regarding this as a mortal offence; and William III profited by this feeling to induce Parliament to consent to fight.

Without Louis' recognition of the "Old Pretender" it is very doubtful if the English Parliament would have joined in the war. Nevertheless, ten days before Louis made his ill-considered *démarche*, William had on his own authority negotiated a treaty which was the foundation of the new "Grand Alliance." On September 7, 1701, the Treaty of the Hague was concluded between the Governments of Great Britain, Austria and the United Netherlands, signed by the Counts Goessen and Wratislaw for the Emperor, by Eck de Panteleon, Heinsius, and others for the Netherlands, and by Lord Marlborough for the English. It bound the three Powers to obtain compensation for the Emperor on account of his rights to the Spanish throne; to occupy the Spanish Netherlands, and the Spanish possessions in Italy (which presum-

[1] Torcy, *op. cit.*, I, 163, 164.

ably were to form the Emperor's compensation); and only to make peace in common.[1] Since July, the Emperor's forces had been fighting the French in Italy, but yet England and Holland did not declare war. It is clear that Louis could have had peace if he had offered to let the Allies transfer the Spanish Netherlands and Spanish Italy to the Emperor, leaving Spain itself to Philip of Anjou. But Louis was himself bent on securing the whole Spanish Empire for his grandson. All his actions make this clear. Before any act of war had been begun even by the Emperor, he had sent a French army on February 6, 1701, into the Spanish Netherlands and had taken into his custody the Barrier Fortresses (Luxemburg, Mons, Namur, Charleroi, Nieuport, Ostend, and others). His recognition of the Old Pretender on September 16, 1701, merely showed that the Grand Monarque had now burned all his boats.

William III died on March 8, 1702, but Queen Anne's Government carried out his policy. In May formal declarations of war were issued: on the 8th by the States-General, on the 14th by Great Britain, on the 15th by the Emperor. The triple alliance of these powers became known in its extended form as the Grand Alliance; the majority of the states of Germany acceded to it, the most important being the King of Prussia.[2] Portugal was detached from its connection with France, on May 16, 1703, by a treaty negotiated through Paul Methuen and Franz van Schonenberg, the British and Dutch ministers at Lisbon. This was a defensive alliance against France and Spain, of a much stricter kind than the Whitehall Treaty of 1662 which is still in force between Great Britain and Portugal. Sweden acceded on August 16, 1703, and Victor Amadeus of Savoy, who had turned his coat several times, on October 25, 1703. France was left with no allies except Spain, and the Electorates of Cologne and Bavaria; this latter state had joined France early in the diplomatic struggle (March 9, 1701); and when one by one the other satellites of Louis dropped off, in 1702 and 1703, Bavaria alone kept to her engagements. She met her fate at the battle of Blenheim.

Though the question of the Spanish Succession was now to be settled by war, the voice of the diplomatist was never silent through-

[1] Dumont, T. VIII, Pt. I, p. 89.

[2] December 30, 1701. The Elector Frederick III had by the "Crown Treaty" with the Emperor, November 16, 1700, become *King in Prussia.*

out the whole struggle. The great victories won by Marlborough and Eugène made Louis' design to "abolish the Pyrenees" impossible. By the year 1706 it was clear to every one that the French had lost the war; and Louis would gladly have given up the struggle. He was not allowed to do so. In 1709 and 1710 he again attempted to shake off the burden of war, and was prepared to make large sacrifices. Again he was rejected; so, desperately fighting on, his soldiers and his diplomatists between them snatched terms of peace from the Allies—not indeed a victorious peace, but a "compromise" peace which involved no great loss to France.

Louis was undoubtedly responsible for beginning the war, although Leopold of Austria did nothing to incline him to peace. But the loss of the fortresses which he had seized in the Spanish Netherlands, the successes of the Allies in Spain, the overwhelming calamity of Blenheim (1704), and the miserable internal condition of France, convinced Louis comparatively early that he must have peace. After the defeat at Ramillies (May 13, 1706) Louis instructed the Spanish Governor of the Netherlands, the Comte de Bergheik, to open negotiations with the Dutch; the offer was that Philip of Anjou should abandon Spain, and all the Spanish Empire, except the two Sicilies and the Milanese.[1] The Allies refused; partly because they did not consider the offer to be sincere; partly because the Emperor thought that the House of Austria could now gain the whole inheritance; and partly because the Maritime Powers now objected (after four years of war) to letting a French prince have power on the Italian shores of the Mediterranean, although they would have consented to this before the war started. So Louis continued fighting, and next year his forces in Spain gained the decisive victory of Almanza (April 25, 1707). It should now have been quite clear that Philip of Anjou could not be driven out of Spain itself—not permanently at least, for the bulk of the Spanish people showed a real attachment to his cause.

In July, 1708, however, Marlborough won another of his brilliant victories at Oudenarde in the Low Countries; accordingly in 1709 negotiations were started again. The President Rouillé, an *homme de robe*, who had been employed before on secret missions by Louis XIV, was sent to Holland, to offer the evacuation of Spain. The negotiations were held at Moerdyck and the Hague (March,

[1] Koch and Schoell, I, 194. Torcy, *Memoirs*, I, 176 ff.

1709) until Marlborough and Eugène learned of them, when the discussions were broken off. Thus Louis' attempt to make a separate peace with the Dutch failed.

Next a negotiation was tried at the Dutch capital; Torcy, the French Minister of Foreign Affairs, was sent to the Hague in May (1709). He chose a time when Marlborough and Eugène were away; but Heinsius refused to treat until the two generals arrived. Marlborough, in addition to being Allies' Generalissimo, was also Ambassador Extraordinary for Queen Anne, a position which he had held since the opening of the war. As soon as he came to the Hague he assumed the lead in the negotiations. With Torcy he was soon on admirable terms, telling how he had served under Turenne and learned the art of war from that great soldier. Eugène and Marlborough both enjoyed long talks with the French minister, explaining to him, without any idea of showing triumph,[1] but simply with the pure interest of soldiers, why the French had failed to hold the line of the Scheldt and what mistakes their generals had made.

There is no doubt that Louis XIV and his ministers were at this time sincerely anxious for peace. "The condition of France," says Torcy, in his account of this negotiation, "grew worse from day to day. Famine reigned there. The finances were exhausted, and the sources to re-establish them were dry."[2] Torcy was empowered to offer the complete abandonment of the Spanish inheritance to the House of Austria. He even went further, and was permitted to offer Strasburg to the Emperor. This was indeed a remarkable concession. Louis empowered Torcy to propose to Marlborough the sum of 2,000,000 livres as a bribe if he could procure Strasburg to be retained by France; if Marlborough could go further and manage not merely to have Strasburg reserved for France, but also Dunkirk and Landau, and the two Sicilies for Philip of Anjou, he was to be given 4,000,000 livres.[3] These offers at least show that Louis looked on the loss of Strasburg as well as of the whole Spanish inheritance as quite probable, unless he could avert this by a huge and lucky bribe—that is, he believed that he only had a gambler's chance. The gamble failed; and

[1] Torcy, II, 149. *Sans aucun air de fanfaronnade.*

[2] *Ibid.*, p. 75.

[3] The letter of the king to Torcy, mentioning these offers for Marlborough, is printed in Flassan, IV, 281–2.

yet, incredible as it may seem, Louis XIV ended the war by keeping Strasburg for France, and his grandson on the throne of Spain.

Torcy, Eugène and Marlborough drew up and signed a preliminary treaty, which was also signed by the Dutch plenipotentiaries. By this treaty Louis was to consent that the whole Spanish Monarchy be given to the Archduke Charles; to cede Strasburg, Breisach and Kehl to the Emperor; to demolish the French Rhine fortresses; to cede Newfoundland to Great Britain; to cede nine north-eastern fortresses, including Lille and Maubeuge, to the United Netherlands. Article 4 stated that if Philip of Anjou would not agree to retire from Spain, "the Most Christian King and the Contracting Princes and States shall take in concert the proper measures to assure the full effect of the convention."[1] An armistice of two months was to be allowed for Louis to procure the consent of his grandson to these terms; at the end of the two months (the French troops having meanwhile been withdrawn from Spain and the Spanish Netherlands—art. 5) Louis must either join the Allies in fighting his grandson, or he must begin the war against them once more. This was asking too much. "You have well foreseen," wrote Louis to Marshal Villars, "that it would be impossible for me to accept conditions, which would only provide for a suspension of arms for two months, and which would put me under the necessity of joining my enemies to dethrone the King of Spain, or to recommence the war against them after having put them in possession of the most important places of my frontier."[2]

Louis could scarcely have induced his exhausted people to undertake a fresh war in order to dethrone a French prince in Spain; he did, however, make efforts to induce Philip to abdicate. It is believed that Philip would have done so, had it not been for the constancy of the Princesse des Ursins, the famous Frenchwoman whom Louis himself had sent to be director of the household of Philip's queen and to act also as an agent of Louis at the Spanish court. The Princesse des Ursins, a woman of great determination and much experience in affairs of state, made Philip answer with a refusal the letter which arrived from Louis XIV requesting abdication.[3] The King of France afterwards recognized that

[1] The full text in Torcy, II, 180 ff.

[2] *Œuvres de Louis XIV*, T. VI, pp. 201–2.

[3] See W. King, *The Princesse des Ursins*, in the *Edinburgh Review*, October, 1927.

Madame des Ursins had acted rightly, and in subsequent peace-negotiations he worked hard (but unsuccessfully) to obtain for her a sovereign principality to be made out of some portion of the Spanish Netherlands.

Louis, finding that the Allies were demanding more than he could perform, broke off the negotiations and revoked his offers. Here was a lamentable failure of the Allies' diplomacy. If the only thing which stood in the way of peace was the demand that Louis should actually fight his grandson, some means of compromise could have been discovered. The truth seems to be, however, that the Allied Governments did not all want peace. The Dutch did, for the war was ruining their prosperity; in England there was a strong peace party, which swept the whole country soon afterwards; even Marlborough, who is commonly represented as selfishly and obstinately determined for war, now wished for peace and sighed for repose. In a letter to Godolphin he had expressed regret at the failure of the peace-proposals, and Godolphin felt it necessary to reply: "I shall keep your opinion in that matter to myself, because if it were known, I am afraid it might discourage people both here and in Holland." [1] Only the Emperor was against it. Leopold I died in 1705; his elder son Joseph I was as opinionated as his father, and expected to become now, in reality, the head of Western Europe. France was to be crushed.

All France was convinced that Louis had offered everything possible, and that now there was nothing left to do but to fight. Extraordinary efforts were made, and Villars fought against Marlborough the terrible battle of Malplaquet (September 11, 1709), in which each side lost about 20,000 men. This was so unlike Marlborough's former successes, that it almost amounted to a defeat; and Louis had reason to congratulate Villars, in sober terms, on having "gained the principal advantage." [2] Thus strengthened, the old king again opened negotiations, and sent plenipotentiaries to Gertruydenburg (March–July, 1710); this time he offered, not indeed to fight against his grandson, but to pay monthly subsidies in lieu of soldiers to the Allies, if they had to dislodge Philip by force from Spain. Even this, however, the

[1] Coxe, *Memoirs of John Duke of Marlborough* (London, 1819), III, 40, 41.

[2] Louis XIV to Villars, September 20, 1709: *Œuvres*, T. VI, p. 204.

Allies refused. They would make France drink the cup of humiliation to the dregs.

As a matter of fact, the fortunes of France from this moment steadily revived. For one thing owing to its folly in prosecuting Dr. Sacheverell, on account of a high Tory, "passive obedience" sermon, the Whig Government fell (August, 1710) and was replaced by Tories who believed in a peace by negotiation, provided that England's commercial and maritime position could be assured. In the second place, Marlborough was relieved of his command in December, 1711, and thenceforward the military superiority of the Allies disappeared. In the third place, the Emperor Joseph I had died in April, 1711, without children, and his brother Charles (the Allies' candidate for the throne of Spain) was now sovereign of all the Austrian territories, and Holy Roman Emperor. If the Allies continued the war and made him King of Spain (in addition to his being Emperor), the "phantom of universal monarchy," as Torcy called it, would be revived in good earnest, at least as much as if a French prince sat on the throne of Madrid. It is no reply to say that the circumstances were different; that France was militarist and Austria pacific. The House of Austria was not, and never had been, pacific; Austria was the intransigeant party (just as in the former war she had refused peace in 1696) all through the War of the Spanish Succession; and her subsequent history has always been that of a military state. The English therefore had excellent reasons for again opening peace-negotiations. But it is quite inexcusable that they began the negotiations (and concluded the preliminaries) without consulting their ally, Austria, with whom they were bound by treaty, and who, with all her faults, had been completely faithful to her engagements. It was these perfidious and separate negotiations which enabled the French (whose courage in the field and diplomacy in the conference-room never showed to more advantage) to snatch from a hopeless war an honourable and not disadvantageous peace.

These separate negotiations began at Paris. To this place was sent secretly in July, 1710, Matthew Prior, who had held important diplomatic positions at the Conference of Ryswick in 1697, at the Paris Embassy before the Succession War, and elsewhere. With Prior was associated a certain Abbé Gaultier, a Frenchman who had been in the household of the Comte de Tallard during his embassy at London, and who had remained there (no doubt as some sort of intermediary) after Tallard had returned to France. Prior entered into negotiations with Torcy, under cover of darkness, in the gardens of the Palace of Fontainebleau. Before returning to England he also had an audience with Louis XIV. The aged monarch was never greater than in those times of his misfortune. " I am sending a minister with you," he said. " You can assure those who govern England and who have sent you that we shall do what we can, myself and the King of Spain, to content them. We both wish peace." He added, referring with dignity to the English against whom he was fighting, and who demanded peace with honour and security to their commerce : " On this foundation peace will be made between two nations descended from the same blood and who are enemies only by necessity ; no time must be lost." [1]

In August, 1711, Prior returned to London, with Nicolas Mesnager, a Rouen merchant, who had already done important diplomatic service for King Louis. The Abbé Gaultier, who had friends in English high society, came back in September. Prior, when returning *incognito* from Paris, had been arrested by the Customs officials at Deal as a French spy. This unfortunate event advertised Prior's mission to the whole world. The Imperialists and Dutch made efforts to stop the negotiations. The British ministry persisted, however ; conferences were conducted secretly in Prior's private house in Duke Street, Westminster. The chief British delegate was Bolingbroke. Gaultier carried on the negotiations for France, along with Nicolas Mesnager. The employing of a business-man, such as Mesnager, was characteristic of the new century, so much concerned with commercial, and especially with colonial affairs. The negotiations at Prior's house turned largely upon the question of Newfoundland, Acadie and Quebec. A British expedition was at the moment on the way to capture Quebec, but it failed disastrously. The discussions took place from August 18 to October 8 ; and on the latter day the preliminaries of peace were signed by Mesnager, Bolingbroke and the Earl of Dartmouth. After the signature, the clever, modest French negotiator was taken down to Windsor and given an audience with Queen Anne. He was also shown over the castle, and pleasantly entertained by Bolingbroke. When he left for France, Lord

[1] See L. G. W. Legg, *Matthew Prior* (1921), 159, 160. The quotations in the original French are in the Hist. MSS. Commission, Portland Papers, V, 41, 42.

Oxford, the Prime Minister, said to Mesnager, in Latin: "Out of two therefore let us make one most friendly nation." [1]

The Anglo-French preliminary terms of October 8, 1711, which were to be the basis of the Peace of Utrecht, were known at any rate in outline to the Allies. By these terms England was to have Gibraltar, Port Mahon, Newfoundland and Hudson's Bay; the Dutch were to be accorded a "Barrier" against France, and the Emperor was to have a "satisfaction" from Spain. The interests of Savoy were carefully safeguarded. The Crowns of France and Spain were never to be joined. The general intention of the preliminaries was communicated to the other allies by the British Government, who urged them to make peace in concert.[2]

The States-General of the United Netherlands unwillingly agreed that a general Congress of Peace should now be held, and at the suggestion of Queen Anne Utrecht was chosen as the meeting-place. January 12, 1712, was fixed as the day of assembling. After the conference had started Dean Swift published a pamphlet —*The Conduct of the Allies*—to justify the conduct of the British Tory ministers, and to prepare the way for the acceptance of the general peace. He pointed out justly that all the conditions stipulated in the Grand Alliance (except one) had been fulfilled by the British Government; and indeed the articles of the Preliminaries of London (which Swift does not mention) show that the British did assure to the Dutch their barrier and to the Emperor his satisfaction. But article 8 of the Grand Alliance prescribed that "none of the powers shall have the liberty to enter upon a treaty of peace with the enemy, but jointly and in concert with the other." [3] That Great Britain had broken this condition Swift could not deny. He argued that the objects of the war had been gained by the year 1711, and that the Allies were unreasonable in insisting

[1] *Ex duabus igitur faciamus gentem unam amicissimam.* See A. Legrelle, *La Diplomatie française et la Succession d'Espagne,* IV, 610. Cp. Torcy, *op. cit.*, III, 143.

[2] Schoell (Koch and Schoell, I, 200) says that the preliminaries were kept secret. Coxe (*Memoirs of John Duke of Marlborough,* III, 447) says they were communicated to the Allies, and published by Count Gallas. Torcy (*Memoirs,* III, 154, 155) says that the Earl of Strafford, the British ambassador at the Hague, was sent to Heinsius to explain that preliminaries had been signed, and that nothing had been done to prejudice Holland.

[3] Torcy, *op. cit.*, III, 157. *The Conduct of the Allies* (Swift's Works, ed. 1814) quotes the article in full, but offers only a weak excuse for breaking it—that the Dutch and Austrians had not fulfilled their military conventions with Great Britain.

on continuing it. If this is so (and there is much truth in it) the British Government should have approached the Allies and said: "The war is won; let us now make the peace; if you will not do so by a certain date, we shall consider ourselves at liberty to negotiate separately." Unfortunately the British Government did not act in this way. It made a private agreement with the French, and then it invited its allies to accede. This course of policy on the part of Great Britain gave the French negotiators at Utrecht and Rastadt an enormous advantage, for they already had the British peace assured, and could afford to be very firm in their attitude to the Dutch and the Austrians. The truth is, the Congress of Utrecht (like that of Rastadt which followed it) only worked out the details of the Preliminaries of 1711. It was at the conferences at Prior's house in Duke Street in August–October, 1711, that the real peace was made.

The Congress of Utrecht was formally opened on January 29, 1712, in the Hôtel de Ville of that city. All the belligerents were represented there: the French plenipotentiaries were the Maréchal d'Huxelles, the Abbé de Polignac, and M. Nicolas Mesnager. The British Government sent Dr. Robinson, Bishop of Bristol, whom Bolingbroke described to Mesnager as "a good Anglican, a good negotiator, honest man, phlegmatic." He had spent thirty-two years in diplomacy at the courts of the Northern Powers. The second British plenipotentiary was the Earl of Strafford (Thomas Wentworth), described in the same conversation by Bolingbroke as "a nobleman fitted for storming his way through an enterprise like a Colonel of Dragoons"—*un seigneur propre à brusquer une entreprise comme un Colonel de Dragons.* He could be counted upon to execute the orders of the queen.[1] Prior was Secretary to the British delegation. The Dutch had ten delegates, the Emperor three. Even the Republics of Venice and Genoa sent their representatives. Philip V of Spain was represented by the French delegation. Meanwhile the war went on; the British troops were kept inactive, and this enabled the Maréchal de Villars to attack and capture a great part of a force of 12,000 Germans and Dutch at Denain, on July 24, 1712. It was not until August 22[2]

[1] Torcy, *op. cit.*, III, 146.

[2] The date usually given is August 19; but the Treaty of Utrecht between France and Great Britain, April 11, 1713 (art. 17), says expressly the armistice was concluded on the 22nd.

of the same year that Bolingbroke and Torcy signed an armistice between the British and French forces, at Paris.[1]

The work of the Congress of Utrecht was transacted very slowly. The sessions lasted from January 29, 1712, till April 11, 1713, when the seven treaties which together form the Peace of Utrecht were signed between France on the one side and, on the other, Great Britain (two treaties), the Dutch (two treaties), Portugal, Brandenburg, Savoy (one treaty each). Altogether, therefore, the Congress lasted over fourteen months, but it was interrupted and in suspense from June to early in September, 1712; and before the Congress ended Great Britain and France had resumed diplomatic relations and had sent ambassadors to each other in December, 1712.[2] The French, who had lost the war, undoubtedly gained greatly by the length of time for which the Congress lasted. They profited by the mutual jealousies of the Allies; their military power perceptibly revived. The instructions issued by Louis to the French delegates show that the French Government was prepared to give up Lille, and to see the Elector of Bavaria transferred to Sardinia. Neither of these things happened. The greatest time was occupied in discussing the commercial treaties, every clause of which was carefully scrutinized by the French Government at Paris, before it was assented to at Utrecht. At last, in spite of the protests of the Emperor, the seven treaties of Utrecht were signed and published, on April 11, 1713.

These seven treaties of 1713, together with the consequential treaties concluded in 1714 between the Empire and France (treaties of Rastadt and Baden), and in 1715 between the Emperor, the States-General and Great Britain at Antwerp, form a *corpus* of conventions of the highest importance, and were a large part of the public law of Europe for nearly 200 years. Indeed, their influence is still felt, and some of their stipulations are even yet operative, for instance the clauses regulating the possession of Gibraltar by Great Britain.

All the treaties signed at Utrecht in 1713 are in the French language. In that between France and Great Britain, France recognized the order of succession to the throne of Great Britain as established by the laws passed under William III and Anne (art. 4). Article 6 stated that the security and liberty of Europe necessitates that the Crowns of France and Spain never be joined

[1] Vast, III, 48. [2] Vast, III, 55.

together, and took note of the renunciation to the French throne made by Philip V at Madrid on November 5, 1712, and of the renunciations to the throne of Spain made by the French princes. By article 9 the fortifications of Dunkirk were to be demolished (this was carried out, and Dunkirk remained unfortified till 1783—Treaty of Versailles). By article 10, the King of France restored to England "the bay and strait of Hudson"; and the Hudson's Bay Company received compensation for damage (art. 11). Article 12 ceded St. Christopher and Nova Scotia (Acadie) to Great Britain; also Newfoundland (art. 13), with a reservation in favour of French subjects who were to be permitted to catch and dry fish on the coast from Cape Bona Vista to the north end of the island, and from there along the western shore to Pointe Riche (this reservation was abolished by the Anglo-French convention of 1904). Article 15 stipulated that the French should not molest the native Indians, friendly or subject to the British in America, nor should the British molest the natives who were in the French interest. The treaty was signed by the Maréchal d'Huxelles and M. Mesnager, and by the Bishop of Bristol and the Earl of Strafford.

The commercial treaty between France and Great Britain secured to their respective subjects reciprocal freedom of navigation and commerce, subject to paying the lawful customs (it must be remembered that until the nineteenth century "freedom of trade" between two nations never meant freedom from paying customs-duties; it only secured merchants from prohibition to trade at all). The customs-duties to be paid were to be no higher than those paid by the most favoured nation (*la nation la plus amie*) which traded with either country (art. 8). Article 17 established, between France and Great Britain, the principle that "free ships make free goods" (*les vaissaux libres rendront les merchandises libres*) except contraband of war; so that if, for instance, England went to war with a third country, French ships should have the right of carrying goods to and from that country. This much-contested principle had already been established between the Dutch (see Franco-Dutch Treaty of Ryswick, September 20, 1697). The recognition of this principle in 1713 is said to have been insisted on, not by the French but by the British, for it was, apparently, chiefly British and Allied goods which had suffered, when being carried in neutral ships, at the hands of French privateers.[1]

[1] Koch and Schoell, I, 209.

The treaty between France and Portugal regulated colonial disputes between them. The treaty between Prussia and France is important because by it Louis XIV, acting for the Spanish Crown, ceded to Prussia Spanish Guelderland (between the Meuse and the Rhine, south of Cleves); and acting on his own account, the French king also ceded to King Frederick I Neuchatel and Valengin on the border of Switzerland. Frederick claimed these (as he also claimed the Principality of Orange) through his mother, who was a daughter of Prince Frederick Henry of Orange. The Principality of Orange, however, Frederick of Prussia now renounced (article 10), so that Louis XIV was able to incorporate it with France. Its possession in law had been contested since the death of the last prince, William III of England, in 1702.

The treaty between France and the Duke of Savoy regulated their disputes about frontiers by the principle of what is now called the crest-line and the watershed (art. 4): "the summits of the Alps and Mountains will serve for the future as limits between France, Piedmont and the County of Nice"; Nice was restored to Savoy. By article 5 Victor Amadeus was recognized as King of Sicily, which was now detached from the Spanish Empire (six years later Savoy exchanged Sicily for Sardinia, and was henceforth known as the Kingdom of Sardinia). By article 6, the male descendants of Victor Amadeus were recognized as heirs to the Spanish crown, in default of the posterity of Philip V, a contingency which, though often, apparently, imminent, has not yet taken place.

In the treaty with the United Netherlands, France engaged to hand over to the States-General, in favour of the House of Austria, the Spanish Netherlands (except High Guelderland, ceded to Prussia, and a part of Luxemburg, which was intended to be erected—though this was never done—into a principality for the Princesse des Ursins, the domineering councillor of Philip V).[1] The States-General were to transfer the Spanish Netherlands to the House of Austria, as soon as they had arranged about the "Barrier"; and the transferred portion was increased through the cession by France of Menin, Tournai, Knoque, Loo, Dixmude, Ypres, Poperinghe and certain minor places. On the other hand,

[1] The reservation in favour of the Princesse des Ursins, though frequently canvassed in subsequent negotiations, remained a dead letter.

the States-General restored Lille to Louis XIV (art. 15). The commercial treaty reaffirms the commercial articles of the Treaties of Nymwegen and Ryswick, among others the maritime declaration that "the free flag makes free goods" (art. 17).

These seven Treaties of Utrecht were all made between the Allies and France. There could be no formal peace made between Spain and the Allies, until the Utrecht treaties had been concluded and had decided who was really King of Spain. When this was done, however, and Philip V had been recognized by all the belligerents, diplomatic relations could be re-established. Accordingly the sessions of the Utrecht Congress were extended and Spanish plenipotentiaries were admitted; and on July 13, 1713, an important treaty was signed between Spain and Great Britain. This treaty stated that the object of the late war would be accomplished by the prohibition of the union of the French and Spanish Crowns, and by a just equilibrium of power (art. 2). This equilibrium had been provided for by the treaties of April 11. The most noteworthy territorial provision of the Spanish Treaty is the cession to Great Britain of Gibraltar, on condition that if the Crown of England shall ever wish to sell or alienate it, Spain is to have the preference over all other princes (art. 10). By article 11, Minorca was ceded to Great Britain; and by article 12 Great Britain and the *Compagnie Anglaise de la traite des nègres* were given the exclusive right of introducing negroes into the various parts of Spanish America. This privilege, called *el Pacto de el assiento de negros* was to last for thirty years from May 1, 1713. The company was to have a convenient ground on the bank of the Plata river for housing its negroes until they were sold; finally article 12 confirmed the treaty already made on March 26, 1713, relative to the Assiento (or privilege conceded), which limited the number of negroes to be imported to 4,800 a year, for twenty years only, the company paying a capitation duty of 33⅓ pieces of eight.[1] The company also had the right to carry back in its empty slave ships the produce of America, and in addition to trade to America in merchandise with one ship of not more than 500 tons burden.

The last article to be noticed is more creditable to Great Britain. It secured to the Catalans, the only people of Spain who had stood consistently by the Archduke Charles, a complete amnesty and all the privileges which the most favoured nation—the people of

[1] The Assiento Treaty is printed in the *General Collection*, III, 375.

Castile—enjoyed (article 13).[1] This exonerates the British Government from the charge commonly levelled against them of having abandoned the Catalans ruthlessly to their fate.

The War of Succession was not ended yet, for the Emperor Charles still claimed Spain for himself, and continued the war. It was now, however, a straight fight between France and the Empire; and Villars proved himself to be a match for the great Eugène. On December 26, 1713, a conference was opened between Villars and Eugène (as diplomatists, not as soldiers) at the Château of Rastadt, a residence of the Margrave of Baden-Durlach. As a diplomatist the ardent Villars did not gain the encomiums which he justly won as a general, but at last peace was signed on March 6, 1714: "*Je viens de gagner ma dernière bataille,*" wrote Villars a month earlier, when, however, the discussion of the position of the Catalans disappointed the Marshal's hopes and deferred the final signature. However, in time he did win his battle. The peace was made only between the Emperor and France; and it required another conference at Baden in the Aargau to procure the adhesion of the Princes of the Empire (June 10—September 7, 1714). No provision was made for the Catalans.

The Treaties of Rastadt and Baden are practically identical, except that the treaty with the Emperor is in French, that with the Empire is in Latin. The treaties were glorious to France; and Villars had reason to congratulate himself on his *dernière bataille,* for he retained Alsace (including Strasburg) for France, and also the fortress of Landau. Only Old Breisach, Freiburg and Kehl were given up to the House of Austria. It was a great triumph for Louis XIV to obtain the restoration of his humiliated and defeated allies, the Electors of Bavaria and Cologne, to their states and to all their prerogatives. The cession by Spain of the

[1] Article 13. Whereas the Queen of Great Britain has continually pressed and insisted with the greatest earnestness that all the Inhabitants of the Principality of Catalonia, of whatever State or Condition they may be, should not only obtain a full and perpetual Oblivion of all that was done in the late War, and enjoy the entire possession of all their Estates and Honours; but should also have their ancient Privileges preserved safe and untouched; the Catholick King, in compliance with the said Queen of Great Britain, hereby grants and confirms to all the Inhabitants of Catalonia whatsoever, not only the Amnesty desired, together with the full Possession of all their Estates and Honours; but also gives and grants to them, all the Privileges which the Inhabitants of both Castiles, who of all the Spaniards are the most dear to the Catholick King, have and enjoy, or may hereafter have and enjoy. *General Collection,* III, 480.

Spanish Netherlands in favour of the Emperor was confirmed; and the Emperor was also to be left in peaceable possession of those parts of Italy which he had occupied in the war, namely Sardinia, the Kingdom of Naples, the Duchy of Milan and the Tuscan ports. Thus Austria gained predominance in Italy. No mention at all is made in the treaties of Rastadt and Baden of the Catalans. Philip V broke his engagement made in the English treaty, and deprived them of their constitutional privileges.

One more question remained to be settled, that of the *Barrier*. It was not considered enough that the Spanish Netherlands should be transferred to the Austrians, to be held as a rampart against France. The Dutch had not sufficient trust in the strength, perhaps not even in the intentions, of Austria; and they claimed that they themselves must have the garrisoning of the Netherland forts on the French frontier. This had been agreed to by Great Britain in a convention, known as the First Barrier Treaty, made on October 29, 1709. The First Barrier Treaty was now replaced by the Second, January 29, 1713,[1] made at Utrecht between Great Britain and the United Netherlands. By this treaty the Dutch guaranteed the Protestant succession in Great Britain, and agreed to send 6,000 troops, if necessary, in defence of it (a guarantee which they actually had to fulfil in 1745). The Spanish Netherlands were to serve as a barrier for the Dutch against France; and the States-General were to have the garrisoning of Barrier Towns. But the Emperor was no party to this treaty, and it required one more Congress, held at Antwerp, in 1715, to bring him into the system. The Irish General Cadogan (one of Marlborough's best soldiers) represented Great Britain, and the veteran diplomatist Van der Dussen, the Dutch. On November 15, 1715, the negotiations of Utrecht were at last liquidated, by a tripartite treaty between Great Britain, the Emperor and the States-General (Third Barrier Treaty).[2] By this, the Dutch agreed to transfer the Spanish Netherlands (which they held in pledge) to the Emperor (the transfer was actually made on February 5, 1716). The Emperor on his part engaged never to cede any portion of it to France. Moreover, a chain of fortresses, lying along the Austro-Netherlands-French frontier, from Namur on the Sambre and Meuse to Furnes and Knoque on the North Sea, were to be held by Dutch troops.

By this means what was at that time the greatest danger-zone

[1] *General Collection*, III, 364 ff.

[2] Dumont, VIII, Partie I, 458.

of Western Europe was to be given over for safe keeping to the Dutch, whose whole interest was in peace and quietness. Further, Great Britain guaranteed the Barrier Treaty " in all its points and articles " ; thus every inducement was held out to the French not to attempt to cross the line into the debatable territory.[1] The inclusion in the Barrier Treaty of the closure of the Scheldt to sea-going ships (according to the principle established by the Treaty of Münster) was a cruel restriction upon the commerce of the Belgic provinces. But commercial restrictions upon the commerce between states were not then (and, unfortunately, are not now) contrary to public sentiment ; and, in the case of the Austrian Netherlands, such restrictions were perhaps inevitable in the eighteenth century in order to assuage Dutch jealousy, and to prevent severe commercial competition between two neighbouring peoples.

Thus Europe was settled after twelve years of war.[2] It must be allowed that the Allies had achieved the objects of the war, as stated in the Treaty of September 7, 1701 (the triple alliance, generally known as the Grand Alliance). They had prevented the acquisition of the " entire inheritance " ; they had procured " equitable and reasonable satisfaction to his Imperial Majesty " ; they had recovered " the Provinces of the Spanish Low Countries that they may be a Fence and a Rampart, commonly called a Barrier, separating and distancing France from the United Provinces " ; and they had detached Milan, Naples, Sicily and the Tuscan ports and islands from the Spanish Crown ; security had been taken " that the Kingdoms of France and Spain shall never come and be united under the same Government " ; and finally the commercial interests of the Maritime Powers had been not merely safeguarded, but greatly advanced.[3] From the British point of view, the treaties of Utrecht were very satisfactory. Great Britain had gained Gibraltar (although this prize was not much appreciated then) ; and she had prevented Antwerp and the Belgian coast from coming under a powerful naval and military state, such as France. In the Emperor's hands, the Belgian provinces, cut off as they were

[1] For further details about the Barrier Treaty, see below, p. 209.

[2] The Treaties of Utrecht of April 11, 1713, are in Vast, III, p. 68 ff., and in Dumont, T. VIII, Partie I, where the other treaties of Utrecht and Antwerp are also given. See also *General Collection,* III, p. 398 ff.

[3] See Preamble to the Grand Alliance, art. 33, 5. (*General Collection of Treaties,* I, 415–18.)

from Austria, and with the Scheldt closed to the sea, were no danger to Great Britain.

The credit for this solution of the Spanish Succession question must be given to William III, the maker of the Grand Alliance; and yet Tory prejudice could induce Dr. Johnson to allude to him as "one of the most worthless scoundrels that ever existed." [1] In the same way, one who actually lived through the time of the war and was excellently informed could sneer at "the unexampled politics of a nation maintaining a war by ultimately pawning itself." [2] This is like much of the carping criticism which another War Government, struggling amid the greatest difficulties for the greatest ends, had to endure from many highly educated men in the years 1914–18.

[1] Boswell's *Life of Samuel Johnson* (*sub anno* 1775).

[2] Swift, *The Conduct of the Allies* (Collected Edition, 1814, Vol. V, p. 23).

CHAPTER XXIV

SCANDINAVIA AND THE SLAVONIC STATES

The history of the Baltic lands and of Europe east of the River Oder, during the seventy-three years between the Peace of Westphalia and the Peace of Nystadt, contains two movements of momentous significance—the attempt and glorious failure of Sweden to form an Empire of the North; and, secondly, the rise of Russia, steadily, though with some severe set-backs, to be a Great Power in Europe. In addition, during this period, the Republic of Poland is seen to become the puppet of neighbouring states.

In the Baltic lands, as in Western Europe, the period is one of wars, but the intervals of peace are shorter; during the long stretch of seventy-three years one hears little more than a tale of wars, punctuated by treaties, which are scarcely better than truces. The diplomatist is less to the fore than in Western politics; his work, when his chance does come, has to be done more quickly, and often it is only half-done. Moreover, in the kingdoms around the Baltic during this period, the diplomatists, much more than in Western Europe, are simply the instrument of their sovereigns; public opinion in their country influences them practically not at all. The destinies of Northern Europe are controlled by half a dozen monarchs, of whom seldom more than one has an intelligible policy, while the rest play fast and loose.

Sweden at this time was a country with a vigorous people, and a particularly vigorous royal family. The country, however, was poor, while its noble class was large, expensive and warlike. Although now a highly industrial country, Sweden was then almost without industries; and for extending their resources the Swedes had to look to the outside. Thus the eyes of the Swedish monarchs were attracted to the corn-lands on the east of the Baltic, particularly to Livonia; to the North Sea, from which the Swedes were cut off everywhere, except at one point (Götheborg); and to the mouths of the great German rivers—the Oder, the Elbe, the Weser—at which they might establish trading posts and fortresses and where they could take tolls.

Before Gustavus Adolphus entered the Thirty Years' War, he had already won Livonia, with its fine port Riga, from Poland; but he had gained nothing from the Kingdom of Denmark, to which Norway was attached in a personal union, and which had three provinces—Halland, Schonen (Scania) and Blekingen—at the southern end of the Kingdom of Sweden. In 1632 the great Gustavus was killed at Lutzen, and his daughter Christina assumed the Crown. The war in Germany was maintained, but in 1643 the Swedish Government also found time to fight Christian IV of Denmark, with whom they had many grounds of dispute, both commercial and territorial. The skill of Torstenson and Wrangel, and the incomparable fighting qualities of the soldiers, brought victory to the Swedes. In 1645 a conference was held (lasting six months) under the mediation of the French minister to Sweden, Caspar Coignetz de Thuilleries, at the frontier town of Brömsebro (in Blekingen). On August 13 the Treaty of Brömsebro was signed by the Chancellor Oxenstjerna and the Dane, Korfits Ulfeld. To Sweden was ceded Halland for thirty years; and her ancient freedom from paying dues for vessels passing through the Sound was confirmed and made more complete.[1]

The Peace of Westphalia left Sweden, through her possession of Western Pomerania, the Duchies of Verden and Bremen, in control of the mouths of the Oder, Ems and Weser. Also, by the Truce of Altmark, 1629, prolonged for twenty-six years by the Truce of Stuhmsdorf, 1635, she remained, *de facto*, in possession of most of Livonia.[2] Thus secure in respect of corn-supply and of foreign trade, and thoroughly capable of defending herself, Sweden might have remained content and at peace for many years; but the Polish-Vasa claim restarted the Northern Question which was only settled after three great wars and a disastrous peace in 1721. John Casimir of Sweden, a son of Sigismund III, still regarded himself as lawful king of Poland and demanded to be at least compensated; and he wholly denied the right of the Swedes to be in Livonia at all. Failing to solve these troubles by diplomacy, after a conference held under French mediation at Lübeck in 1651–

[1] Dumont, VI, Partie I, 315.
[2] *Ibid.*, p. 115 (Truce of Stuhmsdorf, September 20, 1635).

52, Charles Gustavus X of Sweden made war on the Poles in July, 1655.

Charles Gustavus, who was thirty-three years old when the war began, might be regarded as a Northern Alexander. Poland was a vast crumbling state which, like Persia in the face of the Macedonian phalanx, offered a tempting mark to the compact Swedish regiments. In August, 1655, the King of Sweden was over the Polish frontier and was heading straight for Warsaw, with the Poles flying before him. Franz von Lisola, after seventeen years of incessant diplomatic activity, including two missions to England, was out of work, and was beseeching the Emperor to give him either employment or a pension. The Emperor took the opportunity to provide for him by sending him as representative to the Swedish king's headquarters.[1]

Charles Gustavus' heroic marches, 500 miles into Eastern Europe, and his two separate captures of Warsaw, failed to destroy the somewhat intangible Polish state. One by one Russia, Denmark, and finally Austria (on the advice of Lisola, who found mediation impossible) joined in the war against him. His only ally, and a very doubtful one, was Frederick William, Elector of Brandenburg. This monarch, as Duke of East Prussia, was in feudal allegiance to the King of Poland. But he wore the feudal bonds lightly; and by the Treaty of Königsberg, January 17, 1656, threatened with war by Charles Gustavus and the Swedish army, he transferred his allegiance for East Prussia to the King of Sweden, specifically assuring to the king free passage for Swedish troops through Prussia. Ten months later, when Charles was feeling the pressure of Polish and Russian wars severely, Frederick William obtained from him the Treaty of Labiau, November 10, 1656, and was recognized by Sweden as sovereign, free of all allegiance, in East Prussia.

Poland could not stand the battering of the Swedes for ever. The best diplomatist of the Emperor, Franz von Lisola, was pressing forward a scheme for a coalition. In 1657 Poland was laid waste wherever Charles Gustavus went; but "diplomacy against which he had been running a race, reached its goal." Lisola triumphed. Denmark and Austria entered the field;[2] and

[1] See F. Hirsch, *Der österreichische Diplomat Franz von Lisola und Seine Tätigkeit*, 1655–1660, in *Historische Zeitschrift* (1888), XXIV, 474–6.

[2] W. F. Reddaway in the *Cambridge Modern History*, IV, 583.

Frederick William of Brandenburg, with easy loyalty,[1] retransferred his alliance to John Casimir of Poland and received in return Polish recognition of his complete sovereignty in East Prussia. This was registered in the Treaty of Wehlau (September 19, 1657), one of the *chefs-d'œuvre* of the Austrian Lisola's diplomacy; Charles Gustavus received a definite check.[2]

Charles' attention was now wholly absorbed by his war with Denmark. Not the land, nor the sea, could stop him. He marched from Poland to Stettin. He invaded Holstein; he marched across the ice (January, 1658) over the Little Belt to Fyen, and from there, over the Great Belt, to Zeeland on which is Copenhagen. Before he reached the capital he was met by Danish peace commissioners, and the Treaty of Roeskilde was signed (February 27, 1658). Cromwell's envoy, Meadowe, and the French representative, Terlon, had a part in bringing about the negotiation.[3] By the terms of the peace Scania, Halland and Blekingen became Swedish for ever. The treaty had the hearty approval of England and the Dutch, for by establishing Sweden on the eastern shore of the Sound, it seemed likely to ease the stranglehold of the Danes on the passage of trade between North Sea and Baltic.

At this point the Northern War should have ended. Charles might have had to make concessions to Poland, but he could have retained most of his empire. He still felt unsafe, however, and suspicion is the father of war. He demanded that Denmark should close the Sound to foreign armaments. The Danes, who relied on support from the Dutch, felt that they could not concede this demand. Charles began his second Danish War and was besieging Copenhagen when a Dutch fleet passed the Sound and relieved the city. A Conference of Ambassadors of France and England (George Downing was the English representative, de Thou, the French) with the Dutch Pensionary, John de Witt, at the Hague decided that the war must be stopped on the basis of the Peace of Roeskilde and the freedom of the Sound (Con-

[1] Ranke, a warm admirer of Frederick William, merely says: "After a while he forsook their (the Swedes') alliance": *History of Prussia* (trans. 1849), I, 47.

[2] The treaties concerning the transference and finally the abolition of Prussian vassalage are in Dumont. Treaty of Königsberg, January 17, 1656, is in VI, Partie II, 127; Labiau, November 10, 1656, *ibid.*, 148; Wehlau, September 19, 1657, *ibid.*, 191.

[3] Firth, *The Last Years of the Protectorate* (1909), II, 227. Treaty in Dumont, VI, Partie II, 205.

vention or Concert of the Hague, May 21, 1659). This diplomatic understanding of the Western Powers, the Concert of the Hague (which at this time "became a centre for diplomacy"),[1] may be considered as one of the origins of the modern Concert of Europe. It had at first no effect on Charles; he defied it. But armed military and naval intervention on the part of the Dutch convinced him that he must treat with his enemies for peace; before, however, the Peace Congress began he died of a fever on February 13, 1660, at the age of thirty-seven. The Regency of Sweden, through the mediation of Antoine de Lombres, ambassador of Louis XIV, made an excellent peace at Oliva (near Danzig) with Poland and Brandenburg, May 3, 1660.

The Congress of Oliva was almost as celebrated in Northern affairs as the Congress of Münster and Osnabrück was in the affairs of Central and Western Europe. It was a brilliant assembly and was held in the convent of Oliva. The chief Swedish plenipotentiaries were Magnus de la Gardie and Benoît Oxenstjerna; of Poland, John, Count of Lesno, Palatine of Posnania, and George, Count Lubomirski; the Empire was represented by Count Kolowrat and Franz von Lisola. The discussions lasted from the last days of the year 1659, when the deputies arrived at Oliva, to midnight on May 3, 1660, when the treaty was signed. On the last occasion, after the signature, M. de Lombres took his stand in a room between the two apartments of the Swedish and Polish delegations. From the opposite apartments the Polish and Swedish secretaries advanced, each bearing the copy of the declaration of the plenipotentiaries, and preceded by lackeys carrying torches. Step by step the secretaries advanced, measuring their paces so as to reach the mediator at the same moment. They arrived one at the right hand, the other at the left, of M. de Lombres, who, crossing his arms, took the one copy from the Swedish secretary and the other from the Polish and exchanged them, while the Abbot of Oliva intoned the Te Deum. Outside, cannons fired.[2]

By the Treaty of Oliva, John Casimir, a childless man, renounced

[1] Treitschke, *Politics* (trans. 1916), II, 572. The Concert of the Hague is in Dumont, VI, Partie II, 252. There were actually three Concerts of the Hague in 1659 (May 21, July 24, August 14), each being a separate convention designed to bring increasing pressure to bear on Sweden to make peace. See Koch and Schoell, *Histoire abrégée*, IV, 95–7.

[2] Koch and Schoell, IV, 116, quoting Boehm, *Acta pacis Olivæ*, II, 303.

his claim to the Swedish crown and confirmed the Swedish possession of Livonia;[1] some years afterwards he abdicated and retired to the Abbey of Saint Germain des Près at Paris, where his tomb now remains. Sweden kept Livonia, Brandenburg's sovereignty in East Prussia was confirmed, Poland's right to West Prussia, which Brandenburg coveted, was recognized. Two treaties of peace (Copenhagen with Denmark, made under the mediation of Algernon Sydney and Terlon, June 5, 1660, and Kardis with Russia, made without foreign mediation, July 1, 1661) completed the Northern Settlement. Just before the signature of the Treaty of Copenhagen the Danish and Swedish plenipotentiaries nearly separated in anger. They were only prevented by the aged Danish statesman, Annibal Sehested, who came out of his retirement and besought the delegates of each country, in the name of patriotism, to put aside their national hatreds. Thus the Concert of the Western Powers had made a just peace throughout the Baltic.

After the Peace of Oliva and its complementary treaties, the North had nearly fifteen years of rest. The peace broke down owing to several causes. First, there was the curious unreasonableness of mankind which makes neighbouring peoples apt to dislike each other. Secondly, there was the rankling historical memory of the Danes that they had formerly possessed Scania and thus had held both sides of the Sound. Thirdly, there was the not unnatural desire of Frederick William of Brandenburg for Western (Swedish) Pomerania. Lastly, there was the diplomacy of Louis XIV, who managed to retain Sweden, as well as Poland, in his "system." In 1668 Swedish diplomacy joined with that of England and the Dutch, checking Louis XIV by the formation of the short-lived Triple Alliance of the Hague. In 1672, however, the chief power in Sweden was in the hands of Magnus de la Gardie, whose grandfather had been a very capable French soldier and diplomatist in the Swedish service. Magnus maintained the French tradition of his family, and made a Franco-Swedish alliance on April 3, 1672, on condition of Sweden receiving a large annual subsidy. In 1675 Sweden implemented her agreement with France by invading Brandenburg, but was defeated by the "Great Elector," Frederick William, on June 18, at Fehrbellin. Denmark joined in the war to regain Scania, and things

[1] Dumont, VI, Partie II, 303.

would have gone badly for Sweden had not Louis XIV and the Emperor Leopold, after the conclusion of the Peace of Nymwegen and the end of the war in the West, undertaken to mediate in the Northern War. The mediation of the French was particularly successful, and the Treaty of Saint-Germain-en-Laye between Sweden and Brandenburg (June 29, 1679) and of Fontainebleau between Denmark and Sweden (September 2, 1679) made peace practically on the basis of the *status quo ante bellum*. The French mediator, Pomponne, signed both treaties on behalf of Sweden.[1]

The Northern group of states were a separate system from the Western states—a system in which a war for a balance of power was practically certain to occur from time to time unless Western diplomacy took joint action. Unfortunately the Western diplomatists were hopelessly divided by the violent rivalries of the Spanish Succession Question. Western Europe itself was engaged in interstate war from 1702 to 1713; and the Northern group of states was also engaged in a great war between its own members. This is the last time, as the German historian Treitschke points out, that two great wars could go on separately and simultaneously in Europe. "The great drama of the Scandinavian War was being played out at the same time [as the Spanish Succession War] in the Eastern half of Europe, but the two contests had no connection with each other, and are therefore not to be described as European."[2] The Northern War of 1700–21 has little interest for diplomacy. It arose out of the sort of conditions which tempt diplomatists to throw up their hands and almost to believe that war must come. Sweden, a stationary if not declining Power, had more land outside the Scandinavian peninsula than her military and political resources seemed to warrant. Russia, Denmark, Poland and Brandenburg naturally, if not inevitably, reacted against the Swedish Empire on the Baltic and North Sea coast; and of these Powers Russia and Brandenburg at any rate were still far below the limit of normal development and growth to which their vitality and political resources seemed to entitle them. When the martial but peaceful Charles XI died in 1697 and an inexperienced boy became King of Sweden, there was only one thing which could prevent sooner or later a war of balance

[1] Koch and Schoell, IV, 157, 158.
[2] Treitschke, *Politics*, II, 573.

of power, and that was a Concert of the Western great states; but the Spanish Succession Question made such concert impossible.

People are too apt to use loosely the phrase "war of existence." The great Northern War was not a war of existence for Sweden, as is proved by the fact that after twenty years of struggle and after final and decisive defeat, Sweden was left in existence and with nearly the same territory as she still has to-day. The Northern War was simply a war for a balance of power. This does not excuse the conduct of the states which in 1699 made secret treaties to attack Sweden, but it explains their conduct better than calling the war one of brigandage or partition. If they were determined on bringing about a balance of power they could do so only by two means: one, by war; the other, by assembling a conference of the interested states and arranging for a reallotment of the territories in dispute on a basis of monetary compensation for Sweden. This method of buying and selling, which is perfectly unobjectionable if done with the good-will of all parties (including the inhabitants of the ceded territories), only began to be put into practice, and then merely in regard to minor territorial issues, in the nineteenth century. As a general rule, in modern European history rearrangements of territory have been accomplished only within the framework of a general war.

The idea which actually produced the coalition against Sweden may have originated in the mind of Johann Reinhold von Patkul, a wealthy Lithuanian landowner who had protested against the exactions of Charles XI in Livonia and consequently had been compelled to go into exile. Augustus II, Elector of Saxony and King of Poland, frivolous, ambitious, aping the splendour of Versailles, took Patkul into his service. Augustus was desirous of making the Crown of Poland hereditary in his family, and of regaining Livonia from Sweden. The Livonian exile had a scheme for coalition against his enemy and for partition of her trans-Baltic domains. On September 25, 1699, by a treaty signed at Dresden, Augustus II and Frederick IV of Denmark entered into alliance against Sweden. Charles XII had already given cause of war to Denmark by sending military assistance to the Duke of Holstein who was involved in a quarrel with the Danish Crown. The Saxon General, Carlowitz, was sent on mission to Moscow, and Patkul went secretly in his train. The result was an alliance concluded between Augustus II and Tsar Peter at Preobajenski,

November 11, 1699, signed on the part of Augustus by General Carlowitz.[1] Each member of the coalition was to receive back the territories on the Baltic which Sweden had taken from them. The preparations for war could not be concealed.

The scene at the fateful meeting at Stockholm of the Council of Charles XII has been made famous by Voltaire. The eighteen-year-old sovereign is present, inattentive, indifferent, lying back in his chair with his feet on the table. The statesmen and generals talk in low tones about the armaments preparing against Sweden. One or two propose to meet the coalition by negotiation. Suddenly the king sits upright: "Gentlemen," he says, "I have resolved never to make an unjust war, but never to cease from a lawful war until my enemies are destroyed." Shortly after this, news comes that Saxon troops have invaded Livonia from Poland (May, 1700).

This was the beginning of a Twenty Years' War in which Charles refused to hear of compromise; and without compromise diplomacy can do nothing to stop a war which is in progress. Yet he had brilliant military successes which a prudent diplomacy could have most profitably utilized. In August, 1700, Charles XII descended upon the Island of Zeeland and (aided by the armed mediation of the Dutch and English fleets) forced the King of Denmark to make peace by the Treaty of Travendal (August 18, 1700). This peace was indeed generous and prudent on the part of the Swedish king. It inflicted no punishment, no loss, upon Denmark. On November 20, 1700, a great Russian army was annihilated at Narva in Esthonia. In 1702 the Polish Saxon army was overthrown at Klissow in Poland. Lillieroth, Charles' minister at the Hague, had reported that the English and Dutch Governments were most anxious to have the Northern War stopped in view of the approaching Spanish Succession struggle. Chancellor Benoît Oxenstjerna told Charles that with his military prestige so well established he could take advantage of the international situation in the West to end the Northern War on favourable terms and to become the real arbiter of Europe. Charles brushed aside the suggestion. He occupied Warsaw and declared Augustus II to be dethroned. A young Polish deputy of excellent education, character and lineage, came to Charles and conferred with him

[1] Koch and Schoell, IV, 184. The Russo-Saxon-Polish Alliance was secret, and the text of it has not been published, so far as I know. Carlson, *Geschichte Schwedens* (1887), VI, 80, states only the date of treaty.

in Latin about the vacant throne. Charles, impressed with the character of a disinterested nobleman (so rare in his experience of Poland), leapt to a decision: "This is the man to be king." Accordingly, a form of election was carried through at Warsaw under the eyes of the Swedish soldiers, and Stanislaus Leczynski became king (October 4, 1705). The war was transferred to Saxony until, on September 24, 1706, the plenipotentiaries of Augustus signed a treaty in Charles' camp at Altranstadt, acknowledging Stanislaus as King of Poland. Charles knew that Augustus was wholly deceitful and treacherous. The Treaty of Altranstadt was certain not to be kept. It served the purpose, however, of gaining time for Augustus, who callously handed over Patkul to the Swedish king. Patkul, protesting that the law of nations should protect him, was broken on the wheel.

At Altranstadt Charles, who remained for a year at this camp in Saxony, was courted by all the Powers of Europe. Louis XIV sent a diplomatist, M. Besenval (who managed to cross Germany in the train of a Swedish nobleman), to the camp. Besenval was empowered to propose that Charles should be mediator in peace-negotiations between the warring Powers of the West. Charles, advised by his Foreign Minister, Count Piper, who was in the camp, declined (March, 1707).[1]

M. Besenval's interview with Charles was not uninteresting. The Frenchman drove in his carriage to a large dismal villa, and alighted in the courtyard. There were a number of horses standing in the open air, unhaltered, ungroomed, with sacking on their backs. Only one horse was saddled, ready for the king in case he should suddenly want a gallop.

Entering the house, M. Besenval mounted the stair, and was shown into a room where the king was with Count Piper. M. Besenval saw a tall, strong man, in a blue coat with yellow copper buttons, the lower corners of the coat being tied back, so as to show the greasy vest and breeches. At the top the coat was buttoned close up to the throat. The king wore no gloves, and his weathered hands looked the same colour as his sleeves.

M. Besenval bowed, and began his speech in French. A Swedish secretary replied in the Swedish tongue. The Frenchman then awaited a word from the king: but not a word was uttered. M.

[1] G. Syveton, *Au Camp d'Altranstadt*, in *Rev. d'histoire diplomatique* (XII), 1898, 581 ff.

Besenval, nothing disconcerted, spoke again, this time in German, addressing himself to the king. Still silence. M. Besenval began once more, raising his voice, and asked the king to promise him a second audience, in order that he might communicate the terms on which Louis XIV proposed that Charles should mediate peace between France and the Allies. Silence. The king made a sign of dismissal. Besenval saluted and departed. Sadly he drove off to his lodging at Leipzic, and wrote his report to Minister Torcy.[1]

Besenval stayed for a few weeks longer at Leipzic, and had further, but fruitless, dealings with Count Piper. On April 26 a sensation was created by the arrival of the Duke of Marlborough, the second most famous captain of the age, if Charles XII had to be reckoned the first. The victor of Blenheim and Ramillies had left the Hague on April 20, and in less than a week, travelling by way of Hanover and Halle, within a week reached Altranstadt where Robinson, the English diplomatist in attendance upon Charles, received him.

On April 27 Marlborough had an audience with Charles. Superficially there was a great contrast between, on the one hand, the battered Swedish king, with the ancient war-worn uniform and the military boots reaching up to the thigh, and, on the other, the graceful English officer, with the sweet expression, the charming manner, and the well-cut, fashionable clothes. Nevertheless, the two soldiers understood each other. Charles, who had proved so impassive towards Besenval, now, as soon as Marlborough entered the room, advanced to meet him ; then, leaning upon a table, listened complaisantly to the complimentary speech which Marlborough made, and which Robinson translated for the king into Swedish. The duke's words were :

> I present to your Majesty a letter not from the Chancery but from the heart of the Queen, my mistress, and written with her own hand. Had not her sex prevented it, she would have crossed the sea to see a prince admired by the whole universe. I am in this particular more happy than the Queen, and I wish I could serve some campaigns under so great a general as your Majesty, that I might learn what I yet want to know in the art of war.[2]

After the interview Marlborough was able to report in a dispatch to Harley, the Secretary of State, that Charles seemed well disposed to the interests of the Allies. Next morning, April 28,

[1] G. Syveton, *Au Camp d'Altranstadt*, in *Rev. d'histoire diplomatique* (XII), 1898, p. 588.

[2] Coxe, *Memoirs of the Duke of Marlborough*, chap. 55.

at eight o'clock, Marlborough had an interview at Leipsic with King Augustus II, who, for the time being at peace with Charles XII, was able to move freely in his own dominions. Augustus contracted to hire about 5,000 troops to the Allies. Scarcely was the interview with Augustus over, than Marlborough found King Stanislaus Leczynski of Poland at Altranstadt, eager to meet him (April 29). On the same day Marlborough dined with a certain Baron de Görz, an alert diplomatist, who mysteriously maintained magnificent state on the meagre stipend of an ambassador of the Duke of Holstein-Gottorp. After a final interview with Charles XII, Marlborough left Altranstadt on the afternoon of April 29, journeying by way of Berlin, for he had promised to visit the King of Prussia.

In spite of the favourable assurances which Marlborough had received, Charles still remained rather ominously at Altranstadt, causing anxiety to the Imperial diplomatist Sinzindorff, who had wept when he saw the persuasive Englishman depart. Charles was brooding over the religious persecution inflicted by Joseph I in the neighbouring Austrian province of Silesia. In May, Joseph, much to the disgust of his allies, sent off a large number of his troops (who were needed for the war in Flanders) to make the conquest of Naples and Milan for the Spaniards. The departure of the Austrian troops eased the tension in the Saxon theatre of war and Charles XII turned towards Russia. Thus the military diversions of the Emperor in Italy which had angered the Allies "proved the salvation of the Alliance." [1]

Charles XII at Altranstadt in 1707 was at the high-water mark of his power. All his enemies were beaten; the diplomatists of England, the Netherlands and the Empire would have afforded decisive mediation in the negotiation of a peace favourable to Sweden. But Charles' terms were the restoration of everything that Sweden had lost *plus* the forfeiture of the Polish throne by Augustus of Saxony. Peter the Great, however, though he would concede nearly all the Baltic territory that he had occupied, would not give up the strip along the Neva where he was building St. Petersburg. So Charles, oblivious to the fact that he was failing to take the tide at the flood, went off to his doom at Pultava. This battle (June 27, 1709) was really the beginning of the end, although actually it was only half-way through Charles' military career.

[1] I. S. Leadam, *The History of England*, 1702–1760 (1912), p. 114.

With the invasion of Russia an absolute failure; with the finest Swedish army broken, its best generals prisoners, and the king a fugitive at Bender in Moldavia, the old coalition against Sweden naturally revived. Saxony and Russia renewed their alliance, on condition that Augustus should have his Polish throne back, and that Peter should have Livonia, which hitherto had been considered as the Polish share. Denmark renewed its alliance with Saxony, and war went on hotly against Sweden's continental possessions which inevitably dwindled in spite of heroic resistance extending over years. For four years Charles remained at Bender, drawing a large subsidy from the Porte, and maintaining a Chancery through which he conducted a large amount of diplomatic correspondence. His attendants were for the most part hard-fighting and hard-drinking Swedish officers who had escaped with him from Pultava; but he also had a skilful and active diplomatist in Stanislaus Poniatowski, who transacted the king's business with the Porte. Charles maintained his frugal and martial habits and his industry in affairs throughout this long period of exile, except in the last year when he feigned illness and spent eleven months in bed. Magnus Stenbock, Charles' best captain, made a splendid defence of the Swedish Baltic provinces, while the king at Bender was urging the Turks to create a diversion by attacking Russia.

An hour after midnight on November 21, 1714, a booted, spurred, bespattered horseman in a blue military tunic shouted to a sentinel at the gate of Stralsund that he had dispatches for the commandant. The sentinel admitted the courier; it was the King of Sweden. He had ridden through Wallachia, Transylvania, Hungary, Austria and Saxony. He came back to continue *à outrance* the war which he had been trying to direct in his four years of self-imposed exile at Bender.

The return of the unyielding Charles stimulated all his active or potential enemies into new union. During the summer of 1714 (just before Charles left Bender on his long ride through Austria and the rest of Germany) a Congress of Powers had met at Brunswick to try and arrange a general peace; it failed, however, as the Swedish plenipotentiaries had no authority to cede the Baltic provinces.

Anne, Queen of England, died on August 1, 1714, and the new king, George, desirous of obtaining the Duchies of Bremen and Verden from the Swedes, joined as Elector of Hanover in the coalition against Charles in 1715. Prussia also joined in the league (April, 1715). Two years later Peter the Great offered the friendship of Russia to France, and came to Paris to negotiate. He made an offer to the effect that Russia should take the place which the Swedish alliance had filled in the French diplomatic system in the North. The Regent Orleans, however, preferred to stand by the engagements which he had made with Sweden and also with England, for these engagements were incompatible with a military alliance between France and Russia. The Duc de Saint Simon, a very powerful person in French society, pressed Orleans to accept the Tsar's offer; in his famous Memoirs he writes: "We have good reason to repent of our foolish contempt for Russia and of yielding to the fatal charms of England." [1] The Tsar left Paris, "much struck with the luxury which he saw everywhere, and said he feared it would prove the ruin of France" (June 20, 1717).[2]

Although the Regent would not enter into any binding engagements with Russia, he did not reject the Tsar's offer of friendship; for on August 4, 1717, M. de Chateauneuf, French ambassador at Amsterdam, concluded with the Russian ambassador there (and also with the Prussian) a treaty of friendship and alliance for the maintenance of the Treaties of Utrecht and Baden, and of those which should be made for the settlement of the Northern War. It was through this treaty that France acted, with England, as a mediator when the peace-settlement actually took place. Such are the small beginnings from which French historians trace the entry of Russia into Western Europe.[3]

A last effort to save the situation for Charles XII was made by Görz, the Franconian baron who had entered the service of the Duke of Holstein (then an independent duchy, later joined to the Danish crown in 1773). Görz was a flashy, adroit man, incessantly active and intriguing, with a considerable knowledge and experience both of finance and politics. He naturally found the Duchy of Holstein too limited a sphere for his restless genius. He had already (in 1713) made the dangerous journey to Bender, and offered his services to Charles; and when Charles came back from there Görz at once went to Stralsund and took up his abode

[1] Saint Simon, *Memoirs*, XXVIII. [2] *Ibid.*

[3] Flassan, *Histoire de la Diplomatie française*, IV, 385–97; Wiesener, *Le Régent, l'Abbé Dubois et les Anglais* (1893), II, 17–28.

with him. The daring man with his vast plans appealed to Charles' instincts, and he remained with the king, nominally as minister for Holstein, actually as Swedish Prime Minister and Minister for Foreign Affairs. Görz hoped to break up the anti-Swedish coalition by concessions here and there. Prussia could be bought off by the cession of Stettin; Russia by the cession of Ingria, Carelia and Livonia. Görz negotiated on these terms. Even Vellingk, Charles' best diplomatist, who had been in service for thirty-five years, thought that something might be accomplished in this way.[1] There is ground, however, for thinking that Görz knew all the time of Charles' determination not to make such cessions; the Allies' diplomatists suspected this too. Equally dishonest and rash was Görz's engineering, in collusion with Count Gyllenborg, Swedish ambassador at London, but without the knowledge of Charles XII, a Jacobite plot in England with promises of help from a Swedish fleet and army.[2] His object seems to have been to gain Jacobite subsidies for Charles XII rather than to promote a Jacobite revolution. The plot was discovered (January, 1717) and Görz, who was engaged in one of his many diplomatic journeys, was imprisoned for a short time by the Dutch authorities.[3] After being released, he made energetic efforts to negotiate peace with Peter the Great. A Conference was held at Löfö, on one of the Aland Islands, in 1718–19 between Görz and Gyllenborg for Sweden, and Bruce and Osterman for Russia, but without result. Charles, meanwhile, was invading Norway, which was joined to the Crown of Denmark; if he could conquer a province or two he would then have some pledges with which Görz could negotiate. While engaged in this Norwegian expedition Charles met his death in the trenches on December 12, 1718.

On the death of Charles XII his sister Ulrica Eleonora was proclaimed Queen of Sweden; a council of high noble officials administered the kingdom. Görz, who was in Stockholm at the time, on a visit from the Aland Conference which was still going on, was arrested. In March, 1719, after a travesty of a trial, he was executed for treason. He had lived well, maintaining a splendid table and household, occupying magnificent houses; his encouragement of Charles' military obstinacy and his own insincere diplo-

[1] Chance, *George I and the Northern War*, 245. [2] Chance, 184.

[3] For the imprisonment, see *Lettres inédites de Görtz*, in *Rev. d'hist. diplomatique* (1898), XII, 270–3.

macy had probably lengthened the war; nevertheless, he had been labouring for peace, though not always through the best means, and he had not betrayed Sweden.[1]

The new Swedish Government, in which the Chancellor Arved Horn, a very experienced official, held chief power, ended the long war, making use of the diplomacy of Lord Carteret, British Minister at Stockholm, and of M. de Campredon, French ambassador at Stockholm. The cession of the Duchies of Bremen and Verden ensured peace with Hanover, and was Carteret's first success (Treaty of Stockholm between Sweden and Hanover, November 20, 1719). Sweden secured the alliance of Hanover and a payment of one million rix-dollars for Bremen and Verden. The withdrawal of Hanover from the war meant that the coalition was really at an end. Carteret and Campredon also had no difficulty in convincing the Swedish Government that it must sacrifice Stettin to Prussia (Treaty of Peace between Sweden and Prussia, February 1, 1720). Nobody in Sweden took any interest in Stanislaus, who had never any substantial support in his own country; accordingly there was no obstacle in the way of peace with Augustus II of Saxony and Poland. Carteret, in a mission which he undertook to Copenhagen, persuaded the Danes to restore Rügen and Pomerania to Sweden in return for an indemnity of 600,000 dollars. Sweden also renounced her exemption from paying Sound dues.[2] In order to overcome the unwillingness of Denmark to make peace on these terms, Carteret and Campredon undertook, on behalf of Great Britain and France, a guarantee of the union of Schleswig with the Danish Crown.[3] All these negotiations, which were over by the end of the year 1720, were materially forwarded by the presence of a British fleet under Admiral Norris in the Baltic.

With Russia (of which Great Britain wished to restrict the power on the Baltic)[4] Carteret had not so much influence, for Peter the Great knew that the English fleet could not bring much pressure to bear on him. Accordingly in the Treaty of Nystadt in Finland (August 30, 1721) he made no concessions, gaining Ingria, Carelia,

[1] See G. Syveton, *L'Erreur de Gœrtz,* in *Rev. d'hist. diplomatique* (IX), 1895, 420, and (X), 1896, 42.

[2] Treaty of Stockholm between Sweden and Denmark, June 3/12, 1720, in Dumont, VIII, Partie II, 29.

[3] The British guarantee, which was signed by Lord Polwarth, colleague of Carteret, is dated Friederichsbourg, July 23, 1720. The French guarantee was signed at Stockholm, June 3/14, 1720. Both guarantees—conventions and the ratifications—are in Dumont, VIII, Partie II, 32-3.

[4] See Instructions to Carteret in Chance, 334.

Esthonia and Livonia, and even part of Finland, including Viborg and the country to the west of that fortress. The active French diplomatist, Campredon, acting on instructions from the Regent Orleans, had crossed from Stockholm to Russia, and performed valuable services as mediator at the Peace of Nystadt.[1]

The long war was not fatal to Sweden, though it was the end of her martial greatness. Her subsequent history has been one of strong though peaceful development. In the Baltic a stable balance of power was attained. The subjection of Ingria, Carelia, Livonia and part of Finland to Russia was a disaster to the Nordic peoples there, which was not undone until they released themselves at the time of the Russian revolution of 1917. Had they remained under Sweden they would probably have obtained their emancipation sooner and might have taken part in a Baltic federation. But the diplomatists of 1719–20 made the best settlement which was possible after twenty years of war.

The country of which the fate was really sealed by the result of the Great Northern War was Poland. This unhappy land could not maintain itself by its own force ; but a powerful Sweden, fortified by provinces on the eastern and southern coasts of the Baltic, would have supported an independent Poland against Russia ; and this support, combined with the French alliance with both Sweden and Poland, would have been sufficient in all probability, to sustain the Poles. But after 1721 Sweden ceased to be a Great Power and to have any influence upon the destinies of Central Europe ; and with the fall of Sweden, French influence, so often and for so long linked to that country, was diminished, though it did not disappear from the North. "It was by the same Treaties of Westphalia," wrote Louis XIV to his ambassador with Charles XII, "that France and Sweden had acquired provinces in Germany. This reciprocal interest is the solid foundation of their close connection." [2] The Northern Settlement made by the treaties of 1720–21 destroyed this foundation.

[1] Schefer, *La Monarchie Française et l'Alliance Suédoise*, in *Revue d'histoire diplomatique* (1892), VI, 100. The Treaty of Nystadt (in French) is in Dumont, VIII, Partie II, 36.

[2] Dispatch of January 20, 1707, in Geffroy, *Recueil des Instructions données aux ambassadeurs de France : Suède*, 228. For further information on the subject of this chapter, see Carlson, *Geschichte Schwedens* (1887), Band VI ; V. O. Klachevsky, *A History of Russia* (trans. 1926), Vol. IV ; J. F. Chance, *George I and the Northern War* (1909) ; R. N. Bain, *Charles XII* (1895) ; E. Godley, *Charles XII of Sweden* (1928).

CHAPTER XXV

TURKEY AND EUROPE, TO THE PEACE OF PASSAROWITZ

The capture of Constantinople in 1453 was only a stage in the conquest of South-Eastern Europe by the Turks. The famous Suleiman I, who reigned from 1520 to 1566, advanced his standards twice to Vienna, and though he failed to gain Austrian territory, he held the greater part of Hungary. The Habsburgs several times consented to pay tribute to the Porte, which would enter into no definite treaties with Austria, but only into truces for a term of years. Francis I and subsequent French kings, on the other hand, were uniformly friendly with the Porte. France received valuable privileges by acts or charters of the Sultan, known as capitulations. From the sixteenth century nearly all the states of Europe maintained diplomatic missions at Constantinople. One of the Imperial ambassadors, Busbecq, has left graphic *Turkish Letters*.

Ogier Ghiselin de Busbecq, born at Comines in Flanders in 1522, was sent as ambassador to Constantinople in 1554. Busbecq's predecessor, John Maria Malvezzi, had been imprisoned by Sultan Suleiman for two years on account of an Austrian invasion of Transylvania. Malvezzi only emerged from prison to die. Busbecq himself was under surveillance and more or less strict confinement to his villa for part of his time, and he was unable to make peace between the Sultan and the Emperor Charles, although he did manage to conclude a truce. In answer to an inquiry from his friend and correspondent, Nicholas Michault, whether he ever left his villa at Constantinople, Busbecq wrote: "I do not generally do so unless I have dispatches from the Emperor for presentation to the Sultan, or instructions to protest against the ravages and malpractices of the Turkish garrisons. If I wished from time to time to take a ride through the city with my custodian, permission would probably not be refused. . . . What I enjoy is the country and the fields, not the city—especially a city which is almost falling to pieces, and of whose former glory nothing remains except its splendid position." [1] Busbecq was fortunate enough (and brave enough) to be able to undertake a journey into Asia Minor, where he made the first copy of Augustus' *Monumentum Ancyranum* at Angora, and whence he brought back to Europe the lilac, the tulip and the syringa.

The permanent English mission dates from 1583, when William Harborne, a "Turkey merchant," was accredited by Queen Elizabeth to represent her at the Porte. It was not until 1606 that Turkey entered into regular diplomatic relations with European states. In this year, November 11, Achmet I made with the Emperor Rudolf the Treaty of Sitvatorok. For the first time the Turkish commissioners had full powers signed by the Sultan; they referred to the sovereign with whom they were treating as Emperor; and they concluded a definite peace.[2] Regular relations between the two countries were established by the following curious article of the treaty: "When ambassadors go to both Emperors, the ambassador shall treat the Emperor as a father, and the Emperor shall treat the ambassador as a son." [3]

It has often been said that the political demoralization at Constantinople and the frequent palace-revolutions there during the Thirty Years' War were fortunate for Austria and for all Europe, rendered helpless by the religious struggle. But it could be asserted with equal force that the wars of Europe were equally fortunate for the Turks, who might otherwise have been driven out of the Balkan lands by an undistracted Austria and a united Empire. The Porte was in a very bad way at that time, and Sir Thomas Roe, English ambassador at Constantinople from 1621 to 1628, reported on its condition in words which strongly forecast the "sick man" expressions of later statesmen. The dispatches of Roe relating the intrigues of himself and other representatives of Protestant states to arouse the Turks for an invasion of Austria do not make pleasant reading.

When Europe had recovered from her religious wars the Turks

[1] Busbecq, *Turkish Letters* (trans. 1927), 132.
[2] Creasy, *History of the Ottoman Turks* (1858), I, 384.
[3] Treaty (called *Instrumentum Pacificationis*) of Sitvatorok, art. 1, in Dumont, V, Partie II, p. 78. It is in Latin.

had recovered from their political decadence. Their revival was brought about by the administrative abilities of the famous Kiuprili family, which provided the Sultan with almost a dynasty of Grand Viziers. In 1664 Achmet Kiuprili led a great Turkish army from Belgrade into Austria, but was decisively defeated by Montecuculi at the battle of Mohacs near the Convent of St. Gothard on the Raab. A corps of French volunteers had been permitted by Louis XIV to serve with the Austrians. This battle saved Austria and brought about an agreement for a truce of twenty years, signed at Vasvar on August 10, 1664. Against Venice Kiuprili waged an energetic campaign which led to the capture of Candia in 1669. In 1672 Turkey went to war with Poland.

On November 10, 1675, the great Polish soldier, John Sobieski, won a great victory over the Turks at Khoczin. Next year he became King of Poland, with the title of John III. The war with Turkey continued ; but Louis XIV, who had been for years paying a pension of 20,000 livres a year to Sobieski, and 20,000 livres to Sobieski's wife, was labouring to end the Polo-Turkish struggle. Louis' object in this was to free the hands of the Turks for an invasion of Austria. Louis took council with his ministers on the Turkish question on April 15, 1676. Pomponne was absolutely against the project of letting loose the Turkish armies upon Austria. Colbert and Le Tellier did not like the plan of attacking a Christian prince with Mohammedan forces, but thought it justifiable in the present emergency in Western Europe for purely military reasons. Louvois was not present, but his views were well known. Louis decided in favour of assisting Turkey. "And I know one person," he said, in rising from the council table, "who will be happy to see the Turks in Hungary: M. de Louvois."[1] The result of this council, and of the diplomatic labours of M. Forbin, French ambassador at Warsaw, and of M. Nointel, French ambassador at Constantinople, was the Treaty of Zurawna, October 16, 1676, between Poland and Turkey. Poland was released from tribute to Turkey, but surrendered portions of Podolia and of the Ukraine to the Porte.[2] Although Louis XIV's scheme for bringing the Porte into the war against Austria did not immediately

[1] See J. du Hamel de Breuil, *Sobieski et sa Politique*, in *Rev. d'histoire diplomatique* (1893), VII, 501.

[2] Dumont, VII, Partie I, 325.

bear fruit (for Peter the Great of Russia diverted the Turkish armies by a vigorous attack), it helped to bring on the terrible crisis of 1682–83 when the Turks nearly took Vienna itself. Fortunately for Austria and for all Europe, by this time Sobieski had abandoned his dependence upon France and had concluded a treaty of alliance and mutual defence against the Turks with the Emperor, March 31, 1683, under the mediation of Pope Innocent XI.[1]

Two months later the Turkish armies were battering at the gates of Vienna. The Emperor Leopold I invoked Polish aid under the terms of the recently signed treaty. When King John Sobieski arrived with the chivalry of Poland on a height overlooking Vienna, he is said to have looked down on a seething mass of two million Asiatic fighters. In the ensuing battle the Turkish host was destroyed. Europe hailed the victory as presaging the expulsion of the Turks from the Continent. But war in the West, the "War of the League of Augsburg," was already beginning, and Louis XIV himself was encouraging the Turks in their war with the Emperor and was working hard to restore the old alliance with Poland. King John Sobieski, however, in spite of a vigorous and skilful French diplomacy at Vienna, remained loyal to the Imperial alliance.[2] The campaigns of Prince Eugène and Prince Louis of Baden on the Danube are justly celebrated in Austrian history, as is also the great campaign of the Venetian Morosini in the Peloponnese (or Morea). But, as in every other department of European life, the Spanish Succession Question cast its shadow over the hopeful armies of the Emperor on the Danube. The Maritime Powers—the British and the Dutch—were anxious to bring about a pacification which would set the Emperor free to concentrate on the problem in the West. Lord Paget, British ambassador at Constantinople, offered good offices to Turkey. He was warmly supported by the Dutch minister. The representatives of the Maritime Powers at Vienna were equally energetic in advocating a settlement.

A Peace Congress was assembled in the village of Carlowitz (in the district of Mitrovitz in Hungary) on the Danube on

[1] J. du Hamel de Breuil, *Sobieski et sa Politique*, in *Rev. d'histoire diplomatique* (1894), VIII, 73.

[2] See *Polnische Wirtschaft und Französische Diplomatie*, 1692 *bis* 1697, in *Historische Zeitschrift* (1859), 2 Heft, p. 381 ff.

October 24, 1698. There were present representatives of the fighting states—Austria, Venice, Poland, Russia and Turkey. Lord Paget and his Dutch colleague, James Colyer, acted as mediators. This was the first general European congress in which either Russia or Turkey took part. The basis of peace put forward by the mediators was *uti possidetis*—each party to retain what its armies held at the time when the negotiations began. This principle was very favourable to Austria, which had lost nothing and had gained much territory. The Turkish interests were defended by a diplomatist of the celebrated Greek family of Mavrogordato. The terms on January 26, 1699, gave to Austria all Hungary and Transylvania, but not that large region between the Marosh and the Danube called the Banat of Temesvar. Venice obtained the Morea, Poland Kaminiec (i.e. the part of Podolia lost by the Treaty of Vasvar), Russia Azov.[1]

When Charles XII was at Bender he was urgent in putting before the Porte plans for the invasion of Russia. He employed on missions to Constantinople the able Polish diplomatist, Count Poniatowski. In 1711 Charles had his wish, for war broke out between Russia and Poland; and Tsar Peter, who crossed the Pruth into Moldavia, was trapped by the Turkish Grand Vizier Baltaji Mehemet in his camp, but escaped by making the Treaty of the Pruth, July 21, 1711. Peter lost Azov, but saved his life and his army. Nobody has ever succeeded in completely accounting for the astonishing leniency of the Turkish terms; presents were given by Peter, but Baltaji would have had the whole Russian army and all its possessions if he had waited. The words of the Treaty of the Pruth explicitly state that Peter was at the mercy of the Turks: "In as much as by the grace of God the victorious Mussulman army having straitly enclosed the Tsar of Muscovy with all his army in the neighbourhood of the village of the Pruth, he has himself demanded peace. . . ."[2] Count Poniatowski, who was present in the Turkish camp, did everything he could to prevent the giving of terms. At any rate, instead of simply requiring Azov and a few places of minor importance, Baltaji might at least have demanded that Peter should restore the con-

[1] Dumont, VII, Partie II, 448-58. The Peace of Carlowitz was comprised in three treaties of the same date, one with the Emperor, another with Augustus II of Poland, the third with Venice.

[2] Dumont, VIII, Partie I, 275 (in French, from a copy sent to Dumont from Constantinople).

quered Baltic provinces to Charles XII; for the consolidation of Russian power in the Baltic provinces only set Russia free to pursue her designs against the Turkish Empire.

In 1715 the Porte resolved to attack Venice, a feeble and declining state, in order to regain the Morea, in which Venetian rule had proved to be exceedingly unpopular. The Emperor Charles VI only joined in the war after the Morea had fallen before the Turkish armies. The victory of Prince Eugène at Peterwardein, August 5, 1716, led to the siege and capture of Belgrade in the following year. Thoroughly defeated, the Porte again accepted the offer of good offices from the English and Dutch ambassadors. The Maritime Powers, and France and the Empire all wanted the war to cease, because Western Europe was being disturbed by the underground activities of the Cardinal Alberoni, Chief Minister of Spain. A peace-conference took place in tents at the little Serbian town, Passarowitz, in June, 1718, with the British and Dutch diplomatists (Sir Robert Sutton and Count James Colyer) mediating. By the Treaty of Passarowitz, signed on July 21, 1718, Venice gave up the Morea to Turkey, but Austria-Hungary gained the Banat, Belgrade, Northern Serbia, and Little Wallachia. This treaty marks the furthest step that Austria ever made towards Salonica and the Ægean.

During the seventeenth century foreign diplomatists began to exercise an extraordinary influence at Constantinople. The Englishman, Sir Thomas Roe, ambassador from 1621 to 1628, carried considerable weight in the counsels of the Porte. More extraordinary still was the career of James or Jacobus Colyer, the mediator, along with Great Britain, of the peaces of Carlowitz and Passarowitz. He was at the Dutch embassy at Constantinople for nearly forty years, from 1686 to his death in 1725. His sister resided with him at Constantinople, and was high in the favour of the Sultana Validé.[1] During about two years of Colyer's tenure of the Dutch embassy, Lady Mary Wortley Montagu was at Constantinople where her husband was British ambassador (1716–18) before the arrival of Sir Robert Sutton. Lady Mary's letters give an interesting description of life in Turkey in Europe. On the other hand, it was the presence of a Turkish embassy in 1723 at Paris, and the opportunities for conversing with the

[1] A. J. van der Aa, *Biographisch Woordenboek der Nederlanden*, III, 640.

ambassador Mehemet Effendi, which suggested to the observant and philosophic Montesquieu the writing of *Lettres Persanes*, his famous ironical description of Western society.[1]

[1] For further information on the subject of this chapter, see J. von Hammer-Purgstall, *Geschichte des Osmanischen Reiches* (1827), Band VI–VII; Creasy, *History of the Ottoman Turks* (1858); Sir T. Roe, *Negotiations in his Embassy to the Porte*, 1621–1628 (1740); De la Jonquière, *Histoire de l'Empire Ottoman* (1914), Tome I.

PART IV
THE EIGHTEENTH CENTURY

CHAPTER XXVI

TWENTY-FIVE YEARS OF PEACE. I

The Quadruple Alliance of London

The international situation after the Peace Treaties of Utrecht, 1713, was somewhat like that which subsequently existed in Europe after the Treaties of Vienna of 1815. At each of these settlements, 1713 and 1814, an international balance of power had been made which on the whole satisfied the needs of Europe at the time. This balance was not rigid, but could be adjusted, and actually was adjusted, from time to time, in the five and twenty years after each treaty.

France, which had emerged with credit from the War of the Spanish Succession, retained throughout the eighteenth century, down to the Revolution, her eminence, if not pre-eminence, in diplomacy. She was active—too active. "Compared with the majestic and solid order of French diplomacy in the preceding century . . . how poor are the designs of France in their twisted and undecided form, how sterile her efforts in their excessive multiplicity!"[1] Louis XIV at the end of his life had seen clearly into the future. He had counselled his great-grandson of France and his grandson of Spain to abandon the traditional hostility of Bourbon for Habsburg, and to make the two great ruling houses into friends.[2]

The twenty-five years after the Peace of Utrecht were not entirely without wars. There was a brief war in Sicily in 1718; there was a naval war and a land-siege of Gibraltar in 1727; there

[1] Bourgeois, *Manuel historique,* I, 455. [2] *Ibid.,* p. 462.

was a war between 1733 and 1738 in which five important states took part, yet which was neither a general nor a very costly war. Finally, there was a Turkish war.

Only one state or government in this period seemed really to believe in war as a means of adjusting the international territorial system ; this state was Spain. The rest of Europe was obstinately determined to live at peace. But an act of pure aggression, the attack of Frederick II of Prussia upon Austria in 1740 began an era of general wars again, and made a disturbance in the European system which did not really cease until 1815. The Silesian War of 1740, therefore, may be compared with the Crimean War of 1854, which ended the thirty years' peace after the Treaties of Vienna.

The British Government was undoubtedly the leading diplomatic force in Europe in the post-Utrecht period. The settlement of 1713–14 suited Great Britain. The Belgic Netherlands were in the hands of Austria, a non-maritime power. The possession of Gibraltar by Great Britain and the dispossession of Spain from Naples and Sicily ensured that the commerce of the Mediterranean should be unimpeded. The fact that the King of Great Britain was also Elector of Hanover afforded to the British Government a powerful means of influencing diplomacy among the German states.

George I knew that he was only accepted as King of Great Britain in order to ensure the Protestant succession and the maintenance of parliamentary government. With domestic policy he could not interfere, but in foreign affairs his Government permitted him a good deal of influence. The chief minister in the British Cabinet after the fall of the Tories in 1714 was the Secretary of State for the Southern Department, General Stanhope, trained in diplomacy as well as in arms, who had been a hard-fighting soldier in Spain during the Succession War, but who now adopted the Tory policy of peace and entered into alliance with France.

The true diplomatist has no prejudices. If alliance with a recent enemy will promote peace, he has no difficulty in shaking hands. But so long as Louis XIV was alive, France officially thought only of revenge, although the old king himself steadily refused to take any step that would involve the country in another war.[1] The British ambassador at Paris, Lord Stair, took no pains

[1] See Perkins, *France under the Regency*, pp. 372–3.

to show the tact and consideration which might have mollified the injured king.[1] Accordingly Stanhope instructed Cadogan, British Minister at the Hague, to renew if possible the alliance with the States-General and with the Emperor. Cadogan conducted the negotiations with Charles VI at Antwerp in the Austrian Netherlands, and later at Vienna, which Stanhope himself also visited. The alliance of Great Britain, the States-General, and the Emperor was renewed by the Barrier Treaty signed at Antwerp on November 15, 1715. This was a sort of " Locarno " treaty, aimed, not indeed at neutralizing, but at guaranteeing the inviolability of the frontier of the Belgic (Austro-Netherlands) provinces towards France. The chief terms were : (1) The Emperor undertook never to cede any of the towns or fortresses of his provinces in the Low Countries (the Austrian Netherlands) to France. (2) The Emperor and the Dutch agreed to maintain a corps of 30,000 to 35,000 troops in the Austrian Netherlands, the Emperor furnishing three-fifths and the Dutch two-fifths. Of this corps, the Dutch troops were to garrison, under Dutch governors, Namur, Tournai, Menin, Furnes, Warneton, Ypres and Knoque. Only in Dendermonde was there to be a mixed garrison of Dutch and Austrian troops, under an Austrian commander. (3) Towards the maintenance of the Dutch garrisons and of the fortresses entrusted to them, the Emperor agreed to pay annually a sum of 1,250,000 Dutch florins, secured on the revenues of the Austrian Netherlands. (4) The Emperor ceded Venloo and Stevenswerth in full sovereignty to the Dutch. (5) The commerce of the Austrian Netherlands was to depend upon the stipulations of the Treaty of Münster of 1648. (6) Great Britain guaranteed the execution and observance of the Treaty in all its articles, if necessary with all her military and naval forces.[2]

By the Barrier Treaty the Emperor agreed to the imposition

[1] Cp. L. G. Wickham Legg, *British Diplomatic Instructions* (1925), p. xxiv. Stair's conduct indeed showed more than coldness. He even contemplated another war, to be made in alliance with the Emperor, in 1716, for the dismemberment of France! See Syveton, *Un projet de démembrement de la France*, in *Rev. d'histoire diplomatique*, VI (1892), 497–517.

[2] Dumont, VIII, Partie I, 458 ; Koch and Schoell, I, 228–9. This was the third Barrier Treaty. The first was dated October 29, 1709 ; the second was dated January 29, 1713. All three were signed at the Hague. By the first and second treaties (of which the second only remained in force after 1713) the Dutch guaranteed the Protestant Succession in Great Britain with, if necessary, a corps of 6,000 men. See above, p. 180.

of a remarkable servitude over his dominions in the Low Countries; and although the military stipulations did not in practice add much to the degree of safety of the Austrian Netherlands, the presence of Dutch garrisons and governors does not appear to have caused serious friction, nor to have diminished the reputation of the Austrians, which proves that states can give up certain elements in their absolute sovereignty without suffering discomfort or loss of prestige.

Under the Treaties of Utrecht (1713), Rastadt and Baden (1714) the Dutch were to remain in possession of the former Spanish Netherlands until the Emperor should come to an agreement with the Dutch over the Barrier. It was to deal with this that the Congress of Antwerp had met. With the conclusion of the Barrier Treaty of 1715 the Emperor entered into possession of the Austrian Netherlands.

Louis XIV died in September, 1715, leaving a five-year-old great-grandson to occupy the throne. The Regent, Duke of Orleans, would be, in the event of the death of the young king, in the line of succession; so would Philip V of Spain, but he was barred by the Treaty of Utrecht. Orleans therefore had no personal interest in supporting the obvious Spanish desire to upset the Utrecht settlement; indeed, to give such support would merely have been to invite another European war. The Regent was for peace, and had no prejudice against Great Britain. George I, accompanied by Stanhope, set out on a journey to Hanover. They passed by the Hague and stopped awhile. The Abbé Dubois, once the Regent Orleans' tutor, now his chief adviser, came to the Hague under the name of Saint-Albin, giving himself out to be an amateur of books and paintings (July, 1716).[1] He gave to George I and Stanhope assurances that France would not support the Jacobites. The discussions were continued at Hanover, whither Dubois also went, still in the character of Saint-Albin (August to October, 1716). When Dubois left Hanover he took away signed articles of alliance (October 11). The final negotiations took place at the Hague, where the British envoys were Horatio Walpole (younger brother of Sir Robert) and Lord Cadogan. On January 4, 1717, a Triple Alliance was signed on behalf of Great Britain, France, and the United Netherlands. This alliance contained a confirmation and guarantee of the Utrecht

[1] Wiesinger, I, 281.

settlement. France undertook to induce the Pretender to leave Avignon (which was Papal territory) and to go "beyond the Alps."[1] One of its fruits was the arrest by the Dutch of the magnificent adventurer Görz, the adviser of Charles XII (February, 1717), who was scheming for a Jacobite rising in England. The Triple Alliance brought France back actively into the European Concert. It is the real end of the Grand Alliance of Powers which had been formed in order to withstand the domination of Louis XIV. France now, "delivered from this sort of European blockade, breathed again."[2]

The opening of archives and the researches of scholars have brought to light in French diplomatic history of this time a curious feature, which continued to mark it throughout the whole reign of Louis XV. This was *Le Secret*, which before long became almost a department of state, a private foreign office of the Regent and, after him, of the king. Side by side with the known, accredited diplomacy, of which, for instance, under the Regent, the Abbé Dubois was the head, there was another diplomacy maintained by the Regent and Dubois through agents unknown to the regular French ambassadors and acting on different instructions. Thus France had a double diplomacy—the regular, official policy, which was publicly recognized, and the Secret (*le Secret*), which might be employed either to support the official diplomacy, or to control and even undermine it, and which, because it represented the absolute power of the Crown, could commit the nation in advance just as much as could the official diplomatists. This vicious system must have done more than anything else to lower the efficiency of the French diplomatic service. Monarchs of other countries occasionally used a similar double system. The Emperor Charles VI is known to have conducted diplomatic affairs without the knowledge of his Chancellor, Sinzendorff.[3]

The eighteenth century was an age curiously compounded of cosmopolitanism and national egotism. In no period were people of capacity able to pass more easily from country to country and to rise to the highest positions. On the other hand, in no period were the governments more eager to extend their frontiers and

[1] Cp. Instructions to Lord Stair, June 7, 1716: "the removal of the Pretender from Avignon, which we shall always look upon as part of France" (*British Diplomatic Instructions*, II, France, 106).

[2] Wiesinger, I, 465.

[3] *Allgemeine Deutsche Biographie*, XXXIV, 411, s.v. Sinzendorff.

to add to their possessions. The talented stranger became the servant of the national egotism. Cardinal Alberoni, a Parmesan priest, is an instance. He had been discovered by the Duc de Vendôme during the Spanish Succession War in Italy, and had come to Spain with the Duc as secretary in the campaign of 1710, and had remained in the country. The Princesse des Ursins, who was still all-powerful at the Spanish court, took his advice about a new wife for Philip V after the death of his first wife, Marie Louise of Savoy, in 1714. Alberoni suggested Elizabeth Farnese, niece of the Duke of Parma. The marriage was accomplished; and Queen Elizabeth at once dismissed the Princesse des Ursins and induced Philip V to make Alberoni First Minister of Spain. The new minister set himself with the most intense application to restore the strength of that country and to regain its lost territories in Italy.

In August, 1717, Europe was startled by the news that a Spanish fleet had left Barcelona on an obviously warlike expedition. Sardinia, one of the Austrian acquisitions under the Utrecht settlement, fell an easy prey; Sicily, the share of the Duke of Savoy by the Utrecht treaties, was the next objective of Alberoni. An assault upon Naples, an Austrian kingdom since the conclusion of the Spanish Succession War, would follow next. The Spanish expedition was a most cynical and reckless assault upon the Utrecht settlement, a system which, however defective, offered a harassed Europe at that time the only practicable means of peace and progress. It brought Austria back into line with the Maritime Powers.[1] Stanhope at once sent his confidential secretary, Luke Schaub, a Swiss, to Vienna (February, 1718). Schaub, who had previously (1715) been secretary to the British Embassy at Vienna, carried with him a draft treaty which provided for the accession of Austria to the Triple Alliance of Great Britain, France, and the United Netherlands. At Vienna he had the co-operation of Saint Saphorin, another Swiss, who, a diplomatist in the Hanoverian service, was now British and Hanoverian ambassador at Vienna. Charles V seemed ready to agree to a quadruple alliance, yet delayed week after week. Schaub went on to Paris (June, 1718). Dubois went to London, and stayed there for the first nine months of the year 1718. Stanhope crossed over to Paris (June–July, 1718). The Council of Regency was persuaded to join with Great

[1] H. Benedikt, *Das Konigreich Neapel unter Kaiser Karl VI* (1927), p. 188.

Britain in making very strong representations to Vienna. Saint Saphorin, who was a man of ability, and who had considerable influence at Vienna, gave great assistance. At London, Dubois, Secretary of State Craggs in the absence of Stanhope, and Pentenriedter (ambassador of the Emperor) negotiated in concert. The result was the Quadruple Alliance, concluded in London on August 2, 1718.[1] The Four Powers agreed to support each other with certain forces, if any one of them was attacked in its territories. A separate treaty, made for the Emperor and the Duke of Savoy (who was also King of Sicily), arranged that Savoy (subject to his consent) should cede Sicily to the Emperor (who already had Naples under the Utrecht treaties) and should receive Sardinia in exchange. The indefatigable Stanhope made a journey from Paris to Madrid (July 23–August 27) in order to persuade Alberoni and Philip V to give up their designs upon Italy without further fighting, but the Spanish statesmen would not listen to him.

Alberoni's magnificent design was checked. He had intended not merely to conquer the south of Italy, but (in order to break up the diplomatic group of the "Utrecht" Powers at its centre) to dethrone George I through a Jacobite rising supported by Spain and Sweden. The formation of the Quadruple Alliance, proclaiming as it did the solidarity of the "Utrecht" Powers, might by itself have induced Alberoni to retire. Unfortunately his expeditionary force had already conquered Sicily; and Admiral Byng, meeting the Spanish fleet off Cape Passaro on August 11, 1718, annihilated it. This battle was like one of the fights of the next century, Navarino, fought by parties which were nominally at peace with each other. Great Britain actually declared war on Spain on December 18, 1718, and France declared war in the following January. The dramatic end of Charles XII in his invasion of Norway on December 11, 1718, caused a sigh of relief to go through Whig circles in England, for Charles was the only effective ally that Alberoni could find for his Jacobite plots. All the Spanish warlike ventures went wrong at once, and the few hundred Spanish soldiers who actually landed at Glenshiel in Ross-shire in June, 1719, were easily captured. The eccentric but extremely clever and fascinating Lord Peterborough (a hero of the War of the Spanish Succession and an inveterate traveller) went on a mission to the Duke of Parma, the uncle of the Queen of Spain. Peter-

[1] Dumont, VIII, Partie I, 531–41.

borough persuaded the duke to write a letter to his niece, who had complete influence over her weak husband, asking her to obtain the dismissal of Alberoni and assuring her that France and England would not make peace with Spain until that was done.[1] Queen Elizabeth was angry with the First Minister in any case. With all his grand schemes shattered in irretrievable disasters, Alberoni was dismissed from office, and retired to resume his clerical vocation in Italy. Peterborough paid for his success with a spell of imprisonment; for while he delayed in Italy the Pope Clement XI had him arrested and incarcerated in Urbino. The Regent Orleans procured his release.

The only change in the Utrecht settlement effected by the disturbances of 1718 was that Sicily (according to the terms of the Quadruple Alliance) was given up by the Duke of Savoy, Victor Amadeus, to Austria which, in return, gave him Sardinia. This was done after the battle of Cape Passaro and when Victor Amadeus acceded to the Quadruple Alliance in November, 1718. He had shown himself unable to defend Sicily, so the Utrecht Powers transferred the island to Austria, which already had Naples. But Victor Amadeus could have pointed out that Austria had made no better defence of Sardinia against Alberoni's force than he had made of Sicily.

The Treaties of Madrid (France and Spain, March 27, 1721; Great Britain and Spain, June 13, 1721) ended the desultory war. Both Stanhope and George I had held out hopes to Spain of ceding Gibraltar, but opposition in Parliament prevented them from going on with this proposal. The Emperor and Spain did not sign peace, although there were no actual hostilities in progress, until they made the First Treaty of Vienna, April 30, 1725.[2]

During the reigns of Louis XIV, Queen Anne, and George I, the Law of Nations concerning the privileges and status of diplomatists assumed coherence and definiteness. The rule generally adopted was that diplomatic agents in a foreign state should have the same immunities as their sovereigns in similar circumstances.

[1] Bourgeois, *Le Secret des Farnèse*, 369.

[2] For further details on the subject of this chapter see W. Michael, *Englische Geschichte im achtzehnten Jahrhundert* (1896), Vol. I; L. Wiesener, *Le Régent l'Abbé Dubois et les Anglais* (1891); E. Bourgeois, *La Diplomatie Secrète au XVIIIe Siècle*, I–III; L. G. Wickham Legg, *British Diplomatic Instructions, 1689–1789*, Vol. II, France (edited for the Royal Historical Society, 1925); J. B. Perkins, *France under the Regency* (1892).

Thus a diplomatic agent cannot be tried for a criminal offence by the courts of the country to which he is accredited.[1] If his offence is of extreme gravity he may be arrested while a request is sent to his Government for his recall. Count Gyllenborg, Swedish ambassador to England, was arrested and detained for some time in 1717 for engaging in a plot against the Hanoverian dynasty. In 1718 the Prince of Cellamare, Spanish ambassador at the Court of France, was arrested for conspiring against the Government of the Duke of Orleans. The most that can happen to diplomatic agents in these circumstances is recall or expulsion.

In regard to civil jurisdiction, diplomatic agents enjoy almost complete immunity. No interference whatever is legal against their freedom of diplomatic action, or against the property belonging to them as diplomatic agents. In England this rule was defined by statute in consequence of a popular outrage on the carriage and person of the Russian ambassador, Artemonowitz Matueof. The statute passed in 1708 is still valid, declaring that such violence shown to an ambassador or minister is contrary to the Law of Nations, and that all writs or processes against his chattels are void.

[1] Hall, *International Law* (1917), 182.

CHAPTER XXVII

TWENTY-FIVE YEARS OF PEACE. II

Walpole

Stanhope, who was a very finished diplomatist and who spared no labour in making journeys for personal conference with continental statesmen, died in 1721. His successor as Prime Minister was Robert Walpole, who had had much training in administration but none in diplomacy except as the principal author of what might be called an exhaustive " blue book " on the Treaties of Utrecht. Indeed, he may be said to have been entirely without the diplomatic outlook which is cosmopolitan as well as national. But Walpole, if he was wholly national in his outlook, was essentially wise and tolerant. When he took up office in 1720 his remark was: " Nothing is more fatal to England than the state of war. We can only lose as long as it goes on, and when it is finished we have scarcely anything to gain." This maxim, although it cannot be applied without exception, served Great Britain well enough for the next twenty years and could have been applied for a good many more years. Yet Walpole himself was responsible for the blunder which ultimately brought Great Britain into a general war, the British guarantee of the Austrian succession.

Although Great Britain, France and Spain had made peace on February 17, 1720, the Emperor and Spain remained in a nominal state of war, because Queen Elizabeth Farnese of Spain wished to secure Parma and Tuscany for her two sons Carlos and Philip, while the Emperor, naturally, resented the idea of an extension of Spanish influence in Italy. A nominal condition of war between two Great Powers, even if it did not involve actual hostilities, was obviously a very great danger to Europe. Even where states which are not Great Powers were concerned, like the Vilna-Poland nominal condition of war 1920–28, the danger is sufficiently serious. To deal with the Austro-Spanish trouble, as with any other great crisis, a European Congress had now become the acceptable method. Accordingly, a Congress was brought together gradually at Cambrai "in the course of the year 1722." [1] It continued in existence for nearly three years! "More inane congress never met in this world, nor will meet," writes Carlyle [2] —surely a very superficial judgment; for if the Congress of Cambrai did not solve the Austro-Spanish problem, it at least maintained the *status quo* and prevented hostilities—and if hostilities can be put off during a war-crisis for three years, they are not likely to occur at the end of the period.

There were present at the Congress representatives of Great Britain, Austria, Spain, France, the United Netherlands, and of many minor German states. The old cathedral city was enlivened by the accession of a brilliant if rather formal society. "All the ambassadors and all the cooks of Europe have given one another *rendez-vous*," wrote Voltaire, who visited the city on his way to Holland in July, 1722. This letter was written to Dubois, who was Archbishop of Cambrai, and who was in Paris at the time: "it is not thought," wrote Voltaire rather pointedly, "that you will quit the Palais-Royal to visit the sheep of your flock in these parts." The chief British representative was Lord Whitworth, "whom I do not know," said Voltaire. An investigation of the Foreign Office papers gives the impression that Whitworth was the best British diplomatist of the period.

The Congress of Cambrai was dissolved in 1725 with the Austro-Spanish difficulty still unsolved. The solution came about in a remarkable way. In 1720 the Regent Orleans had negotiated through Dubois a treaty with Spain, according to which the Spanish Infanta was to marry Louis XV. Until the marriage should be celebrated the Infanta, who was aged four when the treaty was signed, was to be brought up in France. On December 23, 1723, the Duke of Orleans died. The Duke of Bourbon succeeded to the Regency; Dubois' influence on foreign affairs was ended. Some time in the summer of 1724 the Duke of Bourbon determined that the engagement of Louis XV, who was fifteen years old, should be broken off; for it was now considered inadvisable to wait for the seven-year-old Spanish Infanta to grow up. Accordingly, on April 5, 1725, the Infanta was sent back from Paris to Madrid. This step, which in any case was certain to mortify the Court of Spain, was

[1] Koch and Schoell, I, 240.

[2] Carlyle, *Frederick the Great,* Book V, chap. 3.

made more distasteful by the maladroitness of the French ambassador, Marshal Tessé, who announced it—"having prefaced his communication, not with light adroit preludings of speech, but with a tempest of tears and lamentations, as if that were the way to conciliate King Philip and his termagant Elizabeth."[1] When the French court realized the offence which had been given to Spain, everything possible was done to mitigate it. Tessé was recalled. The Pope was asked to use his influence with Philip V; but the indignation of Spain could not be assuaged. Meanwhile the Duke of Bourbon, after surveying all the other princesses of Europe, had sent a proposal to Stanislaus Leczynski on behalf of his plain-faced daughter, Marie. Stanislaus, who was living in dignified retirement at Wissembourg in Alsace, accepted the brilliant proposal. He was a virtuous, mediocre, unambitious man upon whom greatness was continually being thrust, without any good coming of it.

Before the Infanta was sent back to Spain, Queen Elizabeth, who held all the power over her hypochondriac husband, had determined to make up the quarrel with the Emperor. The Baron de Ripperda,[2] who had been secretary to the Dutch embassy at Madrid, went to Vienna *incognito*, in October, 1724, and arranged (in conversations with Prince Eugène, Stahremberg and Sinzendorff at Eugène's palace) the First Treaty of Vienna, April 30, 1725. It was a secret engagement of alliance between the two countries. In the first place peace was declared, and the state of war which had endured since 1718 was ended. Spain agreed to guarantee the Pragmatic Sanction (establishing the succession in the future of the Emperor's eldest child to all his dominions) and to recognize the Ostend Company, a maritime trading corporation in which the Emperor had for some years been interested. The Emperor on his side contracted to use his influence with the British Government to induce it to surrender Gibraltar.[3] The signature of the alliance was announced; accordingly the Congress of Cambrai was dissolved. The Treaty of Vienna had another repercussion, for France and England, along with Prussia, immediately drew close

[1] Carlyle, *op. cit.*, Book V, chap. 3.

[2] For Ripperda and his negotiations see Syveton in *Revue d'histoire diplomatique*, VIII (1894), pp. 161, 364, 530, particularly p. 373 ff.

[3] Dumont, VIII, Partie II, 106. The Ostend Company is mentioned in the commercial convention which was signed separately by Ripperda at Vienna on May 1, 1725, *ibid.*, p. 117, art. 36.

together, making the Treaty of Defensive Alliance of Hanover (for the mutual guaranteeing of their existing possessions inside and outside Europe), September, 1725. This was "done quietly at Hanover," when George I went over "for the Hanover hunting season."[1] To this union Holland, Sweden and Denmark acceded. When Spain, having demanded Gibraltar of Great Britain and having been refused, opened hostilities by besieging the Rock in February, 1727, no other state joined in the war. Gibraltar held out; and Walpole gave the British fleet orders not to fight, but only to blockade Porto Bello in South America. The Emperor agreed with the British and French Governments that a Congress should meet at Soissons to deal with the crisis.

The Congress of Soissons (which was opened by the Austrian Chancellor Sinzendorff in person) sat for over a year from June 14, 1728, and seemed, like that of Cambrai, to accomplish nothing except to give a dull provincial town the spectacle of many diplomatists in Ramillies wigs diverting themselves with feasts and plays. A sensation was caused by the Spanish representative producing an old letter (of 1721) from George I to Philip V, offering to restore Gibraltar (but only in return for an equivalent, and subject to the consent of Parliament).[2] The Congress, however, did enough to show Spain that agreement with the Maritime Powers was necessary. Pentenriedter, "the tallest diplomatist in Europe," who had once been "crimped" for the Prussian army, represented Austria. The French deputation was led by the First Minister himself, the Cardinal Fleury. Colonel Stanhope, Horatio Walpole and Stephen Poyntz were there for Great Britain. Poyntz was the permanent British member of the Congress; the other two were engaged a good deal in travelling between Paris and London. On November 9, 1729, after negotiations carried on at Seville, where the Spanish court then was, France, Spain, Great Britain and Holland made the Treaty of Seville, reciprocally guaranteeing each other's possessions, and recognizing the claim of Don Carlos to succeed to Tuscany, Parma, and Piacenza.[3] This treaty greatly perturbed the Emperor. Yet in the Congress of Soissons he still failed to find a satisfactory arrangement for the ends which he

[1] Carlyle, *op. cit., loc. cit.* Treaty in Dumont, VIII, Partie II, 127.

[2] See Coxe, *Memoirs of Sir Robert Walpole* (1798), I, 308–9.

[3] Dumont, VIII, Partie II, 158. The Dutch did not accede to the treaty until November 21 (*ibid.*, p. 160).

had in view. On August 27, 1730, Sinzendorff wrote from Vienna to Count Kinsley and Baron Fonseca, the Austrian representatives at Soissons, to terminate the leases which they had taken of houses there, "all the more as in this they will only be following the example of several other ministers, deputies of the Congress." [1] The Congress of Soissons was thus virtually at an end.

The Emperor still held off until 1731. In that year (January, 1731) the last Farnese Duke of Parma, brother of the Queen of Spain, died. The Emperor must now wage a war in order to occupy the Duchy or make up his friendship with Spain and the Maritime Powers. Yielding to prolonged pressure from the aged Prince Eugène (always favourable to an English alliance),[2] he determined for peace, and on March 16, 1731, the Second Treaty of Vienna was signed between Great Britain, Holland and the Emperor, Spain acceding in the following July. The Emperor agreed to limit the trading of the Ostend East India Company with the Indies to, at most, two ships a year. By article 2 Great Britain and Holland, in the fullest, strongest and most express terms, gave their guarantee to the Pragmatic Sanction for the undivided succession of Charles' eldest daughter to the Habsburg dominions. Don Carlos travelled through France to Antibes; from there a British squadron took him and his troops to Leghorn. Early in 1732 he was established in Parma.

The Second Treaty of Vienna and the peaceful settlement of the affair of Parma was a great success for Walpole's diplomacy. Chauvelin, the strong-willed Garde des Sceaux, who was right-hand man to the amiable Cardinal Fleury, had been in favour of France offering firm support to Spain, if the Spanish Government would agree to take action in Italy without arrangement with the Maritime Powers and the Emperor.[3] The attraction of this course to Spain would have been that she need not give commercial concessions in the New World to Great Britain and that she might gain Gibraltar. Fleury, however, would not follow Chauvelin in these bellicose projects; he preferred to hold by his friendly relations with Walpole.[4]

[1] C. Höfler, *Der Congress von Soissons* (1876), II, 264, in *Fontes Rerum Austriacarum*, XXXVIII.

[2] A. F. Pribram, *Österreichische Staatsverträge* (1907) (*Veröffentlichungen der Kommission für neuere Geschichte Österreichs*), I, 467–9. The text of the Second Treaty of Vienna is on p. 491 ff.

[3] Cp. E. Driault, *Chauvelin*, in *Rev. d'hist. diplomatique* (1893), VII, 33–4.

[4] See P. Vaucher, *Robert Walpole et la Politique de Fleury* (1924), pp. 34–49.

The general war which had been staved off since 1713 seemed at last to break out in 1733. In that year (February 1, 1733) Augustus II of Saxony and Poland died. The rulers of Austria and Russia alike determined to continue the Saxon dynasty on the throne. Louis XV and Fleury were persuaded by the fiery Chauvelin to support the claims of Stanislaus Leczynski.[1] The courtiers of Versailles (according to a famous passage in Frederick the Great's works) said that Chauvelin had *escamoté* the war to the Cardinal.[2] The bribery and election were over by September (1733) and Stanislaus, who travelled safely enough from France via Berlin to Warsaw, was installed as king. Almost immediately he was chased away by a Russian army and besieged in Danzig, which ultimately capitulated to the Russian Marshal Münnich. France and Spain were now acting fairly solidly together; for, on November 7, 1733, Louis XV and Philip V had concluded the Treaty of the Escurial, known later as the First Family Compact. The French and Spanish monarchs promised eternal friendship for themselves and their posterity.

In the Western theatre Austrian troops met French troops on the Rhine, and two famous marshals of the War of the Spanish Succession, Prince Eugène and the Duke of Berwick, now aged men, pitted their prestige and their ability against each other. On the whole the French armies did best in the struggle; and the Emperor Charles VI even appealed for Russian help, and 18,000 Russian troops actually marched to the Rhine. In Italy, Spanish and Sardinian troops conquered Milan from Austria, which also lost Naples to the Spaniards. The Maritime Powers (Great Britain and Holland) were incessant in offers of mediation; and, in truth, both the Emperor Charles VI and Cardinal Fleury, chief minister of France, were always ready to make peace. The massive strength of the Russian army in Poland under Marshal Münnich had surprised Europe. Fleury judged that it would be impossible to maintain Stanislaus in Poland in the face of Russian opposition. He might have accepted the good offices of the Maritime Powers, but instead (still under the influence of Chauvelin) he used the services of a neutral German who was in Paris in 1735, being sent there probably

[1] P. Boyé, *Stanislas Leszczynski et la Troisième Traité de Vienne*, pp. 111, 112.

[2] *Histoire de mon temps*, Chap. I (*Publicationen aus den K. Preuss. Staatsarchiven* (1879), IV, 167). *Escamoter* is to make a thing disappear by a conjuring trick.

by the Emperor. This was the Baron von Nierodt, a nephew and agent of the Count of Wied, who travelled with Fleury's letters to Vienna and became (along with Count Sinzendorff the Emperor's Chancellor) a means of direct correspondence with Charles VI. Soon, a more regular diplomatist, M. de la Beaune, who was frequently employed by Fleury upon missions, took up the matter.

One of the obstacles to peace between France and Austria was that Francis, Duke of Lorraine, as the future husband of the Archduchess Maria Theresa, heiress of the Austrian dominions, would also become Emperor. Fleury, however pacific, could not allow that the Emperor and head of the House of Austria should possess a state, Lorraine, almost in the very heart of France. Another obstacle was that France could not easily submit to the loss of his Polish throne on the part of Stanislaus, the father-in-law of the French king. But these two obstacles could be used to cancel each other. Francis of Lorraine could marry Maria Theresa; Stanislaus, renouncing the throne of Poland, could be compensated by being given Lorraine for life; and Francis, in return for giving up Lorraine, could have Tuscany.[1] All this was agreed upon between France and Austria, and the Preliminary Peace of Vienna was signed on October 3, 1735, and hostilities ceased within a month, Spain, reluctantly, joining in the general pacification.

The final treaty of peace was not signed until three more years had passed, apparently owing to the opposition of Chauvelin, and owing to difficulties concerning the transference of Lorraine. On February 12, 1736, Francis of Lorraine married Maria Theresa. On November 18, 1738, the final Peace (known as the Third Treaty of Vienna) was signed.

Before this happened, Chauvelin had been dismissed by Fleury. "Our most violent enemy is fallen," wrote Waldegrave, British ambassador at Paris, to Newcastle, when the Garde des Sceaux lost his office on February 20, 1737. It was really the Imperial Government which insisted on Chauvelin's dismissal as a condition of making peace.[2] By the Third Treaty of Vienna, November 18, 1738, signed by Mirepoix for France and Sinzendorff and three others for the Emperor, Augustus III of Saxony was recognized as King of Poland; the Duchy of Lorraine was given in compensation for

[1] M. de La Beaune to Fleury, August 16, 1735, *apud* Boyé, p. 333.
[2] Driault, *Chauvelin*, in *Rev. d'hist. diplomatique* (1893), VII, 43.

life to Stanislaus (with reversion to France); Francis, Duke of Lorraine, the son-in-law of the Emperor, was to be Grand Duke of Tuscany, the last Medici prince having died in 1737; the Emperor was to have Parma and Piacenza; France guaranteed the Pragmatic Sanction; Don Carlos of Parma was to be King of Naples.[1]

This so-called "War of the Polish Succession" cost many lives, although there were no great battles or intense fighting. Its outbreak was the great failure of European diplomacy, for the death of Augustus II of Poland could have been foreseen, and the succession of that country could have been provided for in a European Congress. The war was the prelude to the Partition of Poland of 1772, from which many of the later evils of Europe came. The decision of Great Britain and the Dutch to take no part in the War of the Polish Succession was probably correct, although it resulted in their becoming isolated in Europe.[2] If Great Britain had fought at all, it would have been on the side of the Emperor, on account of her interest in Hanover, in the Austrian Netherlands, and in the *status quo* of Italy. If, when the war was over, the settlement of Italy was not what Great Britain altogether approved of, it was such as in any case she could not probably have prevented.

The interest taken by Englishmen in the war seems to have been slight. The poet Gray and Horace Walpole travelled in France and Italy immediately after the conclusion of peace. They visited Horace Mann, the English resident at the Court of Tuscany, in 1739. They moved a little in political circles. Yet Gray's letters for the year 1739 make no mention of the war which had just recently passed over the country.

In order that hostilities might be localized, the Dutch had negotiated with Fénelon, the distinguished French ambassador at the Hague, a convention by which France agreed to treat the Austrian Netherlands as neutral (November 24, 1733).[3] Thus the principle of neutralizing the vital parts of Europe was recognized and used effectively, and this was the sole reason why the war did not become general.

Fleury's direct negotiation of peace with Austria re-established his personal power, and enabled him to dispense with Chauvelin,

[1] Koch and Schoell, I, 256–7.
[2] See P. Vaucher, *La Crise du Ministère Walpole en* 1733–34 (1924), p. 42.
[3] Martens, Supp. I, 216.

with whom the Cardinal had *escamoté* the peace just as Chauvelin had *escamoté* the war with the Cardinal.[1] Moreover, Fleury's readiness to establish not merely peace but an "intimate and durable union"[2] with Austria shows the French Ministère des Affaires étrangères ready to abandon the traditional hostility to the Habsburgs if such abandonment suited the interests of France; it foreshadows the Reversal of Alliances and the Habsburg-Bourbon Alliance of 1756.[3]

The conclusion of the War of the Polish Succession by the Treaty of Vienna, although it did not restore to France her influence in Poland, satisfied her views in regard to Italy and Lorraine. "After the Treaty of Vienna," wrote Frederick the Great, "France was the arbiter of Europe."[4] It was her highest point in the eighteenth century. After that comes a slow decline.

[1] See above, p. 221 and note.

[2] These are Fleury's words in his instructions to the Duc de Mirepoix, ambassador at Vienna, 1737 (Bourgeois, *Manuel Historique*, I, 485).

[3] See Vaucher, *Robert Walpole*, pp. 149, 150.

[4] *Œuvres de Frédéric, Histoire de mon temps.* For further information on the subject of this chapter see C. Höfler, *Der Congress von Soissons* (*Fontes Rerum Austriacarum*, Zweite Abtheilung, XXXII, XXXVIII); P. Boyé, *Un roi de Pologne. Stanislaus Leszczynski et le troisième traité de Vienne* (1898); Haussonville, *Histoire de la réunion de la Lorraine à la France* (1860). For a discussion of the guarantees given in 1731 and at other times see J. W. Headlam-Morley, *Treaties of Guarantees,* in the *Cambridge Historical Journal* (1927), II, 156 ff.

CHAPTER XXVIII

A GENERAL WAR

Much blame has been dealt out by historians and publicists to dynastic politics. Yet it is probably true to say that if the European states had each remained in the sole control of a dynastic ruler without any interference from his national public opinion, there would have been fewer wars in the last two or three centuries ; for the egotism of one ruler who might from mere ambition have made a war (as Queen Elizabeth Farnese was prepared to do) would have been checked by the prudent measures of the other rulers. Almost any war can be prevented by *sang-froid* from becoming general ; and experienced statesmen, merely because they have been long at the task, can be counted on to show *sang-froid*. But the public never has this quality. Inevitably inexperienced in the daily business of foreign affairs, the public is subject to intense excitement at times of crisis ; and it frequently compels the responsible ruler or minister to take steps to which his better judgment is consistently opposed. This is how Walpole allowed himself to be forced into a war which he believed to be wholly unnecessary.

The cause of the war of 1740 was restriction of trade between nations—a thing which always tends to promote war and which, nevertheless, the unwisdom of mankind persists in maintaining. To their credit, it must be recognized that diplomatists have never been in favour of trade restriction between nations ; for they know by experience that it makes their business of keeping the peace extraordinarily difficult.

The Spaniards, it is acknowledged, had every legal right in excluding, subject to their treaty engagements, British commerce from South America. Under one of the Treaties of Utrecht the British had the privilege of sending one trading-ship a year to the Spanish main. The privilege had been freely exploited, and the Spanish authorities had administered the limitation to one ship very laxly. A new Spanish minister, the efficient José Patino, like another George Grenville, said that the law must be enforced; and he tightened up the control of the Spanish coastguards and revenue-officers in South American waters, and did away with the extended and illegal British trading. The result was indignation among the mercantile classes of England, indignation which the so-called Patriotic opposition in Parliament exploited in order to discredit the Prime Minister Walpole.

Through the Duke of Newcastle, who was Secretary of State, negotiations were conducted at London and at Madrid. Keene, the British ambassador at Madrid, was a man of sense and moderation. The Convention of the Pardo, signed by Keene and La Quadra on January 14, 1739, provided for the settlement of claims for damages and compensation arising out of the commercial dispute, and for the appointment of a joint high commission to promote a general settlement between the two countries.[1] This excellent treaty was never put into effect. It was received in England with a storm of abuse of which the outrageous character can still be appreciated from contemporary ballads and pamphlets. Walpole and Newcastle could, and ought to, have resigned office, but this would not have prevented war. They made themselves the instrument of an ill-informed public opinion, of party-spirit, and of mercantile Chauvinism; they consented to declare war upon Spain (October, 1739). Walpole's alleged remark when he heard the bells ringing from their church-steeples, that the people would soon be wringing their hands, is apparently authentic.

Walpole hoped to be able to wage a purely maritime war like that which had so fortunately burned itself out in 1727. For a time his hopes seemed to be justified. Neither the gentle and shrewd Cardinal Fleury in France, nor the Emperor Charles VI, anxious about the succession to his heterogeneous dominions, nor Frederick William of Prussia, sick to death and uncertain of the capacity of his son, had the remotest desire for war. "Europe was obstinate for peace." [2] The assault which Frederick II of Prussia suddenly made on Silesia determined the fate of Europe.

It can scarcely be denied that Frederick deliberately and with surprising ease smashed an established system of public law.

[1] Koch and Schoell, I, 270. Full text in Wenck, *Codex Juris Gentium*, I, 293.

[2] Bourgeois, *Manuel historique de politique étrangère*, I, 313. Bourgeois asserts that Walpole wanted a general war. There is, so far as I know, no authority for this statement. Vaucher, *Robert Walpole*, p. 253, emphatically declares (and gives reasons and evidence) that Walpole was for peace.

Diplomatists and statesmen, in the eighteenth century, " carved states as if they were Dutch cheeses." But in doing so, if they neglected to ask the wishes of the governed, they did, as a rule, recognize the necessity of some consent on the part of the governments of Europe. The diplomatic solidarity of Europe was slight and insecure, but it was a fact ; lip-service, and something more than lip-service, was accorded to the Grotian system of public law : namely, that there is a determinate law of nations ; that it is binding on states *inter se* ; and that sovereignty is territorial, with rights of property, to encroach on which, by violence, is stealing.

Thus there was a public law or law of nations, but an unscrupulous state could disregard it. Prussia had only 3,000,000 inhabitants, but it had 80,000 troops. France had only 150,000 soldiers, a professional army which could not easily be expanded. Austria, which had fought an unsuccessful Turkish war from 1735 to 1738, was largely depleted of soldiers.

The condition of the Habsburg monarchy on the death of Charles VI in 1740 closely resembles in certain respects its condition in 1914. In the latter year the end of a long reign (of Francis Joseph) was apprehended, or considered to be not far off ; and the liveliest fears were entertained concerning a possible breaking up of the hitherto united empire. In 1914, however, the danger was chiefly from within, from the internal, nationalist forces making for disintegration. In 1740 the danger was from without, from foreign Powers—Prussia, Bavaria, France, Spain—which could put forward claims to Austrian territory in the new situation created by the death of the last male Habsburg of the direct line, and by the succession of a daughter. Obviously, a situation of this kind, in which the interests of many states were involved and in which the Power chiefly concerned (Austria) was in a tottering condition, was of the greatest danger internationally. The invasion of Silesia by Frederick of Prussia in 1740 was a crime against Europe, not so much because he was nakedly employing the method of force in place of law, but because, in order to assert his particular interest, he took a step which he knew was only too likely to lead to a general war. " Every one was expecting a general war, but what confounded human policy was that the storm began in a quarter to which nobody had turned their eyes." [1] Looked at in this way, the invasion of Silesia by Prussia in 1740 is very like the invasion of Serbia by

[1] Voltaire, *Siècle de Louis XV*, Chap. V.

Austria in 1914, and was undertaken even more cynically. " Powerful reasons obliged me," writes Frederick ," to give at the commencement of my reign marks of vigour and of firmness, to furnish to the military class means of acquiring glory, and to make the nation to be respected by Europe." [1]

Prussia had legal claims, through family connections, to certain parts of Silesia, claims which had never been argued out before a law-court. There was in existence a permanent imperial law-court, charged with the duty of hearing and deciding suits between states of the Empire. The death of Charles VI and the accession of a woman, with all its political uncertainties, to the Austrian throne, provided a very favourable moment for a strong state like Prussia to bring its claim before a law-court, or simply, by direct negotiation, to obtain a concession from Austria. Frederick tried neither of these two methods of peace ; he used the sword. He did this with the certainty of providing a field for general war ; for the feeble but greedy Charles Albert of Bavaria had territorial claims which he would be sure to assert on the occasion of an Austro-Prussian war. France, though she had guaranteed the Pragmatic Sanction in 1738, was nevertheless ready to carry into effect a secret engagement of 1714 with Bavaria, by which she had promised, in case of a vacancy of the Imperial throne, to support the candidature of the Elector of Bavaria. This engagement was not absolutely inconsistent with the guarantee of the Pragmatic Sanction in favour of Maria Theresa's accession to the hereditary Habsburg dominions.[2] A military party, headed by Marshal Belleisle, had at this time gained an ascendancy at the French court and was determined to use the Bavarian affair for a grandiose French military adventure ; Spain and Great Britain were already fighting a maritime war ; in India and in North America French and British people, unofficially, engaged in intermittent hostilities.

The Pragmatic Sanction, an Austrian law entailing the dominions of Charles VI on his elder daughter, had been issued by Charles in 1713,[3] and had been adopted by the Germanic Diet in 1732. It had been expressly guaranteed by Great Britain, France, Spain,

[1] *Histoire de mon temps*, Chap. II (ed. 1879, p. 212). Cp. Oncken, *Das Zeitalter Friedrichs des Grossen* (1895), I, 304.

[2] See Broglie, *Le Cardinal Fleury et la Pragmatique Sanction*, in *Revue historique* (XX), 259.

[3] Text of the Pragmatic Sanction in Pribram, *Österreichische Staatsverträge, England*, I, 499.

Prussia, Bavaria and other states, but the Prussian and Bavarian recognitions had been made subject to certain reserves and might possibly be considered in 1740 as *non avenu* or annulled. It is not in regard to an obligation under the Pragmatic Sanction that the conduct of Prussia and Bavaria is to be condemned, but on the wider ground of obligation not to resort to war over claims for which there exist diplomatic or legal means of settlement.[1]

The designs of the various states which desired to share in the Austrian Succession amounted almost to a scheme of partition. The Habsburg Monarchy as a great Central European union would have ceased to exist. Frederick was, in effect, the spearhead of a phalanx of enemies who would have dismembered the Austrian Empire. Nevertheless, he pretended, until the last moment, that he was mobilizing to fight on behalf of Maria Theresa. Before setting out for Silesia on December 15, 1740, he remarked to the French ambassador, the Marquis de Beauvau (who was quite uncertain whether Frederick was going against France or Austria): "I am going, I believe, to play your game; and if I gain the ace we will share."[2] The adherents to the policy of Chauvelin (then in retirement at Bourges) felt that their hour had struck. "Here is the grandest event which has happened in the Empire and in Europe since time immemorial," Barbier had cried when he heard of the death of Charles VI. Now was the time to break the Habsburg power for ever! Marshal Belleisle and his friends were still living in the traditions of the sixteenth and seventeenth centuries.

Marshal Belleisle, the ardent champion of the dismemberment of Austria, was also one of the agents of *le Secret* of Louis XV, of the cryptic diplomatic service which the king maintained beneath the regular diplomacy of Fleury. "Belleisle can be reckoned among the great men of our century," wrote Frederick the Great; "his genius is vast, his spirit brilliant, he has the audacious courage which leads in war to great undertakings, his imagination works too much, his passion is his profession."[3] The brilliant busy man—general, diplomatist, politician—obtained authority from Louis XV to make treaties of alliance. On May 18 or 28, 1741,

[1] Ranke (*History of Prussia*, Bk. IV, Chap. IV) defends Frederick's breach with Austria on the ground that Austria had broken her treaty by not handing over the Duchy of Berg to Frederick William I. But Frederick could have brought this matter before the Court of Imperial Chamber.

[2] Voltaire, *Siècle de Louis XV*, Chap. VI.

[3] *Histoire de mon temps*, Chap. I (ed. 1879, p. 167).

at the Palace of Nymphenburg, near Munich, he signed, with the Elector of Bavaria, the Treaty of Nymphenburg. Spain also signed this act, and Prussia acceded to it in July, Saxony in September.[1]

The Franco-Bavarian Treaty of Nymphenburg has long puzzled historians, for no copy of it has been found in either the Munich or Paris archives. Marshal Belleisle did not arrive in Munich until May 18, 1741, the date of the reputed signature of the treaty. There was no other French minister at that time at Munich, so it is difficult to see how drafts could have been prepared and discussed in time for Belleisle to sign the treaty on the very day of his arrival. Nevertheless, there is no doubt that France and Bavaria did bind themselves by treaty about this time, probably on May 28, the date of the signature of the Hispano-Bavarian Treaty; and from the known texts of the subsequent Spanish and Saxo-Polish accessions, the French text can be reconstructed. The Allies bound themselves not merely to secure the Imperial Crown for the Elector of Bavaria; but to secure Bohemia, the Tyrol, and Upper Austria for Bavaria; Upper Silesia and Moravia for Saxony; and the Italian possessions of Austria for Don Philip of Spain; France was to have the Austrian Netherlands. The Nymphenburg treaties, in fact, amounted to a scheme of guaranteed partition of the Austrian domains.[2]

Silesia was overrun by Prussian troops in the autumn of 1740, and Bohemia by French and Bavarians in the campaigning season of 1741. George II went over to Hanover in person; but when a French army approached from the Meuse he hastily, in his capacity of Elector of Hanover, made a treaty of neutrality (October 28, 1741), signed by M. de Bussy and two Hanoverian ministers, the Barons Münchhausen and Steinberg. "Ever since the accession of the House of Brunswick, Hanover had been a perpetual source of embarrassment and danger to England, but a German war was one of the very few contingencies in which its alliance was of some real value."[3] Great Britain was now certainly involved in

[1] See A. Schaefer, *Graf Brühl und Friedrich der Grosse*, in *Historiche Zeitschrift* (1866), XV, 125.

[2] Hispano-Bavarian Treaty of Nymphenburg, May 28, 1741, in Martens *Nouveau Supplémens*, I, 721; Saxo-Bavarian Treaty, signed at Frankfort, September 19, 1741, *ibid.*, 728. The reputed French Treaty of Nymphenburg is given in Koch and Schoell, I, 274 (in summary). Frederick of Prussia was able to accede to the plan that Saxony should possess Upper Silesia because he himself was at this time only claiming Lower Silesia from Austria. Cp. *Recueil des Instructions*, VII, par A. Lebon, p. 193.

[3] Lecky, *op. cit.*, I, 393.

a general war, and Walpole, whose averseness from European war was strangely unpopular, lost a division in the House of Commons and resigned (January 28, 1742).

Long afterwards it was discovered that he had been at least twice in communication with the Pretender—in 1734 and in 1739. On the last occasion the Jacobite scholar and man of affairs, Thomas Carte, had come secretly under safe-conduct from France to England and had interviews with Walpole in London. But, face to face with Carte, Walpole expressed astonishment at being considered likely to turn against the House of Hanover; and he dismissed Carte, saying that the safe-conduct would be respected and that his departure would not be opposed. The truth appears to be that Carte had been attracted over to London in order that he might be enrolled among Walpole's unseen cloud of secret agents on the Continent. And Carte had come over, thinking that he could enlist Walpole among the secret supporters of Jacobitism. Each was equally surprised to discover that both were faithful to their own masters.[1]

After Walpole's fall, Lord Carteret became Secretary of State, with Lord Wilmington as Prime Minister. All the interest of Carteret's public life was in foreign affairs. "What is it to me," he said to Chief Justice Willes, "who is a judge and who a bishop? It is my business to make kings and emperors, and to maintain the balance of Europe."[2]

The British Government, which was helping Austria with a large annual subsidy (£300,000), had from the first pressed Maria Theresa through Thomas Robinson, ambassador at Vienna, to cede Silesia to Frederick. The Austrians could defeat their other enemies. They drove the French out of Bohemia, invaded Bavaria, and on February 12, 1742, entered the capital, Munich. This was the same day on which Charles Albert of Bavaria was crowned Holy Roman Emperor at Frankfort. He was the first non-Habsburg prince to be elected in three hundred years and the last; and his election had been viewed with profound concern by "nearly all Germany," as being "entirely the work of France."[3] Maria

[1] Mahon, *History of England* (1853), III, 23, and Appendix. Vaucher, *Robert Walpole*, Appendix II.

[2] Mahon, *History of England* (1853), III, 243. Horace Walpole, *Memoirs*, I, 147.

[3] Report of Prince Emmanuel de Croy in Grouchy, *L'Ambassade du Maréchal de Belleisle à Francfort en* 1742, in *Rev. d'hist. diplomatique* (1894), VIII, 595.

Theresa bowed before necessity. She consented to cede Glatz and Upper and Lower Silesia, except Teschen and Troppau, to Frederick by the preliminary Treaty of Breslau, June 11, 1742, and the Final Treaty of Berlin, of July 28, 1742. Frederick himself gives the chief credit for this peace to the British Secretary of State, Lord Carteret. The greatest credit should be given to Lord Hyndford, who was the English diplomatist accredited to follow Frederick's headquarters.

Here the war might have stopped if Maria Theresa had seized the occasion of peace with Prussia to offer peace to all her other enemies. But her indignation led her to desire revenge—to take Bavaria from Charles Albert, and to annex Alsace and Lorraine from France. The British Government should have withdrawn from the war. Instead, it continued to pay the subsidy to Austria, and in 1743 it sent into the Rhineland an army which fought and won the battle of Dettingen against the French (June 27, 1743). The monarchs of France and Spain made common cause through the Second Family Compact, October 25, 1743. Not, however, until March, 1744, did England and France recognize each other as being engaged in war; down to this time they had only been auxiliaries—England, the auxiliary of Austria, France of Bavaria. The war was still generally popular in England, a country where opinion was more widespread and had more influence upon policy than anywhere else. In Boswell's *Life of Johnson*, under the year 1744, there is an account of the poverty-stricken poet Savage and Johnson (himself equally poor at that time) walking through the night round St. James's Square for want of a lodging. "They were not at all depressed by their situation; but in high spirits and brimful of patriotism, traversed the square for several hours, inveighed against the minister, and resolved they would *stand by their country*."

In August, 1744, Frederick of Prussia, jealous of the Austrian successes, fearful of a *revanche* on the part of the martial Maria Theresa, suddenly began war again, invading Bohemia by marching through Saxony, which had been neutral since the Peace of Breslau. Europe seemed to be settling down to a hopeless condition of perpetual bloodshed as in the Thirty Years' War. The Belgic (Austrian) Netherlands could not be defended against French armies; Alsace was being reduced to ruins by contending Austrian and French soldiers; the Prussians were burning villages in Bohemia, the Sardinians and Austrians in alliance were fighting fiercely with Charles of Naples. A Jacobite rebellion occurred in Scotland; the Highland host invaded England (1745); a British army was defeated at Fontenoy in Flanders (May 11, 1745). The European diplomatic system had absolutely collapsed, and the clock was set back for sixty years. The decline of Europe was never more strikingly shown than when, amid the general failure of the diplomacy of the civilized Christian Powers, the Sultan Mohammed V offered his mediation. The offer was rejected.[1]

Maria Theresa seems even to have let her indignation so far master her as to incline her to a continuance of war for the partial dismemberment or partition of France. Magnificent and heroic woman as she was, she, like so many autocrats, seems to have had little regard for the sufferings of her subjects in war so long as she could, by any effort, preserve her empire in the extent in which she had inherited it.[2]

Nevertheless, there were four events in the year 1745 which gave some prospect of a general peace. One was the death in January of the Elector Charles Albert of Bavaria, who was also the Emperor Charles VII. His son made peace by the Treaty of Füssen, April 15, 1745, with Maria Theresa, and promised to vote for her husband as Emperor.[3] The second was the election of Francis, the husband of Maria Theresa, as Emperor (Sept. 13). The third was the treaty which the British Government made with Frederick of Prussia (Hanover, August 26, 1745),[4] guaranteeing to him the possession of Silesia according to the Peace of Breslau. Finally Maria Theresa consented to treat with the king on the same basis; and the Austro-Prussian Treaty of Dresden, December 25, 1745, made under the mediation of Great Britain, confirmed Frederick in the possession of Silesia and Glatz.

Yet a general peace was not achieved until 1748. "This country and Europe are undone without a secure and lasting peace," wrote Pitt to Newcastle on December 5, 1747. The final impelling force seems to have been the British Government, which subsidized

[1] Koch and Schoell, I, 301.

[2] Cf. Lecky's remarks, *op. cit.*, I, 418–19.

[3] See G. Preuss, *Der Friede von Füssen* (1894). Koch and Schoell, I, 295.

[4] Text in Wenck, *Codex Juris Gentium* (1788), II, 191. Great Britain had given a similar guarantee by the Prusso-British Convention of Westminster, November 18, 1742 (Wenck, I, 640), but this lapsed when Frederick renewed his attack on Austria in 1744.

Russia to send 30,000 men to the Western theatre of war (treaty of December 9, 1747), and at the same time made it clear to Maria Theresa that she could not count on a continuance of British subsidies for a war which was now being mainly fought in Italy. The advance of the Russians predisposed France to peace ; the prospect of decreasing subsidies inclined Maria Theresa to consider a cessation of hostilities.

The chief difficulty in ending a war is often the initial step of establishing diplomatic contact between the enemies. The War of the Austrian Succession had at one time or another involved every state in Europe except Switzerland, Denmark and Turkey ; there was no neutral state with sufficient prestige or diplomatic and other resources to offer good offices with any chance of success. Diplomatic contact was actually established through a famous British prisoner of war in the hands of the French. This was General Sir John Ligonier, captured at Lawfeldt in July, 1747. In the autumn of 1747 Marshal Saxe had some conversation with him. The Marshal said that the King of France would make peace with Great Britain on the basis of the *status quo ante bellum.* He also made the strange proposal that the peace should be negotiated by two soldiers, the Duke of Cumberland and himself at the head of their armies. Ligonier found means to convey this news to the British Government, then directed by Henry Pelham, Prime Minister. The duke could not be altogether kept out of the negotiations (for which his rash character was quite unsuited), but the main work was given to the Earl of Sandwich, an experienced diplomatist. Sandwich—although the war was raging in the Netherlands—crossed to Liège and met the French Minister of Foreign Affairs, the Marquis de Pieseulx (September 11, 1747). A few months later either in case diplomacy failed, or to strengthen its arguments, Great Britain, Austria, the Dutch and Sardinia signed a military convention at the Hague, agreeing to put in the field in the Low Countries an unprecedented Allied force of 192,000 men against the French (January 26, 1748).[1] However, on April 30, 1748, after the general Peace Congress had come together, the Preliminary Treaty of Peace was signed by Lord Sandwich and Saint-Severin, Count Bentinck also adhering for the Dutch. The other belligerent Governments, especially Austria, were very unwilling to join in this triple concert of peace, but at last they gave way.

[1] Koch and Schoell, I, 510.

The general conference assembled at Aix-la-Chapelle on April 24, 1748. Frederick of Prussia, not being a belligerent, was not represented. After the signature of the Preliminary Peace Treaty (which was a separate act of Great Britain, the Dutch and France) long and arduous negotiations were needed before the Final Peace was signed on October 18 (1748). Except that the possession of Silesia was guaranteed to Frederick the Great, that the King of Sardinia received Novara and Tortona in the Austrian Milanese from his ally Maria Theresa, and that Don Philip of Spain, younger brother of Charles III, became Duke of Parma, there were no territorial changes. Nobody was satisfied except Frederick of Prussia and possibly Don Philip.[1]

[1] For further information on this chapter see Le Duc de Broglie, *Fréderic II et Marie Therèse* (1883); *Frederic II et Louis XV* (1885); *Marie Therèse Impératrice* (1890); *Maurice de Saxe et le Marquis d'Argenson* (1891); *La Paix d'Aix-la-Chapelle* (1892). An index to all these works and to M. de Broglie's later volume, *L'Alliance Autrichienne,* has been issued under the title of *Histoire de la Politique extérieure de Louis XV*, 1741–1756 (1899). Evan Charteris, *William Augustus, Duke of Cumberland* (1913), especially p. 323 ff. For the British alliance with Russia which began with a purely defensive union (Treaty of St. Petersburg, Dec. 11, 1742) see R. Lodge, *The First Anglo-Russian Treaty,* 1739–42, in the *English Historical Review* (July, 1928), XLIII, 354.

CHAPTER XXIX

THE REVERSAL OF ALLIANCES

There is a close parallel between the outlook of Frederick the Great after the War of the Austrian Succession and that of Bismarck after the Franco-Prussian. Bismarck, when he had made the modern German Empire, and had annexed Alsace and Lorraine to it, had no other governing idea than to keep these gains. The idea of coalitions, he said, gave him nightmares. Frederick the Great, in the same way, had annexed a most valuable province, continuous with his hereditary dominions, but in doing so he had violated the public law and had risked incurring the animosity of powerful states. All that he wanted now was to be able to keep what he had gained. The seizure of Silesia, he wrote in his *Testament Politique* (composed in 1752), was like one of those popular novels of which the originals achieve a striking success but the imitations always fail.[1]

Oesterreich habe Schlesien nicht vergessen, wrote Frederick in 1752, " and Maria Theresa will, as soon as her domestic affairs have been put in order, march to the attack."[2] Nor was she like Gambetta at a later date who used to say, in reference to the lost French provinces of Alsace and Lorraine : *y pensez toujours, parlez jamais !* Maria Theresa did not make much secret of her intention to recover Silesia if she found an opportunity. Naturally Frederick, like Bismarck after 1870, felt that his attitude must be *toujours en vedette*. Thus the annexation of Silesia in its effect was something like the annexation of Alsace-Lorraine—it imposed an armed peace upon the Powers, which after a prolonged period of tension broke out into a great war.

It was not merely the relations between Prussia and Austria that were at high tension. Great Britain and France were nearly

[1] *Das Politische Testament Friedrichs des Grossen von* 1752 (ed. Küntzel und Mass, 1920), p. 55.

[2] *Ibid.*, pp. 51, 52.

at blows in the five or six years after the Peace of Aix-la-Chapelle. There was an old, unsettled and acrimonious dispute about the frontier of Acadie (Nova Scotia), ceded by France at the Peace of Utrecht. But still more serious in its result upon the relations between the two countries was the obvious design of the French to take possession of the valleys of the Mississippi and Ohio, and to prevent any expansion of the British colonies inland beyond the Alleghanies. "They supported their claim by launching war-ships on Lake Ontario, and by rapidly throwing out supports and founding forts along the Ohio"[1] (1754). The Board of Trade reported to George II that "it was a matter of wonder what such a strange expedition in time of peace could mean, unless to complete the object so long in view of conjoining the St. Lawrence with the Mississippi."[2] In the later nineteenth century similar international rivalries for the partition of another continent (Africa) were prevented from breaking out into war by an international Conference held at Berlin in 1885 and by subsequent negotiations. But in the eighteenth century the local European officials and officers on the frontiers of the colonies were far less under control of their respective Home Governments than they are now, because in those days there was no telegraph and no steamship. Reports and administrative orders travelled with the most painful slowness; "months passed between the order and its execution";[3] and the men on the confines of empire were necessarily exempt from strict control. This made the task of diplomacy in trying to smooth out frontier incidents extraordinarily difficult. Desultory fighting went on between French regular soldiers and British colonial militia in North America in 1754. In May, 1755, the French Government, in order to strengthen its American garrisons, sent out a fleet from Brest for the St. Lawrence. The British Government dispatched Admiral Boscawen with instructions to intercept the French fleet. It avoided the British during a fog, but Boscawen found two French ships, the *Alcide* and the *Lys*, which had become detached from the main body in the mouth of the St. Lawrence. He attacked and captured them. When the news of this reached Europe, about July 15, the French ambassador was recalled from

[1] Lecky, *History of England*, II, 443.
[2] *Ibid.*, 444.
[3] Burke, Speech on Moving the Resolutions for Conciliation with the Colonies, March 22, 1775.

London, but France did not declare war. In July, 1755, General Braddock, acting on instructions which he had brought out from home, led an expedition to attack Fort Duquesne at the junction of the Ohio and Monongahela (now Pittsburg). He was routed, and died of wounds. But the French Government still refrained from declaring war, and even released a captured British warship.

The French were not going to put themselves into the position of aggressors, but war could not be avoided now because it was already going on between France and Great Britain, although not on the grand scale. Throughout the year 1755 the British Government was making diplomatic preparations for war, by concluding subsidy-treaties (for the defence of Hanover) with Saxony and with Russia. On January 16, 1756, Frederick of Prussia and George II of Great Britain bound themselves by the Treaty of Westminster, which has been called " one of the most important treaties in the whole of European diplomatic history." [1] The two monarchs agreed that they would not, during the troubles in America, permit any foreign troops to pass through Germany. This amounted to a guarantee of the defence of Hanover from the French by Prussia, and of the defence of Prussia from the Russians by Great Britain. The treaty was not secret ; the terms were officially communicated to the French Government before they were signed.[2]

Frederick, who never could refrain from making one of his satirical jokes, had complained in his *Testament Politique*, written two years previously, that " the King of England with a sack of guineas " came too often to Germany to attach the German princes to him. But Frederick himself was soon to accept thankfully some of these sacks of guineas. When he made the treaty of alliance with England he informed France that he would not renew the treaty of alliance of 1741 with France which was due to expire in 1756.

Since the Peace of Aix-la-Chapelle, France's diplomacy had been anything but steady. The *double jeu* between the official diplomacy and that of " The Secret " of the King (and " The Secrets " of several courtiers, such as Mme. de Pompadour), made baffling cross-currents

[1] Emil Daniels in *The Cambridge Modern History*, VI, 251. For the treaty see Koch and Schoell, I, 333.

[2] See Arnold Schaefer, *Das Ende des Preussisch-Französischen Allianz*, in *Historische Zeitschrift* (1865), XIV, 136.

in policy. This double policy is said to have begun when Louis XV sent Voltaire in August, 1743, to Berlin to find out the intentions of Frederick in regard to the war in which France was engaged against Austria.[1]

For instance, under the Marquis d'Argenson, who became Minister of Foreign Affairs in 1744 after the death of Fleury, the official policy of France, approved by Louis XV, was to be in alliance with Augustus III of Saxony and Poland. D'Argenson's plan, which was quite sound, was to help Augustus III to make the crown of Poland hereditary in the Saxon line, and so to put an end to the anarchy in that unfortunate country. Poland thus would become a stable state, permanently allied to the King of France, who would sustain it against the encroachments of Russia and Prussia. With this object in view, a treaty of alliance was signed between Louis XV and Augustus III on April 21, 1746, and the Dauphin married the charming and talented Princess Marie Josephe of Saxony and Poland. But the weary and dissipated monarch "took a malicious pleasure in stultifying his own policy."[2] He adopted the cause of his cousin, the Prince de Conti, who, from sheer ambition, wanted to supplant Augustus III on the throne of Poland. The Secret of the King was employed to further this object in Warsaw, while the official French diplomatic agents were receiving instructions to pursue a policy of peace. The Dauphin and Madame de Pompadour had their secret cabinets and diplomacies too; their policy was hostile to that of Conti, whose design came to nothing, and was abandoned in 1755.

Meanwhile the French and Austrian Governments were drawing together. Historians have at last divested themselves of the "anecdotal side" of this evolution.[3] The rapprochement between France and Austria, which the French call the Reversal of Alliances or the Diplomatic Revolution, was not so surprising as it has been considered to be. Diplomacy is the intelligent pursuit of a country's international interest. In the Middle Ages there was little or no diplomacy because states acted blindly accord-

[1] Broglie, *Frédéric II et Louis XV*, II, 52 ff.

[2] Bourgeois, *Manuel historique*, I, 505. On the other hand, the Secret personnel sometimes proved to be wiser and more patriotic than the regular advisers of the Ministry of Foreign Affairs. See Broglie, *Le Secret du Roi*, I, 4.

[3] Cp. A. Tratchevsky, *La France et l'Allemagne sous Louis XVI*, in *Revue historique* (1880), XIV, 242.

ing to tradition; Emperors and Popes fought each other for centuries, as did also English and French, and Scots and English. But since the late fifteenth century, even before Machiavelli explained the idea with a cogency that nobody could deny, states had begun to pursue the policy of adjusting their international relations to suit their interests or necessities. If the French had fairly consistently opposed the Austrian monarchy, it was because they wished to gain dominion in Italy, or to strengthen their eastern frontier. But since the Treaty of Cateau-Cambrésis in 1559 France had given up the Italian dream; and since the acquisition of Alsace in 1648, of the north-eastern (Flemish) fortresses in 1678, and of Lorraine in 1738, the French frontier was fairly secure against the Habsburgs. The highly-intelligent and well-instructed French foreign office could be in no doubt that France's interest no longer required a continual opposition to the Habsburgs. The Treaty of Utrecht, by confirming the exclusion of the Habsburgs from Spain, had removed the really serious danger to France of Spanish-Austrian union. Besides, that France was not absolutely wedded to an anti-Austrian policy was proved by the fact that she had already departed from it. Louis XIV had been in favour of friendship with the Habsburgs at the end of his life. In 1719 a Franco-Austro-British coalition had been made actually against a Bourbon, against the designs of Philip V and Queen Elizabeth Farnese on Naples, and in a short war Philip had been forced to give way. Fleury had decided for a good understanding with Austria in 1738. At the time when the Habsburg-Bourbon Alliance was made nobody in France raised any objection to it.[1] The truth is that in 1756 France had nothing to gain from continual opposition to the Habsburgs, but she had much to gain from Habsburg friendship, namely the Austrian Netherlands or some influence there. In the negotiations which Kaunitz, the Austrian ambassador, conducted at Paris in 1755, it was arranged that if Austria recovered Silesia Maria Theresa would cede the great fortress of Mons to France, and would agree that the Bourbon Duke of Parma in Italy should exchange Parma for the Austrian Netherlands. This exchange-scheme, which was very characteristic of eighteenth-century diplomacy, would not have been, if carried into effect, as repugnant to popular opinion then as it would be now.

[1] Tratchevsky, *op. cit.*, in *Revue historique* (1880), XIV, 248.

The criticism usually applied to the Franco-Austrian alliance, as it affected the interests of France, is to allege that by keeping large French armies occupied in fighting in Germany, it left the French overseas empire starved of defence, a prize to the British maritime power. The answer to this is that France in 1755 was already involved in hostilities with Great Britain (although the formal state of war had not been proclaimed), and that Great Britain, using her wealth and the position of her king as Elector of Hanover, would certainly have done all she could to arrange some continental attack upon France ; so the best thing that France could do was to gain a strong continental ally. Frederick had proved himself to be a very undependable ally in the Austrian Succession War, and by January, 1756, he was bound by treaty with Great Britain. So there was no strong Central European state left for France to ally with, except Austria. There seemed just a chance, too (from the French point of view), that a Franco-Austrian alliance would so obviously make a balance between the strength of the continental antagonists, that they would decide not to fight [1] (for Bernis did not know that Austria and Russia were scheming to partition Prussia). It seems legitimate, therefore, for a modern historian to hold that the Abbé Bernis, who negotiated the Franco-Austrian treaty with Kaunitz, acted on an intelligible, indeed on the only intelligible policy, and that it was not just the personal spite of the mistress of Louis XV, Madame de Pompadour, against the cynical, loose-tongued Frederick, which promoted the alliance. The only conceivable alternative for France to an alliance with Austria in the approaching continental struggle was a policy of neutrality on the Continent, and of concentration upon the maritime and colonial struggle with Great Britain. But this was only possible if Austria and Prussia did not fight each other. If Maria Theresa attacked Frederick, Great Britain, by offering subsidies and soldiers, could almost certainly secure the alliance of one or the other. Britain had means for promoting a coalition on the Continent against France and indeed, by January, 1756, had already done so, although as yet only on a purely defensive basis. Thus from the French point of view the Austrian alliance was simply a necessity. Pitt said later that Great Britain won America on the plains of Germany. This is a mistake. The destiny of North America was settled by sea-power. What the

[1] Bourgeois, *Manuel historique*, I, 509.

R

British war in Germany helped to settle was the maintenance of the balance of power between Austria, France, Prussia and Russia.

From the Austrian point of view the French alliance was not exactly a necessity but rather a very great convenience. When a Government has adopted a particular aim, it is the duty of statesmanship to take every honourable means for ensuring the success of that aim. For allies, Austria had already by the end of the year 1755 secured Russia and was not unlikely to have Saxony; if she could secure the active assistance of France, all the better. France was still the greatest military state in Europe; besides, the alliance with France would prevent the Austrian Netherlands from being occupied or made the scene of hostilities during the war.

The Habsburg-Bourbon Alliance, commonly called the First Treaty of Versailles, was actually signed at Jouy, the country-house of Minister Rouillé, near Versailles, and was dated May 1, 1756. It consisted of two conventions. By the first, Maria Theresa bound herself to observe a perfect neutrality in the dispute between France and Great Britain. By the second convention, Austria and France mutually guaranteed each other's territories in Europe and promised to each other a succour of 24,000 troops in case either party was attacked. The war between England and France was excepted from this guarantee.

It has been said that the French ministers' object in making the first Versailles alliance was to maintain peace in Europe.[1] M. de Broglie believes, on the evidence, that the French ministers had no such illusion.[2] The invasion of Saxony, on the way to Bohemia, by Frederick brought the French guarantee of Austria into operation; and once France was in the Austro-Prussian War, she found, as states have found since, that a limited participation in European grand-scale war is impossible; it is a question of a country's total resources or none. Therefore on May 1, 1757, when war on the grand scale was in full blast, the Second Treaty of Alliance of Versailles was concluded. The contracting parties in the preamble took note of the necessity of reducing the power of the King of Prussia "within such boundaries that he will not in future be able to disturb the public tranquillity." France raised the

[1] C. T. Atkinson, *A History of Germany* (1908), p. 192.

[2] Broglie, *L'Alliance Autrichienne*, p. 375.

number of troops which she was bound to put in the field from 24,000 to 105,000 for the year 1757, and promised to pay a subsidy of 12,000,000 florins a year, until Austria was in possession of Silesia and Glatz. Saxony was to receive Magdeburg, Sweden Pomerania. Maria Theresa, in compensation for the sacrifices of France, was to cede Ostend, Nieuport, Mons, Ypres and other fortresses and towns of the Austrian Netherlands. Except for the first two of these towns, the territories allocated in compensation to France were only to come to her after Austria had been put in possession of her own promised lands. Don Philip was to have the Austrian Netherlands and Luxemburg in exchange for his duchies of Parma and Piacenza, which were to return to Austria.

The Habsburg-Bourbon Alliance-Treaty of May 1, 1757, was not ratified, and is omitted from the collection of French treaties published under the auspices of the Ministère des Affaires etrangères in the latter half of the nineteenth century.[1] It did, however, govern the relations of France and Austria until the next treaty was concluded in December, 1758.

If France could not help entering into this strict "offensive" alliance with Austria, it must be acknowledged that the balance of advantage was with Austria. French historians rightly call the treaty a brilliant success for Chancellor Kaunitz and still more for Stahremberg, Austrian ambassador at Versailles, who obtained more by his negotiation than the Instructions of the Austrian Chancellery had prescribed to him.[2]

Great Britain had four Continental interests to attend to in the coming struggle. One was the defence of Hanover, which the French would certainly try to seize and to hold as a pledge for subsequent concessions; a second was the maintenance of a balance of power between the great Continental states; a third was the preventing of the Austrian Netherlands (with Antwerp at the mouth of the Scheldt) from coming under the control of France; a fourth was the absorption of as much of France's reserves as possible in the Continental theatre of war.

A Prusso-British alliance was just the thing to help ensure these interests. Prussia, although as a whole its military resources

[1] Waddington, *La Guerre de Sept Ans*, I, 154–5.

[2] De Clercq, *Recueil des Traités de la France* (1864), Vol. I. Cp. Koch and Schoell, I, 341. All modern French historians agree that the treaty regulated Franco-Austrian assistance in the year 1757–58.

were not so great as those of France, had the most efficient standing army in Europe, and its dominions were neighbouring to Hanover, some of them (Cleves, Mark, Ravensburg) lying actually on the way between France and Hanover. If Great Britain by assisting Frederick, could prevent the partition of Prussia, she would be maintaining the balance of power. The Prussian army would be a very great help, if not in preventing the French from entering the Austrian Netherlands, at any rate in inducing them to leave. Finally, British financial and military assistance to Frederick would enable him to offer such an effective resistance to the coalition against him that if France was in that coalition (and she was almost certain to be) her military and financial resources would be involved in the struggle for a long time.

That the existence of Prussia as an important power was at stake is indubitable. Frederick, although he did not pay his agents much, was well served in the capitals of Europe and received much useful information. He understood the art of rewarding and bribing: "Give little and often," *donner peu et souvent*, is one of the precepts which he put in his *Testament Politique* of 1752. Among other informants was one Frederick Wilhelm Menzel, a Kanzellist or clerk in the Saxon Secret Chancery at Dresden, which, during the long ministry of Count Brühl, was very carelessly conducted.[1] Menzel was not in the Foreign Department, but as a Kanzellist he knew that important documents of the Foreign Department were kept in certain presses in the Chancery. As in many stories of this kind, the clerk, who had a good record in his office, fell through extravagance. In 1752 he owed money, and his creditor, a man named Rhenitz, pressed for his debt. Menzel could not pay. Rhenitz hinted that he could put him in the way of making something extra. He then introduced Menzel to the secretary of the Prussian legation at Dresden, who took him to von Mahlzahn, the Prussian Minister. The upshot was that the Prussian legation supplied Menzel with a bunch of keys, some of which, after a little filing, were able to open the secret presses in the Dresden Chancery. When the Saxon Court moved to Warsaw (the Elector Augustus III being King of Poland) the Chancery staff, including Menzel, sometimes went

[1] Brühl nominally concentrated all affairs in his hands, drew the salaries, and left the duties to underpaid officials. See A. Schaefer, *Graf Brühl und Friedrich der Grosse*, in *Historische Zeitschrift* (1866), XV, 121.

too, and the presses also. From about Easter, 1753, documents were abstracted from the Chancery and were taken to the Prussian legation, which also followed the court to Warsaw. The dispatches, after being copied by the Prussian secretaries, were returned to Menzel, who put them back in their presses. From 1752 until he was detected in 1757 he received sums amounting to £450 from the Prussian legation.[1]

In the same years Frederick was receiving information out of the Austrian legation in Berlin through one of its second secretaries, one "Weingarten Junior," who was in love with a Charlottenburg chambermaid. The chambermaid seems to have induced him to become a traitor, and he was able to marry her and live on in Brandenburg, doubtless on a small Prussian pension, after the treason was discovered in June, 1756.

The documents of which Frederick obtained knowledge convinced him that Austria and Russia (Saxony also, he alleged) were in agreement to make war upon Prussia with a view to reducing her to the ancient limits of Brandenburg by annexing Silesia, Glatz, Magdeburg and East Prussia. The germ of this plan was in a treaty which had been made during the War of the Austrian Succession by Austria and Saxony. The preamble to this act, the Treaty of Leipsic of May 18, 1745, provided for a partial dismemberment of Prussia, and that "this formidable neighbour be restricted to narrow limits." [2] On April 10, 1756, Esterhazy, Austrian ambassador at St. Petersburg, was able to report that Russia was agreed with Austria on a plan of attack upon Prussia, and for Maria Theresa to have Silesia and Glatz, Saxony to have East Prussia, while Russia would compensate herself with the annexation of Courland.[3] Saxony was not a party to this agreement, although the Saxon ambassador at St. Petersburg, Funk, was (as the Tsaritsa Elizabeth told Esterhazy) [4] kept informed of its contents; and Funk doubtless reported them to Dresden. Frederick, through the treasons of Menzel, would thus have knowledge of the partition-scheme.

Frederick was thus fairly well apprised of his danger. On July

[1] Carlyle, *Frederick the Great*, Book XVI, chap. 15.

[2] Text in Hertzberg, *Recueil* (1790), I, 28.

[3] Arneth, *Maria Theresa und der Siebenjährige Krieg* (1875), V, 46.

[4] Esterhazy to Kaunitz, September 23, 1755: *Preussische und Österreichische Akten zur Vorgeschichte des Siebenjährigen Krieges*, in *Publicationen aus der K. Preussischen Staatsarchiven* (1899), LXXIV, 172.

26 (1756) Frederick's minister at Vienna, Graf von Klinggräffen, acting on instructions, demanded from the Empress Maria Theresa to be assured that her unwonted armaments were not intended against Prussian security. He received for answer that the *bedänklichen Umstände*—circumstances giving cause for thought—moved her to consider what measures were necessary for her security and that of her allies, but that these measures did not intend injury to anybody. When Klinggräffen sent a report of this to Potsdam, Frederick (August 2) directed him again to apply to Maria Theresa for a specific assurance that Austria would not attack him in this or the following year. The Empress on August 21 refused to give the required assurance; and on August 26 Frederick began the invasion of Saxony. He had prefaced this act with an invitation to Augustus to give him unopposed passage through Saxony into Austrian territory. "The estates of the King will be spared, so far as present circumstances allow." [1] Augustus, however, rejected this offer, resolved to do his duty as a neutral and to resist any violation of his territory.

On September 9 Frederick's army entered Dresden. The Saxon king and his army retired to Pirna, leaving behind them with culpable negligence (but such things have happened again since) the secret archives of the Chancery at Dresden. Frederick thus obtained possession of the originals of the "Menzel" documents; they were forthwith edited into a workmanlike memoir [2] and were published at Berlin in the autumn of the same year. The practice of Governments appealing to the educated public opinion of Europe, through the publication of secret documents concerning the origin of a war which was going on, was already becoming well established.

The materials discovered by Frederick at Dresden did not provide any proof that Saxony was a party to the Austro-Russian plan of April, 1756, for partitioning Prussia. Whether the military expediency of marching through Saxony and of occupying Dresden justified Frederick in violating a neutral state is very doubtful, although, on Frederick's side, it can be held that Saxony was not unlikely, after the war should begin, to join the hostile coalition.[3]

[1] Text in Reddaway, *Frederick the Great* (1904), 204.

[2] The Memoir with original *pièces justificatives* is in Hertzberg, *Recueil*, I, 1–64. For the defence of Saxony's neutral attitude see Arneth, *op. cit.*, V, 487–9.

[3] A. Schaefer, *Graf Brühl und Friedrich der Grosse*, in *Historische Zeitschrift* (1866), XV, 151–2. Schaefer admits that Saxony had not formally joined the Austro-Russian alliance of 1755–56.

"I have ground for believing that we can count upon that court," wrote Stahremberg from Paris, alluding to Saxony, on July 25, 1756.[1]

Carlyle calls the preliminaries to this great European war a "topsy-turvying of the old Diplomatic-Political Scheme of Europe."[2] On the Prusso-British side the alliance was a perfectly natural association which, if successful, would preserve the territorial balance of power of Europe. On the other side the Austro-Russian scheme of coalition (joined later by France and Sweden) was certainly immoral in its aim of partitioning Prussia. Frederick was absolutely peaceful after 1748. The cause of the Continental war of 1756 was Maria Theresa's determination to retake Silesia. It is true that Great Britain and France were already practically at war and certain to be absolutely at war soon; but a firm policy and declaration of neutrality on the part of Maria Theresa would undoubtedly have been met by a similar policy on the part of Frederick, whose only desire was to keep what he had. Prusso-Austrian neutrality would have confined the Franco-British war to a purely maritime and colonial contest.

[1] Document in *Preussische und Österreichische Akten, etc.*, p. 476. Cp. Schaefer's article *Der Ursprung des siebenjährigen Krieges*, in *Historische Zeitschrift* (1870), XXIV, 405.

[2] *Frederick the Great*, Bk. XVII, chap. 2 *ad fin.* Cp. Arneth, *Maria Theresa*, IV, 494. Arneth admits that Austria's true interest lay in the English alliance and in peace with Prussia, notwithstanding the *empörende Unrecht* which Austria had suffered at Frederick's hands. For further details see Theodor Bernhardt, *Friedrich II und der Beginn des Siebenjährigen Krieges*, in *Historische Zeitschrift* (1864), XII, 22–68. Bernhardt asks the question, was Frederick justified in beginning the war by marching upon Saxony? He then proves that Prussia was justified in anticipating a war with Austria, but passes over in complete silence the question of justification in attacking Saxony. For the Preliminaries of the Seven Years' War see Volz and Küntzel, *Preussische und Österreichische Akten zur Vorgeschichte des Siebenjährigen Krieges*, in *Publicationen aus den K. Preussischen Staatsarchiven* (1899), LXXIV. See also R. Waddington, *Louis XV et le Renversement des Alliances* (1896); Broglie, *L'Alliance Autrichienne* (1895). For the British efforts to prevent Russia from taking the Austrian side, see *Correspondence of Catherine the Great, when Grand Duchess, with Sir Charles Hanbury-Williams*, 1756–57 (1928), especially p. 89 ff. Hanbury-Williams was British Ambassador at St. Petersburg.

CHAPTER XXX

THE SEVEN YEARS' WAR

In those far-off eighteenth-century days public opinion had not much influence upon the making of wars, although when aroused by victory or defeat it could vitally influence the question of continuing or ending a war. The making of the Continental war (called the Seven Years' or " Third Silesian " War) was an affair of autocratic monarchical governments. The Franco-British war was not made deliberately or by any single act ; it grew out of the tension between the British and French in North America. British public opinion had nothing to do with the inception of this war, as it had with the war of 1740 with Spain—a war largely caused by a worked-up popular clamour in London. The war of 1756 was entered upon by the British with a heavy heart, for political life was at a low ebb : " apathy " was the prevailing note in politics as well as in religion. The Prime Minister, the Duke of Newcastle, who was by no means a bad man, could give no inspiration. " There was no violence, no oppression, no particular complaint, and yet the nation was sinking by degrees, and there was a general indisposition proceeding from the weakness and worthlessness (*sic*) of the minister who would embrace everything and was fit for nothing." [1] After the war was well started, Lord Chesterfield wrote : " Whoever is in, or whoever is out, I am sure we are undone both at home and abroad." [2]

The famous Barrier Treaty of 1715 was of no use in preserving the Austrian Netherlands from French influence, for French garrisons by invitation of Maria Theresa entered Ostend and Nieuport. The Duke of Cumberland, sent to defend Hanover, was defeated by a French army at Hastenbeck (July 26, 1757). Hanover was lost. The duke retreated to Stade near the mouth of the

[1] Doddington's *Diary*, May, 1755, quoted by Lecky, *History of England*, II, 445.

[2] Chesterfield, *Miscellaneous Works*, IV, 198, quoted by Lecky, II, 488.

Elbe and would probably have lost his whole army had he not, through the mediation of Count Lynar, Danish Governor of Oldenburg,[1] made with the French commander, the Duc de Richelieu, the Convention of Closter-seven, September 8, 1757.

Although the Convention was severely criticized then and subsequently in British and Prussian circles, there is reason to believe that the British came off very well and that the French, who if they had pressed the campaign might have captured the whole British army, were the losers. The Convention stipulated for the disbandment of the subsidized troops of Brunswick, Hesse, Gotha and Lippe-Bückeburg, and for the Hanoverians remaining under arms (observing a truce, but without any stipulation about duration) in Stade and on the further (eastern) side of the Elbe. Being not a simple military convention within the competence of the commanders to make, but a political agreement, it required the ratification of the French and British Governments. Pitt, who had become Secretary of State in 1757, recommended George II (who in any case was furious at the Convention) not to ratify it.[2] The Hanoverian army was re-equipped and placed, on the advice of Frederick of Prussia, under Ferdinand, Governor of Magdeburg, brother of the reigning Duke of Brunswick. This resolute act was of a piece with all Pitt's policy. His advent could not be expected immediately to change the fortune of war, but it resulted in a bracing of the torpid public life and an elevating of the national tone. His superb self-confidence was expressed in the famous remark to the Duke of Devonshire: "I am sure that I can save the country, and that no one else can." And as a matter of fact luck did turn very soon, for in the same half-year as Pitt assumed office Frederick chased the French out of most of Hanover by the stunning blow delivered at Rossbach (November 5, 1757). Before this happened Pitt had felt so anxious about Great Britain's chances that he had induced his colleagues to agree to offer Gibraltar to Spain in return for assistance. The offer was delivered at the Court of Madrid through Sir Benjamin Keene, the ambassador who had represented Great Britain since Walpole's time (1727). The Spanish Govern-

[1] Schlosser, *History of the Eighteenth Century* (1845), IV, 117. Koch and Schoell, I, 343.

[2] Lecky, *op. cit.*, II, 490. Smollett for text and arguments for repudiating it (*History of England*, ed. 1800, IV, pp. 163–5 and 214–220). France ratified.

ment, however, refused to depart from its neutrality. Keene was deeply opposed to the idea of ceding Gibraltar. This was the last important business in which he was engaged; "that old and meritorious public servant died at Madrid in the December following."[1]

Frederick's diplomatic position was curious, but in time of war diplomatic abnormality becomes almost the rule. The Elector of Saxony appealed against the invasion of his dominions to the Imperial Diet at Ratisbon. On January 17, 1757, after long debates the Diet by a majority decided to employ its military resources on the side of the Elector against the King of Prussia. The princes of Hanover, Brunswick, Lippe, Waldeck, Hesse and Gotha protested against this resolution of the Diet; they were the subsidiary allies of Great Britain on the side of Frederick. The King of Prussia was not actually put to the ban of the Empire (or outlawed), as he was able to defer the publication of the declaration by putting in a legal plea against a majority decision.[2] In accordance with the Diet's resolution of January 17 steps were taken to levy a contribution on all the states of the Empire and to raise an Imperial army. Actually a small and ill-disciplined Imperial force was raised and was put under command of an Austrian general. It was this army which was broken, along with a French army, at Rossbach.

The Seven Years' War looked as if it were going to divide Europe into two religious camps, like the Thirty Years' War. The opposing coalitions were respectively Catholic and Protestant. Maria Theresa was very devout and was much influenced by her Jesuit chaplains. With her were associated the Catholic Elector of Saxony and the King of France, as well as the Catholic princes of the Empire. Frederick of Prussia was a Protestant (in so far as he had any religion), and he was supported, not merely by Protestant Great Britain, but by the Protestant North German princes. Pitt, when piloting the Prussian subsidy-treaty (£670,000 a year to be given by the British Government) through Parliament spoke of Frederick as "the hero of Protestantism." It is true that the Pope openly hoped for Austrian success and granted permission

[1] Mahon, *History of England* (1853), IV, 167.

[2] He claimed that his case belonged to the class which could only be decided by the individual states (i.e. by the *itio in partes*) not by the Diet. Schlosser, IV, 120.

to the clergy to raise money for the war.[1] On the other hand, Russia and Sweden, which were not Catholic states, were on the side of Maria Theresa and France. The struggle cannot really be regarded as a religious war, because the fortunes of the two religions did not vitally depend upon it; even if Prussia had been partitioned the Austrian and Saxon rulers could not have made the North Germans Protestant. With more justice Frederick was regarded by his supporters as a manly hero fighting against a league of women, priests and parasites—the women being Maria Theresa of Austria, Elizabeth of Russia, and Madame de Pompadour.

The Prusso-British treaty of April 11, 1758, arranged not only for the payment of a British subsidy (£670,000 a year); it also stipulated that neither ally should make peace without the concurrence of the other: "*à ne conclure aucun traité de paix, de trève ou de neutralité . . . que de concert et par un accord mutuel.*" The French on their side had not much heart in the struggle after 1757. They had lost a fine army at Rossbach and were finding the war terribly costly in money. The excesses of their troops, who were very badly supervised by the detestably licentious and indolent Marshal Duke of Richelieu, were giving them a very bad name in Germany. Bernis, the Foreign Minister, was in the spring of 1758 putting forward tentative suggestions for peace with Prussia through the Margravine of Baireuth, sister of Frederick.[2] About the same time Bernis wrote to Richelieu's successor as commander-in-chief in Germany, the Comte de Clermont, on April 24, 1758, that he was desirous of peace, although the king did not like abandoning his friends; he concluded: "the only way to arrive at peace is to push the war with vigour."[3] Bernis' plan now was to disengage France as soon as possible from the heavy obligations to Austria and to use a fortunate victory (if the French army gained one) to try and make peace now; but Maria Theresa was not in a mood for stopping. Stainville, French ambassador at Vienna, who was anxious to become Minister for Foreign Affairs, made himself the instrument of the

[1] Schlosser, IV, 107. Catholicism as one of the bonds of union between Austria and France is given in Kaunitz's famous Memorial drawn up for the Emperor, and sent to Stahremberg, dated August 28, 1756. (Text in Appendix to Broglie's *L'Alliance Autrichienne*, p. 423.)

[2] See A. Schaefer, *Französische Friedensanträge an Preussen vom Jahre* 1758, in *Historische Zeitschrift* (1869), XXI, 112 ff.

[3] Schlosser, IV, 132, from Paris archives.

policy of war until definite success could be achieved. Bernis was removed from the Ministry of Foreign Affairs at the end of the year 1758, and was succeeded by M. de Stainville, who became the Duc de Choiseul. Before leaving Vienna Choiseul (on November 15, 1758), acting on instructions from Louis XV, but without the knowledge of Bernis,[1] had arranged the new terms of alliance which were embodied in the Franco-Austrian treaty of December 30, 1758.

This treaty was secret, like the famous first offensive alliance of May 1, 1757. Its precise terms remained unknown until 1795. France agreed to maintain 100,000 troops in the German theatre of war, and to pay to Austria monthly 288,000 florins. The war was to go on until Austria received Silesia and Glatz.[2] These extremely generous terms given by France to Austria have been severely criticized by historians; and yet they were apparently well calculated to achieve their object, for the next year, 1759, was the worst for Frederick and nearly brought the Continental war to an end. On August 12, 1759, Frederick was completely defeated by Russians and Austrians at the battle of Kunersdorf, near Frankfort on the Oder. He was only prevented from committing suicide by finding that the Russians, to his surprise, neglected to follow up their victory. Good news, too, came from the Western theatre of war, for on August 1 Ferdinand of Brunswick with British and Hanoverian troops had defeated the French at the battle of Minden. On sea and in the colonial theatre of war Great Britain was now in the full tide of success. The naval battles of Lagos and Quiberon Bay and the battle of the Heights of Abraham outside Quebec settled the destinies of empire. But battles at sea and in North America could not save Frederick. The British victory at Minden, however, had been a help. Next year Frederick won the battle of Liegnitz in Silesia against the Austrians, and so saved himself (August 15, 1760), although Berlin had to capitulate to Russians and Austrians on October 9. They only stayed three days. The approach of Frederick, victorious from Liegnitz, compelled them to retire.

In 1760 George II died after ruling for thirty-three years. " An

[1] Waddington, *Guerre de Sept Ans*, II, 466-7.

[2] The treaty was first published by Wenck, III, 185. Dated December 30, 1758, the treaty was not actually signed until March nor ratified until May, 1759. Waddington, *op. cit.*, III, 452.

impartial historian will acknowledge that the reign of George II was in its early part one of the most prosperous and tranquil, and in its latter part one of the most glorious periods in English history; and that the moderation with which the sovereign exercised his prerogative, and the fidelity with which he sacrificed his own wishes in the support of his ministers, contributed in no small measure to the result."[1] His successor, George III, aged twenty-two, though much less martial than his grandfather, was much less tolerant of the trammels imposed on the prerogative since the Revolution of 1688. Almost his first act was to have his tutor and friend Lord Bute sworn of the Privy Council; but he continued Newcastle and Pitt in their offices of Secretary of State. The Prussian subsidy-treaty, which was an annual affair, was renewed for the following year 1761.

Meanwhile, Frederick was still in a very bad way. In October, 1760, the Austrian general Laudohn made a brilliant capture of Schweidnitz in Silesia, and the Austrians were able to pass the winter in that province. The Russians captured Colberg, and so were able to winter in Prussian Pomerania. Although no great battle was fought in this year (1760), it seemed likely to be more fatal to Frederick than the disasters of 1759. A contemporary in London (perhaps Burke) wrote: "His power has gradually crumbled away. . . . In the situation in which he stood after the taking of Colberg we may safely say that there was scarcely a possibility that he could be preserved from destruction by anything that lay within the reach of human endeavours."[2] On the other hand, France was also feeling the strain terribly; and Choiseul, although he had risen to power as the supporter of war, instructed Breteuil, French ambassador at Petersburg, to secure the mediation of the Tsaritsa Elizabeth. When Elizabeth, however, offered her good offices, and Choiseul ordered the ambassador to accept them (March 10, 1761), Louis XV sent contrary instructions, unknown to Choiseul, through "The Secret" (June, 1761).

So the war went on, ruinous for France, and likely to prove fatal to Frederick. Probably what actually saved him was the death of his enemy the Tsaritsa Elizabeth on January 5, 1762. Her nephew, the Duke of Holstein, who succeeded her as Peter III, was an enthusiastic admirer of Frederick, and at once negotiated a suspension of hostilities.

[1] Lecky, *op. cit.*, II, 520.

[2] *Annual Register*, 1761, Part I, 37.

The war ought to have ended in January, 1762. After this date the effusion of blood and treasure was sheer avoidable waste. Austria could not force Frederick to surrender Silesia ; Russia was out of the war ; France had lost her fleet and her chief colonies, and, without sea-power, could not possibly hope to regain them by force of arms. Spain, although she could join in the war, could not supply the sea-power without which France's military efforts were merely bringing her daily nearer to bankruptcy.

In August, 1759, Frederick had written a witty and philosophical letter to Voltaire, mentioning the word peace. Voltaire gave the letter to a mistress of Choiseul, and the mistress showed it to the Minister.[1] In September, 1759, Voltaire received a hint, apparently from Choiseul, to the effect that the King of France was prepared to receive a proposal of peace. Voltaire sent this communication to Frederick through a mutual friend, the Duchess of Saxe-Gotha. Frederick replied to the duchess that he was ready to make peace, but only in conjunction with his allies, Great Britain and Hesse ; and it must be an honourable peace. Whether this meant that he must keep Silesia is uncertain. He would not make difficulties : " I have honour for ten," he wrote.[2]

Frederick sent his news to Pitt, and the two agreed to make a joint declaration on the continuance of the war at the Hague through their ministers there. The declaration was to the effect that their Prussian and British majesties " should think themselves wanting to the duties of humanity . . . if they neglected the proper means to put a stop to the progress of so severe a calamity " ; they therefore proclaimed their readiness to appoint plenipotentiaries who should go to a congress and treat conjointly of a general peace. The Dutch Government presented this manifesto to the diplomatic representatives of Austria and France at the Hague (who, for the purpose, were invited by Louis of Brunswick, commander-in-chief of the Dutch troops, to his château at Ryswick), on November 25, 1759. Nothing came of this declaration.[3]

Two years later, France's financial condition being by this time really desperate, Choiseul (March 26, 1761) sent out a proposal for a Peace Congress, to meet at Augsburg. Austria and Russia

[1] Text of Frederick's and Voltaire's letters in Carlyle, *Frederick*, Bk. XIX, 151–2.

[2] Text of letter of Frederick to the duchess, September 22, 1799, in Carlyle, *Frederick*, Bk. XIX, 104–5.

[3] *Gentleman's Magazine* (1759), XXIX, 603 ; (1760), XXX, 188. Cp. Waddington, *La Guerre de Sept Ans*, III, 489.

also signed the proposal. The British and Prussian Governments at once acquiesced, and named plenipotentiaries. Choiseul, however, before the Congress could meet, thought fit to clear the ground by direct negotiation between France and Great Britain. Pitt agreed and sent an able diplomatist, Hans Stanley, to Paris; Choiseul sent M. de Bussy to London. Hostilities continued all the time. The negotiations broke down (August, 1761), partly because Pitt demanded Minorca (in addition to Canada, which France would have ceded), and partly because he would not agree to withdraw military assistance from Frederick until a general pacification should take place.

Such general pacification was deferred, and new and useless effusion of blood was caused, by the sudden intervention of Spain. Charles III, formerly Charles King of Naples, had now succeeded to the throne of Spain in August, 1759.[1] Charles was a Bourbon with the "family" or "home" sentiment very strongly developed. Choiseul took advantage of this to open a negotiation through Grimaldi, Spanish ambassador at Paris. The affair resulted in the conclusion on August 15, 1761 (two days before the rupture of the London negotiations), of the *Pacte de Famille* or Third Family Compact between the Bourbon monarchs of France and Spain. It was certainly a brilliant stroke of business on the part of Choiseul, for it made Spain "answerable for the sins of France."[2] It was the danger which had hovered over the horizon of William III and his school of great ministers. "The commencement of the War of the Spanish Succession was never yet so fully vindicated as by the conclusion of the Family Compact."[3] The monarchs of Spain and France bound each other to make war and peace in common, and guaranteed each other's dominions as they should be at the conclusion of the next peace.[4] The lure for Spain was, of course, Minorca and Gibraltar. But what can be thought of the statesmanship which exposed the widespread, almost defenceless Spanish empire to the fleets of Great Britain?[5]

Spain had taken part in the London negotiations, and had kept them in being until the armed bullion-fleet should have arrived

[1] Spain and Naples were not united by this. Charles, on going to Spain, made his third son, Ferdinand, King of Naples; Ferdinand's line reigned there until 1860, when it was expelled as a result of the expedition of Garibaldi and "the Thousand."

[2] Schlosser, IV, 170. [3] Mahon, IV, 352.

[4] Wenck, III, 268. Waddington, IV, 607.

[5] Cp. the remarks of Mahon, IV, 357.

safely at Cadiz. For the same reason Pitt, who suspected that Spain and France had concluded an alliance, was of opinion that Great Britain should make war upon Spain while the bullion-fleet could still be caught at sea. It is possible that Pitt had been warned through the Earl Marischal that something in the nature of the Family Compact was going to take place. The Earl Marischal, a Jacobite officer of Frederick, had been on mission in Spain in 1759–60, and again for a short time in 1761. George II, as the ally of Frederick, who was the Marischal's employer, amnestied the old Jacobite on March 29, 1759, on the advice, no doubt, of Pitt.[1] The Marischal visited England in 1759 or 1760. Hans Stanley at Paris had also learned that Spain and France had an agreement, although he did not know the terms.

"There can be no possible doubt that Pitt was honestly anxious to secure peace, but he would not have peace on any lower conditions than those which the military situation seemed to justify."[2] He proposed to break off the British negotiations which were still going on with France, and to make war upon Spain.

On September 18, 1761, there was held one of the most fateful Cabinet meetings in British history. A speedy attack upon Spain would make a prize of the Spanish merchantmen without any new armament or augmentation of the British Navy. "On this principle," explained Pitt later, "I submitted my advice for an immediate declaration of war to a trembling Council."[3] After fruitless discussion, the question was adjourned. Another Cabinet meeting was held, and still one more. Newcastle and Bute were against the war, and Earl Granville (the veteran foreign statesman, Carteret), who was Lord President of the Privy Council, also pronounced against it. On October 5 Pitt resigned. If his expressions seem to imply that he had a passion for humbling the House of Bourbon, an examination of his policy proves that he was actuated by motives of pure prudence and foresight. For the same Cabinet (*minus* Pitt) which refused to declare war against Spain in October, 1761, felt itself compelled to do so on January 4, 1762. The war spread still further, for in April, 1762, Spain made war upon Portugal,

[1] Carlyle, Bk. XIV, 162–3. The Marischal's ancestor had founded Marischal College, Aberdeen, in 1593; hence Carlyle's particular interest. For the question of Pitt's possible knowledge of the Family Compact see A. von Ruville, *William Pitt, Earl of Chatham* (1907), II, 405–6.

[2] Ruville, *op. cit.*, II, 391.

[3] Mahon, IV, 359. Debate in House of Lords, November 22, 1770.

Great Britain's most ancient ally, and the British Parliament had to vote a sum of £1,000,000 towards its defence. In June, 1762, Newcastle, the partner with Pitt in the most famous ministry (1757–61) in all British history, resigned his post as First Lord of the Treasury ; Bute took it, and accordingly became Prime Minister.

At the beginning of the year 1762 Frederick's military position "was wellnigh hopeless." [1] The death of the Tsaritsa Elizabeth and the accession of Peter III in Russia on January 5, 1762, was a stroke of great fortune for Frederick. The Tsar made a truce with Prussia on March 16, 1762, and peace on May 5, according to the *status quo ante bellum.*[2] On the other hand, luck seemed to turn again when Peter was deposed by a palace-revolution on July 9, 1762. However, Peter's wife, who became Tsaritsa or empress as Catherine II, maintained the peace-treaty in force. On July 22 the Russian troops in the Silesian theatre of war began to be withdrawn. Sweden also had made peace with Prussia, on the basis of the *status quo ante bellum* by the Treaty of Hamburg, May 22, 1762. Frederick's military position was thus greatly improved. Bute's plan for a general pacification involved the cession of some pieces of territory to Austria and Russia. Frederick absolutely refused to disclose the terms on which he would agree to peace.[3]

The naval war of Great Britain against France continued to be successfully conducted in 1762, Martinique being captured from the French, Havana and the Philippines from the Spanish (the news of the capture of the Philippines did not, however, arrive at London until after the conclusion of peace). Frederick was doing extremely well in the Silesian theatre ; and Ferdinand of Brunswick, who had about 100,000 British and subsidized German troops, was finding no great trouble in dealing with the French in Westphalia. The subsidy-treaty with Prussia (which was a purely annual instrument, made in 1757, and renewed on the last occasion in 1760) was allowed to expire after the end of its last legal period, on December 12, 1761.[4]

The British Government was quite free to make peace if it chose.[5] Lord Bute resolved to open direct negotiations with the French. As was the custom in those days, without the conclusion of any

[1] Lodge, *Great Britain and Prussia in the Eighteenth Century,* 113.

[2] Hertzberg, *Recueil,* I, 288.

[3] *Ibid.,* 295.

[4] Lodge, 107–8.

[5] Lodge, 115, 123, 133, 135.

armistice, the diplomatists were put in touch with each other. Contact was first made through Count Vitry, the minister at London of the neutral government of Sardinia; and the Duke of Bedford was sent to Paris, the Duke of Nivernois to London.

The French, who were really much exhausted by the war, eagerly entered into the overtures. The Preliminary Treaty of Peace [1] was signed at Fontainebleau on November 3, 1762, between France, Spain and Great Britain, Portugal acceding in the same month. Care was taken by the British Government to safeguard Frederick's interests, and by France to safeguard Austria's. Great Britain and France bound themselves to furnish no more succours for the war in Germany. In addition, the French agreed to evacuate the Prussian territory (in Cleves and Gueldres) which they had occupied on the Rhine. Great Britain obtained from France Canada and Cape Breton Island, but the French kept St. Pierre and Miquelon as unfortified resting-places for their fishermen. In the West Indies Great Britain acquired from France Tobago, Dominica, St. Vincent and Granada, and restored to her Guadeloupe, Martinique and St. Lucia. In Africa the French gave up Senegal and received back Goree; in India they recovered their factories and settlements on condition of maintaining no troops in Bengal. Spain was included in the Preliminary Treaty, and had to cede Florida to Great Britain. France indemnified Spain by ceding Louisiana, in a separate and secret convention. Minorca, which was a British possession, captured by France in 1756, was restored to Great Britain. All Portuguese possessions taken by France and Spain were restored.

The Preliminary Treaty of Peace was submitted to Parliament and was approved in both houses on the same day (December 9, 1762); in the Lords Pitt criticized almost every article of it in a speech which lasted for three and a half hours, yet 319 peers voted for the Government and only 65 against. The Final Treaty of Peace, which does not materially differ from the preliminary terms, was signed by the Duke of Bedford at Paris on February 10, 1763.[2] The British negotiators neglected to insert a stipulation for payment of the ransom, which had been one of the terms of the capitulation of Manilla when captured by Admiral Cornish and General Draper. The Grenville administration, after the fall of

[1] Martens, *Recueil*, I, 92.
[2] Treaty in Martens, *Recueil*, I, 104.

Bute, were unable to obtain it; hence Dr. Johnson's criticism about George Grenville's rather mechanical efficiency: "Could he have enforced payment of the Manilla ransom, he could have counted it." [1]

When the Franco-British Preliminary Treaty was signed Frederick wrote to his friend, the Duchess of Saxe-Gotha (December 6, 1762): "Messieurs the English continue to betray. Poor M. Mitchell [the English diplomatist with Frederick] has had a stroke of apoplexy on hearing it. It is a hideous thing, but I will speak of it no more." [2] As a matter of fact he had little to complain about. With all French support withdrawn from Maria Theresa, Frederick could easily deal with the danger from Austria, which was far more exhausted than the British Government had thought. The only real criticism which he could have against the British treaty was that it did not specify the State to which the French should deliver Cleves and Gueldres when evacuated. Probably none of the negotiators dreamed that anyone but the owner, Frederick, would receive them. But the Austrians threatened to occupy Cleves and Gueldres (as, being at war, they had a perfect right to try to do). Frederick had little difficulty, however, in finding enough troops to take delivery of the territories from the French.

The Habsburg-Bourbon Alliance bound the two parties not to make peace except in common. The French, however, could say, like the British at the end of the Spanish Succession War, that they could not go on fighting for ever, in order to satisfy Habsburg pride and obstinacy. Besides, Choiseul had informed Kaunitz of the negotiations with Great Britain in 1762; and Kaunitz had unwillingly given Choiseul leave to make a separate peace.[3] The Austrians themselves had taken an obligation towards the Empire not to cease from war "until the estates of the Empire which had sent contingents to the Imperial army should have received full indemnification for their costs." [4] However, Maria Theresa had no difficulty in persuading her husband, Francis I, who was Emperor, to declare himself neutral. Thus, free to make peace, she opened negotiations through a Saxon privy-councillor, Baron von Fritsch [5]

[1] Boswell, *Life of Johnson*, sub anno 1771.

[2] Carlyle, Bk. XX, chap. 13.

[3] J. F. Bright, *Maria Theresa* (1897), pp. 179, 180.

[4] Schlosser, IV, 194.

[5] Carlyle, Bk. XX, chap. 13; Schlosser, IV, 195. Koch and Schoell, I, 360.

(although he was not a neutral), with Frederick, and peace was soon, made at the Castle of Hubertusburg, near Leipsig, on February 15, 1763, on the basis of the *status quo ante bellum.* Thus Frederick was absolutely justified in his refusal of Lord Bute's proposals of 1762 for a general pacification with the condition that Prussia should make some cessions to Austria. He retained Silesia exactly as he had it at the opening of the war.[1] With Saxony and Poland Frederick also made peace on February 15, 1763, at Hubertusburg, without cessions or payments on either side. No treaty of peace was needed between Austria and Great Britain, for these two States had never declared war.

The general pacification of 1762–63 was in accordance with the results of the war. The Silesian question was definitely settled. Dominion in North America passed from France to Great Britain. On the British side, notwithstanding the very large gains, it was not an ungenerous peace. By a ruthless determination to exploit the full consequences of military and naval success and financial strength, Havana could have been obtained from Spain and Martinique and Louisiana from France; seen from this point of view, the British annexations were moderate. One serious flaw in the British negotiation was in regard to Newfoundland; the French retained the right to catch fish and to land on the Treaty Shore. This privilege, originally recognized in the Treaty of Utrecht, was a source of much friction throughout the next century and was not adjusted until the Franco-British Entente was made in 1904.

On Frederick the Franco-British separate peace left a deep impression. It wholly estranged him from Great Britain, and is believed to have been the beginning of the eastern policy which led him in 1772 to be one of the partitioners of Poland.[2]

"It is the common result of great wars not to produce great effects," wrote Frederick at the end of the Second Silesian War of 1745. "Europe, which divides itself into two parties at the first raising of the buckler, establishes by the alliances an equality of forces which for the most part prevents one of the parties from gaining the superiority over the other." [3] This statement is

[1] Hertzberg, *Recueil,* I, 295.

[2] Mahon, IV, 378. For further details on this chapter see R. Waddington, *La guerre de Sept Ans* (1899), 5 vols. down to November, 1762; R. H. Soltau, *The Duke de Choiseul* (1909); R. Lodge, *Great Britain and Prussia in the Eighteenth Century* (1923).

[3] *Histoire de mon temps,* ad fin.

certainly not correct if applied to the great wars of the nineteenth and twentieth centuries. It might be considered to be true with respect to the Austro-Prussian struggle of the Seven Years' War, which left the two Powers with territories unchanged; but with regard to France and Great Britain, the associates of the two principal allies, Frederick's remark is quite inapplicable. Far from making no change, the great war of 1756–63 resulted in the loss of a grand overseas empire of France and the transference of colonial dominion to Great Britain.

CHAPTER XXXI

THE DECLINE OF THE EMPIRE

Of the three European empires—the Roman, the Carolingian and the Holy Roman—the third had never been much of a reality. It never wholly lost its international quality, for certain foreign sovereigns were in the seventeenth and eighteenth centuries members of the Empire for particular territories. Thus the King of Sweden had a vote in the Diet (Reichstag) for Pomerania, the King of Great Britain for Hanover, the King of Denmark for Holstein. But the Empire, just like any other state, had no title to exist unless it could preserve peace among its members and could protect the whole body from external attack. The Thirty Years' War and the Seven Years' War had shown the futility of the Empire from this point of view. Goethe, who was practising law in the Supreme Imperial Court of law at Wetzlar in 1772, wrote later in *Faust*:

> Das liebe, heil'ge Röm'sche Reich
> Wie hälts nur noch zusammen ?

Yet, phantom as it seemed to be, the Empire is to the historian, publicist or international lawyer, a deeply interesting organization because in certain respects it was superior to national prejudices, and because it had a court before which sovereign bodies could plead and could be arraigned. There was indeed litigation enough. " The whole German life," wrote Schlosser, " was under the guidance of writing pedants," and in the same sentence he added : " The German always talks and writes instead of acting." [1] As between the sovereign states of the Empire in the eighteenth century, the courts, although often appealed to, were of practically no avail. Frederick the Great solved his legal problems with his brother (or sister) sovereigns by arms.

Joseph II, co-Emperor with his mother, the Empress Maria Theresa from the year 1765, wished to make the Empire a reality,

[1] Schlosser, V, 31.

but, as a Habsburg, his interest in his hereditary Austrian dominions was as strong as his interest in the Empire. In 1777 Maximilian Joseph, Elector of Bavaria, died; with him the Bavarian branch of the House of Wittelsbach became extinct. His heir was Charles Theodore, Elector of the Palatinate, who had no legitimate children; after Charles Theodore the heir of the Wittelsbach dominions was the Duke of Deux Ponts (Zweibrücken). The Emperor, Joseph II, in order to consolidate and round off his territories laid claim to Lower Bavaria and some other lordships, and was able to advance certain feudal pleas in justification. The international situation seemed favourable. Kaunitz thought that France (because of the Habsburg-Bourbon Alliance) and Great Britain (because Frederick had cast her off) would consent to Joseph's scheme.[1]

Charles Theodore, whose country, like that of the Duke in *Jew Süss*, was a prey to mistresses and other parasites, was induced by offers of provision for his illegitimate children, to agree with Joseph II, by treaty signed by his minister Ritter and by Kaunitz at Vienna on January 3, 1778, conceding the claims of Austria. The treaty, which was communicated to the other German courts, conceded about half of Bavaria to Joseph, who was authorized to occupy it forthwith. This he proceeded to do.[2]

Frederick determined to stop this traffic in territory of states of the Empire. He was not alone. The Duke of Deux Ponts naturally protested; so did the Elector of Saxony. Frederick published an illuminating *brochure* on the Bavarian question, composed by the capable Hertzberg,[3] and sent, not one of his regular diplomatists, but a specially appointed agent, to the Diet at Ratisbon and to the Duke of Deux Ponts.[4] This man was Eustace von Görtz, formerly tutor to the Duke of Weimar. Görtz, incessantly active at Ratisbon, at Munich, at Mannheim, aroused public opinion against the Austrian proposals; and then, when the time was ripe, Frederick led 100,000 into Bohemia (July 5, 1778).

There ensued a state of war between Austria and Prussia lasting for over twelve months. Joseph II meant to fight, but his mother,

[1] See A. Beer, *Zur Geschichte des bayerischen Erfolgekriegs*, in *Historische Zeitschrift* (XXXV), 1876, p. 90.

[2] Treaty in Koch and Schoell. See also Kaunitz to Riedesel in Hertzberg, *Recueil*, II, 54.

[3] *Considérations sur le droit de la succession de Bavière* in Hertzberg, II, 1–25.

[4] See A. Beer, *op. cit.*, in *Historische Zeitschrift* (XXXV), 1876, pp. 108, 124, 125.

the co-Empress, was determined on peace. There is an element of unreality about this war in Bohemia and in Austrian Silesia, and yet many men lost their lives, some by arms, more by disease. Frederick, probably, by brusque attacks and rapid marching, after the manner of his younger days, could have gone to Vienna and dictated his own terms—" which is obviously absurd," writes Carlyle, " Frederick's object not being to lay Austria flat, or drive animosities to the sanguinary point, and kindle all Europe into war, but merely to extract, with the minimum of violence, something like justice from Austria on this Bavarian matter." [1] Whether it was precisely justice that Frederick was demanding is another question. He was certainly preventing the Empire from becoming a reality, for he was insisting on decision by the sword instead of by the *Reichskammergericht* at Wetzlar or the Reichstag at Ratisbon. He was asserting Prussian military domination and Bavarian particularism.

While the armies were waiting in entrenched camps, marching, or making raids on small towns and fortresses, the diplomatists were in touch and were actively negotiating. Louis Cobenzl represented Maria Theresa in Berlin; and later the famous baron Thugut was sent, on the initiative of the Empress herself " and much to the discontent of Joseph," [2] from Vienna to Frederick's headquarters in Bohemia. Russia, the ally of Prussia, and France, the ally of Austria, offered good offices. Saxony and probably Sardinia were supporting Prussia.[3] The question was at last liquidated in a Congress which met at Teschen in Austrian Silesia, from March 10 to May 13, 1779. There were present Repnin for Russia, Breteuil for France, Cobenzl for Austria, Hertzberg for Prussia. The Terms of Peace, signed at Teschen on May 13, 1779, arranged that Charles Theodore should be released from the Convention of Vienna of January 3, 1778, and should inherit all Bohemia except a small part (34 square miles) situated between the Inn, Danube and Sulzach which was to be ceded to Austria.[4] The terms of the Peace were guaranteed by the two Mediating Powers, France and Russia.[5]

[1] Carlyle, Bk. XXI, chap. 6.

[2] See A. Beer, *Die Sendung Thuguts in das preussische Hauptquartier und der Friede von Teschen*, in *Historische Zeitschrift*, 1877 (Neue Folge 2), p. 403.

[3] *Ibid.*

[4] There were three treaties signed at Teschen on May 13, 1779, between Austria on the one hand and on the other (1) Prussia, (2) the Elector Palatine, (3) Saxony. Koch and Schoell, I, 454. Martens, *Recueil*, II, 661 ff.

[5] *Ibid.*, pp. 682, 683.

So ended this war of raids and requisitions called in disgust by the Prussians the *Kartoffel Krieg*, the Potato War. It cost Frederick £2,000,000 and 10,000 men, and probably rather more to the Austrians; it put absolute check upon Austria's attempt to advance into South Germany; and it made impossible the development of a strong Empire of the German States under the Habsburg monarchy.

In 1784–5 the Austro-Prussian or Habsburg-Hohenzollern Question was raised again through a plan which Joseph II (inspired by Kaunitz) put forward for exchanging his distant possession, Belgium (the Austrian Netherlands, to be called the Kingdom of Burgundy), for Bavaria. Charles Theodore of Bavaria seemed to approve; the Duke of Deux Ponts, who had the reversionary right to Bavaria, might be won over. But Frederick, now very old, was still ready to oppose Austria, more especially as he was alarmed at this time by the prospect of an Austro-Russian alliance. His minister Hertzberg proposed to him that a League of Princes might be formed in defence of the constitution of the Empire.[1] Frederick thereupon "with his own hand" drafted a project of a league, stating in the first line of the draft that the League had no offensive object, but aimed only at maintaining the rights and immunities of the Princes of Germany.[2] After three weeks' conference in Berlin, plenipotentiaries of Prussia, Saxony, and Hanover signed, July 23, 1785, the Fürstenbund Covenant for maintaining the Peace of Westphalia and other Imperial peace-treaties, and for preserving the integrity of the circles of the Empire. The League was soon joined by Mainz, Deux Ponts, Baden and other princes. Joseph II at once gave up the exchange project. The creation of a Kingdom of Belgium was postponed for forty-five years. Moreover, the constitution of the Empire received a serious shock. Frederick's plan for a Fürstenbund happened to coincide with ideas actually in existence at the time among the smaller German princes for a union of princes, which indeed they hoped would be established on a permanent footing. It was clear that the Emperor had now no real authority outside Austria at all.[3]

Frederick the Great died at Sans Souci in the early morning

[1] See Hertzberg, *Recueil*, II, 364, note.

[2] See P. Bailleu, *Der Ursprung des Deutschen Fürstenbundes*, in *Historische Zeitschrift* (V), 1879, 425, 433.

[3] See K. Obser, *Zur Geschichte des Fürstenbundes*, in *Forschungen zur Brandenburgischen und Preuss. Geschichte* (1892), V, 471–82.

of August 17, 1786. He had practically broken up the Empire and had greatly weakened the respect of peoples for the public law of Europe. He left annexation as a principle in Prussian policy, and war as a normal instrument of that policy. Carlyle tells a story of the last years of the childless old king. Frederick was writing at a table and was constantly interrupted by the ball of one of his small grand-nephews (he was fond of children) who was playing in the same room. At last when the ball had hit the king several times he put it in his pocket. The boy insisted on restoration. The King went on writing. "Will your Majesty give me my ball then?" The king looked up at the tense little figure, "planted firm, hands on haunches, and wearing quite a peremptory air." The amused king gave in and flung back the ball. "They won't get Silesia out of thee," he remarked.[1] A frontier held by bristling bayonets—this was the legacy of the great Hohenzollern: *toujours en vedette*. He had put Prussia into the condition of a besieged fortress.[2]

[1] Carlyle, Bk. XXI, Chap. 8.

[2] See P. Bailleu, *Der Ursprung des Deutschen Fürstenbundes*, in *Historische Zeitschrift* (V), 411. For further information on this chapter see Paganel, *Histoire de Joseph II* (1843); Temperley, *Frederick the Great and Kaiser Joseph* (1915).

CHAPTER XXXII

THE END OF POLAND

Peter the Great set Russia upon two lines of external policy which it followed consistently for something over two hundred years. One line was along the Baltic, the other towards Constantinople. The instruments of his policy were some of the natives, like Mentchikoff and the Dolgoroukis, others Scottish, Swiss or German, especially Germans of Saxony. These foreigners were, naturally, particularly interested in Russia's western advance. On the other hand, in Germany itself, the princes and their advisers viewed with some alarm this Russian movement towards Central Europe. The plan which from about 1725 began to take shape fairly precisely in their minds for meeting this "Russian inundation" was the somewhat curious one of partitioning Poland—the vast republic whose frontierless and inert mass lay between Germany and the empire of the Tsars.

By the Treaty of the Pruth (or Falczi), 1711, the Porte had compelled Russia to agree to withdraw permanently from the internal affairs of Poland.[1] But among the Polish nobles, by inveterate habit attached more to their privileges than to their country's liberty, there were always many who were ready even to call in Russia. In 1716 a party or Confederation of Polish nobles invited intervention of the Russian Czar: "We wish that his ambassador intervene in our affairs as being the Minister of a most just Potentate."[2] In 1724 the Porte compelled Peter the Great to re-establish the Treaty of the Pruth, which the Poles in 1716 had renounced. Only opportunity and force could henceforth decide between these two

[1] Art. 3 of the Treaty of Falczi, July 21, 1711, see Koch and Schoell, IV, 362. Full text in Dumont, Tome VIII, Partie I, p. 275.

[2] See Preamble to the "Preliminaries of the proposed treaty"; text in Dumont, VIII, Partie I, p. 482; also article 5 of the proposed terms, "We have chosen as Guarantors of the peace the Tsar of Russia and the Cham of the Tartars."

contrary clauses, of which one was for the republic its anchor of safety, the other its charter of servitude.[1]

When Augustine II of Saxony and Poland died in 1733, the French envoy at Warsaw, acting on instructions from France, supported the claim to election of the national candidate, Stanislaus Leczynski, father-in-law of Louis XV. This claim had also the support of France's allies, Sweden and Turkey. Against such a coalition Austria naturally advanced another candidate, the son of Augustus II; and the Russian court, to prevent Franco-Swedish-Turkish ascendancy in Poland, supported Austria. Stanislaus, who was living at Wissembourg, travelled to Warsaw disguised as a coachman and was elected by the Sejm on September 4. But a dissenting minority of the Polish nobles took no part in the voting.

The Russian policy was—from the point of view of Russia—thoroughly sound. It was to convert Poland into a protectorate by means of Augustus III of Saxony. France, far away, had no means of preventing this except by arousing to action the two states most directly interested in the integrity and independence of Poland; these were Sweden and Turkey. But the French ambassador, de Castera, vainly strove to move the Swedish oligarchy, and Villeneuve had little more success at Constantinople. France had one more chance: the Russians and Austrians disagreed. Then Louis XV made the final mistake. Moved by fear that Lorraine would be united to the Habsburgs through the marriage of Duke Francis with Maria Theresa, he declared war upon Austria. "Henceforth the Russians had in the East their hands free." [2]

The Russo-Austrian candidate for the Polish throne, Augustus III, was established at Warsaw (October, 1733). The allies then turned against Turkey which had remained passive when it should have intervened. But the Turkish war which Russia undertook in 1736 and Austria in 1737 was a surprising failure. The pasha Bonneval, a French adventurer, reorganized the Turkish army and gave it a plan of defence. A new French ambassador at Stockholm won over the oligarchy of Stockholm to threaten war against Russia. A brisk advance of the Turkish army on the Danube looked like ending with the capture of Belgrade. The Austrian generals and court were disheartened; and, moreover,

[1] Bourgeois, *Manuel historique*, I, 397.

[2] *Ibid.*, 401.

they had received a report from their representative with the Russian army to the effect that the Russians were going to make a separate peace with the Turks.[1] If this report were true (its correctness has never been established) the whole force of Turkey would soon be directed against the failing armies of Austria. Villeneuve was at the Grand Vizier's headquarters, acting as mediator, and for a time even as plenipotentiary for the Emperor Charles VI. By the Treaty of Belgrade (September 1, 1739) Austria renounced its possession of this fortress, the key to the Sanjac and Macedonia, and gave up also Little Wallachia and all the gains made at Passarowitz. The preamble to the treaty mentions Villeneuve as having acted as mediator and "at first as plenipotentiary."[2] The treaty was the greatest stroke of success scored by French diplomacy since the bequest by will of the Spanish king Charles II was secured for France. "Let the Turks pay their dues of gratitude to Mahomet and Villeneuve," cried the Russian Marshal Münnich, when he heard of the Peace of Belgrade. A long lease of life was gained for Turkey-in-Europe. Cardinal Fleury followed up this diplomatic success by making a tripartite alliance—France, Sweden and Turkey (1739).[3] The time seemed ripe for the undoing of the Treaty of Nystadt—for taking Livonia, Esthonia and the Duchy of Courland too, which was now under Russia, from Russia. But the Baltic peoples had to wait till 1918 for their liberation.

By starting the Seven Years' War, Maria Theresa recklessly encouraged the Russians to pour over Poland and Brandenburg. Nothing but the death of the Tsaritsa Elizabeth and the accession of the infatuated Peter in January, 1762, seems to have saved eastern Germany from falling under the Russians. "The caprice of one of their despots made them lose the fruit and interrupted the course of their progress at the hour when a decisive victory was about to confirm it."[4]

Peter III of Russia was assassinated after a six-months' reign. The autocracy of Russia came into the hands of his widow, the

[1] See T. Tupetz, *Der Turkenkrieg von* 1739 *und der Friede zu Belgrad*, in *Historische Zeitschrift* (IV), 1878, pp. 33, 34.

[2] Treaty in Wenck, I, 317.

[3] Treaty between Sweden and Turkey for mutual defence against Russia, Constantinople, December 2, 1739 (Wenck, I, 504). The alliance of France and the Porte had no definite stipulations concerning assistance. It was an "Entente" rather than an alliance; see the Capitulations or Treaty of 1740 in Wenck, I, 540.

[4] Bourgeois, *Manuel historique*, I, 417.

German princess, Catherine of Anhalt-Zerbst. This intelligent and strong-willed woman had wholly identified herself with the ambitions of Russia, that is, of Peter the Great and the great corps of military and civil functionaries which he had founded. In the year after Catherine's accession, Augustus III of Saxony and Poland died (October 5, 1763). The reopening of the Polish throne to an election gave Catherine the opportunity to finish the work which Peter III had broken off in the last year of the Seven Years' War. She had only to secure a Russian nominee on the Polish throne and the protectorate would be completed. French and Austrian diplomacy, impaired by the cross-currents and failures of the Seven Years' War, had now no strength in Eastern Europe.

There was one monarch, however, the King of Prussia, whom nobody could hoodwink. He saw Poland lying at the mercy of Catherine; and judging it inexpedient or impossible to try and save the feeble republic, he resolved to have a share in its destruction. Catherine, on her side not feeling strong enough to act quite alone, offered alliance to Frederick, who sent Count Solms to St. Petersburg to complete the negotiation. On April 11, 1764, the Russo-Prussian treaty of alliance was signed. "This was that unholy alliance which from 1764 till the present day has proved the source of all the misfortunes of the European nations, because it has served as a model for all the treaties since concluded by means of which the fate and internal administration of the weaker states have become wholly dependent on the compacts, arms and diplomatists of powerful foreign nations." [1]

In the public articles of this treaty (which was stipulated to endure for eight years) the two states guaranteed their respective possessions in Europe (Silesia was particularly in Frederick's mind), and to defend each other, in case of attack, with 12,000 men or with all their forces, if necessary. The secret article stated:

> As it is to the interest of H.M. the King of Prussia and of H.M. the Empress of all the Russians, to employ all their care and all their efforts in order that the Republic of Poland be maintained in its right of free election, and that it be permitted to nobody to make the said kingdom hereditary in his family, or to make himself absolute there, H.M. the King of Prussia and Her Imperial Majesty have promised and engaged themselves mutually and in the strongest manner by this secret article, not only not to permit that anyone, whoever it be, undertake to despoil the republic of its right of free election, to make

[1] Schlosser, IV, 383.

the kingdom hereditary or to make himself absolute there in any of the ways that may be possible; but also to prevent and to destroy by all possible means and by a common accord the views and designs which can conduce to this end as soon as they shall be discovered, and even to have in case of need recourse to force of arms to guarantee the republic from the overturning of its constitution and of its fundamental laws.[1]

Considering that the Polish "constitution," thus guaranteed, was no constitution at all, and that the fundamental laws (noble *liberum veto* and right of confederation) were a mainspring of anarchy, the intention of the secret article was obviously cynical and immoral. In effect the Treaty of St. Petersburg arranged for a *condominium* of Russia and Prussia over Poland. But a condominium of two powerful states over a weaker always ends either by one giving way before the other, or by the two partners dividing the territory between themselves. Thus the Treaty of St. Petersburg of 1764 was the basis of the Partition of 1772. Frederick's letter in 1763 to his friend the Electress Marie Antoine of Saxony (who wanted him to use his influence to make her son King of Poland)—"As for me, madame, I wish, if possible, not to meddle at all with this business"[2]—seems disingenuous.

The Treaty of St. Petersburg, which admitted Prussia to condominium in Poland, was a sacrifice for Russia, because the Tsars already could claim a right to intervene (that is, to have the protectorate) in Poland by the Act of the Confederates of 1716. On the other hand, while the St. Petersburg treaty increased, at that time, the influence of Prussia, it also, by bringing Prussia and Russia close together in the Polish affair, menaced Prussia's future security. This menace was met by a century of Prusso-Russian alliance, which was "not the result of an accord freely adopted by both parties nor justified by community of interests. It was the double effect of reciprocal fear and of opposed covetousness."[3] The Partition of 1772 makes this fact all the more apparent.

The unfortunate country was brought quickly to its doom. The Russian soldier and diplomatist, Repnin, openly supported by Russian troops, controlled Warsaw, and on February 24, 1768, succeeded in making a treaty between Russia and Poland by which Russia became guarantor of the integrity of Polish territory, and

[1] Martens, *Recueil*, I, 229.
[2] November 11, 1763. Text in Carlyle, Bk. XXI, chap. 3.
[3] Bourgeois, *Manuel historique*, I, 429.

also of the Polish Constitution and thus acquired from the Republic itself the right of intervention.[1]

Catherine II had thus regained practically sole control over Poland and had gently excluded the participation of Prussia in the condominium. But suddenly a number of Polish nobles protested and formed (as was their constitutional privilege) a military confederation, at Bar. Louis XV and Choiseul seized the occasion to reassert the lost authority of France; they sent money to the Confederates of Bar, and they aroused the Turks. The eminent diplomatist, Vergennes, then ambassador at Constantinople and afterwards Minister of Foreign Affairs, induced the Porte to declare war upon Russia, October 6, 1768. It was the last effort made by France to stop the advance of Russia into Central Europe.

The French resources, however, were not adequate; the diplomacy of Louis XV lacked constancy, and his allies were wanting in strength. The Russians beat the Turks by land and sea. Maria Theresa and Joseph II became apprehensive, and began to ensure themselves against the future by annexing Zips, a district of Poland south of Galicia, on the Hungarian slopes of the Carpathians (February, 1769). If an Austro-Russian war occurred, Frederick of Prussia was bound by the Treaty of St. Petersburg, 1764, to support Russia. Kaunitz, the Austrian Chancellor, did consider the chances of a war in which Austria, with her French ally (the Habsburg-Bourbon alliance still existed) and Turkey, should face Russia and Prussia—a new "seven years' war" which perhaps would not have lasted so long, and might have saved Poland. Decision failed him, however; and in a few months the face of Eastern European politics was completely changed by a proposal put forward by Frederick the Great. This was a plan, which Count Lynar (the Danish diplomatist and Governor of Oldenburg who had mediated in the Convention of Closter-seven in 1757) suggested to him for a tripartite partition of Poland in 1769, and which Frederick communicated to Russia.[2] The three great states of Central and Eastern Europe instead of fighting would divide the carcase. Thus the veteran Danish diplomatist, Count Lynar, from the village to which he had retired, could still, said Frederick the Great, claim to govern Europe.

[1] Martens, *Recueil*, I, 535.

[2] Martens, *Recueil des Traités et Conventions conclus par la Russie*, II, 15.

The Partition of Poland, immoral act though it was, had in its initial stages much that is incidentally interesting and commendable to historians of diplomacy. "It is the first example," writes Frederick, "which history furnishes of a partition, regulated and terminated peaceably between three Powers." [1] It is an instance of international "concert," carried on with the object of maintaining peace, although by the sacrifice of a helpless neutral. There were many exchanges of visits between diplomatists; and the three monarchs, Frederick, Joseph and Catherine, established a friendly understanding.

The first interview of Frederick and Joseph took place at Neisse in September, 1769, in Silesia, where Joseph came ostensibly to take part in a review of Prussian troops. The Spartan young Emperor stayed for three days, under the name of Graf von Falkenstein, at the inn of the Three Kings, refusing to use the grand apartments which Frederick had prepared for him. Although Neisse was not a great city, there was an opera which the two monarchs attended. Monarchs seldom met in the late eighteenth or early nineteenth century without seeing an opera. Frederick gave his youthful admirer a copy of Marechal Saxe's *Rêveries*. Joseph ever afterwards kept the book by his bedside. It was there still when he died—not a page cut.[2]

Joseph at the time of the Neisse interview, restive at the advance of Russia against the Turks, seemed still inclined to declare war against Catherine. It was on returning from Neisse, apparently, that Frederick sent Lynar's partition-plan to Russia.

Frederick returned the Kaiser's visit by attending the Austrian reviews at Neustadt in Moravia from the 3rd to the 7th September, 1770. Frederick and his suite appeared in white Austrian uniforms. The king stood respectfully at the head of Joseph's horse and held the bridle when the Emperor put his foot in the stirrup. The two monarchs went to the play together. Yet in spite of their cordiality, the neighbouring province of Silesia, writes the Prince de Ligne, still cast its shadow between them. The chief subject of discussion was the Russo-Turkish War. Chancellor Kaunitz was in attendance with Joseph. It was just after the Neisse interviews that Joseph II quietly allowed his troops, which were already in occupation of Zips, to extend the occupied area by planting their standards over

[1] *Mémoires*, p. 47.
[2] Carlyle, Bk. XXV, chap. 4.

the frontier in a neighbouring piece of Poland.[1] Frederick the Great declared afterwards that the Austrian occupation of Zips was the thing which contributed most to decide him in favour of the partition of Poland.[2]

In the autumn of the year 1770 Frederick's useful brother Henry was at Stockholm in the palace of Drottingholm on a visit to his sister Louisa Ulrica, who was Queen of Sweden. While there he received an invitation from Catherine II to come to St. Petersburg. It is said that this was not brought about by any suggestion of Frederick, and that "if Poland got its fate from the circumstance, it was by accident, and by the fact that Poland's fate was drop-ripe, ready to fall by a touch." [3] On or about New Year's day, 1771, there was a grand masked ball lasting from six in the evening until five in the morning, given by the Empress at St. Petersburg. Catherine took the opportunity of saying to Henry, *à propos* of the Austrian annexation of Zips: " It seems, in Poland you have only to stoop and pick up what you like of it. If the Court of Vienna have the notion to dismember that kingdom, its neighbours will have right to do as much." [4]

In February, 1771, Henry was back at Potsdam with his news from Russia. Austria was still threatening to make war against Russia, and was secretly intriguing for alliance with the Turks. On July 6, 1771, Thugut at Constantinople actually concluded with the Porte a treaty for the participation of Austria in the war in which Turkey was engaged against Russia; but the treaty was not ratified.[5] Frederick may have suspected the Austro-Turkish negotiation. Anxious to avoid war (and to avoid it profitably), he pressed forward his partition-project. Austria was averse, and put off the negotiation. Events did not move quickly, but early in the year 1772, Frederick and Catherine were in full agreement, and on January 4, 1772, Count Panin and Prince Galitzin for Russia, and Count Solms for Prussia signed a Convention, embodying their partition-scheme, and contracting with each other to take possession on the beginning of spring. Austria was to be invited to share in the partition.[6] Then Austria came into the bargain, stating that her share must be equal to that

[1] Oncken, *Das Zeitalter Friedrichs des Grossen*, II, 501-2.

[2] Martens, *Recueil des Traités et Conventions conclus par la Russie*, II, 15 (Introduction to the Act of February 19, 1772).

[3] Carlyle, *ibid.*

[4] Cp. *Œuvres de Frédéric*, XXVI, 345.

[5] Martens, *Recueil*, II, 19.

[6] Martens, *Recueil*, VI, 71.

of the other two Powers (Act signed at Vienna by Maria Theresa and Joseph, February 19, 1772). The final agreements between the three Powers was dated July 25, 1772, at St. Petersburg.[1] Possession followed by way of military occupation; indeed in May the three Powers had already provisionally seized their shares. The three Powers taxed themselves ("*on se cotisa*," said Frederick)[2] to form a bribery fund; and on April 19, 1773, the Polish Diet "consented" to the Partition. Frederick's share, West Prussia, amounted only to some 13,000 square miles, but it connected East Prussia with Brandenburg. Austria's share, Galicia, was 27,000 square miles, and was a well-defined region geographically, a "glacis" of the Carpathians. Russia obtained 42,000 square miles, White Russia. There remained of independent Poland about 200,000 square miles.

The well-known letter written by Maria Theresa to Kaunitz after she had assented to the Partition stigmatizes it as unjust, against sound reason and as sure to be a bad example.[3] It was said of Maria Theresa that she wept in taking part of Poland: *elle pleurait en prenant.* Frederick of Prussia could not refrain from a gibe. "The Empress Catherine and myself," he said to D'Alembert, "are two brigands; but that devout Queen Empress, how has she settled it with her confessor?"[4]

The Partition of Poland was a brutal crime in the face of a known and acknowledged Law of Nations. Annexations had been made in the seventeenth and eighteenth centuries—many annexations—but nearly all had been made either as indemnities at the end of wars, or as the result of exchanges, or of hereditary succession. Annexation through these means has always been considered legitimate. In modern times, annexation on grounds of nationality is also considered to be legitimate, if effected by way of purchase or exchange, or at the end of a war, and after the holding of a plebiscite. The annexations made by Austria, Russia and Prussia at the Partition of Poland could not be defended on the ground of costs of warfare, of exchange and compensation,

[1] Martens, *Recueil . . . conclus par la Russie*, II, 24. The accession of Maria Theresa and Joseph II of February 19, 1772, is in the same volume, p. 20.

[2] Carlyle, *ibid.*

[3] Arneth, *Geschichte Maria Theresas*, VIII, 375–8, 601–2.

[4] Quoted by Sorel, *The Eastern Question in the Eighteenth Century* (trans. 1898), p. 223.

or of nationality. They were pure brigandage, the robbing of a neighbour, carried out in time of peace by three Powers against a helpless neutral.

This act of international immorality was the result of fear. Russia, Prussia and Austria feared each other. For the moment they eased the tension among themselves by taking each a slice of Poland. Indeed, if the Allies of 1772 had chosen to dismember Poland completely and to leave nothing over, they probably could have done so without meeting serious resistance.[1] The thing was so easy to do, that one or another would wish to do it again. But if one did it, the other two, impelled by their fear, must sooner or later do the same. "There is no worse slavery than that of fear." [2] And at the end, when by three successive partitions Poland had been divided and nothing more remained, the three Powers were left facing each other with the same fear, and with nothing keeping them apart but bayonets and fortresses.

That Frederick himself was conscious of this danger, cannot be doubted. "I would consider it an unpardonable fault in policy," he wrote, "if I worked for the aggrandisement of a Power which could become a fearful and terrible neighbour for all Europe." His final judgment was that: "There were only two courses to be taken—to stop Russia in the progress of her immense conquests, or, what seemed wiser, to endeavour by skill, to derive some advantage from it." [3] The advantage which he gained, as compensation for the increased danger from Russia, was Polish or West Prussia, the province which, long ago as Crown Prince,[4] he had stated to be highly desirable, as joining together Brandenburg and East Prussia.

One curious result of these proceedings was that the Swiss Confederation which had maintained an attitude of isolation throughout the eighteenth century suddenly made up its mind to accept alliance with France, so as to have a powerful friend against any threat of partition.

Since the battle of Marignano, 1515,[5] the Swiss had taken no part in international affairs, but had consistently maintained the

[1] See N. Karéiev, *Causes de la chute de Pologne*, in *Revue historique* (45), 1891, p. 255.

[2] Bourgeois, *Manuel historique*, I, 438.

[3] *Mémoires*, p. 26.

[4] See G. Waitz, *Preussen und die erste Theilung Polens* (1860), III, 9.

[5] See above, p. 41.

policy of neutrality which later, since 1815, has been recognized as their permanent position in international law. At the Peace of Westphalia, 1648, they had gained complete independence from the Empire.[1] For the next seventy years religious dissension, breaking out on occasion into civil war, absorbed the energies of the Swiss. Religious war, however, ceased with the Treaty of Aarau, August 11, 1712, by which the Protestant and Catholic cantons adjusted their difficulties with each other. Externally the Swiss were at least nominally in alliance with France under a treaty of 1663 which, however, expired in 1723. Thereafter the Confederation was absolutely neutral, although individual cantons regularly, by capitulation, hired contingents of Switzers to foreign powers; there were Swiss regiments in the service of France until 1792. As a rule, it was the Catholic cantons which leased troops to France, while the Protestant cantons leased troops to the Emperor and the Dutch. Thus Swiss regiments fought on opposite sides in the various wars of the eighteenth century.

In 1777 the Swiss Confederation, alarmed at the fate of Poland, accepted the alliance which every French envoy to the Swiss had worked for from Du Lac in 1715 to Jean Vergennes. This Treaty of Alliance, May 28, 1777,[2] was meant to endure for fifty years, but was replaced in the French Revolutionary and Napoleonic period by various compacts which ended by binding the Swiss hand and foot to France. Clearly a policy of neutrality and a policy of alliance were mutually incompatible.[3]

[1] The Swiss Confederation had been practically, if not in theory, separated from the Empire since the Treaty of Bâle, made with the Emperor Maximilian, September 22, 1499. See K. Klüpfel, *Die Lostrennung der Schweiz von Deutschland,* in *Historische Zeitschrift* (1866), XVI, 40, 41.

[2] Martens, *Recueil,* II, 507.

[3] For Switzerland, see J. Dierauer, *Geschichte der Schweiz. Eidgenossenschaft* (1913). For further details about Poland, see A. Beer, *Die Erste Theilung Polens* (1873); J. Lelevel, *Histoire de Pologne* (1844); A. Sorel, *La Question d'Orient au XVIIIme Siècle* (1902).

CHAPTER XXXIII

THE SICK MAN OF EUROPE

The European System, as it was understood by statesmen and publicists in the seventeenth and eighteenth centuries, was a balance, equilibrium, or—what comes to the same thing—a recognition by the European states of their mutual interest. This European system had been allowed to be destroyed in Eastern Europe, because France, still in alliance with Austria, had been unable to oppose that Power, because Sweden was still helpless through the rule of its factious oligarchies, and because Great Britain and France were still hopelessly divided by the memories of the Seven Years' War : indeed, Great Britain and France, the two most powerful states of Western Europe, were soon to be at war with each other over the American Revolution. Europe approached the great crash which was to be caused by another, the French Revolution, without a vestige of general Concert ; publicists like Gentz might cry, when the militant French Revolution came, that it was destroying the " System," but in truth the System had gone long before this ; there was no consciousness of common interest, no capacity among the European states of acting in general Concert.

There were five great partitions planned in the eighteenth century. One, that of the east and south Baltic provinces of Sweden, was carried out largely by Peter the Great, when Western Europe was engaged in the Spanish Succession War. A second, the partition of the Habsburg dominions, was undertaken by Prussia, France and Bavaria in 1740, but was checked by the resistance of Maria Theresa and by the intervention of Great Britain. The third was the Austrian *riposte* against Prussia ; in 1756 Prussia would have been partitioned by Austria, Saxony and Russia, but for the resistance of Frederick and by the intervention of Great Britain. The fourth was the Partition of Poland in 1772. The fifth was Turkey, which Catherine and Joseph II planned to share in 1787.

The first Partition of Poland prevented the Russo-Turkish War of 1769–74 from becoming a general war among the Central and Eastern Powers. The Russians finished off the last campaign in a way that was fairly satisfactory to their ambitions. The Treaty of Kutchuk-Kainardji was signed by Field-Marshal Romanzow and the Grand Vizier Mousson Zadé Mehemet on July 10, 1774. The Sultan and the Tsaritsa recognized the Tartars of the Crimea and the Kuban to be independent—an obvious compromise, preparatory to the Tartars being annexed to Russia. The treaty, as a matter of fact, recognized the annexation of Kertch and Yenikale, the two fortresses at the east end of the Crimea, commanding the entrance to the Sea of Azov, and the annexation of the town of Azov at the north-east end of the sea. Russia also obtained Kinburn at the mouth of the Dnieper with a strip of land on the left bank of the river. A Russian minister was to be permanently resident at Constantinople, and he was to have the right of making at any time representations on behalf of the worshippers at the Greek Church which the Russians were to be allowed to build at Constantinople.[1]

Russia did not secure these privileges for nothing. Catherine II had to acquiesce in Joseph II taking from Poland the Bukovina (to the north of Moldavia) and in Frederick II extending the boundary of West Prussia to include an additional 200 Polish villages.

Catherine II, though by origin and training a German princess, had wholly identified herself with the national aspirations of her people, that is to say, of the politically conscious and vocal part of her people, the military and the civil service. Like them she regarded Russia's historic mission as leading to Constantinople, and to dominion over all the land held by the Turks in Europe. Austria, however, would not tolerate this ; therefore, as in the case of Poland, Catherine had to consent to share. Joseph II came to visit her at Mohilev in 1780. Catherine tried to direct Joseph's attention to Italy, where there was a fair field for further Austrian extension ; but Joseph had other views. In 1782 (November 12) he sent to Catherine his own plan, drafted partly in accordance with what he had learned about Catherine's views. Moldavia and

[1] The religious articles are 7 and 14. Text of Treaty of Kutchuk-Kainardji in Martens, *Recueil,* II, 287 ff., in the original Italian with a French translation.

Wallachia were to form one Christian state; Thrace with Constantinople were to be another; both states would be vassals to Russia and perhaps under Russian princes. Russia herself would receive the land between the Dniester and the Bug. Austria would have Serbia and Bosnia. France's susceptibilities (the Habsburg-Bourbon Alliance was still in force) would be met by her receiving Egypt.

How often has the estate of the "Sick Man" been ideally partitioned? Catherine took advantage of the negotiations with Joseph II to add to Azov the Kuban and the Crimea (1784). The French ambassador at Constantinople, Saint-Priest, persuaded the Sultan to acquiesce in these annexations, and not to make a new Russo-Turkish war. In April, 1787, Joseph made another journey to Russia, travelling in a simple carriage or *calèche de voyage* with one officer and two servants.[1] He met Catherine at Kherson. The two monarchs journeyed down the river Dnieper with the brilliant company of diplomatists who were with Catherine—Prince de Ligne, Count Cobenzl, Ségur. Joseph's serious conversations seem to have been reserved for the Comte de Ségur who was French minister at the court of Catherine II. Joseph was not impressed with the displays of smiling villages and happy peasants which Catherine's minister Potemkin produced. "There's more brilliance (*éclat*) than reality here," he said. "Constantinople," he remarked, "is an object of jealousy and discord which will always render impossible an accord among the Great Powers for the partition of Turkey."

The Russian ambassador at Constantinople, Bulgakoff, had come to Kherson to receive instructions from Catherine; he went with the court as far as Sebastopol [2] and then returned to his post. There he proceeded, according to his instructions, to make fresh demands upon the Sultan, and some stormy negotiations ensued in the course of which the Porte threw the ambassador into prison. This flagrant breach of one of the oldest rules of international courtesy naturally brought on at once the war which was coming. The Russians, under Suvorov, were steadily, although not brilliantly, successful against the Turks. Joseph II, after trying by a surprise attack on Belgrade in the night of December 2, 1787, to seize that fortress and failing, declared war on February

[1] Count Ségur, *Memoirs and Recollections* (trans. 1827), I, 122.
[2] *Ibid.*, p. 124.

10, 1788. On December 16, 1788, the terrible Suvorov stormed Oczakov (near Odessa). In 1790 the Austrians captured Belgrade. The advance of the Russian and Austrian armies upon Constantinople seemed certain and the partition of Turkey inevitable, when Joseph II died on February 20, 1790.

Once more Turkey was to be saved by the dissensions of Europe. France and Great Britain had viewed the progress of the Austrian and Russian armies with increasing misgiving. In the summer of 1783, after the conclusion of the Franco-American-British War, the French Government (whose foreign policy was then directed by Vergennes) had proposed to Great Britain joint diplomatic intervention in favour of Turkey; but Charles James Fox, Secretary of State for Foreign Affairs, had coldly refused. The eminent Vergennes died on February 13, 1787. His successor, Count Montmorin, a safe professional diplomatist, had a falling dynasty on his hands. On May 5, 1789, the French Estates-General met, and after this there was little leisure at the *Ministère des Affaires étrangères* for foreign policy. But Pitt, the British Prime Minister, now gave firm diplomatic support to Turkey, and even mobilized the fleet. The Emperor Leopold, brother of the late Joseph II, was too much concerned at the possible consequences of the French conflagration to allow himself to be further involved in the Turkish war. He made (through Prusso-British-Dutch mediation) the Peace of Sistova on August 4, 1791, and handed back Belgrade to the Turks.[1]

On their side the Russians were gaining ground. On December 22, 1790, Suvorov stormed Ismail on the Kilia branch of the Danube; the defenders and many of the inhabitants were put to the sword.

> There was an end of Ismail—hapless town!
> Far flashed her burning towers o'er Danube's stream,
> And redly ran his blushing waters down.

The death of Potemkin, Catherine's chief adviser, in 1790 had on Russian operations an effect somewhat similar to that which the death of Joseph II had upon Austrian. The Prussian and British Governments (which had been in alliance along with the Dutch since 1788) continued their diplomatic pressure at St. Petersburg; and

[1] Martens, *Recueil*, V, 244.

Catherine's eyes began to stray towards Warsaw where Kosciusko and other Polish patriots were carrying out important reforms. A second Partition of Poland would compensate her for unavoidable self-denial in the south-west. The Empress bowed (Treaty of Jassy, January 9, 1792) so far as to fix her boundary at the Dniester, keeping Oczakov, soon to be overshadowed by the new city of Odessa. The Prussian and British ministers at St. Petersburg had done their best to make Catherine give back Oczakov to the Turks, or at least to recognize it as neutral territory between Turkey and Russia.[1] But Catherine would not retire from the Dniester.

[1] See *Mémoire* of Whitworth and Goltz, St. Petersburg, June 29, 1791, in Martens, *Recueil,* V, 281. The Treaty of Jassy is in the same volume on p. 291. Also for further particulars see E. Driault, *La Question d'Orient* (1905).

CHAPTER XXXIV

THE LAST YEARS OF THE ANCIEN RÉGIME

The eighteenth century has sometimes been called the Age of Reason, or the Age of the Benevolent Despots. The ground for both these descriptions may be discerned in the terms of the proclamation which Joseph II issued on November 28, 1780, after the death of his mother when he became sole ruler of the Habsburg dominions. He stated that he was going to keep in view only the benefit of the whole community, without regard to the prejudices or privileges of the peoples whom he ruled. In the same way the monarchs in their foreign policies professed to act by pure reason, in disregard of prejudice.

This is seen in the concerted action among the Roman Catholic continental monarchs with regard to the Jesuits. The wealthy and powerful Order, strongly entrenched in every Catholic country and court, was essentially international and papal. Its directing force was in its headquarters at Rome. The monarchs of Portugal, Spain, Naples, and France first each suppressed the Jesuit Society in their own country before, in 1769, Charles III of Spain formally demanded from Pope Clement XIII the dissolution of the whole Order. But Clement XIII died before anything further was done (February 2, 1769), Joseph II was at Rome at the time of the Papal Conclave, and partly through his influence, Lorenzo Ganganelli, Clement XIV, was elected. Whether he had promised before election to suppress the Order is unknown; he certainly proceeded slowly. Bernis, the architect of the Habsburg-Bourbon Alliance of 1756, now a Cardinal at Rome, maintained the pressure. The long-deferred bull of abolition was at last issued by Clement XIV on June 21, 1773. It is a curious document, justifying the suppression of the Order on the ground that it had for long departed from its original profession of poverty, and had mixed itself in political affairs.[1] The Papacy lost—for forty years at any rate—

[1] Text of Bull in Martens, *Recueil*, II, 231.

its strongest international army; and from this time the influence of the Papacy in diplomatic affairs, which had been steadily dwindling, may be considered definitely at an end. In 1782 the next Pope, Pius VI, took the step, unprecedented for some hundreds of years, of paying a personal visit to his brother sovereign, Joseph II, who was engaged on what was considered to be an anti-clerical policy. Pius was a dignified, handsome man, not without experience in practical affairs; but he was unable at Vienna to make Joseph II or Kaunitz modify their policy at all. Kaunitz, a "Voltairian," who had once had Jean-Jacques Rousseau for a secretary, was particularly anti-clerical.

Most of the continental monarchies of pre-Revolutionary Europe had no consistent policy unless the convenience and interest of the sovereigns can be considered to be policy. The only kingdom which kept itself completely clear of war was Denmark, where a skilful foreign policy was pursued by Johann Hartwig Bernstorff (1712–71), Struensee (1731–72) and the younger Bernstorff, nephew of Johann Hartwig (1735–97). In 1773 (May 21) the Treaty of Tsarskoye Selo, between Denmark on the one hand and Russia (as head of the House of Holstein-Gottorp) on the other, put an end to a territorial controversy which might have led to war at almost any moment. By this treaty the House of Holstein-Gottorp, in the person of its younger branch, gave up Holstein to the Danish Crown and received the Danish county of Oldenburg instead. Both parties agreed to use their influence in the Empire to have Oldenburg erected into a duchy; and they also agreed to guarantee the exchange.[1]

The last twenty years before the French Revolution were filled with wars or war-crises. The Seven Years' War was no sooner over than Spain and Great Britain fell to disputing about their subjects' rights on the Mississippi, in the Gulf of Mexico, in the Atlantic and Pacific. In 1770 a Spanish expedition seized Port Egmont, the chief British settlement or capital of the Falkland Islands. Charles III of Spain expected France to join him under the Family Compact, but Louis XV felt that he could not afford a war yet. So Charles had to evacuate the Falkland Islands and to declare that he viewed the expedition "with displeasure." This declaration amounted to an apology on the part of Spain. At the same time it explicitly reserved any claims of sovereignty

[1] Martens, *Recueil*, II, 173.

which Spain or Great Britain might have. But as sometimes happens in diplomatic history this matter, being left to the anodyne of time, settled itself. British sovereignty over the Falkland Islands became unquestioned.[1]

In 1776, however, Great Britain became involved in war with her American colonies. France, as soon as the Americans had proved their military strength by the battle of Saratoga (October 16, 1777), made a treaty of alliance with the United States, February 6, 1778.[2] In March the French and British Governments recalled their ambassadors at London and Paris, and in June hostilities between the two countries began without a declaration of war. It was the day of revenge for which Choiseul had carefully prepared in his years of office after the Seven Years' War (he was dismissed in 1770). He had built up a fleet and had acquired Corsica, an important base in the Mediterranean, from the Genoese in 1768. France, although restrained by Vergennes, a stiff Puritan, who hated the courtiers and made no attempt to be popular,[3] was crying out for her revenge. At this time Aranda, who as Spanish Prime Minister had planned the expedition against the Falkland Isles in 1770, was ambassador at Paris. He did everything that he could now to bring Spain into the war against Great Britain. Charles III held back, hoping to receive Gibraltar as the price of neutrality. Failing in this, he made the secret treaty of Aranjuez with France, April 12, 1779, and declared war in June.

The British navy was perfectly well able to deal with the Spanish and French fleets, and to relieve Gibraltar, had it not been hampered by the war against the American colonists. It was the object of the British Government, therefore, to detach one or other of its enemies from their alliance; and to this end Richard Cumberland (private secretary to the Secretary of State for the Colonies) spent eight months at Madrid in 1780, while the war was going on, and the red-hot cannon balls were being shot from Gibraltar. Contact between the British and Spanish Governments had been made, in the first place, through an Irish priest, Thomas Hussey, formerly a chaplain in the Spanish embassy in London. Cumberland's negotiation, however, came to nothing, for the Spaniards would

[1] See Julius Goebel, *The Struggle for the Falkland Islands* (1927), p. 358 ff.

[2] Treaty of Friendship and Commerce, Martens, *Recueil*, II, 587. Treaty of Alliance, *ibid.*, p. 605; both dated at Paris, February 6, 1778.

[3] For Vergennes' simple and uncorrupted life see Tratchewsky, *La France et l'Allemagne sous Louis XVI*, in *Revue historique* (1880), XIV, 257.

only make a separate peace if they received Gibraltar. This the British Government refused, and Gibraltar remained uncaptured.

Vergennes, by the exercise of watchfulness and tact, managed to preserve the anti-British diplomatic union nearly to the end of 1782, by which time the British Government was ready to concede independence to the American colonies. Before this the coalition against Britain had greatly increased. The war between Great Britain and the Colonies, and still more the war between Great Britain and France, occasioned an immense amount of friction with neutral and maritime states. As Great Britain had the strongest fleet and could assure her own supplies, it was her interest to stop all neutral trade with France in naval and other stores. The Scandinavian states and the Dutch felt the British naval pressure. Vergennes at once declared France's adhesion to the principle that "free ships make free goods" (July, 1778). In March, 1780, Catherine II (Russia was now becoming a grain-exporting country) issued a declaration of her demands for the maritime rights of neutrals;[1] of these rights one was that "the effects belonging to the subjects of the said belligerent Powers shall be free in all neutral vessels, except contraband merchandise." France and Spain made no difficulty in assenting to the Russian declaration. The British Government maintained that the navy acted towards neutrals strictly according to the Law of Nations, and that redress of irregularities could be obtained from the Court of Admiralty. In the Instructions issued by the Secretary of State (Lord Stormont) to Sir James Harris, ambassador at St. Petersburg, relative to the Russian declaration, and especially with regard to the article concerning enemy goods in neutral ships, the following words occur: "You will take the greatest care not to drop a syllable that can be construed into an acquiescence in the erroneous doctrine which that article endeavours to establish." Great Britain had need to be careful of her sea-power, for there was nothing else left to defend her. The country had never been in such a frightful international situation. The whole of Europe was either actively or passively hostile. Even Portugal, England's oldest and most faithful ally, turned against her.

In order to defend their view of neutral rights at sea, the states which adhered to Catherine's Declaration formed a "Convention for an Armed Neutrality," in July, 1780. Their subjects were

[1] Martens, *Recueil*, III, 158.

to have freedom to trade with the belligerents in everything except contraband; and only articles were to be considered contraband which were specifically recognized as such in existing treaties between the neutral states and the belligerents. The states which signed or subsequently adhered to the principles of the Convention of Armed Neutrality were Russia, Denmark, Sweden, the United Netherlands, Prussia, Portugal, the two Sicilies, and the Empire.[1] The Contracting Powers agreed to defend their neutral rights at sea with their naval forces, if necessary. In spite of this very threatening league, the British Government managed to avoid hostilities with any of the members except Holland (the neutral with the largest carrying trade), against whom Great Britain declared war on December 20, 1780. In the negotiations of 1782–84 the British Government declined to recognize the principles of the Convention of Armed Neutrality, and they nowhere appear in the peace-treaties.

Negotiations for peace were conducted at Versailles from July, 1782. The Americans, represented by Franklin, Adams, Jay and Laurens, although bound by their treaty of alliance with France to make peace only in common, concluded separate and so-called *provisional* articles of peace on November 30, 1782. On the British side this peace was negotiated and concluded by Richard Oswald, not a professional diplomatist, but a merchant who was engaged in the American trade and was familiar with the personalities of American politics.[2] Vergennes was irritated when informed of this separate peace, but in truth no harm was done, for all parties were sick of war, and, as the British navy again commanded the sea (after Rodney's victory of Les Saintes, April, 1782, and the relief of Gibraltar), there was nothing to fight for once the question of American independence had been settled. The preliminary treaty of peace between France and Great Britain was signed at Versailles on January 20, 1783. France regained one of the islands lost at the end of the Seven Years' War, Tobago, and also Senegal. France, in addition, obtained a concession which greatly satisfied her feelings of dignity; she re-acquired the right to fortify Dunkirk (forbidden by the Treaties

[1] The Russo-Danish Convention was signed at Copenhagen on July 9, 1780, and forms the first of the series. All the Acts and Conventions are in Martens, *Recueil*, III, 158 ff.

[2] For Oswald, see *The Autobiography of Alexander Carlyle* (1910), p. 87.

of Utrecht, Aix-la-Chapelle and Paris); the British overseer or "control" was therefore withdrawn. No relaxation, however, was made in the rule that no French troops could be maintained in Bengal.

The preliminary articles of peace between Great Britain and Spain were signed at Versailles on the same day as the French treaty, January 20, 1783; Spain retained her conquest, Florida, and also acquired Minorca again. The preliminary peace between Great Britain and the Dutch was signed at Paris on September 2, 1783. The Dutch gained no advantage.[1]

These pre-Revolutionary years were not politically happy for the Dutch. The Republic was divided by the old animosity which always appeared in times of peace between the Burgher (or aristocratic) party and the Orange (or popular) party. At the same time in 1783–84, a determined attack upon the special position of the Dutch on the Scheldt was made by Joseph II.

There was something to be said on Joseph's side. He was claiming to free the Austrian Netherlands from the unreasonable servitude which had been imposed upon it by the Barrier Treaty of 1715 (and previously, under the Spanish régime, by the Peace of Westphalia in 1648). The treaties of 1648 and 1715 had closed the Scheldt to ships coming from or to the sea. Thus Antwerp had nothing except inland trade, a condition of affairs which was extremely unpopular among the educated classes of the Austrian Netherlands.[2] The Dutch, who held lands and forts on both sides of the estuary of the Scheldt, were permitted to fire on ships coming from Antwerp.[3] Another servitude upon the Austrian Netherlands was imposed by the Barrier Treaty of 1715. This permitted the Dutch to garrison Namur, Tournai, Menin, Furnes, Warneton, Ypres and Knoque, and to receive an annual indemnity for their expenses from the Austrian Netherlands. This "Barrier" was really a farce, for on the only occasion when it was seriously wanted, in the War of the Austrian Succession, the Dutch garrisons were withdrawn from the fortresses in 1745, in order that the Dutch should preserve their neutrality. From 1745 to the end of the Seven Years' War in 1763, there were no Dutch garrisons at all

[1] The final treaties of peace which did not differ materially from the provisional articles were signed by Great Britain, as follows: With France, at Versailles, September 3, 1783; with Spain, at Versailles, September 3, 1783; with the United States, at Paris, September 3, 1783; with Holland, at Paris, May 20, 1784. The Preliminary and Final Treaties are all in Martens, *Recueil*, I, 497–565.

[2] Koch and Schoell, I, 483.

[3] Schlosser, V, 347.

in the Barrier fortresses. They were restored at the end of the Seven Years' War; but in 1782, yielding to the pressure of Joseph II and also to the necessities of their war with Great Britain, the Dutch again, although under protest, withdrew their garrisons.

Kaunitz, in official conversations in the year 1782 with the Dutch Minister at Vienna, Count Wassenaer, had referred to the Barrier fortresses, as being, on account of the alliance between Austria and France, of no account. "*Elles n'existent plus*," he said.[1] Joseph next formally demanded the cession of Maastricht and other places; and by a note of August 23, 1784, he claimed that the Scheldt should be immediately opened. An Austrian warship was sent down the river from Antwerp, but the Dutch fired on her from the fort of Saftingen and compelled her to return.

An acute war-crisis ensued. The Prince de Ligne, who was Governor of Antwerp, was ready to attack the Dutch forts on the Scheldt, but was restrained by the Austrian Government until it should ascertain the attitude of France. Louis XVI was in a difficulty, for he was bound by the now very unpopular Habsburg-Bourbon Alliance, while, on the other hand, French public opinion supported the Dutch, and Mirabeau (later the famous revolutionary nobleman) wrote a much-talked-of pamphlet in their favour.[2] Vergennes, who was now nearing the end of his career at the *Ministère des Affaires étrangères* (he died in 1787), managed the crisis with considerable skill. He offered mediation, and made it clear not merely that there would be no military support for Austria, but that the French were backing the Dutch. A Conference, consisting of Vergennes, Count Mercy, Austrian ambassador to France, and MM. Berkenrode and Brantzen representing the United Netherlands, was held at Versailles from December 8, 1784, to September 20, 1785. At the last the Austrian representative declared that, unless the Dutch agreed by September 21 to pay the compensation demanded by the Emperor, war would begin. The Dutch representatives then confided to Vergennes that their instructions only authorized them to offer five and a half million florins—just over half the sum upon which the Emperor insisted. Vergennes thereupon undertook that France should pay the other half.[3] Preliminary articles were then signed.

[1] Schlosser, V, 347–8. *Réflexions sur une Conversation ministérielle entre le Prince de Kaunitz et le Comte de Wassenaer*, 1782. Koch and Schoell, I, 484.

[2] *Aux Bataves sur le Stathouderat* par le Comte de Mirabeau (1788). An eloquent incitement to Revolution.

[3] Koch and Schoell, I, 487–8.

The definite Treaty of Peace and Friendship was made at Fontainebleau, between Joseph II and the Dutch, November 8, 1785. The Treaty of Münster, 1648, was explicitly restored (by article 2), and therefore by implication the Barrier Treaties were annulled. The forts of Lillo and Liefkershoek were ceded by the Dutch to Joseph, who, on his side, desisted from his demand for Maastricht. The Dutch agreed to pay nine and a half million florins (France paying half), as compensation to Joseph for the abandonment of his other claims. The generosity of France was well worth to her; for she avoided a costly war and secured complete diplomatic ascendancy in the United Netherlands, through firm understanding with the Burgher party. The net result of the treaty was that the Dutch no longer could claim to have garrisons in the Austrian Netherlands, but that the Scheldt (under the provisions of the Treaty of Münster) remained closed to trade from or to the sea. France guaranteed the Treaty of Fontainebleau, and also made a separate defensive alliance with the Dutch.[1]

This settlement (which could hardly be regarded as final) was the best possible in the circumstances. France came out of a difficult situation without loss of prestige, indeed with real credit as a peace-maker. It was the last notable work of Vergennes—"the man of the imposing and mysterious air, the glacial politeness, the stiff manners, who believed that the sure means of controlling events was to temporise."[2]

The British Government, which had as vital interests in the Scheldt and in the international situation of the Dutch as had the French, took no part in the crisis of 1784–85. Its long-standing influence in the United Netherlands was now practically all gone. In 1786 the Burgher party, strong in its alliance with France, proposed that the House of Orange should be deprived of the hereditary Stadtholdership (instituted in 1747). Sir James Harris, British minister at the Hague, was at his wits' end how to support the Orange party, the one which was still friendly to Great Britain. On June 28, 1787, Princess Wilhelmina, wife of William V of Orange and sister of King Frederick William II of Prussia, was stopped by Burgher forces at the boundary of Holland when

[1] Treaty of Fontainebleau, November 8, 1785, in Martens, *Recueil,* IV, 55. Treaty of Alliance, November 10, 1785, *ibid.*, p. 65.

[2] Tratchewsky, *La France et l'Allemagne sous Louis XVI,* in *Revue historique* (1880), XIV, 255. For a criticism of Tratchewsky and defence of Vergennes see A. Sorel, *Vergennes et sa politique,* in *Revue historique* (1881), XV, 273 ff.

journeying in her carriage from Nymwegen with intention to proceed to the Hague. After a brief detention the princess was sent back to Nymwegen. Sir James Harris wrote from the Hague on June 29 to the Marquis of Carmarthen, Secretary of State for Foreign Affairs: "*Check to the Queen*, and in a move or two check-mate is, I fear, the state of our game. . . . My bile runs through the pores at the end of my fingers, and mixes with the ink as I write." [1] Carmarthen replied: "My dear Harris,—Don't be so disheartened by a check to the Queen; let her be covered by the Knight, and all's safe. . . . If the King her brother is not the dirtiest and shabbiest of Kings, he must resent it, *coûte que coûte*."

The crisis was no local affair of domestic politics in the United Netherlands. "The great object in dispute, as I take it," wrote Harris to Carmarthen (July 13, 1787), "is not so much how this country is to be governed, but whether France shall, by the exercise of undue influence, get the direction of the Republic into her own hands, or whether it shall be restored to a state of independence, and at liberty [*sic*] either to return to the ancient system or to form such political connections as may appear the most suitable to its interests." [2]

On hearing the news, Frederick William II at once demanded redress for the insult offered to his sister; and Harris, on instructions from Pitt, negotiated a convention for British naval support to Prussia.[3] A Prussian army, commanded by the Duke of Brunswick, entered into Holland in September, 1787, and occupied Amsterdam. The Dutch yielded, and recognized the Stadtholdership as hereditary. The French Government, which had little energy left since the death in 1787 of Vergennes (and, anyhow, had no money), simply acquiesced in these results. Montmorin, skilful, cautious, aware of the disabilities of France, did not invoke the guarantee-provisions of the Treaty of Fontainebleau. Harris had already stated his opinion to Carmarthen in the previous year: "France will never fight for this country, not even if England was to attempt to reduce it by force." [4]

[1] *Diaries and Correspondence of James Harris, first Earl of Malmesbury* (1844), II, 329.

[2] *Ibid.*, p. 336.

[3] The Prusso-British Convention was not signed until October 2, 1787, but was agreed upon in the previous August. See *Diaries, etc., of Malmesbury*, II, 351, where the stipulations of the Convention are also given.

[4] *Ibid.*, p. 210.

The *status quo* was further consolidated when the British, Prussian and Dutch Governments entered into a Triple Alliance. This was made by three instruments. A treaty was made between Great Britain and the United Netherlands, signed at the Hague, April 15, 1788. Another, between the United Netherlands and Prussia, was signed at Berlin, on April 15, 1788. The third, the most difficult of all to achieve, was concluded on June 13, 1788, by Harris and Alvensleben (Prussian Minister to the United Netherlands) at Loo, where the King of Prussia was staying with his sister.

This last treaty, which set the seal to the Triple Alliance, was Harris's *chef d'œuvre.* Frederick William was wavering, uncertain whether to reverse the policy of Frederick the Great by binding himself and Great Britain together. A strong body of advisers and courtiers pressed him towards an anti-British policy. Only Hertzberg was in favour of an alliance with Great Britain (indeed, he was the architect of it), but, alone, he could not move the king.[1] Harris had an interview with the king at Loo at seven in the morning of June 12 (1788): "I employed no art, or any words which bore the remotest reference to duplicity; I stated things precisely as they were, and after recapitulating, as well as my memory would allow me to do, all which had passed between the two Courts, from the signature of the Convention of the 2nd October, 1787, to this day, I explained away, as I went along, every circumstance which could wear the appearance of delay or unwillingness on our part to unite ourselves by the closest political bonds with his Prussian Majesty." The king was impressed with Harris's words and views. The English diplomatist had taken the precaution to give the king's *valet de chambre* a hundred ducats on the previous day, with the promise of another hundred if the valet refused admission to Stein (the chief opponent of the English alliance) until after Harris had his interview with the king. The plan worked excellently: "Mr. Stein twice presented himself at the closet-door, and was twice sent away."

Harris had a second interview with the King of Prussia after midnight of the same day, June 12. On the following morning, at nine o'clock, the king sent for Harris and told him that, with a few small alterations, the Prusso-British Draft Treaty could now be signed. "Being thus agreed as to the Articles, Mr. d'Alvens-

[1] For Hertzberg's position at this crisis, see P. Bailleu, *Graf Hertzberg*, in *Historische Zeitschrift* (1879), VI, 462.

leben and myself went into my apartment at the palace; and in the presence of the Great Pensionary, Mr. Vander Spiegel, proceeded to the signature, and we entitled the Treaty, *The Provisional Treaty of Loo*." [1] On the Prussian side the initiative had come entirely from the king, and caused considerable agitation among his ministers.[2]

The first of the three treaties (that between Great Britain and the United Netherlands), April 15, 1788, provided for a mutual guarantee of the territories of the Contracting Parties, who were bound to succour each other with specified numbers of forces—Great Britain to provide, in case of need, 10,000 men and 20 ships, the United Netherlands to provide 6,000 men and 16 ships. Great Britain also guaranteed the Hereditary Stadtholderate in the House of Orange according to the constitution of 1847. On his side, the Prince of Orange undertook "to maintain this form of government against all attack." This article (No. 3), concerning a matter of domestic politics, is of a kind that is rare (although by no means unique) in international conventions. No limit was prescribed for the duration of the treaty.

The treaty concluded between Prussia and the United Netherlands followed the lines of the Anglo-Dutch Treaty, in the guarantee of the Stadtholderate; it was stated (article 10) to have a duration for twenty years.

By the third treaty, concluded at Loo on June 13, 1788, Great Britain and Prussia undertook to act in concert to maintain the independence and the Government of the United Netherlands according to the engagements which they had contracted by the treaties of April 15. Further, the Treaty of Loo included a guarantee of each other's territories, in case either party were attacked in consequence of its carrying out the stipulations of the treaties of April 15.

The Triple Alliance, although modern opinion would be unfavourable to the provisions for the guarantee of the Dutch constitution, was an instrument of peace, in so far as it secured the

[1] *Diaries, etc., of Malmesbury*, II, 424–7. The three treaties which composed the Triple Alliance of 1788 are in Martens, *Recueil*, IV, 372–85. The Treaty of Loo required ratification and renewal by a subsequent Final Treaty which was signed by Hertzberg and Ewart at Berlin on August 13, 1788 (Martens, *Recueil*, IV, 390).

[2] R. Duncker, *Friedrich Wilhelm II und Gra Hertzberg*, in *Historische Zeitschrift* (1877), I, 6.

integrity of the United Netherlands, and withdrew that debatable territory from international contests. It belongs to the type of regional peace-guarantees of which in modern times the Locarno treaties are the most celebrated examples.

Fortified by confidence in the Triple Alliance, Hertzberg, the Chief Minister of Frederick William II, aspired to take advantage of the war of Russia and Austria against Turkey, which broke out in 1788, in order to win great concessions for Prussia. Hertzberg considered himself as a follower of Frederick the Great and accepted as a principle of policy that monarch's ironical praises of Chance. He said that his "system" was to have "none," and to act "only according to circumstances."[1]

Joseph II, besides having a Turkish war on his hands, had also a revolt in Hungary and Belgium. Hertzberg planned to enter into friendly agreements with Poland and Turkey, and then to offer armed mediation (supported by the Triple Alliance) in the Austro-Turkish War. By this means Austria would be induced to retrocede Galicia to the Poles; and the Poles, out of gratitude, would have to cede Danzig and Thorn to Prussia. Austria could compensate herself by taking Wallachia and Moldavia from the Sultan.

Joseph II, through his secret agents, learned something of Hertzberg's plan. He could not possibly, he felt, maintain the costly Turkish war and withstand Prussia. He could not allow the Monarchy to be drawn into a "double war, which would be its ruin," wrote Joseph to Kaunitz.[2]

For a time fortune favoured Hertzberg. The Austrian armies suffered reverses at the hands of the Turks; the Russians, although winning battles under Suvorov in Bessarabia, were distracted by a sudden attack in July, 1788, made by Gustavus III of Sweden. This talented and energetic monarch invaded Finland with the object of recovering Livonia and Carelia, the provinces lost by the Treaty of Nystadt, 1721. The smouldering revolts in Hungary and Belgium became acute. In the midst of this shattering of his hopes, Joseph II died (February 20, 1790).

[1] Sorel, *L'Europe et la Révolution française* (1887), I, 523, quoting *Archives du Ministère des Affaires étrangères.*

[2] Beer, *Joseph II, Leopold II und Kaunitz* (1873), p. 327 (Nov. 17, 1788). For Hertzberg's plan to obtain Austrian consent to the proposed cession of Danzig and Thorn, see M. Duncker, *Friedrich Wilhelm II und Graf Hertzberg*, in *Historische Zeitschrift* (1879), I, 18, 19.

The new Emperor was Joseph's brother, Leopold. Added to the international complexities of the time was the fact that the French monarchy, since May 5, 1789, plunged in an internal crisis, could play no part in foreign affairs. Hertzberg went on with his game, and made an alliance for mutual guarantee of territories with the Poles (March 29, 1790)—" an alliance which should be a mark in the history of perjuries, and a scandal even in a century which had seen the War of the Austrian Succession." [1] Besides making this treaty, Prussia, through its minister at Constantinople, Baron Dietz, had made a treaty of mutual defence and guarantee with Turkey on January 31, 1790. Frederick William II, however, deferred the ratification of this treaty for five months.[2] The Prusso-Polish and Prusso-Turkish alliances perhaps saved Turkey from defeat and partition in the contemporary war with Austria and Russia.

Hertzberg persuaded Frederick William to mobilize his army, to lead it into Silesia, and to ratify the Turkish alliance treaty, which the king did in his headquarters at Schönwalde. Leopold II, a subtle man, with long views and strong will, was his own minister. The aged Chancellor Kaunitz, though still alive, no longer directed affairs. Leopold saw that Great Britain's greatest interest—as always—was in the Netherlands. He therefore offered to restore the old constitution in the Austrian Netherlands ; at the same time he declared that if Prussia made war, he would rather give the Austrian Netherlands over to France than concede Hertzberg's demands. He entered into direct communication, by letter, with Frederick William II ; and he sent the Prince of Reuss and Spielmann to the invading Prussian army's headquarters at Schönwalde, and proposed that a peace-congress should meet in the neighbouring town of Reichenbach. Frederick William consented. The congress opened on June 26 (1790) and sat for one month. The British Minister at Berlin, Ewart, was present, resolute to do everything to prevent a great continental war. A party soon defined itself around the King of Prussia, hostile to the influence of Hertzberg. The Poles (as Lucchesini, the Prussian minister, reported from Warsaw) refused to consider giving up Danzig and Thorn. Frederick

[1] Sorel, *op. cit.*, II, 68. The treaty, signed by Lucchesini for Prussia, and by Malachowski, Sapieha and others for Poland, at Warsaw on March 29, 1790, is in Martens, *Recueil*, IV, 471.

[2] Treaty and Prussian ratification in Martens, *Recueil*, IV, 466–71.

William shrank from the only alternative to pushing his demands, the alternative of war with Austria. Like another Frederick William, sixty years later, in a similar situation at Olmütz, he gave way. Leopold II must have been slightly amused to receive from Prussian headquarters a sort of *ultimatum* which embodied the terms for which he was contending. Prussia would give up her demands if Austria would not annex Wallachia from Turkey. He concealed his emotion and accepted the articles, which were signed at Reichenbach on July 27 (1790). Austria agreed to make peace with Turkey on the basis of the *status quo ante bellum.*[1] The settlement was a great victory for European peace. It was also a success for Austria, for at the death of Joseph II and at the accession of Leopold II, with a war in progress with Turkey, with war threatened by Prussia, with the Triple Alliance diplomatically hostile to her, with revolts in her dominions, she had indeed been in a desperate position.[2] On the other hand, Leopold's success in preserving the *status quo* was gained at the expense of the Austrian dominion on the Danube. Had Prussia not interfered in 1790 Austria would have undoubtedly forced the Turks to cede at least Belgrade, which her army had taken.

The Convention of Reichenbach marks a turning-point in the history of Europe. The extreme tension of the last few months was relaxed. The decisive struggle between Austria and Prussia was postponed for three-quarters of a century. Austria escaped from the most serious crisis through which she had passed since the accession of Maria Theresa. Prussia stepped down from the commanding position she had occupied since the death of Frederick the Great.[3]

The Russo-Swedish War which had broken out in 1788 was composed by the Peace of Verela (August 14, 1790) on the basis of the *status quo ante bellum.*[4] The contemporary Russo-Turkish War ended (as noted above) in the first month of 1792 with the Peace of Jassy, the Russian frontier being advanced to the Dniester. The French Revolution was now in progress, anxiously watched by the Powers of Europe; but it was still a purely domestic affair.

[1] The final peace-terms between Austria and Turkey were signed at Sistova, on August 4, 1791. See above, p. 281.

[2] See M. Duncker, *Friedrich Wilhelm II und Graf Hertzberg*, in *Historische Zeitschrift* (1877), I, 10, 13, 41.

[3] R. Lodge in *The Cambridge Modern History*, VIII, 334.

[4] Martens, *Recueil*, IV, 519.

Not until April (1792) did the Girondins begin the great French Revolutionary Wars: a new era then started for Europe and the world.[1]

[1] For further details see A. Geffroy, *Gustav III et la Cour de France* (1867); R. N. Bain, *Gustavus III and his Contemporaries* (1894); A. Beer, *Joseph II und Kaunitz* (1873); Heigel, K. T., *Deutsche Geschichte vom Tode Friedrichs des Grossen bis zur Auflösung des Alten Reiches* (1899).

EPILOGUE

The Triple Alliance of 1788, signed ten months before the fateful meeting of the Estates-General at Versailles (May 5, 1789), is the natural termination of the diplomacy of the Ancien Régime. The public tranquillity of Europe seemed assured and Pitt looked forward to a long period of peace in which he could complete his economical reforms.

When the absolutely sovereign state came into existence at the time of the Renaissance, Europe entered upon a condition of international anarchy in which only two public principles seemed to be recognized—security and aggrandisement.

The first principle is perfectly natural. No state can help trying to secure its existence any more than an individual can. It was upon this principle that diplomatists constructed the policy of equilibrium or balance of power, thus converting the international anarchy into a " system," though one that was never very stable. The " system " was at any moment liable to be disturbed by the other principle, by a monarch seizing an occasion to aggrandise his state by invading his neighbour's property. To prevent this, international jurists developed the theory of a Law of Nations which should regulate relations between all sovereign states. The diplomatists at once seized upon the Law of Nations and inscribed its practice in their treaties.

The Law of Nations, however, as elaborated by Grotius, would have kept the European states in a fixed or static condition. Such a condition was impossible to maintain permanently, at least before the establishment of frontiers which follow the boundaries of nationality. Accordingly, to meet the need for change, diplomatists claimed the right, at the end of every war, to make new contracts and to re-allot territories and to adjust and alter frontiers, in accordance with the physical and moral force of the respective combatants at the conclusion of hostilities. These contracts (called treaties), when once made, were considered to be permanent, and were jealously guarded by the diplomatists, until dissolved by a fresh outbreak of war. But no means were found for avoiding changes without war.

Yet it must not be thought that the diplomatists were blind to this evil, or that they hopelessly resigned themselves to the idea that change must come and that it could only come through war. This was the devilish doctrine which Treitschke later preached; [1] but it finds no authority with eighteenth-century diplomatists, not even with Frederick the Great, who wrote on the side of the Law of Nations, although he deliberately violated its greatest precept. From the beginning, from the institution of sovereign states at the Renaissance, diplomatists worked strenuously at various means of meeting the need for change and development in the international states-system, by marriage-contracts, by exchanges, by transactions of various kinds carried out in conferences and congresses. It is true that no diplomatist went so far as to say boldly that the interests of states should be adjusted between themselves by the higgling of the market, by buying and selling (at an international conference) just as the interests of private estates are adjusted in the municipal life of any country. Nor did they seriously attempt to find an international tribunal before which international disputes could be settled as the disputes of individuals are settled by the municipal courts inside the sovereign state. It was left for the late nineteenth century to achieve the establishment of an international court.

Before the nineteenth century diplomacy progressed no further towards durable peace than a system of balance, to be adjusted from time to time in conference or congress. This is the system which in the much clearer and fuller form given to it by the Congress of Vienna (1815) was called the Concert of Europe. But although the earlier diplomacy, that of the years of 1451–1792, had the idea of Concert and acted upon it on a vast number of occasions (and ended with a congress at Reichenbach), it was corrupted by the *raison d'état* of the "Benevolent Despots." The invasion of Silesia in 1740 and the Partition of Poland of 1772 were the shipwrecks of the old diplomacy. The European system of equilibrium and acknowledged right was cynically annulled by the three enlightened autocrats, Frederick II, Catherine II, Joseph II. When

[1] *Politik* (1899), I, 60–75; II, 360–363. Cp. Davis, *Political Thought of H. von Treitschke* (1914), Chap. VIII.

the militant French Revolution and the old Monarchies joined issue in the Great War the system disappeared, but it had been already ruined by the old Monarchies themselves. Then came Napoleon Bonaparte who, using diplomacy simply as the handmaid of war, tried to make a new European system, all his own, under French dominion. For a time his system existed, tottered, then fell to ruin likewise. It was left to the statesmen and diplomatists of the Congress of Vienna to reconstruct the European system on a basis of compromise between the principles of the old Europe which had preceded the Revolution, and the principles of the new Europe which in the Revolution had grown to self-consciousness.

INDEX

(Treaties, Pacts, etc., are grouped under the heading "Treaties.")

Achmet I, 201
Adovno, Jeronimo, 47
Adrian VI, 48
Aeneas Silvius, *see* Pius II
Agnadello, 34, 50
Aigues Mortes, Conference of, 53
Aix-la-Chapelle, Congress of, 234
Alberoni, 205, 212–4
Albert of Brandenburg-Culmbach, 54
— of Poland, 31
Albret, Charlotte d', 29
Alembert, 275
Alençon, 68
Alexander VI, 10–11, 29, 37
— VII, 124
Alfonso II., of Naples, 11, 26
Almanza, 167
Alva, Duke of, 56, 66
Amboise, Georges d', 29, 33, 39, 46
Anhalt, Christian of, 86–7, 94
Anjou, Duke of, *see* Philip V
Anne, Queen, 168, 173, 175
— de Beaujeu, 23, 25, 37
— of Brittany, 23, 24, 29
Anstruther, Sir R., 94
Aranda, 285
Argenson, Marquis d', 239
Arlington, Lord, 127, 133, 136
Arques, 78
Arthur, Prince of Wales, 37, 38, 39
Arundel, 136
Assiento, 178
Augsburg, League of, 145
— War of League of, 126
Augustus II, 190–2, 194, 221, 223, 268
— III, 221, 222, 239, 244, 250, 268
Avaux, Comte d', 107–10
Avignon, 124

Bacon, F., 24, 37, 39
Baden, Louis of, 203
— Ludwig Wilhelm of, 145
Badoer, 34
Baireuth, Wilhelmina, Margravine, 251
Balbasez, 139
Baltaji, Mehemet, 204
Bar, Confederation of, 272
Barnet, 17
Barrier Fortresses, 166, 173, 177, 180, 209, 288–9
— Treaties, *see* Treaties
Bavaria, Joseph Ferdinand, Electoral Prince of, 156–60
Bayezid II, 10
Bayonne, Conference of, 66
Beachy Head, 147
Beauvau, 229
Beauvilliers, 164
Bedford, Duke of, 258
Bellay, Guillaume du, 52
Belleisle, 228–30
Bellings, 136
Bender, 195, 204
Bentinck, Earl of Portland, 150, 158
— Count, 234
Bergheik, 167
Berkenrode, 289
Bernis, 251, 252, 283
Bernstorff (elder), 284
— (younger), 284
Berwick, Duke of, 221
Besenval, 192–3
Bessarion, 18
Bethlen, Gabor, 96
Beunigen, 130, 138
Beverning, 139
Bismarck, 236
Black Prince, 16
Blenheim, 158, 166, 167
Boineburg, 152
Bolingbroke, 172, 174, 175
Borgia, Alfonso, *see* Calixtus III

Borgia, Cesare, 29, 33
— Rodrigo, *see* Alexander VI
Boscawen, 237
Bossuet, 153
Boswell, 232
Boufflers, 151
Bouillon, Duc de, 80
Bourbon, Cardinal of, 70, 71, 77
— Duke of, 217, 218
Braddock, 238
Brantzen, 289
Breisach, 139
Breitenfeld, 101
Bremen, 184, 195, 198
Brenteuil, 253
Brill, 74
Brinon, Jean, 50
Brulart de Léon, Charles, 100
Brun, 113
Brunswick, Congress of, 195
— Louis of, 254
Buckingham, Duke of, 92, 95
Bukovina, 279
Burghley, Lord, 62–4, 67, 74, 75
Burke, 153, 253
Burnet, 146
Burton, 78
Busbecq, 200–1
Bussy, 230, 255
Bute, 253, 257

Cadiz Expedition, 94
Cadogan, 180, 209, 210
Caillières, 149
Calais, 64, 65, 66, 79–80
Calixtus III, 8, 9
Cambrai, 71, 79, 80
— Conference of, 118
— Congress of, 217–9
Campredon, 198
Candia, 202
Cardona, Ramon de, 36
Carlos, Don, *see* Charles III of Spain
Carlowitz, General, 190–1
— Conference of, 203–4
Carlyle, 217, 247, 266
Carmarthen, 291
Carte, 231
Carteret, 198, 231, 256
Castel de Rios, 164
Castel Rodrigo, 127–8, 131
Castera, de, 268
Castlemaine, Lady, 134
Catalans, 179
Catherine II, 257, 270, 272, 273, 279–82, 299
Cecil, Robert, Earl of Salisbury, 75, 80, 90–1
— Sir William, *see* Burghley
Cellamare, 215
Cerdagne, 25, 37
Charles I of England, 92, 94–5, 96, 98
— II of England, 119, 128–30, 133, 136–8, 142
— II of Spain, 147, 154, 157–8, 162–3
— III of Spain, 220, 223, 233, 235, 255, 283, 285
— IV of Lorraine, 121, 139
— V (Emperor), 16, 32–55
— VI (Emperor), 162, 169, 171, 178, 205, 209, 211, 220, 221, 222, 227, 228, 229
— VII (Emperor), 228, 230, 231, 232, 233
— VIII (of France), 1, 11, 24–7, 28, 37, 38, 40
— IX of France, 61, 64, 66, 68, 97
— X of Sweden, 185–6
— XI of Sweden, 138, 147, 189, 190
— XII of Sweden, 190–9, 204–5, 213
— Albert of Bavaria, *see* Charles VII
— Archduke, *see* Charles VI
— Louis of the Palatinate, 106, 111, 152
— the Bold, 9, 12–21, 23
— Theodore of the Palatinate, 263, 264
Charnacé, 97–8, 101
Chateauneuf, 196
Chauvelin, 220, 221, 222, 229
Chemnitz, Bogislav Philip, 113
Chièvres, Seigneur de, 42, 46
Chigi, 109, 112, 124
Choiseul, 252, 253, 254, 255, 259, 285
Chouart, Paul de, 77
Christian IV, 94–5, 98
Christina of Sweden, 184
Claude of France, 32
Clement VIII, 47, 48, 51, 53
— XI, 214
— XIII, 283
— XIV, 283
— of Bavaria, 145
Clermont, 251
Cleves, Anne of, 53
— William of, 85, 87

Cloth of Gold, Field of, 45
Cobenzl, 280
Coignetz de Thuilleries, 184
Colbert, 133–4, 202
— de Croissy, 131, 133–5, 136
— — Madame, 134
Cologne, Conference of, 106
Colyer, 203–4, 205
Commines, Philip de, 6, 13, 18, 19, 21, 25, 27, 28
Concert of Europe, 299
Condé, 65
— (Enghien), 115, 118, 119, 130, 138
Confederates, Act of (1716), 267, 271
Constantinople, Fall of, 7
Contarini, 108–9
Conti, 239
Corsica, 285
Créqui, Duc de (Maréchal de France), 123–4, 140, 144
Crimea, 279, 280
Crimean War, 2
Cromwell, Thomas, 53
Cumberland, Duke of, 234, 248–9
— Richard, 285

Dartmouth, Earl of, 172
de Guereau, 67, 68
Denain, 174
de Silva, 67
Dettingen, 232
Deux Ponts, *see* Zweibrücken
Devolution, War of, 126–8, 131, 132
Devonshire, Duke of, 249
Diesbach, 18
Dietz, 295
Djem, 9–13, 26
Dohna, Christopher von, 87, 92
— Christopher Delphique, 129
Donauwörth, 85
Döring, Matthew, 7
Downing, 186
Dresden, 190
Dreux, 65
Dubois, 210–12, 217
Dunes, 115, 118
Dunkirk, 140, 176, 287
Duquesne, Fort, 238

Eboli, Duchess of, 56
Ecclesiastical Reservation, 55
Eck de Panteleon, 165
Edward IV, 17, 19, 20, 21, 24
Eleonora Louisa of Eisenach, 144
Elizabeth, Queen of England, 56–81, 96
— of England, Queen of Bohemia, 91, 94, 95, 96
— Charlotte of Orleans, 145
— Farnese, Queen, 212, 216, 217, 225, 240
— of Russia, 245, 251, 253, 257, 269
Ernest Augustus of Brunswick, 152
Essex, Earl of, 80
Esterhazy, 245
Estrades, Comte d', 130, 140, 155
Estrées, Gabrielle d', 79
Eugène, 167–9, 179, 203, 205, 218, 221
Ewart, 295

Fabricius, 91
Faisans, Île de, 119
Falklands, 284–5
Fehrbellin, 138, 139
Ferdinand I, Archduke of Austria (and Emperor), 55, 64
— II (Emperor), 91–2, 99–100, 105
— III (Emperor), 106
— V of Spain, 5, 25, 34, 35, 37
— of Brunswick, 249, 257, 291
— Joseph (Electoral Prince of Bavaria), 156–60
Feria, Count de, 64
Finland, 198–9
Fleurus, 147
Fleury, 219, 220, 221, 222, 223, 224, 226, 229
Flushing, 74
Foix, Gaston de, 36
— Paul de, 66
Fonseca, 220
Fontainebleau, Conference at, 54
Fontenoy, 233
Forbin, 202
Forest, Jean de la, 53
Fornovo, 26
Fortescue, 154
Fox, Richard, Bishop of Durham (later Winchester), 38, 39, 40
Francesco II of Milan, 52
Franche Comté, 124, 126, 130, 131, 133, 138, 139
Francis I of France, 5, 16, 40–54
— I (Emperor), 222, 233, 259
— II of Brittany, 23
— II of France, 61, 63, 64

Franco-German War, 2
Frederick (III) I of Prussia, 146, 166, 177
— II of Prussia, 2, 208, 221, 224, 226–76, 299
— II (Emperor), 47
— III (Emperor), 7, 8, 9, 17, 21
— IV of the Palatinate, 86, 90
— V, 90–94
— Henry of Orange, 96
— of Würtemberg, 87
— William (Great Elector), 111, 138, 139–40, 142, 144, 146, 185–6, 188
— — II, 290–4, 296
Fresno, 138
Fresse, Jean de, 54
Fritsch, 259
Fronde, 115, 116, 118
Froude, 68
Fürstenberg, 145
Fürstenbund, 265

Galitzin, 274
Gambetta, 236
Gardie, Magnus de la, 188
Gattinara, 39–47
Gaultier, 171–2
Gent, B. de, 113
Gentz, 131, 153
George I, 195, 208, 210, 213, 219
— II, 230, 237, 238, 252–3
— III, 253
— William of Brandenburg, 88, 103
Gertruydenberg, 170
Gibraltar, 175, 181, 208, 249, 255, 285–6
Görtz, Eustace von, 263
Görz, Baron de, 194, 197–8, 211
Grandson, 20
Granvelle, 56
Granville, *see* Carteret
Gravel, 116, 132
Gray, 223
Gregory XIII, 70, 71, 72
Gremonville, 128
Grenville, George, 226, 259
Gresham, 65
Grotius, 102, 105, 298
Guise, Duke of, 64, 65, 68, 70, 72
Gunpowder Plot, 84
Gustavus Vasa, 96
— Adolphus, 94–102, 104, 184
Gustavus III, 295
Gyllenborg, 197, 215

Habsburg, Maritime Design, 95–6, 98–100
Habsburg-Bourbon Alliance, 224, 242, 259, 280, 283
Hague, Congress of (1625), 95
— Concert of the, 187
Hamburg Conference, 106, 107
Hanbury-Williams, 247, note 2
Harborne, 201
Harley, *see* Oxford
Haro, Don Luis de, 118, 119, 123
Harrach, 160
Harris, 286, 291–3
Havre, 65, 66
Heinsius, 164, 168
Henrietta Maria, 116
Henry II of France, 25, 54–61
— III of France, 70–2, 77
— IV of France (Henry of Navarre), 60, 70, 72, 77–88, 133
— VII of England, 24, 34, 37, 38, 39
— VIII of England, 39–54
— of Prussia, 274
Henry Esmond, 154
Hertzberg, 294, 295
Hippolithus a Lapide, 113
Hohenlohe, Gustav von, 145
Horn, Arved, 198
Howard of Effingham, 56
Hundred Years' War, 1, 7, 18, 20, 44
Hunyadi, John, 8
Huxelles, Maréchal d', 174, 175

Indulgence, Declaration of, 138
Innocent VIII, 10
— X, 112
— XI, 145
Isabella of Spain, 25, 37, 39
Ismail, 281

James I of England, 64, 81, 90–4
— II of England, 135, 165
— III (Old Pretender), 165, 166, 231
— IV of Scotland, 35, 38
Jeannin, 81, 82
Jesuits, 60, 283–4
Jew Süss, 263
John of Capistrano, 8
— Casimir, 72, 184, 188
— of France, 16

John George of Saxony, 102–3
Johnson, Dr., 182, 232, 259
Joseph I, 170, 171, 194
— II, 262–83, 288–90, 294, 296, 299
— Father, 100, 105
Julius II, 32–5, 39, 40

Kara Mustafa, 143
Katharine of Aragon, 37, 38, 39, 51
Kaunitz, 243, 259, 263, 273, 275, 284, 289, 294, 295
Keene, 226, 249–50
Kherson, 280
Kinsley, 220
Kiuprili, Achmet, 202
Klesl, 92
Klinggräffen, 246
Klissow, 191
Knox, 63
Kolowrat, 187
Kosciusko, 282
Kunersdorf, 252

Ladislas of Hungary, 31
Lagos, 252
Lang, Bishop of Gurk, 35
La Quadra, 226
La Tremoille, 30
Lawfeldt, 234
League, Holy Catholic, 70–1, 77–9
— Catholic (Germany), 87, 88, 94, 95, 100, 101, 103
Leczynski, Stanislaus, King, 192, 194, 198, 218, 221, 223, 268
Lee, Archbishop of York, 50
Leibniz, 151–3
Leicester, Earl of, 74–5
Leith, Siege of, 63
Lens, 115
Leo X, 41–8
Leopold I, 132, 137, 139, 144, 146, 150, 155–6, 161–2, 167, 170, 188
— II, 281, 295–6
— Archduke, Bishop of Passau, 87
Lesno, 187
Le Tellier, 202
Liège, 15
Liegnitz, 252
Ligne, Prince de, 273, 280
Ligonier, 234
Lillieroth, 191
Lionne, Hugues de, 116, 117–8, 128
Lisola, 131–2, 137, 154, 185–7
Livonia, 97–8, 183–4, 188, 195, 197, 199
Lobkowitz, 132, 137
Lombres, 187
Longueville, Duc de, 109
Loredano, Leonardo 35
Lorraine, Cardinal of, 64, 70
— Duchess of, 54
— — Tuscany Exchange, 222–3
Louis XI, 5, 6, 9–22, 51
— XII, 28–30, 32, 33, 35, 39, 40
— XIII, 100, 101
— XIV, 2, 34, 93, 117–78, 188, 199, 202, 203, 207, 210, 214, 240
— XV, 23, 211, 217, 221, 239, 240, 250, 252, 253, 268, 272, 284
— XVI, 289
— Frederick, Duke of Würtemberg, 90–1
— of Hungary, 51
Louise, daughter of Francis I, 42
— of Savoy, 50–2
Louvois, 143, 147, 202
Lubomirski, 187
Lucchesini, 295
Ludovico, Duke of Milan, 25, 27, 29, 30
Luther, 47
Lutter, 95, 98
Lutzen, 102
Lutzow, 107
Luxembourg, 136, 139, 147
Lynar, 249, 272, 273

Maastricht, 138, 139
Machiavelli, 33
— Age of, 2
Mahlzahn, 244
Maitland of Lethington, 63, 64
Malmesbury, *see* Harris
Malplaquet, 170
Malvezzi, 200
Mancini, Marie, 119
Manilla Ransom, 258–9
Mantua, Congress of, 9
Mantuan Succession, War of, 100–1
Manuel, Juan, 47
Manzoni, 159
Margaret of Anjou, Queen of England, 17
— of Austria, 33, 52
— of Burgundy, 21
— Tudor, Queen of Scotland, 38

Maria Antonia of Austria, 144, 155
— Theresa (of France), 118, 121–2, 154
— — (Empress), 222, 228–75, 296
Marie Antoine of Saxony, 271
— Joseph, Princesse, 239
— Leczynski, Queen of France, 218
Marignano, 41, 43, 44, 276
Marischal, Earl (Keith), 256
Marlborough, Duke of, 137, 167–9, 193–4
Martinitz, 91
Mary of Burgundy, 21, 23
— of Guise, 63
— Queen of Scots, 63, 64, 67, 70, 73, 75
— Tudor, Queen of England, 56
— — Queen of France, 39, 40
Mathenesse, J. de, 113
Matthias Corvinus, 10
— (Emperor), 91–2
Matueof, 215
Maurice of Nassau, 78
— Prince, 152
— of Saxony, 54–5
Maurier, du, 88
Mavrogordato, 204
Max Emmanuel, Elector of Bavaria, 144, 157, 159, 160
Maximilian I, 6, 22, 24, 25, 27, 29–30, 33, 35, 42, 45
— of Bavaria, 85, 87, 100, 101, 103, 111
— Joseph, of Bavaria, 263
Mayenne, Duke of, 70
Mazarin (Mazarini), 101, 108, 116–22, 154
Meadowe, 186
Medici bank, 20
— Cardinal Raffaelo de, *see* Clement VII
— Catherine de, 66, 71
— Cosimo de, 5
— Marie de, 88
Meinders, 139
Mendoza, 68, 70
Menzel, 244–6
Mercy, 289
Merode-Westerloo, 159
Mesnager, 172, 174, 175
Methuen, Paul, 166
Metz, 54–6, 60, 111, 121
Minden, 252
Mirabeau, 289
Mirandola, 41
Mirepoix, 222
Mitchell, 259
Mohacs, 51, 202
Mohammed II, 8–10
— V, 233
Mohilev, 280
Monmouth, Duke of, 137
Montague, Lady M. W., 205
Montecuculi, 202
Monterey, 137
Montesquieu, 42, 206
Montgomery, 61
Montmorency, Constable, 56
— Duke of, 71
Montmorin, 291
Monumentum Ancyranum, 201
Morat, 21
More, Sir J., 45
Morea, 204, 205
Moreo, 70
Mornay, Paul de, 77
Morosini, 203
Moryson, Fynes, 85
Münchhausen, 230
Munn, 223
Münnich, 221, 269
Murray, 35

Nanfan, Richard, 40
Nantes, Edict of, 82, 145
Napoleon I, 300
Narva, 191
Neisse, 273
Neuburg, Philip William of, 145, 152
Neustadt, 273
Newcastle, 253, 257
Nice, Conference of, 53
Nicholas V, 8
Nicodemus, 5
Nierodt, 222
Nivernois, 258
Noailles, Maréchal de, 147
Nointel, 202
Norris, Sir J., 78
— Admiral, 198
Novara, 30

Oczakov, 281, 282
Oldenburg, 284
Oliva, Congress of, 187–8
Olivarez, 73

Orange, Principality of, 177
— William I of, *see* William the Silent
Orleans, Duchesse de (Madame), 134–6
— Duke of (Regent), 196, 210–11, 214–5, 217
Ostend Company, 218, 220
Othello, 87
Oudenarde, 167
Oxenstjerna, Axel, 104, 113, 184
— Benoît, 187
— John, 108
Oxford, Earl of, 173

Paaw, Adrian, 113
Pace, 45
Paget, Charles, 81
— Lord, 203–4
Palatinate, Charles of the, 145
— Ravaging of, 147
Pallavicini, 78
Panin, 274
Paris, Conference of, 2
Parma, Alexander Farnese, Duke of, 75, 78
Partitions in Eighteenth Century, 278
Partition of Poland (First), 274–5, 278–9, 299
Passano, 50
Passaro, Cape, 213–4
Patino, 226
Patkul, 190, 192
Paul III, 53
Pavia, 16, 49, 51
Pelham, Henry, 234
Penaranda, 108, 113, 117–8
Pentenriedter, 219
Peter the Great, 190–1, 194–5, 203, 267, 270
Peter III, 253, 257, 269
Peterborough, Lord, 213–4
Peterwardein, 205
Philip II, 55–80
— III, 81, 91–2
— IV, 127, 154–5
— V, 162, 168, 174, 175, 177, 178, 210, 212, 217, 221, 240
— Archduke of Austria, 32, 37, 39
— of Burgundy, 8, 13, 14
— Don, 235
Philipsburg, 139
Pieseulx, 234
Piper, 192–3
Pitt (Elder), 249, 252, 254, 256, 257
— (Younger), 281
Pius II, 8, 9
— IV, Creed of, 62
— V, 67
— VI, 284
Plessis-Praslin, 124
Polignac, 174
Politiques, 71, 79
Pompadour, 239, 251
Pomponne, 139, 189, 202
Pondicherry, 151
Poniatowski, Stanislaus, 195, 204
Pontchartrain, 164
Porto-Carrero, 160
Potemkin, 280–1
Poyntz, 219
Prado, Don Antonio de, 119
Pragmatic Sanction, 218, 220, 223, 228–9
Prague, Defenestration of, 91
Prignani, Abbé, 134
Prior, M., 171–2, 174
Public Weal, War of, 14
Pultava, 194

Quebec, 252
Quiberon Bay, 252

Ramillies, 167
Rammekins, 74
Raphael, 33
Ratisbon, Kurfürstentag, 99–100
Ravaillac, 88
Ravenna, 36, 39, 40
Reichenbach, Congress of, 295, 299
Réné, Duke of Lorraine, 17, 21, 23, 26
Repnin, 271
Restitution, Edict of, 99, 102
Reunion, Chambers of, 142–4, 149–50
Reuss, 295
Revolutionary Wars, French, 2
Richelieu, Cardinal, 60, 72, 96, 100, 101, 104–5, 115
— Duc de, 249, 251
Rinçon, 51, 53
Ripperda, 218
Ritter, 263
Robinson, Bishop of Bristol, 174, 175, 193
— Thomas, 231

Rocroi, 115
Roe, Sir T., 96–8, 106, 201, 205
Rogers, 75
Romanzow, 279
Rome, Sack of, 51
Rossbach, 249, 250
Rouillé, Président, 167
— Minister, 242
Rousillon, 25, 37
Rudolf II, 86, 201
Rupert, Prince, 152
Ruvigny, 130
Ryswick, Congress of, 149

St. Bartholomew, Massacre, 68
St. Jean de Luz, 119
St. Quentin, 56
Saint Saphorin, 213
Saint-Séverin, 234
Saint Simon, 196
Sacheverell, 171
Salzburg, Archbishop of, 110–11
Sandwich, Earl of, 234
Saratoga, 285
Satyre Ménippée, 78–9
Savage, 232
Saxe-Gotha, Duchess of, 254, 259
Saxe, Marshal, 234
Schaub, 212
Scheldt, 114, 181–2, 290
Schinner, Matthäus, 35, 40
Schlosser, 262
Schmalkalde, League of, 52, 85, 90
Schönborn, P. von, Elector of Mainz, 152
Schonenberg, 166
Schwabisch-Hall, 88
Scott, Sir Walter, 12
Secret of Louis XV, 211, 229, 238–9, 253
Ségur, Agent of Henry III, 71
— diplomatist of Catherine II, 280
Sehested, 188
Servien, 109–10, 117
Sforza family, 48
— Francesco, 5
— Ludovico, *see* Ludovico
Sherburne, 38
Sicily-Sardinia Exchange, 177, 213–4
Sigismund of Austria, 17, 19
— III of Sweden and Poland, 84, 96–7, 184
Silesia, 227–8, 233, 235, 236, 254, 260, 266, 299
Simonetto of Camerino, 8
Sinzendorff, 194, 211, 218, 219, 220, 222
Sixtus V, 72, 73
Slawata, 91
Smerwick, 68
Smith, Sir T., 65–6
Sobieski, John, 144, 202, 203
Soissons, Congress of, 219
Solms, 270, 274
Somme Towns, 14–15, 18, 21, 23
Sophia of Brunswick, 152
Spanish Succession War, 126
Spens, Sir J., 94
Spielmann, 295
Stahremberg, 218, 243, 247
Stainville, *see* Choiseul
Stair, 208–9
Stanhope, James, 160, 208–13, 216
— Col. William, 219
Stanley, 255, 256
Steinberg, 230
Steinkirke, 147
Stenbock, 195
Stormont, 286
Strafford, 174, 175
Stralsund, 98–9
Strasburg, 124, 141, 143, 144, 149–51, 161, 179
Suffolk, Charles Brandon, Duke of, 40
Suleiman I, 51, 53, 200
Sutton, 205
Suvorov, 281
Swift, 173
Sydney, Algernon, 188

Tallard, 158
Taxis, J. B. de, 70
Temple, Sir R., 128–30, 139
Terlon, 186, 188
Tessé, 148, 218
Tewkesbury, 17
Thirlby, Bishop of Ely, 56
Throckmorton, 68–9
Ticino, 30, 41
Tilly, 94, 95
Torcy, 163, 164, 168, 172, 175
Torstenson, 184
Toul, 54–6, 60, 111, 121
Trautmannsdorf, 102, 109–10

Treaties, etc.
Aarau, 277
Aix-la-Chapelle (1668), 126, 130–2, 141
— (1748), 234–5, 238
Altmark, 98, 184
Altranstadt, 192
Anglo-Scottish (1502), 38
— (1586), 64
Anhausen, 87
Antwerp (1609), 81–2
— (1715), 175
Armed Neutrality, 286–7
Arras (1435), 13, 14
— (1482), 22
Augsburg (1555), 55, 62, 84–6
— League of (1686), 145
Austro-Dutch (1673), 137
Baden, 179
Bâle, 30
Barrier (First), 180
— (Second), 180
— (Third), 180–1, 209–10, 248, 288
Barwalde, 101
Belgrade, 269
Berlin (1742), 232
— (1785), 265
— (1885), 237
Blois (1498), 29
— (1504), 32, 33
Breda, 126–7, 140
Breslau, 232
Brömsebro, 184
Bruges (1521), 47–8
Calmar, Union of, 96
Cambrai (League), 33, 39, 41, 137
— (Peace), 52
Carlowitz, 204
Cateau-Cambrésis, 1, 56–7, 60–1, 65, 66, 240
Chambord, 54–5
Cherasco, 100
Cleves, 127
Closter-seven, 249
Cognac, 51
Compiègne, 105
Conflans, 14
Copenhagen, 188
Crépy, 53
Dirschau, 99
Dover (1670), 135–6
— (1676), 142
Edinburgh, 64

Treaties, etc., continued—
Escurial, 221
Étaples, 24, 25, 36
Everlasting Compact, 18
Family Compact (First), *see* Escurial, Treaty of
— — (Second), 232
— — (Third), 255
Fontainebleau (1631), 101
— (1679), 189
— (1762), 258, 259
— (1785), 290, 291
Franco-Austrian (1758), 252
Franco-British Entente (1904), 176
Franco-Dutch (1662), 126
Franco-Papal-Venetian (1524), 48–9
Franco-Prussian (1679), 142
Franco-Swedish (1672), 188
Franco-Swedish-Turkish (1739), 269
Franco-Swiss, 277
Friederichsbourg, 198 and n.
Friedwald, 55
Granada, 31
Grand Alliance (1689), 145–7
— — (1701), 165, 173, 181, 211
Greenwich, 80–1
Gremonville, 128, 132, 141
Hague (1701), *see* Grand Alliance
Hamburg, 257
Hampton Court (1562), 65
— — (1689), 147
Hanover, 219
Hastenbeck, 248–9
Holy League (1511), 35, 36, 37, 38, 50
Hubertusburg, 260
Jassy, 282, 296
Joinville, 70–1, 73
Kardis, 188
Königsberg, 185
Kutchuk-Kainardji, 279
Labiau, 185
Leipsic, 245
Locarno, 209
Lodi, 29
London (1604), 81
Lubeck, 95
Madrid, 51, 54
Magnus Intercursus, 36–7
Malus Intercursus, 39
Medina del Campo, 37, 38

Treaties, etc., continued—
Milan, 103
Monesuch, 72, 76, 78
Monzon, 103
Moore, 50
Munich, 87
Münster, *see* Westphalia
Noyon, 42
Nymphenburg, 230
Nymwegen, 126, 140, 141, 142, 145, 149, 151, 178
Nystadt, 183, 198–9
Oliva, 187–8
Osnabrück, *see* Westphalia
Pardo, 226
Paris (1635), 105
— (1657), 115
— (1763), 2, 258
— (1783), 288
— (1815), 2
Partition (First), 159
— (Second), 161–4
— (First Polish), 274–5
Passarowitz, 205
Passau, 55, 99
Péronne, 16, 18
Picquigny, 19–20, 24
Pisa, 124
" Piteous Peace " (Liège), 15
Prague, 102–4, 105
Prusso-Polish (1790), 295
Prusso-Swedish (1720), 198
Prusso-Turkish (1790), 295
Pruth, 204, 267
Pyrenees, 119–23, 141, 147, 154–5
Quadruple Alliance (1718), 213–4
Rastadt, 179
Ratisbon (1630), 100
— Truces (1684), 141, 142, 144–5
Reichenbach, 296
Rhine, League of, 116, 128
Roeskilde, 186
Ryswick, 126, 150–1, 155, 158, 161, 162, 165, 176, 178
St. Germain-en-Laye, 189
St. Jean de Maurienne, 101
St. Petersburg, 270, 272
Scheyern, 52
Seville, 219
Sistova, 281
Sitvatorok, 201
Southampton, 95
Stockholm, 198

Treaties, etc., continued—
Stolbova, 97
Stuhmsdorf, 184
Teschen, 264
Tordesillas, 27
Triple Alliance (1668), 128–31, 134–5, 140, 188
— — (1717), 210–12
— — (1788), 292–4, 298
Troyes, 66
Tsarkoye Selo, 284
Turin, 148
Universal Peace (1518), 42–4, 45, 48
Utrecht, 2, 175–8, 207, 210, 211, 214, 225, 237, 288
Vasvar, 204
Venice, League of, 26, 28
Verela, 296
Versailles (1756), 242
— (1757), 242–3
— (1782), 287
Vervins, 80, 82–3, 97
Vienna (First, 1725), 218
— (Second, 1731), 220
— (Preliminary, 1735), 222
— (Third, 1738), 222, 224
— (1778), 263, 264
— (1815), 2, 207
Wehlau, 186
Westminster (1674), 138
— (1756), 238
Westphalia, 2, 30, 59, 88, 110–4, 115, 116, 117, 140, 142, 143, 145, 147, 149, 199, 277
Whitehall (1662), 166
— (1670), 136
Xanten, 88, 91
Zurawna, 202
Treitschke, 153, 188
Tremblay, *see* Joseph, Father
Trent, Council of, 60, 62
Trèves, Conference at, 9, 17
Turenne, 115, 127, 136, 138

Ulfeld, 184
Ulrica Eleonora, Queen of Sweden, 197
Union, Evangelical, 87, 88, 90–4
Unton, Sir H., 78, 79
Urban VIII, 105
Ursins, Princesse des, 169–70, 177, 212

Utrecht, Adrian of, *see* Adrian VI
— Congress of, 173–5

Vassy, Massacre of, 65
Vateville, 155
Vauban, 128, 136, 144
Vellingk, 197
Venaissan, 124
Vendôme, 147, 212
Verden, 184, 195, 198
Verdun, 54–6, 60, 111, 121
Vere, Sir F., 78
Vergennes, Jean, 272, 277, 285–7, 289, 291
Versailles, Conference of, 289
Victor Amadeus, 148, 166, 177, 214
Vieilleville, Maréchal de, 54, 56
Vienna, Conference of, 106
— Congress of, 299–300
Villars, 169, 179
Villeneuve, 268–9
Villiers, 150
Vilna-Poland Dispute, 216
Vincent II of Mantua, 100
Vitry, 258
Voltaire, 191, 217, 239, 254

Wade, 69
Waldegrave, 222
Wallenstein, 95, 98, 100
Walpole, Horatio, 210, 219
— Horace (son of Sir R.), 223
— Sir Robert, 216–26, 231
Walsingham, 68, 75
Warwick (Kingmaker), 17
Wassenaer, 289
Weingarten, 245
Werth, Johann von, 105
Westphalia, Congress of, 2, 106–8
White Mountain, 94
Whitworth, 217
Wilhelmina of Orange, 290–1
Willes, 231
William of Neuburg, 88
— the Silent, 56, 61, 70, 72
— III of Orange, 130, 137–9, 144–51, 157–8, 161, 165, 175, 177, 182
— V of Orange, 290
Williamson, 150
Willoughby, 78
Wilmington, 231
Winwood, 81, 90
Witt, Cornelius de, 137
— John de, 128–31, 137, 138, 140, 186
Wolsey, 39–48
Wotton, N., 56
— Sir H., 88
Wrangel, 184
Wratislaw, 165

Yolande of Savoy, 21
York, James, Duke of, *see* James II

Zadé Mehemet, 279
Zips, 273–4
Zweibrücken, 151